Primary Prevention and Promotion in the Schools

Primary Prevention of Psychopathology

George W. Albee and Justin M. Joffe
General Editors

VOLUMES IN THIS SERIES:

Primary Prevention and Promotion in the Schools

Editors
Lynne A. Bond
Bruce E. Compas

Primary Prevention of Psychopathology
Vol. XII

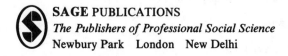

SAGE PUBLICATIONS
The Publishers of Professional Social Science
Newbury Park London New Delhi

For information address:

SAGE Publications, Inc.
2111 West Hillcrest Drive
Newbury Park, California 91320

SAGE Publications Ltd.
28 Banner Street
London EC1Y 8QE
England

SAGE Publications Inda Pvt. Ltd.
M-32 Market
Greater Kailash I
New Delhi 110 048 India

Printed in the United States of America

Library of Congress Cataloging-in-Publication Data

Main entry under title:

Primary prevention and promotion in the schools.

(Primary prevention of psychopathology; v. 12)
Based on papers presented at the Vermont
Conference on the Primary Prevention of Psychopathology,
University of Vermont, June 1987.
Bibliography: p.
Includes index.
1. School psychology—United States—Congresses.
2. Personnel service in education—United States—
Congresses. I. Bond, Lynne A., 1949–   . II. Compas,
Bruce E. III. Vermont Conference on the Primary
Prevention of Psychopathology (1987 : University of
Vermont) IV. Series.
RC454.P683 vol. 12 [LB1027.55] 616.89′05 s 89-10130

ISBN 0-8039-3526-9

FIRST PRINTING 1989

Contents

Preface

In many countries throughout the world, schools comprise one of the greatest investments of the nation's people—investments of finances, talented personnel, and commitment of time and energy by youth. These investments reflect the great promise that schools are believed to hold for their communities, the promise to promote healthy, multifaceted development among their participants. As such, schools have been a logical context in which to focus efforts to prevent the emergence of behavioral and psychological problems and promote psychological well-being.

This volume brings together examples of this nation's most current thinking on ways to integrate prevention and promotion into the schools. The authors have led recent efforts to develop, implement, and evaluate effective preventive and promotive interventions in the schools, to conduct basic research on those factors that underlie effective psychological development during the school years, and to restructure the very models upon which school-based prevention and promotion efforts are grounded.

In June of 1987, the contributors to this volume participated in a Vermont Conference, at the University of Vermont, titled "Primary Prevention Research in the Schools." This conference grew from encouragement and financial support from the National Institute of Mental Health, with particular leadership from Joyce Lazar, Chief, Prevention Research Branch, and Juan Ramos, Deputy Director for Prevention and Special Projects. Chaired by Lynne Bond and Bruce Compas, Professors of Psychology at the University of Vermont, and Carolyn Swift, Director of the Stone Center for Developmental Services and Studies, the conference drew together educators and mental health professionals to consider models and research that utilize schools as the context for the prevention of problematic learning, behavior, and emotion, and the promotion of behavioral and psychological well-being.

In selecting contributions for this conference, we felt it important to emphasize two aspects of school-based prevention/promotion programs. First, we wished to present examples of programs that are based on broad theoretical models of human development and behavior. These theoretical frameworks provide a common set of concepts and parameters to use in comparing various school-based prevention/promotion programs. Further, by drawing on broader theoretical models, we can integrate the applied field of primary prevention with more fundamental areas of psychological theory and research. Second, we have attempted to present programs that are based on strong sets of empirical data. These include data concerning the etiology and prediction of a variety of problems that serve as the targets of school-based prevention efforts, as well as controlled evaluation of the effectiveness of these programs. We believe that the chapters in this volume represent outstanding examples of theory-based prevention programs that have been exposed to intensive empirical evaluation. As such, they reflect some of the best that the field of primary prevention has to offer.

A theme that persists throughout the various contributions to this volume is the importance of considering the social contexts in which children function, and in particular, the school environment itself. Many of the contributors have identified the necessity to avoid models of intervention that are exclusively "person-focused" and result in a process of holding children responsible for the causes of and solutions for their own problems. There is an emerging understanding of the importance of considering the ongoing transactions between children and their environments in the development, maintenance, and ultimately, prevention of problems in learning, behavior, and emotion, as well as in the promotion of adaptive functioning.

This is the twelfth volume emerging from the Vermont Conferences on the Primary Prevention of Psychopathology, a conference series that began in 1975 as a result of discussions between George Albee, of the University of Vermont, and Faith and James Waters, of the Waters Foundation. Supported for seven years by the Waters Foundation, and subsequently by the National Institute of Mental Health, the Vermont Conferences have brought together professionals from a variety of disciplines—psychology, medicine, social work, biology, sociology, education, and nursing, among others—to examine models, research, and programs of practice for the prevention of psychological dysfunction and the promotion of psychological well-being. Over the years, conference participants have examined issues of prevention and promotion as they pertain to building competence and coping across the life span, environmental influences and psychopathology, political action and social change, sexual responsibility, health psychology, family transitions, and a decade of progress from the mid 1970s to 1980s.

As has been true for each of the Vermont conferences and publications, a small group of committed and creative individuals were responsible for the completion of this conference and volume. These include several individuals from the University of Vermont: George Albee, a general editor of the series on Primary Prevention of Psychopathology and an energetic participant of the conference planning committee; Justin Joffe, a general editor of the series who advised us from his new distant home in London, England; Paula MacKay, Conference Coordinator; and Melissa Perry, Conference Assistant. Beyond the walls of the University of Vermont, several people were centrally important in making this conference and publication possible: Carolyn Swift, Cochairperson of the conference, whose broad understanding and experience in prevention contributed in many essential ways to the conference; Joyce Lazar, Chief of the Prevention Research Branch at NIMH who inspired the notion for this particular conference and who, with Juan Ramos, Deputy Director for Prevention and Special Projects at NIMH, both facilitated a contract to fund the meeting of the contributors to this volume and assisted us in the planning of and presentations in the conference. And, of course, we want to acknowledge all those individuals involved in schools throughout the world who have been committed to using the educational system to promote the healthy development of community members.

—Lynne A. Bond
—Bruce E. Compas

PART I

Models for the Design and Evaluation of School-Based Primary Prevention Programs

Sound and systematic efforts to prevent a variety of learning, emotional, and behavioral problems in school-aged children and youth depend on two general factors: (1) a strong theoretical model to guide research and program development; and (2) the use of rigorous methods to measure and evaluate the effectiveness of such programs. A general theoretical model should determine the goals of the intervention program and the methods used to achieve these goals. Appropriate evaluation methods are essential to determine whether goals are met and to identify areas for continued program growth and development.

In the opening chapter, Robert and Tweety Felner describe a transactional-ecological model for understanding primary prevention programs and, in doing so, provide a framework for the evaluation and comparison of the school-based prevention programs described in this book. Robert Felner, Professor of Psychology and Director of Clinical Training at the University of Illinois, Urbana-Champaign, and Tweety Felner, a doctoral candidate in Early Childhood/Special Education at the same institution, have integrated the transactional model of human development with the ecological perspective to generate a comprehensive model for prevention.

The Felners describe three general approaches to primary prevention: person-focused, transaction-focused, and environmentally or ecologically focused programs. They describe examples of each and use their transactional-ecological framework to compare these programs in terms of intervention goals, targets, and foci. Throughout their chapter, the authors emphasize the importance of viewing children and their problems in terms of the broad social contexts in which these problems develop, and the authors warn against the tendency of many programs to focus on promoting children's adaptation to the exclusion of altering children's ecological contexts.

11

Evaluation of the effects of school-based primary prevention programs is dependent on the use of powerful and appropriate research designs. Jean Ann Linney provides a discussion of the steps necessary for successfully evaluating the effects of school-based prevention programs. Linney, Associate Professor of Psychology at the University of South Carolina, outlines the components of evaluation research designs needed for drawing causal inferences about the effects of a program.

Going beyond the important issues pertaining to research design and evaluation, Linney discusses characteristics of schools that may impede the successful evaluation of prevention programs. Drawing on ecological models of the school environment, she describes the norms and rules that may constrain prevention research in schools. Based on her ongoing work involving the evaluation of school-based programs for the prevention of substance abuse, Linney offers a number of strategies for optimizing evaluation research in school settings.

1

Primary Prevention Programs in the Educational Context: A Transactional-Ecological Framework and Analysis

Robert D. Felner
Tweety Yates Felner

Prevention efforts in educational settings are now well into their third generation. Initial work in this area, focused on establishing the viability and appropriateness of mental health interventions in these settings, was generally based on what would be best characterized as a *secondary prevention* stance (Zax & Specter, 1974). These secondary prevention programs were innovative in their timing, the locations in which they were delivered, and their staffing patterns (e.g., nonprofessionals). But, in other ways, they resembled more traditional clinical models as they often focused on individual children, the use of early behavior problems or symptoms to identify children at increased risk for the development of more serious disorder, and the reversal or treatment of such emergent problems (Felner, Jason, Moritsugu, & Farber, 1983).

From these early efforts, a second generation of programs evolved that strove to be more truly primary preventive. This shift, from secondary to *true* primary prevention required extensive modifications in the ways we think about mental health interventions. The newly evolving primary prevention models targeted entire populations of children and youth, and developed strategies that reduced the incidence of the *initial* onset of disorder. No longer was the identification or remediation of early signs of problems emphasized; rather, the focus shifted to the development of resilience and the modification of environmental conditions that predispose children and adolescents to increased risk and vulnerability to dysfunction.

13

The first truly primary preventive initiatives in educational settings have now yielded preliminary data on their effectiveness. These data have spawned third generation preventive interventions that build on and refine the strategies of their predecessors. Not surprisingly, given the relatively recent emergence of such programs, these efforts often seem to have little more in common than a general set of preventive goals and the fact that they are associated with educational settings. Attempts at integration have been based on little more than broad considerations of the target goals of the various programs (e.g., competence development or substance abuse prevention). With few exceptions (Cowen, 1985), there is a lack of well-developed, integrating frameworks that enable us to look across programs and examine their assumptions, goals, and principles on a common metric. Such frameworks are, however, necessary if we are to develop a coherent knowledge base for prevention.

With this backdrop in mind, a central aim of the current chapter is to first provide an integrative framework to guide the development of prevention efforts for children and youth. Next, we will illustrate ways in which the use of this framework may facilitate the identification and elaboration of key conceptual issues that characterize existing programs in educational settings. In accomplishing this, we will examine the implications of our model both for past prevention initiatives and, particularly, for the future development of more systematic and effective intervention efforts.

In addressing the issue of how best to arrive at a framework to organize our thinking about preventive efforts generally, and in educational settings in particular, perhaps the best place to start is with what appear to be some very innocent questions. These are: (1) What are the program's goals?; (2) Who or what does the program *target*?; and (3) What and where is the *focus* of intervention? While these questions appear straightforward, the ways that preventionists have arrived at their preferred answers is complex and, all too often, not based on any clear systematic rationale.

Intervention Goals, Targets, and Focus: The Need for a Guiding Model

To oversimplify, a careful examination of the programs in the remainder of this volume and elsewhere (e.g., Cowen, 1985; Price, Cowen, Lorion, Ramos-McKay, & Hitchins, 1988) reveals that a major dimension on which we can sort prevention programs is on the degree of outcome specificity that is sought. Some programs seek to prevent very specific undesirable developmental outcomes (e.g., substance abuse, school failure, and specific DSM-III-R disorders). By contrast, other programs seek to modify antecedent conditions that may impact normal developmental trajectories and a host of problematic developmental outcomes. Although both types of programs may share certain elements, the fundamental difference in the degree of outcome specificity sought is critical for prevention, and this issue needs to be brought more sharply into focus than has typically been done.

That is, in considering primary prevention strategies we need to be clear about how the targets of interventions are guided by implicit or explicit models of pathways to disorder and adaptation. Of equal or greater concern than the desired outcomes are the underlying developmental or etiological processes reflected in the goals of the program. We also need to consider the degree to which the particular view of the critical etiological/developmental pathways required by the program's goals is explicitly articulated or intended and the evidence that is used to support that view. In considering specific outcome focused efforts, versus more generic, antecedent condition approaches, we see the influence of two quite different perspectives on pathways to disorder. The former reflect a *specific disease prevention* model that rests heavily on classic medical and public health paradigms. These perspectives hold that dysfunction is caused by specific disease agents that interact with individual vulnerabilities, which are also specifiable. By contrast, the *antecedent condition* perspective is based on the assumption that, at least for a wide range of developmental outcomes, efforts to identify a specific etiological agent is neither appropriate nor supported by data.

Guiding Models to Pathways of Disorder

In questioning the assumptions that underlie specifically targeted programs, we must examine the appropriateness of the analogy between biological disorders for which specific "germs" have been found and socioemotional or learning problems. Addressing this issue, Sameroff and Fiese (1988) note, "While clear linkages have been found between some 'germs' and specific biological disorders, this has not been true for behavioral disorders . . . behavioral disturbances in the vast majority of cases are the result of factors more strongly associated with the psychological and social environment *than any intrinsic characteristics of the affected individuals*" (p.4) [emphasis added]. Supportive of this position are a number of recent studies that demonstrate that children's functioning at any particular time is not linearly related to their functioning at later ages. Instead, the effects of contexts children encounter in the future must be considered as they shape developmental trajectories through their interaction with children's personal characteristics (Felner & Lorion, 1985; Sameroff & Fiese, 1988). Indeed, quite different combinations of risk factors may lead to very similar developmental outcomes, just as divergent outcomes may be attained by children with highly convergent psychological or biological characteristics (Bronfenbrenner, 1979; Sameroff & Chandler, 1975).

This is not to say that there are not some specific conditions that are associated with very specific forms of dysfunction. For example, we are aware that the simple lack of appropriate information may often play a critical role in the pathways to certain devastating developmental outcomes (e.g., teen pregnancy), or that certain quite different coping styles or social skill patterns may be associated with the presence of depressed mood or aggressive behavior. When viewed this way, the specific etiology strategy also shows at least some promise. How then to resolve the question? To some extent a quote from Tevye in Sholem Alechem's "Fiddler on the Roof" is appropriate here, "They are both right—and also wrong."

Much of the seeming discrepancy between the two positions may be accounted for by adopting a developmental perspective for explaining both pathways to disorder and the goals and assumptions of prevention programs. As noted by Sroufe and Rutter (1984), the principles of development that apply to healthy or "normal" growth also apply to the emergence of disorder. A corollary we can draw from this view is that the point in the developmental history of the disorder selected as our focus may lead to quite different notions of specificity. As depicted in Figure 1.1, conditions that exist earlier in the sequence, that are more distal from the onset of the problems, especially "diagnosable" ones, may predispose youth to vulnerability to a wide variety of difficulties. By contrast, for children who are more vulnerable due to a failure to develop important early competencies or skills or who have experienced circumstances that are developmentally hazardous, the specific emergence and/or manifestation of disorder may depend on clearly identifiable, quite specific conditions that describe the child's recent, proximal experiences (Bell, 1986; Felner, Farber & Primavera, 1983; Sameroff, 1987; Sameroff & Fiese, 1988). What is important to understand here is that the latter, more proximal conditions will generally fail to produce negative consequences in the absence of the earlier predisposing circumstances.

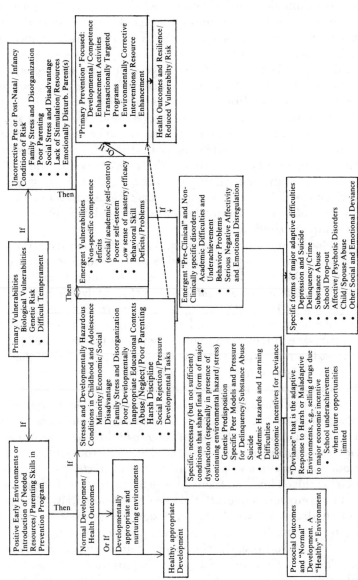

Figure 1.1

This conceptualization, although helpful, still fails to provide a clear framework for understanding the actual trajectories to disorder. That is, a broad developmental perspective lacks sufficient specificity for articulating just what the mechanisms and processes are that shape vulnerability, resilience, and the emergence of one specific outcome over others. The necessity of such specificity for the development of effective prevention efforts is underscored by Felner and Lorion (1985) who state: " . . . a preventive intervention involves the systematic alteration and modification of processes related to the development of adaptation and well-being or disorder, with the goals of increasing or decreasing, respectively, the rate or level at which these patterns occur in the general population . . . " (p.93). As these authors make clear, the focus of preventive interventions needs to be on the *mechanisms and processes* from which disorder and competence result, *not* the endpoint conditions.

A developmental model that we and our colleagues have argued is a particularly appropriate one to guide prevention programs and research that elaborates what the processes of concern should be is one we call a *transactional-ecological model* (Felner, Silverman, & Adan, 1988; Seidman, 1987). Here, a conceptual synthesis of the highly complementary transactional and ecological models of development is accomplished. A full discussion of the separate models is well beyond the scope of this chapter, but there are some aspects of each that bear on the current issues that we need attend to, however briefly.

The transactional model, as articulated by Sameroff and his colleagues (Sameroff & Chandler, 1975; Sameroff & Fiese, 1988), emphasizes the reciprocal effects of children on their environmental contexts and contexts on children. Here, the degree of difficulty of the *dynamic transactions* between the individual and the environment, as well as their adaptive adequacy, is shaped by the characteristics and competencies children bring to them, as well as the nature of the environment they confront. Sameroff & Fiese (1988) note that, "The problems of children (and youth) are no longer seen as restricted to children (and youth). Social experience is now recognized as a critical element of all behavioral developments, both normal and abnormal" (p. 40). Similarly, Sarason and Doris (1979) argue that a transactional model emphasizes that individuals and their environments can never be understood separately and that the direction of developmental influences is always reciprocal.

To this model we have joined the elements of the ecological perspective in certain key ways. This framework has its roots in both developmental and community psychology and has been articulated by

Bronfenbrenner (1979), and others (e.g., Barker, 1968; Lewin, 1951; Rappaport, 1987; Vincent & Trickett, 1983). As does the transactional perspective, this orientation emphasizes the "progressive, mutual accommodation between an active, growing human being and the changing properties of the settings in which the developing person lives" (Bronfenbrenner, 1979; p. 21). To our minds, however, a critical set of additional principles and guiding assumptions are yielded from the synthesis of the ecological and transactional perspectives. First, our focus is expanded to include the ways in which person-setting interactions are impacted by relationships *between settings*, as well as by the broader contexts in which settings may be nested. Now we see that the degree to which each of the settings in which a child develops separately influences the outcomes obtained and the extent to which the experience of one setting modifies that of another are both essential factors to consider in understanding developmental outcomes and mounting prevention efforts. Second, a focus on those settings in which a child may never be directly involved, but which shape his or her more direct developmental circumstances (e.g., parental work settings), is also yielded from this perspective. Finally, the influence of broader social and political systems on the more proximal systems that define a child's day-to-day experience is also of concern (Bronfenbrenner, 1979).

There is an additional, implicit corollary of the ecological perspective that is not addressed by the transactional model and that we feel must be explicitly understood if we are to develop prevention programs that do not require us to assume that the locus of risk or deficit is in the child. That is, this view allows us to see that the adaptive significance and appropriateness of children's behavior cannot be evaluated without a complete understanding of the full set of contexts that shape children's lives, and this view allows us to see some problems of children as *intelligent and effective* adaptations to disordered contexts. Such a view reveals the need to focus not only on children in the educational context, but on other settings that define their world and their relationship to the educational context.

Several examples may be helpful here. At the system-system level, Cauce, Felner, and Primavera (1982), demonstrated that the effects of support from family and peers on inner-city adolescents may interact to promote quite different outcomes. They reported that adolescents who had high levels of peer support, but relatively low levels of family support, had positive self-concepts but did more poorly in school. By contrast, when support from family members, but not peers was high, the reverse pattern of adjustment was found. These authors also showed how the pattern of findings obtained might have been quite different as a function of variation in either the child's age or socioeconomic circumstance.

Similarly, in analyzing the developmental outcomes of children at risk due to perinatal factors, Sameroff and Chandler (1975) provide a clear example of the interplay between individual-setting and setting-setting effects. Children who are more vulnerable because of the experience of such birth complications are shown to be at particular risk for the actual emergence of enduring deficits in families that fail to provide developmentally enriched environments. Further, the probability that such families will fail to provide such enriched circumstances, as well as the likelihood that the child will encounter other settings with the characteristics necessary to off-set family context deficits (e.g., developmental-enhancement focused day-care), are both directly linked to social class and economic opportunities.

In addition to showing the utility of the synthesis proposed, these examples illustrate how an analysis of individuals, not only in their current proximal context, but in the full range of systems that may influence them, may help to avoid unintended consequences of interventions and to understand unexpected ones. For example, interventions that simply seek to enhance the social support that inner-city adolescents receive from peers may be helpful in reducing immediate self-concept problems and perhaps transient depression. However, for some students who perhaps do not also receive high levels of academically oriented family support, we might actually obtain a decrease in school performance.

The Transactional-Ecological Model and Prevention

A full consideration of how the integration of the transactional and ecological perspective may be accomplished is well outside our mission in this work (the interested reader is referred to Felner & Lorion, 1985; Felner, Silverman, & Adan, 1988; and Sameroff & Fiese, 1988). But, in our progress toward a conceptual framework for developing and evaluating models of prevention programs in educational contexts, we can now specify some clear postulates that can be derived from this synthesis for guiding and analyzing prevention efforts. These include:

1. Disorder is seen to result from deviation in normal developmental trajectories and processes, and the primary goals of prevention

efforts are thus to short-circuit these deviations and restore the child to the more typical, appropriate pathways.

2. This model also allows for the understanding that some of the problems we seek to prevent may be adaptive and stem from *normal, typical* processes in disordered circumstances. Such an understanding reduces the degree to which we need to infer the presence of pathology in the person, and it allows us to shift our focus from the individual as the target of intervention to the environment and/or the interface between the child and the environment. An understanding of the *contexts* in which a pattern of behavior evolved and is currently maintained is key to understanding the degree to which a behavior is adaptive or dysfunctional, rather than the diagnosis of some static outcome.

We can now provide an added corollary to Sroufe and Rutter's (1984) argument that the same developmental processes that produce healthy outcomes also produce deviance: *what might appear to be deviant outcomes may be those that any healthy child or adolescent would exhibit in the environments and systems that define the context of their lives. That is, at least in some instances, what might have been seen as a disorder or disease may be better understood as a result of the child's appropriate, predictable, and highly adaptive attempts to adjust to contexts and conditions that require responses which are incompatible with those that are required in other contexts in which they may live.* Thus, we need no longer see the target population as either defective or potentially defective for us to find them of concern. Rather, they may simply be normal children exposed to developmentally hazardous circumstances that produce actions or developmental outcomes that are problematic.

3. A transactional-ecological model puts the focus of prevention programs on the nature of the interactions between children and their environments. It is impossible to understand the origin, the adaptiveness, or the appropriateness of a child's behavior without a thorough understanding of the contexts in which it has evolved and occurs, or the relationship of the child to those environments. Without such understanding the planning of preventive efforts to alter problematic developmental processes cannot be accomplished.

This point is especially important for those formulating prevention models for preschool and school-aged youth. These groups, more than almost any others, are captives of and influenced by systems and settings they neither selected nor always volunteered to participate in, (e.g., families, schools, peer groups). Attention to setting effects may be even more crucial than is the case for other groups.

4. The locus of disorder or dysfunction can be and often is outside

the individual. Thus, the *appropriate targets of at least some prevention efforts are the processes and contexts that children experience rather than children themselves.*

5. Finally, the multicausal model of behavior and psychological development/adjustment that is embodied in our transactional-ecological perspective underscores the need for the central emphasis of primary prevention efforts to be on broad-based antecedent factors and processes rather than the prevention of specific disorders. This does not mean that understanding specific pathways to the final form of dysfunction is unimportant. Rather, the appropriate *primary* focus of preventive interventions is on processes, and since many of the processes with which we are concerned are associated with a broad range of problematic outcomes, an overemphasis on target-disorder specificity is inappropriate.

Using the proposed model and its corollaries as the prism through which to view prevention efforts, let us now consider how its application to current program efforts may be useful in elaborating important similarities and differences among them.

Models of Intervention

Although from a transactional-ecological perspective, effective intervention at any point on the continuum of the transactional process (i.e., the individual, the transaction itself, the environment) will influence all elements of that process, *the extent to which the intervention does so intentionally* and *the point on the continuum that is of primary concern* are critical distinguishing characteristics. Further, from an understanding of how an intervention addresses the question of "point of intervention" focus, one can ascertain the risk or developmentally hazardous conditions that are of concern. Although not always clearly articulated by those who have mounted prevention efforts, knowledge of the developmental hazard or individual deficit the program seeks to address is essential for determining the underlying model that guides it. Finally, the extent to which prevention programs embody a "victim blaming" stance (Rappaport, 1987) can only be understood once the first two dimensions (i.e., intervention target and risk locus) have been articulated.

In the remainder of this section we develop and examine a schema for organizing prevention programs into three broad models. This schema results from the primacy we accord to the modification of processes as the central focus for prevention efforts. It distinguishes among programs by that point on the transactional continuum on which the processes lie that are to be modified and are thought to be the source of risk. This approach yields three broad models that distinguish among prevention programs:

1. Person-focused interventions that seek to reverse or forestall the development of deficits in the person. These deficits are seen as being brought by the person to either all situations, or to specific risk situations.
2. Transaction-focused programs that view the locus of risk as residing in a unique combination of person and environmental conditions. Such programs, regardless of whether they focus their intervention efforts on one or the other side of the transaction, or both simultaneously, make *explicit* their primary emphasis on reshaping the interactions that are developmentally problematic.
3. Environmentally focused programs that place both the locus of risk and the primary point(s) of intervention on elements of the social and physical environment.

As noted above, across, and within each of these transaction continuum keyed program models, another set of distinctions has particular theoretical and practical import. Key among these distinctions are the ways in which programs allow us to view the *nature* and *locus* of risk factors, the specificity of programs' outcome targeting, the degree to which programs emphasize the avoidance of negative outcomes or the enhancement of positive ones, and the extent to which the individual is seen as being to blame for the developmental outcomes of concern. Distinctions among representative programs, and the broader program models, on these dimensions will be highlighted throughout our discussion of the broader program models.

Before moving on, there is an important caveat that must be raised. Specifically, we know from discussions at the VCPPP conference where this chapter was presented, that although there is considerable agreement from prevention specialists about our program model categories, there is less acceptance of the categories to which we have assigned specific programs. We recognize that there are exceptions to the way many of the general case programs we discuss have been carried out, and that focusing on these exceptions would make some programs eligible for inclusion in categories their promulgators would find more congenial. Throughout our discussion we will provide representative examples of such exceptions. We will also suggest ways that programs in one category may, in the future, be integrated with efforts in others. These issues notwithstanding, we feel that the overall schema we offer below is an essential step in developing a systematic conceptual and empirical knowledge base for prevention. Hence, we ask that the focus be on the general processes that are embodied in what would be a prototypic example of the programs we discuss, rather than on a debate about whether this or that specific instance of a program is in the correct category.

Person-Focused Interventions.

This rubric has been used previously by Cowen (1985) to distinguish between person- and situation-focused programs. Although it is not our intent to use his categories in the same fashion, our work owes a debt to that predecessor. For us, programs that are person-focused are those which emphasize the person side of the transactional model. They do not attend to problematic transactions except insofar as they seek to remedy the deficits that individuals bring to their interactions with their social world. These programs virtually ignore aspects of the social and physical environment with which individuals are attempting to cope, or the environment's role in shaping the problematic developmental trajectories that are to be remedied by the intervention.

A first set of these programs are those that focus on children or adolescents who are at risk as a function of displaying initial signs of behavioral, emotional, or other related difficulties. The degree to which such programs can appropriately be labeled as primary preventive in their focus is, at best, debatable. That is, since clear signs of disorder are already present such programs are, at least for the *primary* prevention purist, perhaps better labeled *secondary* prevention or *early intervention* programs. Others however, (e.g., Kellam, Branch, Agrawal, & Ensminger, 1975; Jason, Ferone, & Soucy, 1979) see these efforts within the domain of primary prevention. For this reason, we begin with these programs that are at primary prevention's outermost boundary.

Critical to the basis of these programs is the view that children with emergent, early stage behavior problems are at higher risk for subsequent disorder. These difficulties are thought to evolve into more serious disorder if not checked and reversed early in their course. The primary goal of these interventions is the reversal or alleviation of the emerging problem behaviors or emotional difficulties. Less attention is paid to the mechanisms responsible for the ways in which the early difficulties are linked to later disorder. Of particular note is the general failure of such programs (at least in their intervention components) to attend to ways in which the *reaction* of the environment (e.g., other persons) to such children may maintain or exacerbate the difficulties. Instead, the primary emphasis is on changing the child through therapeutic or behavior-change focused activities, such as the "good behavior game" (e.g., Kellam et al., 1975), consultation with teachers on behavior management strategies, and the use of nonprofessionals in activities with children that approximate one-to-one therapy or tutoring models (e.g., Cowen, Trost, Lorion, Dorr, Izzo, & Isaacson, 1975; Jason, Ferone, & Soucy, 1979).

As illustrated in Figure 1.2, models of risk may be viewed on a continuum, ranging from those that place the locus primarily in the person, to those at the interface of the individual and the environment, to those fully external to the person. Given this view, programs that rely on early behavior problems to *define* risk are at a point on the continuum only slightly less internal-individually focused than those that emphasize genetic risk. Here, at least, the risk characteristic may be modified (in contrast to genetic vulnerability). However, in the instance of behavior problems as risk factors, what may be viewed as the definition of the developmentally hazardous circumstance is no less *within* the organism than a genetic deficit. That is, risk defined in this fashion is seen to be independent of the setting in which the organism is functioning at any particular point in time. Thus, at least implicitly, programs targeted at children with such risk characteristics see children as bearing a great deal of responsibility for their own dysfunction and its course, with both the locus of disorder and the target of the intervention being in the individual.

The next level of person-focused efforts comprise what are perhaps the major subset of school-based primary prevention programs attempted to date. These programs generally start with the view that the individual is lacking in certain essential knowledge, skills, or abilities, although difficulties are not yet clearly present. The general form of these programs is to attempt, though a variety of activities and the delivery of structured curricula, to teach the hypothesized lacking skills, abilities, and information to the persons at risk. By contrast to behavioral-risk focused programs, these efforts do not require the identification of specific persons with these risk characteristics. Instead, they may be delivered to whole groups of children and adolescents in naturally occurring groupings (e.g., classroom groups). It is thought that such a model of delivery will not be harmful to those who are not deficient in the particular skills/information, while teaching the requisite skills to those with existing or potential skill/information deficits.

The most basic of these programs involves information dissemination. These include efforts that have sought to provide information

	Conditions of risk located within the person – person-centered risk and programs	Risks are seen to arise from *specific* combination of environmental and person-level factors – transactional risk points and programs	Environmental risk and hazards – here the risk is posited as entirely external to individual environmentally-focused, change efforts as programs
The continuum of locus of risk toward which prevention efforts are targeted			
Target of change of programs that are focused on risk(s) on that point on the continuum	Prevention programs' target of change are conditions in or characteristics of *the person*	Prevention efforts focus *intentionally* and explicitly on problematic transactional circumstances	Prevention programs of this type seek to reduce environmentally hazardous conditions and enhance needed resources or protective conditoins
Representative risk conditions for that point on the continuum that may be specifically targeted by program efforts, or used as risk markers for selecting populatoins	• Biological vulnerabilities • Genetic Risk • Physical trauma • Emergent behavioral problems	• Non-specific competence deficits (e.g. social skills/ decision-making) • Life Transitions • Problem Peer Interactions • Specific Skill Deficits and Related Environmental Demands/ Hazards • Ability Deficits for Anticipated Future Context Demans • Developmental/ Environmental Mismatches • Poor match of child characteristics and parent expectations	• Health Care Deficits • Social and Economic Disadvantage • Racial Prejudice • Lowered/ Inappropriate expectations of others • Disorganized, damaging, hazardous, and inappropriate developmental contexts • Conditions that remove or impede control, dignity, self-esteem, and opportunity • Environmental incentives for "maladaptive" behavior

Figure 1.2

about the harmful effects of certain substances (e.g., drugs, tobacco) or risk-taking behaviors, and the causes of diseases or unwanted outcomes (e.g., AIDS, pregnancy, and nutritional deficits). At the core of these programs is the provision of certain basic information about the topic of concern. Frequently, an additional goal is that of inducing fear or anxiety sufficient to motivate the use of the newly learned information. Thus, a lack of knowledge (as well as accompanying motivation) is assumed to be the basis of risk.

These information-focused programs tend to focus on very specific behavioral outcomes, and within the context of the current model, they are targeted at that point in the developmental trajectory that is very close to the emergence of the condition(s) of concern. There is little attention to other factors that may make the individual more or less vulnerable to engaging in the problem behaviors. Further, the target behaviors are not viewed as emergent symptoms of other conditions but rather as quite specific, circumscribed dysfunctions. The viability of these assumptions has come under serious question of late, and data on programs that emphasize factual information have been very disappointing (Schaps, Bartolo, Moskowitz, Palley, & Churgin, 1981). Indeed, there are some data to suggest that these efforts, when not used in combination with other competence enhancement strategies, may actually increase, at least initially, the likelihood of the undesired behaviors (Goodstadt, 1978).

A much broader set of individually focused program efforts are those that seek to enhance specific competencies through direct training or by providing experiences that promote the acquisition of the skills. Cowen (1985) notes that a basic assumption of these efforts is that, "Acquiring such skills and/or having such experiences is presumed to radiate positively to adjustment" (p. 39). Adjustment here is used in the general sense, independent of particular settings or situational circumstances. These programs are based on the view that individuals who have deficiencies in the competencies that are emphasized in the training program are at greater risk either for maladjustment in a broad range of areas and/or for specific disorders. These programs are far more proactive than those that focus on the remediation of early behavioral dysfunction and, thus, more truly primary prevention focused. Still, it must be clear that at their heart they remain deficit reduction models that largely ignore, except in a very general sense, the contribution of factors external to the individual in the trajectory to disorder.

Programs of this sort have tended to focus on specific subsets of competencies. At their broadest levels such programs focus on: (1)

cognitive skills and abilities; (2) behavioral skills; and (3) coping with affective arousal, distress, self-regulation, and negative affect states or psychological self-appraisals. Extensive work in each of these areas has demonstrated that when well-executed, such efforts can be very effective in training to criterion (Cowen, 1985). However, the extent to which increases in these skills have generalized to nontraining settings, or more importantly to *actual changes in adjustment and behavioral functioning*, is less clear, with adequate long-term follow-up data not yet available for a definitive answer to this issue.

Cowen (1985) notes that these program efforts are based on a "three-step conceptual paradigm." The primary elements of this are: (1) identification of skills or competencies, through empirical investigation, that are associated with the presence or absence of adequate adaptation; (2) the development of age-appropriate programs to impart these skills; and (3) demonstration of the outcomes of the intervention efforts. Although this is fine as a general strategy for developing such programs, this formulation ignores the *mechanisms* of development of these abilities and/or for understanding why the particular skills targeted are adaptively important. Implicitly, this is a strategy that relies heavily on epidemiological approaches, which, at their core, are still deficit-focused, seeking to identify the immunological element that is lacking. Without further attention to just how these abilities or skills modify the essential transactions between individuals and their environments, such a formulation falls short of the goals and requirements of a systematic model to guide prevention.

Even a partial review of the programs that concern themselves with each of the component competencies that have been addressed to date is well outside the focus or scope of this chapter. However, it may be helpful to discuss briefly some of the most prevalent generic models in each category to provide some idea of how these programs concretely manifest the above issues. In the category of cognitive competencies are those programs that attempt to enhance and develop basic academic and intellectual abilities. Whether targeted toward parental stimulation of infants and toddlers with educationally relevant materials or toward preschoolers and primary graders who may require tutoring due to risk for academic failure (e.g., Jason & DeAmici, 1977; Pierson, Walker, & Tivnan, 1984; Ramey & Campbell, 1984; Schweinhart & Weikart, 1980), these programs can be distinguished by their heavy reliance on achievement measures and intelligence test scores to determine their success.

Yet another group of cognitively focused programs that have achieved widespread adoption and recognition are those that seek to enhance the interpersonal cognitive social problem-solving skills (ICPS) of their target groups. These are exemplified in the work of Spivack, Shure and their colleagues (e.g., Shure & Spivack, 1982) and others (e.g., Elias, Gara, Ubriaco, Rothbaum, Clabby, & Schuyler, 1986; Gesten, et al., 1982; Weissberg, Caplan, & Sivo, this book). This ICPS approach has sought to identify the elements of successful social problem solving and to teach them to children in preschools and the primary and secondary grades. The generation of alternative problem solutions, the development of viable plans for attaining desired ends, and the identification of the consequences of behaviors selected are, among others, all key elements of these ICPS programs.

These ICPS efforts, like the intellectual enhancement programs, are focused on addressing a deficit that impedes the person in all areas of functioning. They again fail to attend to the nature of the transactions that are problematic, or the ways the characteristics of particular environments play a role in the difficulties experienced. These programs are, however, compatible with the T-E perspective of multicausal pathways to deviant developmental trajectories and outcomes, as a key presumption of ICPS efforts is that the skill deficits are antecedent to a wide array of disorders.

Behavioral skill-building programs. These programs take several forms. Those that are broad-based, multi-outcome-focused seek to teach skills that are generic (e.g., negotiation, role-taking, adaptive assertiveness) while others emphasize task specific skills such as those required to resist pressure from other people to engage in undesirable behaviors (e.g., substance use, sexual behavior, risk-taking). In both instances the persons at risk are seen as lacking important behavioral skills that are necessary to negotiate important social interactions. A key distinction, however, is the extent to which particular circumstances in the environment are necessary for the lack of these abilities to be of concern. In the case of skills that are thought to be necessary to prevent *specific* difficulties, it is at least implicit that the environment plays a key role in the emergence of the difficulties, such that if the external pressures were not present the problem behavior would not ensue. By contrast, the lack of more *generic* social skills is thought to increase the probability that individuals will have difficulties in all spheres of their lives and to increase their *overall level of vulnerability* to a range of disorders and life problems.

A final group of individually focused programs seeks to reduce the *psychological* vulnerabilities and increase individual affective self-regulation capabilities. Based on the work of Lazarus, Kanfer, and others (Kanfer & Stevenson, 1985; Lazarus & Folkman, 1984;

Meichenbaum, 1985) these programs seek to enhance individuals' abilities to cope with stress or other affectively negative states, to regulate and moderate their affective responses, especially in emotionally arousing circumstances, and to improve their self-esteem and sense of mastery/efficacy.

Coping-skills programs are based on recent work (Meichenbaum, 1985) that suggests that cognitive-behavioral strategies for stress-innoculation, resistance to or dealing with anger, as well as the active seeking of support in emotionally taxing situations can be taught and may be of critical value for enabling people to function effectively in a wide array of situations. Similarly, deficits in adequate emotional self-regulation capacities have been linked to impulsivity and poor problem solving. Hence, individually focused skill-development preventive efforts have paid increasing attention to remedying these deficits (e.g., Pentz & Pentz, 1986). Finally, given the consistent association found between a heightened level of feelings of personal efficacy, self-worth, and competence in children and adolescents (Dweck & Leggett, 1988), programs such as those by Bry (1982) have begun the quest for strategies that are effective in instilling these psychological characteristics in youngsters who may otherwise have more negative views of themselves and their ability to effect outcomes in their lives.

Building on the above efforts and similar ones that demonstrate the potential of programs that seek to facilitate the development of single, quite specific sets of skills are a new generation of individually focused skill-building efforts. These attempts recognize that many of the above views of the skills and competencies necessary for adequate functioning are not incompatible on either conceptual or programmatic levels, and that they may be complementary in synergistic ways. These new efforts attempt to combine in one program what are perceived to be the most essential abilities and skills *across* the cognitive, behavioral, and affective domains. Botvin's Life Skills Training approach, discussed elsewhere in this book, is a primary example of one such program. Other work (for a more complete discussion, see Michelson, 1987) has compared the relative efficacy of programs such as those which teach social skills or cognitive interpersonal social problem-solving abilities with those that combine across these and other skills. The data have generally supported those programs that combine elements.

At the core of these combined efforts, at least implicitly, is a recognition of the multicausal nature of the pathways to dysfunction. For example, although children may be taught problem-solving skills, if deficits exist in their self-regulatory or emotional coping capacities they may be unable to delay their response sufficiently well to engage in the problem-solving process when they are in affectively charged situations. Similarly, if children are able successfully to engage in the problem-solving process they must: (1) have the desired behavior available to them in their skills repertoire; (2) have a sufficient sense of confidence in their ability to carry it out; and (3) have the values and motivation to select the desired behavior.

There are several features of individually focused program efforts that are noteworthy as they relate to our model. First, in many instances what is being done is most compatible with a rehabilitation, or reconstructive, view of prevention. This approach still views the person as the seat of the disorder and, indeed, deficient in certain fundamental ways that, should they come to the attention of a clinician, might result in the diagnosis of disorder. This approach is flawed, for several reasons. At its most troublesome, despite whatever else is said to the contrary, it pulls our focus away from the essential role of the environment, as well as away from the interplay between the person and the environment, and puts the focus squarely on the individual. In addition, such a stance is *fundamentally incompatible* with the values of a community or preventive psychology that seeks to avoid blaming victims for the difficulties they encounter. Finally, and again in a way that is incompatible with a T-E approach to prevention, such an approach requires us to view all troublesome behaviors and outcomes as the result of some deficit in the person rather than one possible response that any healthy, adequately functioning individual might have to the disordered or developmentally hazardous environmental circumstances they confront.

Transactional Programs

The key factors in the categorization of programs in our model are (1) the point on the transactional continuum on which they intentionally focus, and (2) the locus of the risk that they explicitly or implicitly address. Programs that fall within the transactional category are focused, *intentionally* and *explicitly*, on one or more sets of transactions that individuals may engage in that predispose them to increased risk for dysfunction. In these approaches, a set of characteristics of the person as well as a set of characteristics of the environment must be identified, such that *only when they combine* do they increase risk and distort normal developmental growth patterns. Here the locus of risk is seen to arise from persons with particular characteristics entering or developing in certain settings and contexts that would not be problematic for others. What is at least implicit in these programs is that some specifiable predisposition or coping deficit must be present *within* the child or adolescent *and there must be some specifiable trigger(s) or hazard(s) in the environment that must be experienced* in order for the developmental difficulties to emerge.

Like the individually focused programs discussed above, programs such as these, although transactional in nature, most often focus their change efforts on that side of the risk equation that deals with the person's contribution. Again, these programs also tend to focus on affective, behavioral, and cognitive skill deficits, and/or genetic-constitutional conditions that interact with certain circumstances to produce disorder. One key set of programs of this type are those that Cowen (1985) labeled situation-focused. He notes that highly stressful life circumstances or life crises may place heavy demands on the person's cognitive, affective, and behavioral coping skills such that those with less than excellent abilities in all these areas and/or deficiencies in the availability of other coping resources may be at heightened risk.

A number of school-based programs have been developed that seek to help children cope with major life crises and transitions through the provision of emotional and instrumental support by peers or nonprofessionals (e.g., Bogat, Jones, & Jason, 1980; Jason et al., 1988; Felner, Norton, Cowen, & Farber 1981; Pedro-Carroll & Cowen, 1985; Pedro-Carrol, Cowen, Hightower, & Guare, 1986). Other programs have attempted to teach specific behavioral and cognitive problem-solving skills and abilities that may be required by the transitional tasks (e.g., Elias et al., 1986; Felner & Adan, 1988).

More generally, based on empirical literature that links the failure to effectively cope with stressful life events and transitions to heightened risk for a broad array of dysfunction (see Felner, 1984, for a more detailed discussion), program efforts in this group fall into what we have labelled broad-based antecedent efforts rather than belonging with those that target the prevention of specific disorder. Of course, that is not to say that a priori target outcomes, such as school behavioral dysfunction, may not be the priority of such efforts (e.g., Cowen & Hightower, 1986). Rather, it may also be a number of positive preventive "spillover-side effects" of such programs that reduce the incidence of nontargeted dysfunction.

Yet another major set of transactionally focused school-based programs are those that focus on difficulties that may arise from problematic peer interactions. Here, both specifically targeted and broad-based antecedent efforts are found. Illustrative of the former are those efforts that seek to teach children or adolescents *specific* skills or abilities to deal with *specific* elements of the peer culture or environment that may influence the probability of the target outcome. An excellent example of this type of program is provided by the work of Rotheram (Rotheram, 1988; Rotheram, Armstrong, & Boorsem, 1982) in which children are taught refusal skills and adaptive assertiveness strategies for dealing with pressures from peers to engage in substance abuse. Other investigators have employed similar models and approaches in attempting to prevent health risk behaviors (e.g., those relating to teenage pregnancy, AIDS, and smoking and those that may produce other forms of personal injury, such as drinking and driving; Levy, Iverson, & Walberg, 1975; Pentz, 1983; Perry & Jessor, 1985). A second strand of these peer-focused transactional programs is exemplified by the work of Coie and his colleagues, discussed elsewhere in this volume. Although it is the skill deficits that are proximally addressed by the intervention, what makes these programs such excellent exemplars of transactional models is they explicitly see the source of risk (and the problematic element of the developmental trajectory that both causes and maintains the risk) as the *interactions* between children and their peers.

Taking a somewhat different tack are those programs that seek to *anticipate* those skills and abilities that may be required of children at some *future point* in their development. Representative of these programs are those that focus on the early development of cognitive and social skills (e.g., High Scope's efforts, Project Head Start) that may be required to adapt to demands that will emerge as salient when the child enters new, developmentally keyed settings or situations. By equipping children with those competencies that may be required to master the demands of these settings it is argued that children will be able to avoid potentially developmentally hazardous circumstances (e.g., peer rejection, being placed in special classes, problematic teacher labeling), so that positive effects will continue even when initial program effects (e.g., IQ gains) seem to disappear. It should also be noted that the underlying philosophy of many of these programs emphasizes the replacement or enhancement of resources that may otherwise be deficient in the child's environment, the lack of which results in the failure of vulnerable children to develop the desired competencies. In this way, these programs move far to one side of the transactionally focused continuum, bridging nicely to the fully ecologically based models discussed in the next section. This process is reflected in Schweinhart's work, discussed elsewhere in this volume.

The ICPS work (Shure & Spivack, 1982) is an ability building program that illustrates how a program that was initially purely individually focused can evolve toward a more integrative T-E perspective in ways that enhance its efficacy. Their findings revealed that a curriculum-based approach was effective in teaching children ICPS in ways that were successfully reflected on verbal assessments. However, the generalization of this learning to actual behaviors was less satisfactory. To address this concern the project introduced an element that sought to modify the interaction styles between children and teachers. This element involved the teaching of teachers to use *dialoguing*, a process by which children were asked to employ ICPS procedures throughout the school day, in multiple contexts and interactions. The assumption was that children may fail to demonstrate the requisite ICPS skills in desired situations as a function of the types of transactions that have been modeled or required of them in their actual daily experiences. Spivack and Shure have provided at least some data to indicate that the modification of student-teacher transactions in this fashion may result in improved behaviors in multiple situations throughout the school day (Shure & Spivack, 1982).

A set of transactionally focused program efforts that are sometimes overlooked as school-related strategies, but which impact heavily on adaptation in educational settings, are those that focus on the enhancement of parents as resources for their children. Programs may vary from those that target very basic processes of early attachment to those that seek to increase the role of the parent in the educational life of the child. In the former case, programs often focus on children who may be at risk because of difficult temperament or the presence of physically handicapping conditions (e.g., blindness, hearing loss). These conditions have been shown to be associated with parental response styles that reduce their availability to the child as developmental resources and increase the probability of other developmental deficits. Programs that target these conditions seek to facilitate the development of interaction patterns between the parent and child that more closely approximate typical, developmentally positive patterns (e.g., by teaching mothers of blind infants or toddlers how to *elicit* facial reactions to their presence from their children that enhance bonding and that may otherwise not occur due to the child's condition; Fraiberg, 1977).

A second set of parent-focused programs recognizes the importance of positive interrelationships between two of the primary systems in which children and adolescents spend most of their time; the family and the school. Based on the recognition of these relationships, a number of programs seek to involve parents who may otherwise be less invested in their child's academic school-related socioemotional development in activities in the home in ways that complement and support school efforts (Jason et al., 1988).

A final, often overlooked, transactional prevention strategy is that of matching the child's skills and developmental levels to the demands of the environment, as in educational readiness matching. For example, it is quite normal for children during the first ten or more years of life to show 6–12 month developmental delays or spurts in physical, cognitive, and affective functioning (Schwartz & Johnson, 1981). Despite arguments to the contrary in the educational literature, the usual determination for school entry (e.g., kindergarten or first grade) is heavily based on chronological age and any normative fluctuation in development would certainly not preclude a student's entry. However, if a student happens to have the misfortune of timing a delay period rather than a growth spurt along any of these developmental lines, to the beginning of school, it is clear that there may be serious risk of (1) the student having difficulties or failure experiences that result in self-labeling or attributions of ineptitude or incompetence in particular area(s), especially when they use peers as a reference standard; (2) negative labeling and expectations by teachers that occur independently or simultaneously with these self-labeling processes; and (3) the development of a work style in which there are very low levels of problem-solving persistence in the face of even initial failure. Any of these occurrences of circumstances may place the child on the beginning of a development trajectory toward serious academic and emotional difficulties, especially if allowed to persist.

Some tutoring programs are aimed at the alleviation of precisely these conditions (e.g., Jason et al., 1988). However, rather than simply attending to the children as if they have deficits when in fact at least the initial difficulties arise from normal processes, we can also attend to modifying their experience with the environment so that the original conditions either do not arise or do not persist. Additionally, correcting these problems early on without blaming children may also be important in improving the children's experiences with the environment. For example, in recent work by the current authors and their colleagues, (Felner, Felner, Evans & Blau, 1986), we have shown that holding back children in first grade who are not making satisfactory academic progress may be very successful in putting them back on track. However, when the failure experiences are allowed to persist by not holding back those children who are near or below what is a truly adequate level of academic or social performance, then failure continues and later adjustments in the person-setting relationships (e.g., by holding the student back in later grades) are far less successful in producing enduring positive upturns in academic functioning. Once expectations of failure and labeling processes are allowed to endure and solidify and/or building-block skills are not adequately developed, the child may actually begin to be the carrier of the dysfunction. What is so distressing about this is the understanding that there was absolutely nothing deficient in this child initially! Rather, the difficulties are simply the tragic consequences of a poor match between *arbitrary* regularities of the environment and the child's own growth regularities.

These are but a few current examples of transactional programs or the way a T-E perspective may guide educational perspective in ways that reduce developmental risk. Strongly supported by the basic research efforts of Sameroff and Chandler (1975) and that which has followed on transactional influences on development (Sroufe & Rutter, 1984), these programs have much promise as being more viable and fully attentive to the actual range of developmental processes involved than the more individually focused, deficit models. Nonetheless, most of these efforts still require that the person be seen as one of the targets for change and that at least part of the risk circumstance be present in the individual in a way that implies some individual level of deficit. A few efforts that are much closer to approximating a truly transactional stance in their conceptualizations explicitly recognize that the deficit is not real, in the sense of being a general flaw in the person, but is completely dependent on the situational context for its definition. Finally, some transactional programs also recognize that whatever difficulties the person brings to the transactions of concern may have arisen not because of some inherent, individually related vulnerability, but because of prior exposure to developmentally noxious environmental circumstances. Now we turn to programs that focus on contexts in which children and adolescents grow.

Environmentally and Ecologically Focused Prevention Efforts

The goals of environmentally/ecologically focused programs can, generally, be summarized as either (1) providing necessary resources or conditions in the person's environment to facilitate development and coping efforts or (2) the modification or removal of conditions in the environment that are developmentally hazardous. Although seemingly simple when conceptualized in these ways, actual preventive efforts along these routes have often been dismissed as overly difficult and requiring unrealistically high levels of social engineering or large scale social system change (Cowen, 1985). Hence, these programs, at least when conservative definitions of prevention programs are employed, are the least frequently attempted of all prevention efforts, especially in educational contexts.

Despite this paucity of direct efforts, if we attend to what Bronfenbrenner (1979) has called *experiments in nature* (in our case naturally occuring prevention efforts) and to system-change efforts that have not had mental health outcomes as their primary focus (but which nonetheless bear on such outcomes), then there are significantly more examples that show the promise of such approaches.

First, it must be understood that a critical underlying assumption of environmental level approaches is that the locus of risk with which we are concerned is entirely outside the child. That is not to say that children exposed to hazardous environmental circumstances may not develop important skill deficits or needs for enhancement that are addressed by the programs in the prior two categories. It is simply that the presence of such difficulties and needs are not seen to result from any flaw or inherent characteristic of the child but, rather, from the contexts in which they have developed or are currently operating. Here, a lack of appropriate life skills *is itself something that is an appropriate target of prevention efforts* and environmentally focused preventive efforts are, in their timing, *antecedent* to the evolution of these deficits.

It is also the case that environmentally focused programs do not see individuals as in any way to blame for their risk status or disorder. Indeed, when risk is viewed from this perspective it is far more appropriate to view children as being at risk rather than to talk about high-risk children. In this case children are not high-risk, circumstances are, and it is the exposure to these circumstances that is the concern. To return to a central earlier point, the underlying perspective of these programs is that *any* normal or typical child or adolescent, when exposed to the conditions of concern, may begin to show the emergence of problematic developmental outcomes and disorder.

Finally, although environmentally focused efforts may target a specific disorder because of the particular concerns of the intervention team, these efforts will, with few exceptions, produce positive adaptive consequences in a wide array of domains as well as reduce risk for a host of dysfunctional outcomes.

Context-focused efforts may have as their target a number of particular elements of the environment, either singly or in combination. The family system, peer group, and the school's social, organizational, and physical characteristics are among those to which educationally related efforts are most often targeted.

At the family-context level, programs that enable parents to provide the levels of educational and social stimulation that are necessary for a child's optimal development (e.g., parenting enhancement programs, programs that train parents to provide necessary early stimulation; Johnson, 1988) are illustrative of the wide array of needed and potentially powerful interventions that may be tried appropriately under the flag of school-based primary prevention. So too are programs that attempt to provide children with adequate levels of nutrition (e.g., Olds, 1988). Emergent school-based efforts to assist homeless children and their families by providing necessary stabilization and food resources also fall into this category. One has only to understand that factors such as inadequate nutrition, early educational experiences, and other forms of deprivation explain far more of the variance in identifying those at risk than does, for example, any assessment of social skill levels, to agree that efforts targeted at these circumstances must be included in the continuum of primary prevention models to which educators must attend.

Similarly, a number of programs (e.g., Bry, 1983) have attempted to build on the powerful influence of peers during elementary and secondary school in shaping developmental course and outcome. Some of these efforts focus on the potentially positive roles peers may play by attempting to enhance the levels of social support available to one another, and the key role such support may play during times of heightened stress. Other programs have turned to a focus on reducing the detrimental influences that peers may have in modeling or providing pressure to engage in behaviors that may be hazardous to the physical or emotional health of youth (e.g., substance abuse, risk-taking behaviors; Bukowski, 1985; McAlister, et al., 1980) and/or through their treatment of one antoher, especially during high risk times.

Finally, the most overlooked, and perhaps among the most promising of these programs, are those that seek to understand the ways in which elements of the school or home environment may be structured, developed, or reorganized to make them more appropriate to the competencies and developmental requirements of most children. For example, in one of the few programs intentionally addressing these factors, Felner and his colleagues (Felner, Ginter & Primavera, 1982; Felner & Adan, 1988) have demonstrated that the reorganization of the school structure during the transitions to junior and senior high school may have a significant and lasting impact on the academic and emotional well-being of students, especially those who may be from economically disadvantaged backgrounds.

Focusing on large junior and senior high schools that had multiple elementary or junior high schools feeding into them, these authors sought to reduce the flux and complexity of the school environment students were entering, reduce their exposure to threatening older students, and increase the levels of peer and teacher support available. All of this was accomplished in several quite straightforward ways. Students entering schools in the School Transitional Environment Project (STEP) were assigned to core classes in groups of 60–80 students, all students in their first year in the setting. Hence, the number of other students that STEP children needed to get to know and interact with, at least during the majority of the day, was significantly reduced. In addition, to reduce the fear and confusion students might feel in attempting to adapt to a new and often overwhelming school setting, core classes were scheduled in rooms that were in close physical proximity to one another. Finally, teachers' roles were restructured to make them the administrative-counseling link between the school, the student, and the student's family. All components are based on a T-E model of adaptation to life transitions that specifies that modification of certain elements of the environment may facilitate the accomplishment of necessary adaptive tasks accompanying major transitions (Felner, Rowlison, & Terre, 1986).

Long-term two- and five-year follow-ups of various trials of the program have been conducted. Compared to controls and students in the same schools in years prior to STEP's inception, the drop-out rate of STEP students (which is nearly 50% in the control samples) is reduced by more than 50% (Felner & Adan, 1988). Moreover, demonstrating the broad-based antecedent preventive effects of this program are findings that show that control students, as compared to program students, show significant decrements in self-concept and increases in behavioral and emotional difficulties, delinquent acts, and reported likelihood of illicit substance use. All of this is accomplished in a program that, once established, requires very low levels of additional funding.

Additional support for the potential efficacy of ecologically based school-climate reorganization-focused program efforts is provided by data that demonstrate the relationships of such structural and environmental elements of schools as their perceived social climate, classroom sizes, school disciplinary policies, overall size/population, and physical condition to the academic performance, levels of behavioral and emotional problems, and associated dysfunctions (e.g., drug use, crime; Moos, 1979). Further, it is clear from many years of research on teacher expectations that modifications in the interactions of teachers with students, especially those that reflect expectations of success or behavior problems, may be inordinately powerful in shaping the adaptive outcomes that are obtained by children whom they teach (Rist, 1970; Rosenthal & Jacobson, 1968).

Almost all of the above environmental interventions also demonstrate the degree to which the joining of the ecological perspective to the transactional viewpoint can enrich prevention program planning and success. At the most obvious level we see that attention to the match between children, their resources and needs, and the environments in which they function can have enormous power for facilitating our understanding of the meaning, origin, and maintenance of particular behaviors or affective reactions that might otherwise be attributed to deficits or disorder inside the individual. A less obvious advantage of this synthesis of perspectives is that it focuses attention on the systems that may not directly describe the context of the student's daily experience but profoundly shape the proximal developmental context.

For example, the interactions between teachers and administrators or the economic climate and conditions in which the school system is functioning may shape teacher burnout and expectations of students, as can the nature of the school's physical environments (class sizes, building conditions, etc.). In quite different ways we again see the importance of setting-setting conditions in which the child's proximal contexts are nested: social policies that shape the quality and availability of preschool programs or daycare for children in a school district may influence the general performance levels of children within the district or the extent of behavior problems that may be present among children in each classroom. These conditions will also profoundly influence children's more proximal educational context, including: (1) the attention and support they have available from teachers; (2) teacher performance expectations and morale; and (3) the level of support for prosocial behavior children receive from their peer group, either through direct statements or through modeling.

As we move to fourth generation prevention programs, the potential power and utility of ecological approaches have also been demonstrated in remarkable fashion by non-mental-health professionals. Calling into question Cowen's (1985) contention that broader societal-system based changes may be too difficult or too far in the future to attempt at this juncture, and indeed demonstrating that such changes may be necessary for more individually-focused programs to have any enduring impact, are those efforts that have changed the very nature of the opportunities and experiences perceived available to children at risk because of social disadvantage. One such example is the "I Have a Dream Foundation," begun by the now famous pledge of one very generous individual to guarantee college educations to a group of disadvantaged inner-city sixth-graders, as well as to provide support services and exposure to cultural opportunities and career paths previously not part of these children's direct experiences. The "I Have a Dream Foundation" has now grown across the country. Chapters match corporate and wealthy individual sponsors with groups of school children from economically disadvantaged backgrounds and have demonstrated just how powerfully the broader social context in which learning takes place may influence the socioemotional and academic adjustment of students. This program exposes students to new and different experiences and possibilities, as well as expands the opportunities children and adolescents have for pursuing these possibilities through the provision of essential economic and interpersonal resources in a systematic fashion. Thus, participating students have been made to feel greater control over the outcomes they attain and have achieved far greater academic and personal success than would have otherwise been predicted.

Efforts such as this and others like it (e.g., the city of Boston's program to guarantee jobs to all graduates of inner-city high schools) demonstrate just how powerfully systems in which the school environment is nested may influence the impact of programs mounted within the school context. They also underscore the need for and potential of school-community partnerships in the development of innovative and effective prevention strategies that attend to the full set of developmental contexts and systems that impact on the whole child when mounting school-based prevention efforts. Without attention to factors such as those attended to by the "I Have a Dream Foundation" or by the STEP program that at smaller levels seek to restructure the developmentally noxious environments in which many of our children live and grow, programs that seek to enhance the skills of children or increase their resistance to engaging in substance abuse and other risk behaviors may have disappointing results. Although skills or information may be learned, the continued motivation for utilization of these competencies may be lacking as the incentives and models for doing otherwise may not be clearly present in the broader context in which the child and/or school setting is nested.

What is common across the above ecological efforts and others is the understanding that nearly all children and youth have "thresholds of vulnerability," and that the nature of the environments they confront may influence the degree to which they are successful in staying above this threshold and the degree of jeopardy of their developing disorder. Further, any preventive intervention must attend both to the direct system level conditions involved and the system-system interactions that shape these contexts. Implicit is the assumption that attempting to teach children and adolescents skills and abilities to deal with environments that are well beyond what should reasonably be expected of any typical individual at that developmental level is neither appropriate nor the most effective way of addressing these problems.

Implementation and the Transactional-Ecological Perspective

Before we close, a few comments are necessary about the practicality of T-E based approaches to prevention and the advantages and disadvantages that they may offer educational contexts. The T-E perspective puts a premium on the match between the program's elements and the demands and regularities of the settings in which it is being mounted. Similarly, program efficacy will be determined by the degree of difficulty of the transactions required of the program and setting to accommodate to one another. That is, it is important that our programs be ecologically congruent with the demands and regularities of the settings and schools in which they will be mounted.

If these issues are not attended to in the development of primary prevention programs, even the most promising strategies will ultimately yield disappointing results. Programs developed under the optimal conditions that usually accompany initial field-trials in prevention research, once exposed to more typical conditions, may not be able to be implemented with sufficient fidelity to retain their efficacy or essential characteristics. Regularities of host settings that are focused on responding to demands beyond those to which the program seeks to attend (e.g., economic factors, pressure for increased test scores), may systematically distort the program's intended functioning in such a way that what actually occurs is little more than a vague approximation of the program as designed. Dangers here include the wasting of valuable time and resources, the erroneous conclusion that prevention doesn't work when, in fact, it has not really been attempted as intended and, most tragically, the emergence of socioemotional problems in students that could have otherwise been prevented.

One answer here may be to attempt to get settings to be better at hosting prevention efforts. Indeed, of late, we increasingly hear statements about the inadequacies of the settings in which we are attempting to mount prevention efforts and comments about the need for "teacher proofing" programs or for additional training for teachers (Kumpfer, 1988; Goodstadt, 1988; Swisher, 1988). To our mind this approach is all too reminiscent of victim blaming (Ryan, 1971) and the process that has characterized the individual psychotherapy domain. That is, approaches have continued to be developed that ignore the needs, traditions, and circumstances of many of the clients they are trying to serve, especially those most in need. Thus, we continue to hear disadvantaged populations disparaged as poor potential clients, and find that individuals with such backgrounds tend not to avail themselves of services (Felner & Lorion, 1985). In prevention, unfortunately, some of the more recent comments about settings in which we are trying to reach at-risk and disadvantaged populations are becoming all too reminiscent of this therapy model. A clear alternative to this view for therapy is that the therapy procedures and delivery models we have developed do not sufficiently take into account the realities of the circumstances of those they are intended to serve.

For prevention, the lesson should be clear. We cannot afford to continue to develop programs that do not adequately attend to the ecological contexts in which they will be mounted. As we have described, these setting-setting relationships are critical to the impact of each setting, respectively, on its participants. We must do the hard work of developing programs and models that can be mounted with fidelity. An effective prevention program that will be predictably and systematically vulnerable to host-setting threats to fidelity (or that requires the introduction of extensive human or economic resources into the setting that cannot realistically be expected to endure or be replicated) must be understood for what it truly is, neither a viable nor an effective program.

In addition to pointing us toward these conceptual issues, the T-E perspective also offers some direction for solutions. Illustratively, one of the clearest advantages that stems from it is the support provided for broad-based antecedent approaches to prevention. Currently, schools are being bombarded with separate programs, demands and constituencies that want them to provide time and resources for the prevention of a wide array of disorders. Drop-out rates, teen pregnancy, substance abuse, youth suicide, emotional and behavioral problems and, not least, academic failure, are but a few of the prevention targets schools are being asked to address. The knowledge that all of these conditions may be addressed with a common set of weapons and strategies, as well as a theoretical framework that provides guidelines for the development of these strategies, may go far in reducing the confusion and frustration that educational personnel and staff experience in attempting to deal with the issues that have been laid at their doorstep. Moreover, broad-based, integrative programs may require the least diversion of resources from other tasks to which the school must also attend.

A second critical component of the model for educational-setting based intervention is the increased emphasis that it gives to those ecological and environmental approaches that are perhaps the most ecologically congruent with the demands and nature of educational settings. By attending to regularities and circumstances that characterize these settings that may be developmentally hazardous or at odds with the capacities and needs of the children in them, and building-in access to necessary resources as part of the *fabric* of these settings, prevention may occur without the disruption and diversion of important resources that may be required in other parts of the educational endeavor.

Summary

In the preceding pages we have presented a conceptual framework that can guide the development of the next generation of primary prevention efforts and serve as a foundation on which to build a systematic knowledge-base for prevention. In our presentation we have attempted to articulate not only the ways it may be helpful to attain these future ends, but also how employing this perspective to view our past efforts may provide us with a more integrative understanding of where we have been and, thus, enable us to draw on the wisdom that can be yielded from our experience to provide the broad outlines of the "House of Prevention" that we hope will be built on this foundation. It is also our hope that what we have discussed will enable readers to bring to their consideration of the remainder of the chapters in this volume, and to future prevention work, perspectives and questions beyond those raised directly by their authors. At the very least, we hope that the ways we have proposed for viewing the levels of analyses employed, the points on the transactional continuum targeted, the implicit assumptions about routes to disorder and its nature that are reflected in alternative programs strategies, and the issues of implementation lurking below the surface, will help future preventionists to consider not only what is there but also what might be.

References

Barker, R. G. (1968). *Ecological psychology: Concepts and methods for studying the environment of human behavior*. Stanford, CA: Stanford University Press.

Bell, R. Q. (1986). Age-specific manifestations in changing psychosocial risk. In D. C. Farren & J. D. McKinney (Eds.). *Risk in intellectual and psychosocial development* (pp. 177–185). Orlando, FL: Academic Press.

Bogat, G. A., Jones, J. W., & Jason, L. A. (1980). School transitions: Preventive intervention following an elementary school closing. *Journal of Community Psychology, 8*, 343–352.

Bronfenbrenner, U. (1979). *The ecology of human development: Experiments by nature and design*. Cambridge, MA: Harvard University Press.

Bry, B. (1983). Empirical foundations of family-based approaches to adolescent substance abuse. In T. Glynn, C. Leukefeld, & J. Ludford (Eds.). *Preventing adolescent drug abuse: Intervention strategies*. National Institute on Drug Abuse Research. Monograph No. 47. DHEW Publication No. (ADM) 83–1280. Washington, D.C.: U.S. Government Printing Office.

Bry, B. H. (1982). Reducing the incidence of adolescent problems through preventive intervention: One- and Five-Year Follow-up. *American Journal of Community Psychology, 10*, 265–276.

Bukowski, W. J. (1985). School-based substance abuse prevention: A review of program research. In S. Grisworld-Ezekoye, K. Kumpfer, & Bukowski, W.J., (Eds.). Childhood and chemical abuse: Prevention and intervention. *Journal of Children in Contemporary Society, 18*, (1)(2).

Cauce, A. M., Felner, R. D., & Primavera, J. (1982). Social support systems in high-risk adolescents: Structural components and adaptive impact. *American Journal of Community Psychology, 10*, 417–428.

Cowen, E. L. (1982). Research in primary prevention in mental health. *American Journal of Community Psychology, 10*, 239–367.

Cowen E. L. (1985). Person-centered approaches to primary prevention in mental health: Situation-focused and competence-enhancement. *American Journal of Community Psychology, 13*, 31–48.

Cowen, E. L., & Hightower, A. D. (1986). Stressful life events and young children's school adjustment. In S. M. Auerbach & A. L. Stolberg (Eds.), *Crisis intervention with children and families*. Washington, D.C.: Hemisphere Publishing Corporation.

Cowen, E. L., Trost, M. H., Lorion, R. D., Dorr, D., Izzo, L. D., & Isaacson, R. V. (1975) *New ways in school mental health: Early detection and prevention of school maladjustment*. New York: Behavioral Publications, Inc.

Dweck, C. S., & Leggett, E. L. (1988). A social-cognitive approach to motivation and personality. *Psychological Review, 95*, 256–273.

Elias, M. J., Gara, M., Ubriaco, M., Rothbaum, P. A., Clabby, J. F., & Schuyler, T. (1986). Impact of a preventive social problem-solving intervention on children's coping with middle-school stressors. *American Journal of Community Psychology, 14*, 259–275.

Felner, R. D. (1984). Vulnerability in childhood: A preventive framework for understanding children's efforts to cope with life stress and transitions. In M. C. Roberts & L. Peterson (Eds.). *Prevention of problems in childhood: Psychological research and applications*. New York: Wiley-Interscience.

Felner, R. D., & Adan, A. M. (1988). The school transitional environment project: An ecological intervention and evaluation. In R. H. Price, E. L. Cowen, R. P. Lorion, J.

Ramos-McKay, & B. Hitchins (Eds.). *Fourteen ounces of prevention: A casebook of exemplary primary prevention programs.* Washington, D.C.: American Psychological Association.

Felner, R.D. & Felner, T. Y. (in press). Primary prevention: Conceptual and methodological issues. In J. Rappaport & E. Seidman (Eds.) *Handbook of community psychology.* NY: Plenum.

Felner, R. D., Farber, S. S., & Primavera, J. (1983). Transitions and stressful life events: A model for primary prevention. In R. D. Felner, L. A. Jason, J. N. Moritsugu, & S. S. Farber (Eds.). *Preventive psychology: Theory, research, and prevention* (pp. 191–215). New York: Pergamon.

Felner, R. D., Felner, T. Y., Evans, E., & Blau, G. (1986). *Modifying environmental relationships to correct developmental trajectories: The case of grade retention.* Unpublished manuscript. Auburn University, AL.

Felner, R. D., Ginter, M. A., & Primavera, J. (1982). Primary prevention during school transitions: Social support and environmental structure. *American Journal of Community Psychology, 10,* 277–290.

Felner, R. D., Jason, L. A., Moritsugu, J. N., & Farber, S. S. (1983). Preventive psychology: Evaluation and current status. In R. D. Felner, L. A. Jason, J. N. Moritsugu, & S. S. Farber (Eds.). *Preventive psychology: Theory, research, and practice* (pp. 3–10). New York: Pergamon Press.

Felner, R. D., & Lorion, R. P. (1985). Clinical child psychology and prevention: Toward a workable and satisfying marriage. In J. M. Tuma (Ed.). *Proceedings: Conference on training clinical child psychology* (pp. 91–95). Baton Rouge, LA: Section on Clinical Child Psychology, American Psychological Association.

Felner, R. D., Norton, P. L., Cowen, E. L., & Farber, S. S. (1981). A prevention program for children experiencing life crises. *Professional Psychology, 12,* 446–452.

Felner, R.D., Rowlison, R.T., & Terre, L. (1986) Unravelling the Gordian knot in life change inquiry: A critical examination of crisis, stress, and transitional frameworks for prevention. In S.W. Auerbach & A.L. Stolberg (Eds.) *Children's life crisis events: Preventive intervention strategies.* Washington, DC: Hemisphere/McGraw Hill.

Felner, R.D., Silverman, M., & Adan, A.M. (1988) *Primary prevention: Relevance and principles for the prevention of youth suicide.* In the Proceedings of the Department of Health and Human Services Secretary's Task Force on Youth Suicide. Department of Health and Human Services.

Fraiberg, S. (1977). *Insights from the blind: Comparative studies of blind and sighted infants.* New York: Basic Books.

Gesten, E. L., Rains, M., Rapkin, B., Weissberg, R. P., Flores de Apodaca, R., Cowen, E. L., & Bowen, R. (1982). Training children in social problem-solving competencies: A first and second look. *American Journal of Community Psychology, 10,* 95–115.

Goodstadt, M. (1988). *School-based drug education research findings: What have we learned? What can be done?* Presentation to the First National Conference on Prevention Research Findings: Implications for Alcohol and Drug Abuse Program Planning. (NDA/NPN). March, Kansas City, MO.

Goodstadt, M. S. (1978). Alcohol and drug education. *Health Education Mongraphs, 6,* 263–279.

Jason, L.A. & DeAmici, I. (1977) An approach in providing mental health services to low-income parents. *International Journal of Family Counseling, 5,* 2–33.

Jason, L. A., Ferone, L., & Soucy, G. (1979). Teaching peer-tutoring behaviors in first- and third-grade classrooms. *Psychology in the Schools, 16,* 261–269.

Jason, L. A., Betts, D., Johnson, J., Smith, S., Krueckeberg, S., & Cradock, M. (1988). *An evaluation of an orientation plus tutoring school based prevention program.* Unpublished manuscript: DePaul University, Chicago, IL.

Johnson, D. L. (1988). Houston parent-child development project. In R. H. Price, E. L. Cowen, R. P. Lorion, J. Ramos-McKay, & B. Hitchins (Eds.). *Fourteen ounces of prevention: A Casebook of exemplary primary prevention programs.* Washington, D.C.: American Psychological Association.

Kanfer, F. H., & Stevenson, M. K. (1985). The effects of self-regulation on concurrent cognitive processing. *Cognitive Therapy and Research, 9,* 667–684.

Kellam, S. G., Branch, J. D., Agrawal, K. C., & Ensminger, M. E. (1975). *Mental health and going to school: The Woodlawn program of assessment, early intervention, and evaluation.* Chicago: University of Chicago Press.

Kumpfer, K. (1988). *School-based prevention programming: Challenges.* Presentation to the First National Conference on Prevention Research Findings: Implications for Alcohol and Drug Abuse Program Planning. (NIDA/NPN). March, Kansas City, MO.

Lazarus, R., & Folkman, S. (1984). *Stress, appraisal and coping.* New York: Springer.

Levy, S. R., Iverson, B. K., & Walberg, H. J. (1975). Adolescent pregnancy programs and educational interventions: A research synthesis and review. *Journal of Reviews of Social Health, 103,* 99–103.

Lewin, K. (1951). *Field theory in social science: Selected theoretical papers.* New York: Harper.

McAlister, A., Perry, C., Killen, J., Slinkard, L., & Maccoby, N. (1980). Pilot study of smoking, alcohol and drug abuse prevention. *American Journal of Public Health, 70,* 719–721.

Meichenbaum, D. (1985). *Stress inoculation training.* New York: Pergamon.

Michelson, L. (1987). Cognitive-behavioral strategies in the prevention and treatment of antisocial disorders in children and adolescents. In J. D. Burchard & S. N. Burchard (Eds.). *Prevention of delinquent behavior* (pp. 275–310). Beverly Hills: Sage.

Moos, R. H. (1979). *Evaluating Educational Environments.* San Francisco, CA: Jossey-Bass.

Neale, J.M., & Oltmanns, T.F. (1980). *Schizophrenia.* NY: John Wiley.

Olds, D. (1988). Prenatal/early infancy project. In R. H. Price, E. L. Cowen, R. P. Lorion, J. Ramos-McKay, & B Hitchins (Eds.). *Fourteen ounces of prevention: A casebook of exemplary primary prevention programs.* Washington, D.C.: American Psychological Association.

Pedro-Carroll, J. L., & Cowen, E. L. (1985). The children of divorce intervention project: An investigation of the efficacy of a school-based prevention program. *Journal of Consulting and Clinical Psychology, 53,* 603–611.

Pedro-Carroll, J. L., Cowen, E. L., Hightower, A. D., & Guare, J. C. (1986). Preventive intervention with latency-age children of divorce: A replication study. *American Journal of Community Psychology, 14,* 277–290.

Pentz, M. A. (1983). Prevention of adolescent substance abuse through social skills. In T. J. Glynn, C. G. Leukefeld, & J. P. Ludford (Eds.). *Preventing adolescent drug abuse: Intervention strategies. National Institute on Drug Abuse Research Monograph, 47.* DHHS Pub. No. (ADM) 83–1280. Washington, D.C.: U.S. Government Printing Office, pp. 195–232.

Pentz M. A., & Pentz, C. A. (1986). A social competence approach to stress prevention in early adolescents. *Annals of Behavioral Medicine.*

Perry, C. L., & Jessor, R. (1985). The concept of health promotion and the prevention of adolescent drug abuse. *Health Education Quarterly, 12,* 169–184.

Pierson, D. E., Walker, D. K., & Tivnan, T. (1984). A school-based program from infancy to kindergarten for children and their parents. *The Personnel and Guidance Journal*, 448–454.

Price, R. H., Cowen, E. L., Lorion, R. P., Ramos-McKay, J., & Hitchins, B. (1988). *Fourteen ounces of prevention: A casebook of exemplary primary prevention programs.* Washington, D.C.: American Psychological Association.

Ramey, C. T., & Campbell, F. A. (1984). Preventive intervention for high-risk children: Cognitive consequences of the Carolina Abecedarian Project. *American Journal of Mental Deficiency, 88*, 515–523.

Rappaport, J. (1987). Terms of empowerment/exemplars of prevention: Toward a theory for community psychology. *American Journal of Community Psychology, 15*, 121–148.

Rist, R. C. (1970). Student social class and teacher expectations: The self-fulfilling prophecy in ghetto education. *Harvard Educational Review, 40*, 411–451.

Rosenthal, R. R., & Jacobson, L. (1968). *Pygmalion in the classroom.* New York: Holt, Rinehart, & Winston.

Rotheram, M. J. (1988). The children's assertiveness training program. In R. H. Price, E. L. Cowen, R. P. Lorion, J. Ramos-McKay, & B. Hitchins (Eds.). *Fourteen ounces of prevention: A casebook of exemplary primary prevention programs.* Washington, D.C.: American Psychological Association.

Rotheram, M. J., Armstrong, M., & Booraem, C. (1982). Assertiveness training in fourth and fifth grade children. *American Journal of Psychology, 10*, 567–582.

Ryan, W. (1971). *Blaming the victim.* New York: Vintage Books.

Sameroff, A. J. (1987). Transactional risk factors and prevention. In J. A. Steinberg & M. M. Silverman (Eds). *Preventing mental disorders: A research perspective.* DHHS Pub. No. (ADM) 87–1492 Washington, D.C. U.S. Government Printing Office, pp. 74–89.

Sameroff, A. J., & Chandler, M. J. (1975). Reproductive risk and the continuum of caretaking casualty. In F. D. Horowitz, M. Hetherington, S. Scarr-Salapatek & G. Siegal (Eds.). *Review of Child Development Research*, Vol. 4. Chicago: University of Chicago Press.

Sameroff, A. J., & Fiese, B. (1988). *Conceptual issues in prevention.* Unpublished manuscript. Brown University: Providence, R.I.

Sarason, S. B., & Doris, J. (1979). *Educational handicap, public policy and social history: A broadened perspective on mental retardation.* New York: Free Press.

Schaps, E., Bartolo, R. D., Moskowitz, J., Palley, C. S., & Churgin, S. (1981). A review of 127 drug abuse prevention program evaluations. *Journal of Drug Issues*, Winter, 17–43.

Schweinhart, L. J., & Weikart, D. P. (1980). *Young children grow up: The effects of the Perry preschool program on youths through age 15* (Monographs of the High/Scope Educational Research Foundation, No. 7) Ypsilanti, MI: High/Scope Press.

Schwartz, S., & Johnson, J. H. (1981). *Psychopathology of childhood.* New York: Pergamon Press.

Seidman, E. (1987). Toward a framework for primary prevention resesarch. In J. A. Steinberg & M. M. Silverman (Eds.). *Preventing mental disorder: A research perspective.* DHHS Pub. No. (ADM) 87–1492 Washington, D.C.: U.S. Government Printing Office, pp. 2–19.

Shure, M. B., & Spivack, G. (1982). Interpersonal problem-solving in young children: A cognitive approach to prevention. *American Journal of Community, 10*, 341–356.

Sroufe, L. A. & Rutter, M. (1984). The domain of developmental psychopathology. *Child Development*, 55, 17–29.

Swisher, J. (1988). *Overview of alcohol and drug abuse prevention education in schools in the United States*. Presentation to the First National Conference on Prevention Research Findings: Implications for Alcohol and Drug Abuse Program Planning. (NIDA/NPN). March, Kansas City, Mo.

Vincent, T. A. & Trickett, E. J. (1983). Preventive intervention and the human context: Ecological approaches to environmental assessment and change. In R. D. Felner, L. A. Jason, J. N. Moritsugu, & S. S. Farber (Eds.). *Preventive psychology: Theory, research, and practice* (pp. 67–86). New York: Pergamon.

Zax, M. & Specter, G. A. (1974). *An introduction to community psychology*. New York: Wiley.

2

Optimizing Research Strategies in the Schools

Jean Ann Linney

When children are a primary target of preventive intervention, a logical place to deliver such intervention is the school. By law, all children between certain ages are required to attend school, thus, the school system provides a place of ready access to large numbers of children where they are essentially a captive audience. Further enhancing the attractiveness of the school as an intervention site is the possibility that a large number of children, regardless of demographic characteristics or ability, can be involved in the intervention activity. For many kinds of preventive intervention the school as an intervention site offers an opportunity to provide children with skills, knowledge, or services that their families might not give them. For example, arguments for sex education in the schools are the importance of preventing adolescent pregnancy and the fact that many families either do not provide their teen-aged children with adequate information for prevention or do not provide the atmosphere in which the information can be processed and understood (Reppucci, Mulvey, & Kastner, 1983).

Some of the earliest and most successful efforts at prevention were school based. In the public health field where some models of mental health prevention are rooted, health screenings have been very effective in identifying early the physical health needs of children, and when coupled with service provision, in reducing the severity of the problem and its damaging effects in other areas. In mental health and the prevention of psychopathology there have also been a number of notable efforts in the schools, such as the Primary Mental Health Project targeting at-risk students (Cowen, Trost, Lorion, Dorr, Izzo, &

Author's Note: Completion of this work was facilitated by grant support from the National Institute on Drug Abuse (DA04022).

50

Isaacson, 1975). Skill development prevention programs have been implemented in the school with the goal of enhancing specific skills and competencies to deal more effectively with problematic situations (e.g., Elias, Gara, Ubriaco, Rothbaum, Clabby, & Schuyler, 1986; Rotheram-Borus, 1988; Shure & Spivack, 1978). The school has been a forum for intervention to promote positive social attitudes and peer relations (Aronson, Blaney, Stephen, Sikes, & Snapp, 1978; Schofield, 1982; Slavin, 1980). Alternative schools, changes in school curriculum, and modifications in school procedure (e.g., Felner, Ginter, & Primavera, 1980) are examples of systemic, organizational level primary prevention to reduce the incidence of adjustment and learning problems. Recently, most school-based preventive intervention with children has targeted specific social problems such as sexual abuse, abduction, substance use, suicide, and the effects of family conflict and divorce.

Despite many preventive efforts in the schools, we are too often disappointed with the lack of evaluative research on the effects and effectiveness of these programs. Three independent reviews of research in community psychology (e.g., Lounsbury, Leader, Meares & Cook, 1980; McClure, et al., 1980; Novaco & Monahan, 1980) conclude that the majority of research in this area is methodologically inadequate. Admittedly these reviews are based on research published ten years ago, however in more revent reviews of specific types of school-based preventive intervention the conclusions are essentially the same (e.g., Flay, 1985). It is still the case that methodological shortcomings severely limit the conclusions that can be drawn from community and school-based interventions.

The goal of this chapter is to overview the essentials of a prevention research study that make it methodologically adequate to allow causal inference, to discuss some of the unique factors inhibiting the design and implementation of school-based research, and to suggest strategies for working more effectively with schools to optimize research needs and balance the service-research seesaw that often undermines the fidelity of both the research and the intervention.

Necessities for Causal Inference

The goal of scientific inquiry generally is to derive causal statements (Cook & Campbell, 1979) using an agreed upon set of rules or research methodology. Within the behavioral sciences, paradigms of scientific inquiry are based in the theory of construct validation

(Cronbach & Meehl, 1955) and rely on experimental manipulation and comparison for determining cause-effect relationships. An experiment allowing causal inference must "involve at least a treatment, an outcome measure, units of assignment, and some comparison from which change can be inferred and hopefully attributed to the treatment" (Cook & Campbell, 1979, p.5). This methodology applies equally to research in prevention. In a prevention experiment the treatment is the preventive intervention or manipulation; the outcome measure is the desired effect. To infer a causal relationship between the treatment/intervention and the outcome, it is necessary to have a comparison group of some kind, i.e., a group of participants who do not receive the treatment or preventive intervention. With an appropriate comparison group, differences between the groups following intervention can be attributed to the effect of the treatment. This causal attribution is based on the critical assumption that the groups are equivalent prior to the introduction of intervention. If the groups are equivalent then it is generally reasonable to assume that over the course of the study the factors impinging on the subjects of the investigation are equivalent except for the treatment, and, thus, any differences between the groups are likely to be the result of the intervention.

Equivalence of the comparison groups in any experiment is determined by the assignment rule for the units of study (Judd & Kenny, 1981). A random assignment rule for subjects is the most desirable way to accomplish group equivalence. As Cook & Campbell describe:

> One of the great breakthroughs in experimental design was the realization that random assignment provided a means of comparing the yields of different treatments in a manner that ruled out most alternative interpretations. Random assignment requires experimental units, which can be plots of land in agriculture, individual persons in social psychology and even neighborhoods in some criminal justice research. Treatments are then assigned to these units by some equivalent of a coin toss, a process of random selection which determines the treatment that each receives. Given a sufficient number of units relative to the variability between units, the random selection procedure will make the average unit in any one treatment group comparable to the average unit in any other treatment group before the treatments are applied. (Cook & Campbell, 1979, p. 5)

A methodologically adequate study is one in which causal inference can be drawn. To make causal inference an experiment must have a specifiable intervention, delineated outcomes, and two equivalent groups at least one of which receives the intervention. As simple as this appears, accomplishing these elements can be problematic in community prevention research for both practical and conceptual reasons (Cowen, 1978; Heller, Price, & Sher, 1980; Linney & Reppucci, 1982; Lorion, 1983). The field context for research reduces the degree of control that the researcher has to maintain the integrity of the intervention, establish adequately reliable and valid measures, and establish the equivalence of the comparison groups. Without the control of the laboratory setting, research in the field is subject to a variety of threats to validity and causal inference (e.g., historical events differentially affecting the groups, nonrandom selection or assignment, differential loss of subjects, diffusion of treatments) (Campbell & Stanley, 1966; Cook & Campbell, 1979). These threats constitute rival hypotheses that offer plausible alternative explanations to the treatment-outcome causal inference. For example, multiple treatment interference confounds the treatment-effect causal inference with the alternative explanation that the effect observed is attributable to another coexisting program rather than to the experimental program under study. The presence of an equivalent comparison group and random assignment to condition are adequate to rule out most of the internal validity threats to causal inference.

The school context and its unique ecology introduce conditions that blur or confound the necessary comparisons in a prevention study and exacerbate potential threats to the validity of the research design. To maximize the validity of any school-based research, understanding the ecology and culture of the school setting is crucial. With this ecological perspective, some of the most serious threats to validity can be anticipated and planned for in the design and implementation of research on preventive intervention. The ecology of the school introduces some unique constraints that differentially affect entry to the system, intervention implementation, and design considerations.

Ecological Norms That Constrain
School-Based Prevention Research

The school is an organizational system with a set of values and norms that maintain its ecology. Sarason (1971), O'Neill and Trickett (1982), and Trickett, Kelly, and Todd (1972) have written insightfully about the ecological patterns of the school that regulate and maintain this system, and make change difficult. For prevention research, many of the same constraints become problematic for entry to the system, implementing the intervention as intended, and accomplishing the minimal design requirements. Specific ecological features can seriously threaten the collection of outcome measures and the assignment of procedures used to form the comparison groups. The following section highlights five ecological norms in the school setting that have substantial impact on the research process.

1. *Schools define themselves as innovative, but not experimental.* Our school systems provide an educational service to the community and generally enjoy community consensus that the product they provide is important and necessary. With this community support, the school represents an interesting type of organizational setting in which risk taking (e.g., innovation, change) does not threaten the organization's existence. This feature coupled with their service nature ought to make the school an organization amenable to implementing preventive intervention.

Although prevention makes intuitive sense as an approach to some of our more pressing problems, prevention is innovative and requires a modicum of risk taking and future oriented thinking. It is an activity that invests resources on the wager that problems will develop in the future without the preventive program. In mental health prevention there are no parallels to medical vaccines that will prevent teenage suicide, teenage pregnancy, juvenile delinquency, or school vandalism. Essentially all preventive intervention at this time is experimental, that is, neither the effects of intervention are known nor their preventive efficacy.

Generally schools think of themselves as innovative, but not experimental. Educational historians have shown repeatedly that schools reflect community attitudes and tend to mirror changes that have already occurred in a community (Katz, 1973). Rarely are public schools the leaders in innovation. The philosophy of the public education system is rooted in a democratic responsiveness to the community, so when there is sufficient support or pressure from the community, change comes about. Relative foci in the curriculum are reflective of community political and social trends. For example, the current public education emphasis on science and math comes more from political and industrial concerns about America's ability to compete in the high tech world of the future, than from within the school system. By design, the education system reflects the perceived needs of the community. It is intended to be flexible and have the potential for innovation, but it is not expected to be experimental, because experimental implies untested, with unknown effects. The idea that a program is untested is usually not desirable for school administrators or school board members.

The school's need to be responsive to the community contributes to this hesitation to be experimental. Programs that have some evidence for effectiveness in other communities are often more acceptable to school officials. In rare circumstances, such as when the perceived threat from the problem to be prevented is very high, such as with the current concern about AIDS, schools are generally more accepting of newly developed, experimental programs. Generally however, schools are skeptical of programs that will change the relatively smooth functioning of their system and may be difficult to justify to their community constituencies.

From the perspective of research design, the aversion to experimental status has important implications for the inclusion of control or comparison groups. Generally no one wants to be in the control group in a prevention study. Apart from the degree of disruption to the school that accompanies participation as a control school, if it should turn out that the intervention works, who would choose to be excluded from it? When a prevention study is presented to a school system, discussion about control groups often reduces the chance of successful entry and cooperation. Sometimes a school will make their participation in the research contingent on assignment to a specific condition. While this ensures participation, it immediately introduces selection as a threat to the validity of the design. Unless the "choice of condition" is a designated facet of the research design, this will threaten internal validity by confounding the assignment rule.

2. *Schools are primarily service settings sympathetic to consideration of psychological and social factors that mediate learning and academic achievement, but service and research needs compete in any preventive intervention.* Schools face growing pressure to be more accountable for academic outcomes, and periodic evaluation of students and teachers pervades the academic calendar. Accountability for outcomes does not always carry over to nonacademic areas. For nonacademic concerns, the school may be expected to provide a service, but the outcomes of that service are infrequently evaluated. The service provision ethic that characterizes schools frequently undermines the research component of an intervention. This may happen in several ways. At the most basic level, there is little felt need for research or evaluation in a nonacademic area. Hence the committment to the research facet of an intervention is minimal at the outset. Once the intervention is implemented, completion of research assessment measures is usually a low priority given the other demands placed on students and staff in the

school setting. In secondary prevention programs, preintervention data is often easier to collect because it is consistent with school procedures requiring documentation for providing specialized services. Other data collection typically becomes difficult and researchers should be prepared to collect as much of their data as possible using nonschool personnel and resources.

The service needs of the school setting also affect the selection criteria for participation in an intervention and may undermine random assignment procedures. Every school-based researcher has been faced with a personal plea from a teacher or counselor to include a student or not to include a student in an intervention regardless of design considerations. These requests can ultimately threaten the methodological viability of the project. For example, in a carefully designed randomized secondary prevention study, a teacher threatened to withdraw her entire grade level from the study if two boys did not receive the intervention. These kinds of service demands can quickly undermine the integrity of a research design.

Although the domain of school involvement in student's lives has broadened in the last 50 years to include health education, driver education, physical education, family life education, and now drug education, in some areas, many school personnel, especially at the secondary level, do not see these and other nonacademic areas as within their realm of responsibility (i.e., not part of the service each teacher is contracted to provide). Generally, elementary school teachers are more open to including broad mental health goals and related activities in the classroom curriculum than are secondary school teachers. For interventions that involve the school staff in implementation or delivery, the degree to which the intervention is viewed as consistent with the service role of the staff will determine the school's receptiveness to the intervention and the degree to which the intervention is implemented as it was intended.

3. *The highly regulated school system may facilitate entry, but inhibit implementation.* Every grade level has a detailed, usually state mandated curriculum. These curriculum books are often several inches thick describing in almost scriptlike fashion what is to be accomplished in a school year. Schools have detailed policies regarding the regular functioning of the building. Bells ring and people move at certain times and there are rules that govern the nature of that movement. Personnel policies dictate staff behavior. Policy and procedure govern the interaction of school personnel with community members. As in any complex organization, there are operating mechanisms that maintain

the barriers between the school and the community, and between the units within the school.

As a highly regulated system, or what might be called a *tightly coupled system* (Zald, 1980), it is possible to seek entry into a school system at an administrative level and gain access to each of the systems under that administrative umbrella. However, a flip side of the high level of regulation is that it is often practically difficult to implement the intervention within this complex system. In recent years with the growing concern about raising academic standards, falling SAT scores, etc., schools have been more accountable to document instructional minutes. This has made it increasingly difficult to implement individual level preventive programs involving school time, as these compete for school minutes with academic, regulated, and required activities.

4. *Teachers as decision makers in the classroom may redesign the intervention during implementation.* While heavily regulated, the school system protects the professional autonomy of the teaching staff. As professionals, teachers and school personnel view themselves as somewhat autonomous within the domain of the classroom. They believe in their professional judgment and increasingly expect to be involved in any experimental programming that involves their classroom or their time. This is a double-edged sword. On the one hand these professionals are educated about research design and do have tremendous expertise and insight relative to the students and school functioning. These attributes can be very helpful in developing and implementing programs. This can also introduce tremendous variability in the implementation of an intervention, especially if school personnel are delivering the intervention. School teachers and other selected school personnel are what Weatherly and Lipsky (1977) have named "street level bureaucrats." They have a great deal of control over the implementation of a program and if unconvinced of its significance, they can prevent it from occurring (i.e., despite administrative support, these individuals may exercise bureaucratic decision making in their classroom). Front line school personnel can be the greatest asset or the worst enemy of a prevention research program. They can run interference or throw up roadblocks, and working closely and collaboratively with them is essential.

5. Prevention *and* treatment *are blended by school personnel and the community.* Within the school ecology, treatment is roughly equivalent to remediation, and early remediation is seen as preventive. For example, retention in early grades is viewed as preventing later problems. For both schools and communities, "If it's not broken, don't fix it"

seems to be a guiding maxim. Prevention as an idea is embraced hypothetically, but not implemented unless there is an apparent problem developing. In recent experience, implementing a substance abuse prevention program for high risk youth (Forman & Linney, 1987), school staff expressed strong hesitation about referring students because of their concern that parents would take issue with such a referral. There was surprising resistance from parents both generally and in specific instances following referral, on the grounds that their child was not a drug abuser and therefore did not need intervention. This resistance reflects a general confusion or blending between the concepts of prevention and treatment. Citizens often interpret prevention as early treatment or assume that if a professional person thinks their child needs prevention, that means that the child will get the "disease." This blending of concepts results in a generalized denial of the need for prevention for specific individuals. In the school setting, concern about labeling, creating self-fulfilling prophecies, and setting negative expectations for the student are given as justifications for not providing prevention targeted to individuals at risk.

Communities also have a tendency to resist the notion that prevention is needed in their own locale. An illustration of this phenomenon is reported by Silverman and Silverman (in press) in surveys of parent and student perceptions of substance use in their community. They surveyed several hundred parents in the greater Atlanta area and surrounding counties. More than 90% of the parents felt that substance use among teenagers had reached epidemic proportions and was a crisis in this country. However, less than a third believed that it was a problem in their community. These beliefs would mitigate against implementation of a prevention program.

The lack of differentiation between prevention and treatment has serious implications for the types of schools, classes, and students included in an intervention, and threatens the validity of the test of the intervention. In secondary prevention programs the students referred for inclusion are likely to be past the at-risk stage. They are more likely to be exhibiting symptoms and fall more clearly into a treatment population. With such a population, a preventive intervention may be "too little too late," and the experimental test would likely indicate that the intervention is ineffective. In fact, with such a population, the intervention might be inappropriate. Lorion, Cowen, and Caldwell (1974) have shown that targeting the intervention to the right population is essential for testing and demonstrating effectiveness.

In primary prevention strategies that involve all students or require some change in school operations, often only selected settings volunteer or are volunteered for participation. The units that become available for intervention often have the most serious problems and have exhausted other available options. The intervention becomes a kind of last resort. Given the degree of problematic behavior, there seems to be administrative relaxation of regulations, and these schools are permitted to be innovative and stray from standard policy. With this sample of participants the test of the intervention may have limited generalizability. With the general level of misunderstanding about prevention it is incumbent on the researcher to ensure that the population involved in the research is appropriate.

Collaborating with Schools to Facilitate Implementation

It is evident that prevention research in the schools is complicated by the ecology of the school. These ecological concerns make collaboration between school staff and researchers an essential component of the planning and implementation of prevention research. Research models involving collaboration with participants have been discussed by others (e.g., Chavis, Stucky, & Wandersman, 1983; Rappaport, et al., 1985), yet are rarely adopted in a significant way for a number of reasons. Most researchers are trained in the tradition of keeping subjects blind to experimental conditions, thus excluding them from most phases of the research. While this prevents some validity threats, it may introduce other practical threats when applied in the field setting. Collaboration is time consuming and complicates the timetable of a research project—another reason it may be avoided by researchers. However, in the context of the complex ecology of the school, collaboration with staff is essential.

Staff in the schools are crucial to the successful implementation of any program whether or not it includes research. Staff involvement in the planning stages increases the likelihood that implementation problems can be anticipated and enhances staff commitment to the success of the project. Staff can offer insight into school routines and procedures that may point to new ways of introducing the program and collecting relevant data. Staff knowledge about the accuracy of various sources of information can enhance the validity of any data collected from archival sources. They may also suggest sources of data that would be unknown to the outsider (e.g., in house recording procedures). As part of the collaboration process, these staff become invested in the program and are most effective in selling it to their colleagues. Collaboration can slow the development phase of the project, yet the potential benefits both for program implementation and research validity will outweigh the cost of initial time loss.

Accomplishment of productive collaboration requires that the researcher establish a relationship with school representatives as consultants, where school staff are expert consultants to the research team and work with them in a mutual problem-solving capacity. A consultative-collaborative process will enhance the credibility of the research and build trust between the school and research personnel. The school is most likely to become involved in a project that meets a felt need or problem. This is a logical starting point for collaboration. With an intervention area identified, collaboration should begin with selected school personnel who are interested and concerned about the same issue. The initial meetings with these individuals should focus on identifying mutual concerns, common goals, and discussion of possible intervention strategies. With each successive meeting, the researcher may become more specific in describing an intervention and associated research needs. Throughout the collaborative process, both the research and intervention needs should be discussed, such as who will be involved, selection criteria if applicable, comparison groups, and pre- and post-assessment strategies. Fairweather and Tornatzky (1977) suggest contracting with constituent collaborators on specific research issues. For example, if two or more intervention conditions are designed with input from the constituent group, all agree in the contract to accept random assignment to the intervention condition with the understanding that the most effective intervention will be implemented more broadly at the conclusion of the research.

In some cases, the collaborative process should also involve parent and community groups. When the focus of the prevention program is one that is not directly within the domain of the school (e.g., pregnancy prevention, substance use), then support from community groups, the PTA, and other parent representatives provides the school the sanction they need to intervene in these areas. School staff are less concerned with adverse community reaction when organized, elected parent/citizen groups have supported a program. Collaboration and consultation among research team, school staff, and community representatives will ultimately facilitate the process of entry and implementation and in so doing, enhance the validity of the research.

Collaboration in research areas may raise some questions about a form of experimental bias resulting from the fact that school staff are not blind to experimental conditions. This can be problematic; however, bias in assessment can be balanced by use of outcome measures that do not rely solely on the opinion or judgment of those involved in the intervention. These indices might include relatively objective data such as school attendance rates, scores on standardized achievement tests, or data from other sources such as parent and peer ratings where less bias would be predicted, or in which bias is directionally opposite to predicted intervention outcomes. Collaboration would enhance knowledge about the scope of the research projects and, thus, reduce some validity threats from hypothesis guessing, and compensatory rivalry and demoralization (Cook & Campbell, 1979).

Optimizing Research Design in the School Setting

Preserving the internal validity of the intervention and establishing the construct validity of the intervention are primary tasks for the prevention researcher. In the sections that follow, strategies for accomplishing these ends in light of the ecological demands of the school are discussed.

Forming Comparison Groups

A comparison group design is necessary for even a minimally rigorous prevention study. Without a comparison group it is not possible to link causally any observed effect with the intervention. There are too many other explanations, including such simplistic alternatives as student maturation and the influence of other activities or programs. The strongest causal inferences can be drawn when the comparison groups are created by random assignment. In field research, while it is often complicated to achieve random assignment, it is not impossible, and this option should not be discarded easily. There are many opportunities for random assignment, particularly if the research is collaboratively planned well in advance of implementation. In many instances a random assignment rule is the most defensible rule for providing limited services.

When there is resistance to random assignment it is frequently because the commitment to service provision outweighs the commitment to research, or because one or more of the conditions to which a school or student might be randomly assigned is undesirable. The first issue is one that researchers have little influence upon, but the second can be minimized with a multiple comparison design in which one intervention is compared with another. For researchers, a logical first study is to compare an intervention with the absence of the intervention or "treatment as usual" serving as a control condition. But from the school perspective, no one wants to be in the control group since, by definition, that is the group in which no effect is expected (or even desired). Participation in an assessment-only control condition is disruptive and time consuming for a school, and without some promise of future service, the payoff is nonexistent. Inclusion of a no-treatment, assessment-only condition is likely to reduce school agreement rates and lead to difficulty in data collection. If a no-treatment control group is necessary, the researcher should anticipate resistance from schools and carefully plan the presentation to school staff to optimize participation. The promise of future service is a reason some schools will participate in a multiple comparison design as diagrammed in Table 2.1-a.

In almost any area of prevention, there are competing models of intervention. In the substance abuse area, for example, a drug education and information program (Intervention A) might be compared with a coping skills training program (Intervention B). Selected components of the interventions could be varied, such as who delivers the program, frequency and duration of the program, and included as additional comparison conditions. This type of comparison design is more palatable for a school. Whichever condition they are randomly assigned, there will be some identifiable benefit. In these circumstances the acceptance of random assignment rules is increased, and the strength of the research conclusions greatly enhanced.

Rather than the elementary question: "Is there an effect with this intervention?," the multiple comparison design addresses the question of differential efficacy, or depending on the conditions, incremental efficacy. Forman and Linney (1987) randomly assigned schools to three conditions in a substance abuse prevention program: a self-awareness training program for students, a coping skills training program for students, and a coping skills training program for students and parents. This design allows for comparison of both differential effects between coping skills and self-awareness curricula, and incremental effects of a coping skills intervention with students only versus students and parents.

A key issue in the use of the multiple comparison design is that implementation success is enhanced by employing a research design with basic methodological rigor that more closely matches the needs of the schools and avoids readily anticipated hesitations. In addition this design forces clearer specification of each intervention, that is, better construct definition. In differentiating two or more interventions, the researcher is forced to identify components that are similar and different among the conditions and to specify more clearly those

TABLE 2.1 School-Based Prevention Research Designs

2.1-a: Multiple Comparison Design with Pre-Post Assessment

	Pre	Implement Program	Post(1)	Post(2)	Post(i)
Intervention A (R)	0	X	0	0	0
Intervention B (R)	0	X	0	0	0
Intervention C (R)	0	X	0	0	0
Intervention i (R)	0	X	0	0	0

2.1-b: Randomized Cohort Comparison Design

	Time 1		Time 2		Time 3		Time 4
Cohort 1 (R)	0	X	0		0		0
Cohort 2 (R)	0		0	X	0		0
Cohort 3 (R)			0		0	X	0

2.1-c: Nonequivalent Control Group Design with Pre-Post Assessment

	Pre		Post(1)	Post(2)	Post(3)
Group 1	0	X	0	0	0
Group 2	0		0	0	0

NOTE: X indicates intervention implementation; 0 indicates assessment; (R) indicates random assignment to condition.

expected to produce effects. In the Forman and Linney (1987) substance abuse prevention project, attention, peer support, a discussion forum, and information about substances are common to all three intervention conditions. Outcome differences between conditions can be attributed to causal factors other than those. The question that cannot be addressed in this design is the relative effect of any of the programs compared to no intervention; however, for many prevention efforts that question is either not of interest or is ethically not defensible.

The multiple comparison design is substantially more complex for the management of the research. In essence two or three interventions are being designed and implemented simultaneously. Nevertheless, the benefit in cooperation from the school sites may outweigh this cost. The design also reduces the likelihood of several threats to internal validity, specifically compensatory equalization and compensatory demoralization or rivalry (Cook & Campbell, 1979). When one treatment condition is clearly less desirable than others, the recipients of that less desirable intervention have a tendency to compensate for the perceived deficit by providing additional services, resources, or specialized treatment. This type of equalization is very likely in a school setting given the mandate to provide for the needs of students and to provide services in some standardized manner. If compensatory services are provided, then the experimental comparison is destroyed. Alternatively when a condition is less desirable, the recipients may experience a sense of demoralization and give up or feel some rivalry with the more desirable condition and actually work harder at the methods they have available. In either case the research comparison is no longer valid since the control condition is not unaffected, and treatment-as-usual no longer exists.

Alternatives When Comparison Groups Are Unavailable

There are circumstances in which the identification of control groups is very difficult, if not nearly impossible. When more than one condition of a design cannot be implemented in a single school, other schools can form comparison conditions (nonequivalent control group design). This would be necessary if the intervention were systemic or organizational in nature, or if spillover effects sufficient to threaten the integrity of the separate interventions are likely. In some areas (e.g., small communities) other schools may not be available to serve as comparisons. In these circumstances there are several options and the selection of one would be determined by the nature of the intervention and the outcome measures.

Comparison groups can be created within a single setting with the intervention phased in sequentially to separate subgroups or cohorts within the available population. This design is diagrammed in Table 2.1-b. In this design, a subset of classrooms or students might be randomly selected to receive the intervention in the first phase or cohort. The remaining units would serve as a comparison until the postassessment, when a second cohort would begin the intervention, while the third cohort served as a comparison. This design is very useful in circumstances where the intervention is delivered in units such as a classroom. By phasing in the intervention, no-treatment comparison groups are formed. Continued assessments for all students provide comparisons and follow up analysis. The design also allows replication of the effects with each successive cohort. Practically, this design allows both the school and the researcher to work out implementation problems with the first cohort so that each successive cohort should have cleaner implementation. Threats to the validity of this design primarily relate to spillover effects from the intervention and practice effects on the assessment. However, the presence of a comparison group makes the design more defensible than the case study one-shot intervention, which would be the alternative. If the units in each cohort are randomly determined, the design has added rigor.

A second alternative in the absence of comparison units is the use of base rates and norms for comparison. This type of design shares some of the logic of time series designs by comparing observed effects to those that might be predicted by base rate data or available norms for a similar group. As an illustration, suppose an intervention designed to prevent the onset of drug use in middle school students is implemented school-wide and there is no comparable middle school to serve as a comparison. Survey data on onset and incidence rates from that locale could be used to predict the substance use rates for that school in the intervention year and the years following. Outcome data on substance use following the intervention could be compared with the predicted rates. This design has a number of flaws but does allow some type of comparison. The major threats to validity are the influence of historical variables and other programs implemented during the research period.

A related design involves the use of archival data from a demographically similar setting. The use of such a nonequivalent control group allows comparison on selected variables, but because no random assignment is involved, selection threats remain prominent, and potential validity threats due to history may be problematic.

Unit of Analysis and Assignment Rules

The unit of analysis and the units assigned to intervention conditions are important concerns in field research and prevention. Psychologists are accustomed to thinking about individual persons as research subjects, the unit of analysis, and the locus of intervention. In field research those individuals are more obviously enmeshed in other environments than perhaps is apparent in the laboratory, and for school-based research those environments (e.g., classrooms, schools) are often part of the assignment to conditions.

In school-based research, individual students, classrooms or schools could be the units randomly assigned to intervention conditions. Each more inclusive level presents a source of variance, such as schools have a social climate and set of environmental presses that exert influence on the classrooms and students in each school. Assignments to schools and classrooms is generally not random, but rather correlated with residential patterns, SES, ability, and achievement. Hence, the individuals who share membership in the more comprehensive level (e.g., classroom) are not random or independent units. This interrelationship introduces a significant confounding variable in a research design, may limit the generalizability of the findings, and has implications for the data analysis.

When intervention is implemented at other than the individual level, it is necessary to consider an alternative unit of analysis and assignment. For example, desegregation as an intervention is generally at the school district level, and sometimes an entire community. The effects of that intervention may be at multiple levels including student, teacher, school, and community; however, the locus of intervention is the community or school district. Community and organizational level interventions generally preclude random assignment of students or schools to condition of participation. Media interventions present similar problems for assignment. In these situations the unit of assignment is not the individual, but rather the school, district, or community, even though effects may be expected at the individual level.

For most interventions, effects for individuals are ultimately desired and assessed. The individual is the most common unit of analysis. When the unit of assignment and the unit of analysis differ (e.g., schools are randomly assigned to treatment A or B and the results are analyzed for student change), caution is warranted in the statistical analysis because the units being examined are not independent and share variance from the next more inclusive level. When analysis and assignment units differ, the statistical power of the design will be affected (Cohen, 1977; Rosenthal & Rosnow, 1984) and the generalizability of the findings restricted. For example, if classrooms are randomly assigned to conditions then the sample size of independent units equals the number of classrooms, not the number of students (which is likely to be 15 to 20 times larger). It is very common for classes or schools to be assigned to conditions and analyses conducted as if the students were the unit of assignment. Without sufficient knowledge of the variables determining groupings (e.g., classes, schools), assignment by group introduces a third variable that may interact with the treatment in undetermined ways and a selection by treatment interaction becomes a significant threat to external validity.

When students are the unit where change is expected, students should be randomly assigned to conditions whenever possible. This implies that all comparison conditions be provided in each school in order to eliminate confounding of school by treatment interactions.

While this is not always possible, there are interventions that would allow such an assignment rule. For example, Linney, Seidman, and Rappaport (1985) implemented a school based program similar in model to the Primary Mental Health Program (Cowen, et al, 1975), in which first and second grade students at risk for academic and adjustment problems were paired with nonprofessional change agents. The design involved both intervention schools and control schools. In the control schools no intervention occurred, but students were identified as if the intervention were to be implemented. In the intervention schools teachers identified students for the program and from that group, half of the students were randomly chosen. These children received the intervention, while those not chosen formed a control group within the intervention schools. This design allowed for effects attributable to teacher and school to be controlled because the design allowed these variables to influence equally the treatment and control students. This kind of randomized procedure is appropriate for many skills training programs so long as the conditions are discreet, and compensatory threats can be ruled out or minimized.

When it is not possible to assign randomly students within a school, intact classrooms might be considered as a unit of assignment. Classrooms within the school could be randomly assigned to different conditions controlling the effects of school, although teacher effects and classroom climate variables remain potentially confounded with the intervention. The larger the sample size of classrooms to be assigned the more robust the design.

Sometimes the intervention conditions are such that not more than one can be implemented in a single school. In this instance the school is the unit of assignment and students, teachers and classes are nested in schools. The number of units assigned (i.e., schools) is the sample size of the study. If four schools are assigned to two conditions, regardless of the number of students in each of those schools, the students can not be considered to have been randomly assigned, and the sample size of independently assigned units is four.

When there are more than two or three schools participating in a study, a random assignment with schools yoked or clustered by similar characteristics should by used. Even in a single locale, schools vary widely in the nature of their student body, characteristics of the instructional staff, size, physical environment, and a host of other variables. These characteristics should be considered potential influences on the intervention outcomes and some effort made to control for these and ensure that they are equivalently distributed across the experimental conditions. If the number of units is large and the variability relatively low, then random assignment should accomplish the necessary equivalence. When the variability is high, a very large sample size would be necessary to achieve equivalence with a simple random procedure. Alternatively, a yoked random assignment procedure is appropriate. Schools should be clustered into groups equal to the number of treatment conditions, i.e., with three intervention conditions from groups of three schools with the schools in each cluster similar on predetermined variables. A variety of demographic characteristics are obvious matching variables for this clustering. Variables such as school size, racial composition, urban-rural status, teacher experience levels, teacher-student ratios, achievement levels, and SES indicators may be considered. Once clustered, each cluster is randomly assigned to an order that determines group assignment. For example, with three groups, there are six possible orders (1-2-3, 1-3-2, 2-3-1, 2-1-3, 3-1-2, and 3-2-1). Using a random number table, each cluster would be assigned to an order and the first school in the cluster assigned to the condition corresponding to the first number of the order, the second school to the second numbered condition, and the remaining school to the third condition.

In the process of soliciting schools for participation in research there will inevitably be refusals. If a random assignment procedure is performed prior to participation agreement, refusals may undermine the random assignment. Refusal may be related to the intervention condition presented or some other variable. Whatever the reason, the sample remaining is no longer a random sample nor a randomly assigned sample because self-selection has confounded the assignment rule. To preserve the randomness of the assignment rule, school participation commitments should be solicited and then the random assignment procedures followed. If the sample of schools commonly involved in the intervention research was large enough these issues would be of less concern. Unfortunately, it is rare that a sample of schools would be large enough to dismiss concerns about randomness.

Determining Fidelity of Implementation

In any laboratory research, it is customary to verify and monitor the experimental procedures to insure the construct validity of the manipulation and rule out other causal explanations such as experimenter bias, demand characteristics, or inconsistency in procedures (Rosenthal & Rosnow, 1984). In field research there is a parallel need to establish that the intervention was implemented as intended. If program implementation deviates from design, then the test of its effects is not valid. To establish the construct validity of the manipulation, the interventions need to be carefully specified along as many dimensions as possible, including content, dosage (level or frequency), and conditions of implementation.

The first task in specifying the intervention is to describe the program content and components, specifically what is involved and what constitutes the intervention. For example, many substance abuse prevention programs provide information about the effects of drugs. Skills training in assertiveness, decision making, or communication constitutes the intervention for some person-centered programs. Personal attention or support may constitute the intervention or a component of the intervention. In system-focused intervention the content of the intervention might be teacher/student ratio, racial group ratio, minutes of instructional time, a policy or decision rule regarding student placements.

Every prevention program has a content that needs to be specified, and its implementation verified. In the laboratory it would be unheard of to introduce an experimental manipulation and not check to see that the manipulation was noticed by the subject. In the field we too often leave the implementation to chance, assuming that a program will be implemented as described. It is often only at the conclusion of a project, when data is being analyzed, that a failure in implementation is noticed or hypothesized. Verification is particularly crucial when the intervention is a training program or information transmission administered by someone outside of the research staff. For example, in a coping skills training program, a teacher may shorten the time period allotted to training in order to finish an unrelated activity (changing the dosage level). Specific exercises may be omitted for one reason or another. These changes in the procedure in essence change the intervention and threaten the construct validity of the intervention.

Verification procedures can be more or less intrusive depending on the nature of the intervention. With a self-contained curriculum such as a skills training program or information package, those sessions can be systematically monitored by audio tape for later verification or randomly observed with an observer recording the occurrence of specified components. A less intrusive procedure, but more open to error both conscious and unconscious, is the use of a recording form for the leader/instructor in which he or she reports to what extent each of the procedures was followed. This information provides the researcher with an estimate of the degree to which the program has actually been implemented.

The need for verification is equally important with system-focused intervention. For example, if a prevention intervention is based on a maximum teacher/student ratio, this figure may fluctuate throughout the school, depending upon class, schedules of teacher leave, or new student admissions. The researcher needs to specify the way in which this variable is defined and some limits above and below that figure, which constitute the acceptable range to be considered implementation. These figures should be monitored periodically throughout the research period. Similarly, when the intervention involves a policy change, such as the use of in-school suspension to prevent school drop-out and classroom disruption, evidence of the systematic use of these procedures needs to be established.

The notion of specification and verification of intervention may seem trivial; however, without this data the researcher cannot draw conclusions about the effects of any program. If the outcome data indicate no effect, is that evidence that the program is ineffective or was there no effect because the intervention was not implemented as intended?

Measurement of Outcomes

The research on any prevention project can only be as valid as the assessment strategies and instruments employed. Like any other research it is essential that the measures used be reliable and valid and that the data be collected carefully and systematically. Multiple measures of relevant constructs are essential.

In prevention research most of the desired outcomes are future events (e.g., reduction in school drop-out rates, adjustment problems, or school failure) and may be low frequency events (e.g., prevention of teenage pregnancy or suicide). The time dimension and delayed occurrence of some desired outcomes necessitates longitudinal research designs that involve continued assessment of relevant variables. Researchers need to be acutely aware of the time frame for change in the target populations, and not only make predictions about when relevant changes will occur, but establish an assessment timetable that allows a sufficient number of data collection points to detect the timing of changes. For example, Linney (1986) has shown that the effects of a court-ordered school desegregation fluctuate over time with some immediate change apparent, followed by reversals of those immediate effects. The timing of assessment may distort conclusions about effects. Some interventions would be intended to have effect after a significant transition. For example, in school drop-out programs targeted at the transition to middle school or high school, one would not expect to see an effect for one to two years following the intervention (i.e., intervention in 8th grade before the transition to high school with effects in 10th or 11th grade when drop-out rates increase).

What is suggested here is more than another naive call for longitudinal research. Rather prevention research needs to be conceived and studied in the context of the changes experienced by the target population and the natural ecological evolution of the school setting. School-based prevention research should involve some ongoing monitoring of change and intervention effects, and targeted assessments at times where change is predicted to be most apparent. These latter times might be determined by developmental theory, and rational or empirical evidence on transitions.

Given that most prevention project outcomes are future events, and the desired effect is typically the absence of a negative event, more than any other type of research, prevention research forces us to think more carefully about the constructs to be assessed and to define networks of variables that may be affected by the intervention. Our philosophy of science does not allow us to conclude cause-effect relations by accepting the null hypothesis (no effect). Hence, in order to demonstrate some cause-effect relation research needs to demonstrate that the intervention caused, or produced, some effect. This makes it necessary to postulate mediating variables that may be affected by intervention and to specify positive events that may be associated with the absence of the negative event that is the focus of prevention. For example, if an intervention is intended to prevent teen suicide the researcher needs to specify what correlates of nonsuicide will be affected by the intervention. If the intervention involves skill acquisition in the area of stress management and cognitive restructuring to reduce feelings of depression, then the assessment should demonstrate that skills are acquired, and that affect levels change following the intervention. Intervention in this area might also involve building peer support networks to prevent isolation. Here again the assessment should involve a measure of the level of peer support. Related indicators might include school social climate, level of involvement in school activities, and average attendance rates. These variables would be indicators of a broader construct hypothesized to covary with the targeted domain.

Appropriate outcome measures should be defined during the design of the intervention with the theoretical rationale for the intervention providing a framework for variable selection. In the process of specifying the intervention, the researchers need to hypothesize about

the way in which the intervention will bring about the changes desired. These hypotheses guide the assessment plan in terms of target
variable specification, mediating variables, and related constructs.

Like any good assessment plan the outcome measures should include multiple methods of assessment, multiple sources of data, and
multiple levels of analysis. Several conceptual schemas have been proposed to represent levels of analysis for effects (Bronfenbrenner,
1979; Rappaport, 1977; Seidman, 1987). These commonly include a
set of increasingly inclusive levels such as individual, small group or
family, organization, and community.

School-based prevention is likely to have an impact on multiple
levels surrounding the locus of intervention. For example, a student-
centered intervention to prevent academic failure is likely to have an
impact on classroom operation, teacher behavior, and school or district special placement patterns. These multilevel effects should all be
included in an assessment plan. They provide insight into the effects
of the intervention, its generalizability and longevity, and offer potential explanations for an intervention's failure. Every prevention assessment plan should include at minimum, assessment at two levels of
analysis.

For almost three decades researchers have been urged to include
multiple methods of assessing a construct (Campbell & Fiske, 1959).
Oftentimes the alternative methods include data collection from a
different source. In school-based prevention research, there are several obvious sources of data including student self-report and teacher,
parent, and peer reports of students. In addition, observation procedures might be used. The rigor and validity of prevention research
will be enhanced by the inclusion of multiple methods of assessment.
An important rule of thumb in designing an assessment plan is to ask
the question "How else could I know that?" for each variable included.
This ought to result in at least two types of measurement for each
variable included in the assessment.

Data collection in the context of the school is often difficult to
accomplish, and the assessment can become particularly problematic
if multiple assessments are called for over a long period of time.
There are numerous sources of archival data and unobtrusive methods that can be included in an assessment plan to reduce the data
collection problem. There are several advantages to this strategy in
addition to the practical matter of collecting data (Webb, Campbell,
Schwartz, & Sechrest, 1966). Use of unobtrusive indicators allows for
a greater number of data collection points. It virtually eliminates concern about reactivity and practice effects from the assessment and

adds to the construct validity of the outcomes by providing an alternative source of data. Furthermore, to the extent that multiple measures converge with a given outcome, the validity of that outcome is enhanced. Schools currently keep many records about students including grades, attendance, health records, standardized achievement test scores, and discipline reports. Other indicators can be readily observed, such as attendance at various kinds of student events as indicators of student morale and school involvement, school graffiti, and use of school services such as guidance or counseling services.

Generally schools are amenable to collection of data from students, and from records and archives about students. There is, however, a distinct evaluation anxiety when the skills or knowledge of school personnel are being studied. Repeatedly, school personnel find reasons not to complete assessments about themselves. In a pre-post study of teachers' use of certain classroom techniques, a substantial number of teachers refused to complete the postmeasures, stating that the researchers should simply duplicate their pretests, because they would just say the same thing (Linney, 1978). In other situations, teachers have sharply criticized the instrument format and then refused to complete it, when the format was essentially identical to that being used with students and parents who did complete it (Forman & Linney, 1987). There are enough instances of diverted assessment efforts involving teachers to conclude that their evaluation anxiety is real and can be anticipated. Collaboration in the research planning process is one potential strategy to ameliorate this problem.

School personnel already have their days filled without a prevention research study. Therefore, it is very important to formulate an assessment strategy that will be easy to explain and administer, and will consume as little time as possible given the competing concern for completeness. Use of outside personnel for data collection is highly desirable to reduce the workload on school staff. Additionally, use of archival, nonreactive measures contributes to the minimization of intrusion, and the paperwork required of school staff.

Conclusions

School-based prevention research presents some unique challenges to the research team. These challenges include those common to field research and the special problems of prevention. In addition the school presents an environment not particularly conducive to prevention or research. Nevertheless, it is clear that school-based prevention research can be accomplished with substantially greater methodological rigor than in the past. Accomplishing this will necessitate a broader contextual understanding of the school setting in which the prevention is to be implemented, and substantial collaboration with key school personnel. Throughout the intervention research process, the seesaw of service and research demands will create tension. This teeter-tottering will present infinite opportunities for diversion threatening the fidelity of implementation and the validity of the research procedures. The research/intervention team needs to be aware of this tension throughout, and make decisions from the metaperspective in which the competing demands can be balanced.

It is critical for the research/intervention team to remain in touch with the day-to-day implementation of the project. This is important not only for the overall validity of the project, but also to communicate to those in the school and on the front lines of implementation that the project is an important, truly collaborative effort. Ultimately the success of school-based prevention research rests on understanding and accepting the culture of the school, and working with it to optimize research needs and assess the likelihood of real world program implementation.

References

Aronson, E., Blaney, N., Stephen, C., Sikes, J., Snapp, M. (1978). *The jigsaw classroom.* Beverly Hills, CA: Sage.

Bronfenbrenner, U. (1979). *The ecology of human development: Experiments by nature and design.* Cambridge, MA: Harvard University Press.

Campbell, D. T. & Fiske, D. W. (1959). Convergent and discriminant validation by a multitrait-multimethod matrix. *Psychological Bulletin, 56,* 81–105.

Campbell, D. T. & Stanley, J. C. (1966). *Experimental and quasi-experimental designs for research.* Chicago: Rand-McNally.

Chavis, D. M., Stucky, P. E., & Wandersman, A. (1983). Returning basic research to the community: A relationship between scientist and citizen. *American Psychologist, 38,* 424–434.

Cohen, J. (1977). *Statistical power analysis for the behavioral sciences.* New York: Academic Press.

Cook, T. D. & Campbell, D. T. (1979). *Quasi-experimentation: Design and analysis issues for field settings.* New York: Rand-McNally.

Cowen, E. L., Trost, M. A., Lorion, R. P. Dorr, D., Izzo, L. D., & Isaacson, R. V. (1975). *New ways in school mental health.* New York: Human Sciences Press.

Cowen, E. L. (1978). Some problems in community program evaluation research. *Journal of Consulting and Clinical Psychology, 46,* 792–805.

Cronbach, L. J. & Meehl, P. E. (1955). Construct validity in psychological tests. *Psychological Bulletin, 52,* 281–302.

Elias, M. J., Gara, M., Ubriaco, M., Rothbaum, P. A., Clabby, J. F., & Schuyler, T. (1986).

Impact of a preventive social problem solving intervention on children's coping with middle school stressors. *American Journal of Community Psychology, 14*, 259–276.

Fairweather, G. W. & Tornatzky, L. (1977). *Experimental methods for social policy research.* Elmsford, NY: Pergamon Press.

Felner, R. D., Ginter, M., & Primavera, J. (1980). Primary prevention during school transitions: Social support and environmental structure. *American Journal of Community Psychology, 10*, 277–290.

Flay, B. R. (1985). What do we know about the social influences approach to smoking prevention?: Review and recommendations. In C. Bell & R. Battjes (Eds.), *Prevention research: Deterring drug abuse among children and adolescents.*

Forman, S. G. & Linney, J. A. (1987). Adolescent substance abuse prevention. Paper presented at the annual meeting of the American Psychological Association, August, New York City.

Heller, K., Price, R. H., & Sher, K. J. (1980). Research and evaluation in primary prevention: Issues and guidelines. In R. Price, R. Ketterer, B. Baden, & J. Monahan (Eds.), *Prevention in mental health* (pp 285–313). Beverly Hills, CA: Sage.

Judd, C. M. & Kenny, D. A. (1981). *Estimating the effects of social interventions.* Cambridge: Cambridge University Press.

Katz, M. R. (1973). *Class, bureaucracy and schools: The illusion of educational change in America.* New York: Praeger.

Linney, J. A. (1978). *A multivariable, multilevel analysis of a midwestern city's court ordered desegregation.* Unpublished doctoral dissertation, University of Illinois at Urbana-Champaign.

Linney, J. A. (1986). Court-ordered school desegregation: Shuffling the deck or playing a different game. In E. Seidman & J. Rappaport (Eds.), *Redefining social problems* (pp. 259–274). New York: Plenum.

Linney, J. A., & Reppucci, N. D. (1982). Research design and methods in community psychology. In P. C. Kendall & J. N. Butcher (Eds.), *Handbook of research methods in clinical psychology* (pp. 555–566). New York: Wiley.

Linney, J. A., Seidman, E., & Rappaport, J. (1985). *Interventions with children: The volunteers in schools program.* Unpublished report, University of Illinois.

Lorion, R. P. (1983). Evaluating preventive interventions: Guidelines for the serious social change agent. In R. D. Felner, L. A. Jason, J. N. Moritsugu, & S. S. Farber (Eds.), *Preventive psychology: Theory, research and practice* (pp. 251–268). New York: Pergamon.

Lorion, R. P., Cowen, E. L., Caldwell, R. A. (1974). Problem types of children referred to a school-based mental health program: Identification and outcome. *Journal of Consulting and Clinical Psychology, 42*, 491–496.

Lounsbury, J. W., Leader, D. S., Meares, E. P., & Cook, M. (1980). An analytic review of research in community psychology. *American Journal of Community Psychology, 8*, 415–441.

McClure, L. W., Cannon, D., Allen, S., Belton, E., Connor, P., D'Ascoli, C., Stone, P., Sullivan, B., & McClure, G. (1980). Community psychology concepts and research base: Promise and product. *American Psychologist, 35*, 1000–1011.

Novaco, R. W. & Monahan, J. (1980). Research in community psychology: An analysis of work published in the first six years of the American Journal of Community Psychology. *American Journal of Community Psychology, 8*, 131–146.

O'Neill, P. & Trickett, E. (1982). *Community consultation.* San Francisco: Jossey-Bass.

Rappaport, J. (1977). *Community psychology: Values research and action.* New York: Holt, Rinehart, & Winston.

Rappaport, J., Seidman, E., Toro, P. A., McFadden, L. S., Reischl, T. M., Roberts, L. J., Salem, D. A., Stein, C. H. & Zimmerman, M. A. (1985). Finishing the unfinished business: Collaborative research with a mutual help organization. *Social Policy, 15*, 12–24.

Reppucci, N. D., Mulvey, E. P., & Kastner, L. (1983). Prevention and interdisciplinary perspectives: A framework and case analysis. In R. D. Felner, L. A. Jason, J. N. Moritsugu, & S. S. Farber (Eds.), *Preventive psychology: Theory, research and practice* (pp 234–244). New York: Pergamon.

Rosenthal, R. & Rosnow, R. L. (1984). *Essentials of behavioral research: Methods and data analysis.* New York: McGraw-Hill.

Rotheram-Borus, M. J. (1988). Assertiveness training with children. In R. Price, E. L. Cowan, R. P. Lorion, J. Ramos-McKay (Eds.), *Fourteen ounces of prevention: A casebook for practitioners* (pp. 83-97). Washington, DC: American Psychological Association.

Sarason, S. (1971). *The culture of the school and the problem of change.* Boston: Allyn & Bacon.

Schofield, J. W. (1982). *Black and white in school: Trust, tension or tolerance.* New York: Praeger.

Seidman, E. (1987). Toward a framework for primary prevention research. In J. A. Steinberg & M. M. Silverman (Eds.), *Preventing mental disorders: A research perspective.* (pp. 2–19). Washington, D. C.: U.S. Government Printing Office.

Shure, M. B. & Spivack, G. (1978). *Problem solving techniques in child rearing.* San Francisco: Jossey-Bass.

Silverman, W. H. & Silverman, M. (in press). Comparison of key informants, parents, and teenagers for planning adolescent substance abuse programs. *Psychology of Addictive Behaviors.*

Slavin, R. E. (1980). Cooperative learning. *Review of Educational Research, 50*(2), 315–342.

Trickett, E., Kelly, J. G., & Todd, D. (1972). The social environment of the high school: Guidelines for individual change and organizational development. In S. Golann & C. Eisdorfer (Eds.), *Handbook of community mental health.* New York: Appleton-Century-Crofts.

Weatherly, P. & Lipsky, M. (1977). Street-level bureaucrats and institutional innovation: Implementating special education reform. *Harvard Educational Review, 47*, 171–197.

Webb, E. J., Campbell, D. T., Schwartz, R. D., & Sechrest, L. (1966). *Unobtrusive measures.* Skokie, IL: Rand-McNally.

Zald, M. N. (1980). *The federal impact on the deinstitutionalization of status offenders: A framework.* Paper commissioned by the Panel on Deinstitutionalization of Children and Youth, Assembly of Behavioral and Social Sciences, National Research Council, June, 1980, Washington, D. C.

PART II

Populations of Special Interest for School-Based Prevention Programs

Our schools have been given the task of fostering a wide range of skills and competencies in children. Schools are expected to contribute to the development of not only academic skills, but also essential social and interpersonal competencies. Thus, school-based prevention efforts have focused beyond problems related to learning and intellectual competence to include problematic behaviors ranging from substance abuse to delinquency and dysfunctional interpersonal relationships. In this second section of the book, we examine several of these important problem areas and prevention programs that have been designed to deal with them.

Chapter 3, by Lawrence Schweinhart and David Weikart, addresses the importance of fostering positive development in early childhood and the effects of these efforts on later cognitive and social functioning. Schweinhart and Weikart, of the High/Scope Educational Research Foundation, have directed the longitudinal Perry Preschool Study and the Preschool Curriculum Comparison Study. These authors provide an overview of the role of early childhood in human development, emphasizing the consequences of early experiences for children who grow up in poverty.

Schweinhart and Weikart describe the essential characteristics of good early childhood programs for children in poverty, concentrating on their work with the Perry Preschool Project. The effects of this program have been shown to be significant and long lasting, and include substantial gains in intellectual competencies and social adjustment among participants even 15 years after participation. The authors compare their own work with other childhood interventions and identify what they believe to be the elements that distinguish successful programs from those whose effects have been more short lived.

When considering prevention efforts with school-aged children, the prediction and prevention of learning disabilities are goals that are close to the heart of the educational mission of our schools. In the second chapter of this section, Howard Adelman, Professor of Clinical

Psychology at the University of California at Los Angeles, addresses the prevention of learning disabilities within the broader framework of the prediction, early identification, and prevention of learning problems. Adelman makes the distinction between learning disabilities, a diagnostic category that focuses on the individual child, and the concept of learning problems, which includes difficulties in learning encountered by youngsters that result from a range of personal and environmental factors.

Adelman provides a critical evaluation of current methods used to predict, identify, and prevent learning problems, outlining the many conceptual and methodological problems that have plagued this field. Drawing on a model of learning and learning problems that emphasizes person-environment transactions, he offers a number of directions for the field to pursue in the development and implementation of a continuum of programs that range from prevention to treatment of chronic problems.

Abuse of tobacco, alcohol, and other drugs represents one of the most pressing problems facing school-aged youth today. In the next chapter, Gilbert Botvin and Linda Dusenbury discuss school-based programs designed to accomplish the dual goals of preventing substance abuse and promoting competence in children and adolescents. Botvin, an Associate Professor of Psychology and Director of the Laboratory of Health Behavior Research at Cornell University Medical College, and Dusenbury, an Assistant Professor of Pyschology in the same program, provide an overview of the nature and causes of substance abuse, several theoretical perspectives that have been used to understand substance abuse, and an evaluation of contemporary approaches to the prevention of substance abuse.

The authors describe the Life Skills Training (LST) Program, a comprehensive intervention developed by Botvin and his colleagues to teach a broad range of personal and social skills in order to prevent the abuse of a wide range of substances. The review of issues involved in the implementation of the LST program and documentation of its efficacy provide insights into effective strategies for implementing prevention programs within school-based curricula.

In the final chapter of this section, Magda Stouthamer-Loeber, Assistant Professor of Psychiatry and Psychology at the University of Pittsburgh, and Rolf Loeber, Assistant Professor of Psychiatry at the Western Psychiatric Institute of the University of Pittsburgh School of Medicine, address the prediction of delinquency. The Loebers summarize a large number of studies that have attempted to predict delinquency based on earlier child behavior. Utilizing the "relative improvement over chance" as a measure of predictive power, they highlight the importance of earlier aggression, stealing, and drug use as strong predictors of later delinquent behavior.

The Loebers discuss a number of conditions that increase the likelihood of continuity in antisocial behavior in children, including specific characteristics of early childhood behavior and conditions in children's family and peer environments that are associated with delinquency. The authors emphasize the need to examine a wide variety of personal and environmental factors as sources of risk for delinquency, rather than searching for a single marker for the development of this problem. They conclude by outlining the implications of prediction studies for the development of programs to prevent delinquent behavior.

3

Early Childhood Experience and Its Effects

Lawrence J. Schweinhart
David P. Weikart

The experiences of young children can affect them into adulthood. Variations in social class and program experience have been shown to affect children's development of skills and dispositions, their school success, and eventually their adolescent and adult socieconomic success and social responsibility.

Persons raised in poverty usually do worse than their middle-class peers educationally and later socioeconomically. However, good early childhood development programs have shown that they can partially offset the negative effects of poverty and produce a variety of modest but definite benefits into adulthood. Further, it appears that, in early childhood programs, child-initiated learning activity more effectively prevents juvenile delinquency than does teacher-directed academic instruction.

The Role of Early Childhood Experience in Human Development

The transactional understanding of human development views behavior as the result of the continuous interplay of the person's maturation and experiences in settings. Persons and settings achieve stable patterns of relationship even as they shape and reshape each other. People grow in the traditional settings of childhood family, schooling, work place, and adulthood family. Each setting is a context for the formation of habits of interaction between the individual and other persons. Any *intervention* is an attempt to influence the habitual interactions that characterize traditional institutional settings.

Several aspects of child development converge to make the preschool years an opportune time for social intervention. *Physically*, preschool-aged children have matured to the point that they have achieved both fine- and gross-motor coordination and are able to move about freely and easily. *Socially*, children are able to move away from familiar adults and social contexts, into new settings. The fear of strangers is now not so common as it was earlier, and youngsters welcome relations with new peers and adults. *Mentally*, children have developed the abilities to speak and listen and can use objects for their own purposes. Piaget sees the preschool-aged child moving from the preoperational stage to the concrete-operational stage, developing the ability to learn from symbols (Piaget & Inhelder, 1969). When this development is completed at age 6 or so, schools begin instruction in the symbol-based skills of reading, writing, and arithmetic.

Introductions to new settings are crucial times for human development because they entail the creation of new patterns of habitual interaction. Since the individual is the new element in the setting, the person's initial behavior in the setting is the key element in the creation of these new patterns. Thus, the best times in life for interventions are just before individuals enter new settings. Intervention should focus on changing the individual's initial behavior in the setting so that it promotes the formation of desirable patterns of interaction in the new setting. If expected behavior in the new setting were based only on appearances, desirable behavioral change could be limited to changes in observable behavior. But when expected behavior in the setting is rooted in underlying skills and dispositions, the desirable behavioral change must also be rooted in these skills and dispositions. Thus, an early childhood program just prior to school entry should focus on developing the child's skills and dispositions that underlie adaptive functioning in the school setting. The skills to be developed in early childhood are not the abstract skills of reading, writing and arithmetic. Nor are they merely numbers and letters, the presumed building blocks of these skills. Rather they are the thinking skills appropriate to early childhood—putting things in groups and in series, solving problems in space and time and in social situations. The dispositions to be developed in early childhood are intellectual curiosity, persistence in completing activities, and an open friendliness towards adults and other children.

The special importance of early childhood derives from the fact that it stands at the beginning of schooling and the process of school success or failure. While family experience precedes schooling, the criteria for children's success or failure in family matters are not nearly so clearcut or universal. The institution of schooling is characterized by its emphasis on, if not preoccupation with, evaluation of the performance of individuals. By contrast, the evaluation of the job performance of adults is much more uneven in application. Adult jobs have tremendous variety, some demanding mental skills, others social skills, and still others physical skills. The criteria for success in the role of student are virtually universal in developed countries.

Early Childhood Experience in Poverty

In 1985, children under age 6 constituted the age group in the U.S. with the greatest percentage of its members living in poverty—23% as compared to a 14% rate overall and 13% of people aged 65 and over. Half of all Black young children and two of every five Hispanic young children were poor. Just 16 years earlier, only 15% of young children lived in poverty (Congressional Research Service & Congressional Budget Office, 1985; U.S. Bureau of the Census, 1986, p. 27).

Consequences of Early Childhood Poverty

Young children whose families live in poverty lack educational and economic resources. They are more likely to fail in school than their middle-class peers because their families have less to spend on such educational and cultural goods as toys, books, family trips, and postsecondary education; their parents have experienced educational failure and are less prepared to support educational success; and they often live in stress-producing settings.

Poverty begins to be perpetuated over time to the extent that it leads to, or is associated with, school failure and other social problems. When impoverished teenagers and adults become parents, poverty becomes intergenerational. In the United States some, but by no means all, children raised in poverty are also poor as adults. Two out of five children from the poorest fifth of families remain in the poorest fifth as young adults, seven out of ten in the poorest two fifths (Hill & Ponza, 1983). Poverty increases the likelihood that children will fail in school (National Assessment of Educational Progress, 1983) and that they will drop out of high school (National Center for Education Statistics, 1983). It is also associated with high rates of criminal activity (Loeber & Dishion, 1983) and teenage pregnancy (Moore, Waite, Caldwell, & Hofferth, 1978).

The fewer years of school adults have completed, the more likely they are to live in poverty. In 1985, the adult poverty rate for high school dropouts was 19%, but only 10% for high school graduates and

4% for those who had attended college (U.S. Bureau of the Census, 1986, p. 29). While the strong relationship between years of school completed and subsequent socioeconomic status has not been questioned, some have asked how much this relationship is attributable to education and how much to the characteristics of persons who go to school longer. Jencks and his colleagues (1979), after careful review of the pertinent data for men, concluded that amount of schooling was "the best readily observable predictor of a young man's eventual status or earnings," but that "only part of the association between schooling and success can be due to what students actually learn from year to year in school" (p. 230). The implication is that if students are led to attend school longer without changing their more enduring characteristics, there may be no positive effect on their subsequent socioeconomic status. By the same token, if *early childhood* experiences lead students to attend school longer, it is the result of such enduring characteristics of students and their educational environments.

Escaping the Consequences of Poverty

Childhood poverty does not always lead to educational and socioeconomic failure. Three out of ten children from the poorest fifth of families achieve middle-class status as young adults, i.e., the top three fifths of the income distribution (Hill & Ponza, 1983).

A case in point is that of the Southeast Asian boat people, the second wave of refugees who resettled in the U.S. beginning in 1978. These people were not as well educated or familiar with English and Western culture as the first wave of Southeast Asian refugees who came when Saigon fell in 1975. Despite their lack of education, their initially poor English speaking ability, and the trauma of relocation, many of these people were able to move from poverty to a near-poverty self-sufficiency, and many of their children found their way to success in school. The percentage for whom welfare assistance was the sole source of income, was almost 80% when they first came to the U.S., but dropped to only 30% three years later (Caplan, Whitmore, & Bui, 1985). Their unemployment rate in the U.S., initially 86%, plunged to 25% after 44 months. Their children, in schools in low-income and inner-city areas, demonstrated a remarkably high level of academic achievement; 27% of them had an A average, their overall average was a B, and their California Achievement Test scores exceeded national norms (Caplan, Whitmore, Bui, & Trautman, 1985).

While these people were still themselves limited to low-paying jobs and near-poverty status, the educational attainments of their children will surely move many of them into the middle class. They appear to be duplicating the historic pattern of movement of ethnic refugee groups into the American socioeconomic mainstream. The explanation for this situation surely lies to some extent in their disposition to achieve success through hard work and education. They virtually all rated as *most important* educational achievement, a cohesive family, and a belief in the value of hard work and as *least important* seeking fun and excitement and desire for material possessions (Caplan, Whitmore, Bui, & Trautman, 1985).

Indeed, most people in poverty at a given time do not remain there long: 24% of Americans were poor at least one year between 1969 and 1978, but only 3% were poor during eight or more of those years (Duncan, Coe, & Hill, 1984). However, this does not negate the long-term relationship between educational attainment and income, nor the fact that children born to parents who have little education and income are likely to fail in school. Perhaps it is the lifelong experience of limited opportunities and opportunities not taken that makes people lose hope in the payoff from hard work and education. If so, the question is how to enable children to develop the skills and dispositions to avoid the lifelong experience of failure and missed opportunities.

Experience in an Early Childhood Development Program

Good early childhood care and education programs based on a developmental approach can help offset the harmful consequences of poverty in children's lives. Such programs provide poor children with opportunities for intellectual, social, and physical learning and development that they would not otherwise have. They provide opportunities for children to develop their abilities to have meaningful conversations with adults and other children and to form social relationships of balanced give-and-take. Such programs, because the authority of adults is bounded by respect for the thinking of individual children, exemplify democracy in education.

The principal characteristic of a good early childhood development program, as defined here, is that children initiate their own learning activities—choosing them within a framework created by the teacher and carrying them out as they see fit, unconstrained by the teacher's definition of the "correct" answer or the "correct" use of materials. Child-initiated activity is distinguished from random activity by its purposefulness; it is distinguished from teacher-directed activity by the fact that the child controls what happens. As an example of child-initiated activity, consider children electing to paint pictures of their own design during a class session. It is not a random activity, because the teacher has provided the paint, the paper, the space, and the conditions of use as a framework within which children's self-directed activity can occur. It is not a teacher-directed activity, because the children, not the teacher, are designing and painting the pictures. Further, as teacher and child later discuss the painting, it is the child who informs the teacher about the painting's intention and content.

Early childhood development programs are programs in which young children spend time receiving child care and/or education. Child care programs maintain hours of operation that permit mothers or other primary caregivers to occupy themselves by employment or schooling. Seven out of ten children under 5 receiving child care receive it in homes, either their own or other people's (U.S. Bureau of the Census, 1983 p. 5). Some early childhood programs have education as their sole purpose; these programs typically operate only a few hours a day, from two to five days a week. As should be clear by now, early childhood *education* should not be equated with direct instruction in academic skills; rather, it should be construed broadly, to include indirect teaching and activities that promote children's intellectual, social, and physical development.

Early childhood education and child care are not necessarily mutually exclusive. Children may be enrolled in both child care and early childhood education programs at the same time. Some child care programs include organized educational activities, and all of them provide some kinds of learning opportunities for children. However, all child care programs could provide organized educational activities. Today, one out of two mothers in the U.S. are employed outside the home while their 3- and 4-year-olds receive child care of some sort (U.S. Bureau of the Census, 1983). According to parent reports, two fifths of the children receiving child care are also exposed to programs of organized educational activities. One out of two U.S. mothers of 3- and 4-year-olds are not employed outside the home, but one third of them report that their children are enrolled in an early childhood education program (National Center for Education Statistics, 1982).

The more income and education U.S. parents have, the more likely are their 3 and 4-year-olds to be in early childhood programs that provide organized educational activities. For families with annual incomes below $10,000, the enrollment rate in such programs is only 29%, while it is 52% for families with annual incomes above $20,000. The enrollment rate for 3- and 4-year-old children of elementary school dropouts is 23%, but it is 58% for children of college graduates (National Center for Education Statistics, 1982).

The federal government spends about $1 billion a year on Head Start, which serves one in five poor 3- and 4-year-olds, and about $1 billion a year on various subsidies to child care programs for poor and near-poor children. In 1986, 22 states spent state funds on early childhood education programs prior to kindergarten, especially for children who were poor or otherwise at risk of school failure, at an aggregate funding level of a third of a billion dollars. In 1984, only 8 states provided such funding, at an aggregate level of only $160 million (Schweinhart, Koshel, & Bridgman, 1987).

Early childhood is a time of life when, at least for some, the stream of poverty and school failure can be diverted to a more successful course. The available evidence suggests that one way to accomplish this is to provide early childhood development programs. This idea first became popular among leading educators and social scientists in the 1960s. It led to a variety of experimental programs and, in accord with the spirit of the times, to a limited number of scientific evaluations of the effectiveness of these programs. Despite some early findings that cast doubt on the overall efficacy of the national Head Start program (Westinghouse Learning Corporation, 1969), the later findings of studies of early childhood development programs suggest a possible pattern of causes and effects that stretches from early childhood into adulthood.

Poor children are likely to perform poorly as they enter school because they have not developed, to the same extent as their middle-class peers, the skills and dispositions expected of children in school; this lack of development is manifested in low scores on tests of intellectual ability. Although children who have not developed in this way may be advanced in other respects not relevant to school success, their lack of preparedness for school can lead to unnecessary, preventable placement in special education or retention in grade, low school achievement, and eventually dropping out of high school. Once a pattern of school failure or success is established in the first days of school, it easily can become an enduring characteristic (Schafer & Olexa, 1971). As documented earlier, school failure is associated with poverty, teenage pregnancy, and crime. Poor children who attend good early childhood development programs become better prepared in the skills and dispositions called for in kindergarten and first grade and, thus, they begin a more successful career in school and life.

The High/Scope Perry Preschool Study

The High/Scope Foundation's Perry Preschool study has investigated program effects beyond schooling and found them in many areas of early adult life (Berrueta-Clement, et al., 1984). The Perry study had an experimental group of 58 participants in the early childhood development program and a control group of 65 persons who had no early childhood program. These individuals were selected for the study at age 3 to 4 on the basis of parents' low educational and occupational status, family size, and children's low scores on the Stanford-Binet Intelligence Test. Pairs of children matched on IQ, family socioeconomic status, and gender were randomly assigned to the two groups, groups that were virtually identical on many demographic characteristics.

The Perry Preschool Program used the High/Scope curriculum (Hohmann, Banet & Weikart, 1979), an educational approach based on Piaget's interactional theory of child development. Most children attended the program for two years at ages 3 and 4. The classroom program was in session five mornings a week for seven months of the year, with home visits by a teacher to each parent once a week. Classroom groups had about 25 children and 4 teachers, for a teacher-child ratio of between 1 to 5 and 1 to 6. Other studies mentioned here investigated many kinds of early childhood programs, but all of them were high quality programs.

During their school years, children who had attended the Perry Preschool Program experienced greater success in school than the control group—better intellectual performance at school entry, fewer years spent in special education classes, and better attitudes towards school (Schweinhart & Weikart, 1980). At age 19 program participants were better off in a variety of ways than the control group. As shown in Figure 3.1, the program apparently *increased* the percentage of participants who were: literate, from 38% to 61%; enrolled in postsecondary education, from 21% to 38%; and employed, from 32% to 50%. The program apparently *reduced* the percentage of participants who were: classified as mentally retarded during school years, from 35% to 15%; school dropouts, from 51% to 33% pregnant teens, from 67% to 48%; on welfare, from 32% to 18%; and arrested, from 51% to 31%.

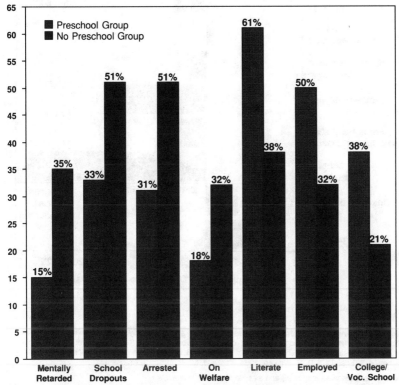

Note. — All group differences are statistically significant, p < .05, two-tailed.

Figure 3.1 High/Scope Perry Preschool Study Age 19 Findings

**Cost-Benefit Analysis of
the Perry Preschool Program**

Good early childhood development programs for poor children can be an excellent investment for taxpayers, according to the cost-benefit analysis of the Perry Preschool Program and its long-term effects. In a book titled *Investing in Our Children*, the Research and Policy Committee of the Committee for Economic Development (1985), an organization of leading business executives and educators, summarized the analysis this way:

> If we examine the Perry Preschool Program for its investment return and convert all costs and benefits into current values based on a 3% real rate of interest, one year of the program is an extraordinary economic

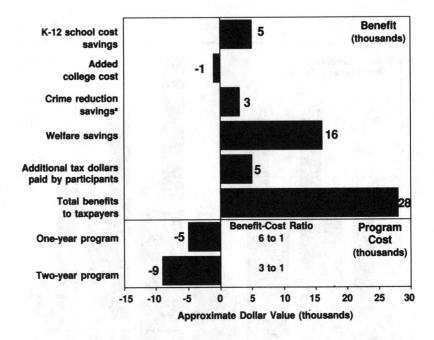

Note. Table entries are constant 1981 dollars, discounted at 3% annually. Adapted from *Changed lives: The effects of the Perry Preschool program on youths through age 19* (Monographs of the High/Scope Educational Research Foundation, No. 8), p. 91, by J. R. Berrueta-Clement, L. J. Schweinhart, W. S. Barnett, A.S. Epstein, & D. P. Weikart, 1984, Ypsilanti, MI: High/Scope Press.

[a]Savings to citizens as taxpayers and as potential crime victims.

Figure 3.2 Perry Preschool Program Per-Child Costs and Benefits to Taxpayers

buy. It would be hard to imagine that society could find a higher yield for a dollar of investment than that found in preschool programs for its at-risk children (p. 44).

The total benefits to taxpayers for the program (in constant 1981 dollars discounted at 3% annually, depicted in Figure 3.2) were about $28,000 per participant, about six times the size of the annual program operation cost of $5,000 per participant. For each program participant, taxpayers saved about $5,000 for special education programs, $3,000 for crime, and $16,000 for welfare assistance. Additional postsecondary education costs added about $1,000 per participant. Because of increased lifetime earnings (based on more years of school completed), the average participant was expected to pay $5,000 more in taxes.

One year of the Perry Preschool Program cost about the same as one year in a special education classroom, about 80% as much as one year of a college education, and less than half as much as imprisoning a criminal for a year. The Perry Program was a novel program under development rather than a test of cost-efficiency. It was relatively expensive because it maintained a teacher-child ratio of 1 to 6. The same kind of program has demonstrated equally good results when it had a teacher-child ratio of 1 to 8 or even 1 to 10 (e.g., Schweinhart, Weikart, & Larner, 1986a). With such ratios the program would cost as little as $3,000 per child (in 1981 dollars).

**The Effectiveness of Good
Early Childhood Programs**

As might be expected, many studies address the short-term effects of early childhood development programs, while only a handful have been able to examine effectiveness ten years or more after the programs end. Yet the weight of the evidence from all these studies points in the same direction. In addition to the Perry study, the longitudinal studies reviewed here were carried out by Gray, Ramsey, and Klaus (1982) in Tennessee; a Head Start program in Georgia (Monroe & McDonald, 1981); and three independently conducted programs in New York evaluated by the state Department of Education (Irvine, 1982); Levenstein, O'Hara, and Madden (1983); and Palmer (1983).

As shown in Table 3.1, these studies indicate that good early childhood programs for poor children help prevent school failure. First, they help improve children's intellectual performance as school begins; this improvement, on the average, reaches a maximum of 8 points on intelligence tests and lasts from the end of the early childhood program to age 8. Second, good early childhood programs help reduce the need for poor children to be placed in special education programs or to repeat grade levels because they are unable to do the work expected of them. Third, participation in these programs leads to a lower high school dropout rate.

The array of findings of early childhood program effects may be divided into short-, mid-, and long-term results. The evidence indicates that good early childhood programs for poor children:

- *do* improve children's intellectual and social performance as they begin school. These effects have been found in many studies of Head Start and other programs. (McKey et al., 1985)

TABLE 3.1 Documented Effects of Good Preschool Programs
for Poor Children

Findings by Study	Program Group	Control Group	Probability of Error[a]
Intellectual ability (IQ) at school entry			
Early Training	96	86	<.01
Perry Preschool	94	83	<.01
Harlem	96	91	<.01
Mother-Child Home	107	103	—
Special education placements			
Rome Head Start	11%	25%	<.05
Early Training	3%	29%	<.01
Perry Preschool	16%	28%	<.05
New York Prekindergarten (age 9)	2%	5%	<.01
Mother-Child Home (age 9)	14%	39%	<.01
Retentions in grade			
Rome Head Start	51%	63%	—
Early Training	53%	69%	—
Perry Preschool	35%	40%	—
Harlem	24%	45%	<.01
New York Pre-Kindergarten	16%	21%	<.05
Mother-Child Home	13%	19%	—
High school dropouts			
Rome Head Start	50%	67%	<.05
Early Training	22%	43%	<.10
Perry Preschool	33%	51%	<.05
Additional Perry Preschool findings			
Literacy (average or better score)	61%	38%	<.05
Postsecondary enrollments	38%	21%	<.05
Arrests	31%	51%	<.05
Teenage pregnancies	64%	117%[b]	<.10
19-year-olds employed	50%	32%	<.05
19-year-olds on welfare	18%	32%	<.05

NOTE: Adapted from *Changed lives: The effects of the Perry Preschool program on youths through age 19* (Monographs of the High/Scope Educational Research Foundation, No. 8), pp. 2 and 102, by J. R. Berrueta-Clement, L. J. Schweinhart, W. S. Barnett, A. S. Epstein, & D. P. Weikart, 1984, Ypsilanti, MI: High/Scope Press.
[a]Statistical likelihood that the difference between the groups could occur by chance; "<.01" means that a particular group difference could occur by chance less than 1 time out of 100, "<.05," less than 5 times out of 100; .05 is usually considered the criterion for statistical significance.
[b]Average of more than one pregnancy per female.

- *probably* help children achieve greater school success. Half a dozen experimentally designed studies found a mid-term effect of lower percentages of poor children being placed in special education programs and repeating grade levels (Lazar, et al., 1982).
- *can* help young people achieve greater socioeconomic success and social responsibility. This evidence comes largely from the Perry Preschool study (Berrueta-Clement et al, 1984) since few studies have been able to document long-term effects because of the difficulties of conducting such research.

The Limits of Early Childhood Development Programs

These findings apply to children who live in poverty and are at risk of school failure. There is less evidence of early childhood program effectiveness for children who are not poor or otherwise at risk of school failure. Evaluation of the Brookline Early Education Project (BEEP) in Massachusetts found that, after a comprehensive five-year intervention program, the school problems of participating middle-class children were reduced somewhat. At the end of grade two, 14% of BEEP's participants exhibited inappropriate classroom learning behavior, as compared to 28% of the control group; 19% of participants had difficulty in reading vs. 32% of the control group (Pierson, Walker, & Tivnan, 1984). It appears that a preschool effect found for poor children would also apply to middle-class children, but to a lesser extent.

Lasting benefits have been achieved only by *good* early childhood development programs—ones characterized by: (a) a child development curriculum with appropriate assessment procedures; (b) teaching teams that are trained in early childhood development and continue to receive such training and related supervision; (c) administrative leadership that includes support for the curriculum; (d) classes with a teacher, teaching assistant, and no more than 20 4-year-olds; (e) systematic efforts to involve parents as partners in their children's education. Such programs may be expensive, but a good, expensive early childhood development program with a high return on investment makes more economic sense than a program that costs less initially, but is less cost-effective in the long run because it provides little or no return on investment.

The wise investor seeks the greatest *return* on investment at the lowest *risk*, but will take a greater risk for the reasonable prospect of a higher return. The public preschool investor seeks a return on investment like the one described here, at minimum risk. The investment

risk level is acceptable, we believe, for an early childhood development program that serves children who live in poverty and that meets
the standards of quality described above. Of course, acceptable risk is
still risk; highly probable findings *could* have occurred by chance, and
educational research designs are never perfect. But the accumulation
of similar findings is our best guide to truth and wise investment.

The primary risk in early childhood programs lies in the degree to
which they meet standards of quality. Program quality consists of a
variety of policy variables such as group size, teacher educational background, type and degree of parental involvement, degree of administrative support, type of curriculum model, and degree of implementation. Each of these program aspects can vary substantially, and an
important task is to identify the crucial level for each variable that is to
be associated with quality. Research efforts have addressed only a few
of the myriad possibilities. For example, the National Day Care Study
(Ruopp, Travers, Glantz, & Coelen, 1979) addressed questions of
group composition and teacher (caregiver) characteristics in early
childhood programs. Several studies reviewed later (Karnes,
Schwedel, & Williams, 1983; Miller & Bizzell, 1984; Schweinhart,
Weikart, & Larner, 1986a) have examined the question of early childhood curriculum differences.

Experience in a Direct
Instruction Preschool Program

The primary alternative to child-initiated activity is teacher-
directed instruction, which is virtually synonymous with formal schooling in the minds of many people. Teacher-directed instruction, common in the nation's public schools, produces a standard product by
relying on standard practices—lectures, teacher-centered discussions,
and paperwork. Some would like these practices to be standard in
early childhood education as well, because they think they are superior to child-initiated activity in fostering children's development. The
stakes are high in the pursuit of educational success for all children,
and some would pursue measured educational success single-
mindedly. If children's low achievement-test scores are the problem,
they have reasoned, then effective teaching should increase children's
achievement-test scores; other goals are secondary. The application of
behavioral analysis to such objectives resulted in the early childhood
teaching approach called Direct Instruction by its designers (Bereiter
& Engelmann, 1966) and copyrighted by SRA Associates as DISTAR.

Direct Instruction programs seek to make teacher-directed instruction more efficient and predictable, even "teacher proof," by scripting the teacher's spoken words and the child's likely reponses. For this reason, some have called them *program*-directed rather than teacher-directed (Walsh, 1986). But, as in all teacher-directed instruction, the *teacher* transmits spoken and written information to children and checks to make sure the information has been received through questioning, paperwork, and tests. The teacher initiates all the activities; children initiate none of them. These activities may be developmentally appropriate, but sometimes they are not—as when flashcards are used to teach reading or arithmetic to very young children, a practice promoted by Glen Doman's Better Baby Institute. Questions have single correct answers and are not open-ended. The teacher identifies the child's entry-level skills, then presents instruction along predetermined lines, based on these skills. Interaction among children is not a part of the curriculum model.

**The High/Scope Preschool
Curriculum Comparison Study**

One important potential outcome of a good program for children at risk is a reduction in antisocial behavior such as crime and delinquency. One of the few longitudinal studies comparing early childhood curriculum approaches has found some evidence that child-initiated learning programs help to prevent juvenile delinquency better than do teacher-directed instruction programs (Schweinhart et al., 1986a).

The High/Scope Preschool Curriculum Comparison study traced the effects on young people through age 15 of three well-implemented early childhood curriculum models—a Direct Instruction curriculum, a High/Scope curriculum, and a child-centered Nursery School curriculum (Schweinhart et al., 1986a). Sixty-eight impoverished children in Ypsilanti, Michigan, were randomly assigned by objective criteria to attend these programs at ages 3 and 4, with children assigned to groups so as to equate the groups' ethnicity, sex, age, and average IQ; siblings were assigned to the same group. The three resultant groups did not differ significantly on any measured background characteristic, except that the Nursery School group mothers averaged 10.9 years of schooling, while the mothers of children in the other two groups (which did not differ from each other) averaged 9.5 years of schooling. This pre-existing group difference did not measurably affect the results (Schweinhart et al., 1986a, p. 26). Seventy-nine percent of the sample was interviewed at age 15.

The Direct Instruction approach taught language, reading, and arithmetic in the manner described earlier. The Nursery School approach, the antithesis of Direct Instruction, allowed children to initiate their own play activities, with the teacher keeping them safe from harm but not interfering. In the third alternative, the High/Scope curriculum, children initiated their own activities, but the teacher also maintained an active role by arranging the room to promote children's active learning, making plans and reviewing activities with children, interacting with individual children throughout the program day, and leading small- and large-group sessions.

The mean IQ of the children who attended these three high-quality early childhood programs rose a remarkable 27 points during the first year of the program, from 78 to 105, and remained in the normal range thereafter, with a mean IQ of 94 at age 10. Although the Direct Instruction group showed a temporary IQ advantage over the other groups at the end of the program, the three groups did not significantly differ in their IQs and school achievement scores at any other time. Prior to analysis of the age-15 data, the conclusion was that well-implemented early childhood programs produced a positive effect regardless of which curriculum model was used (Weikart, Epstein, Schweinhart, & Bond, 1978). This conclusion was consistent with other research documenting the effectiveness of a great variety of early childhood programs (e.g., Lazar et al., 1982, p. 57).

But in this study at age 15, both the High/Scope and the Nursery School groups reported engaging in about half as many delinquent acts as the Direct Instruction group—averages of 13 in the Direct Instruction group, 7 in the Nursery School group, and 5 in the High/Scope group. These group differences applied to both boys and girls. Defining a high-rate offender as one who reported 16 or more delinquent acts, as shown in Figure 3.3, 44% of the Direct Instruction group were high-rate offenders, as compared with only 6% of the High/Scope and 11% of the Nursery School groups. The High/Scope and Nursery School groups each reported only about one fifth as many acts of property violence as the Direct Instruction group and about half as many acts of personal violence, drug abuse, and in-family offenses. While any single group difference in a study of this size could occur by chance, the patterns of group differences in self-reported delinquency were consistent across 17 of the 18 items in the delinquency scale.

Several other findings also fit into this pattern:

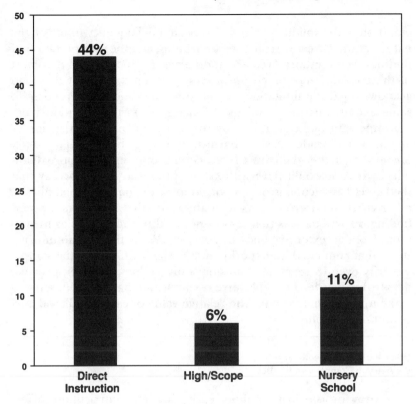

Note. — Group differences are statistically significant at p < .01, two-tailed.

Figure 3.3 High/Scope Preschool Curriculum Study: Percentages of Curriculum Groups Reporting 16 or More Delinquent Acts

- None of the High/Scope group and only 6% of the Nursery School group reported that their families felt they were doing poorly, while this was the case for 33% of the Direct Instruction group.
- None of the Direct Instruction group had ever been appointed to a school office or job, while this was the case for 12% of the High/Scope group and 33% of the Nursery School group.
- Sports participation, another possible alternative to delinquent activities, was reported by 94% of the High/Scope group and 72% of the Nursery School group, but only 44% of the Direct Instruction group.

Bereiter (1986) and Gersten (1986), defending their Direct Instruction approach, raised a variety of questions about the study—its general design, the validity of the self-reported delinquency findings, the nature of the Direct Instruction curriculum, and the interpretation of findings. Schweinhart, Weikart, and Larner (1986b) argued that most of these claims were based on misinterpretations and that they had acknowledged the limitations of the study in the original report. To some extent, this methodological fencing distracted attention from the important question raised by the study: Is Direct Instruction in language and academic skills harmful to young children? This study *cannot* say whether the Direct Instruction group reported more delinquency than it would have without the program. But it *does* say that the Direct Instruction group reported more delinquency than did the other curriculum groups. As with any study that first reports a new finding, its weakness is that it does not lead to conclusions as firm as those from an extensive body of research. While this was an unusual study that combined an experimental design with substantial sample integrity over 15 years, it is but one study. It does, however, provoke debate that may lead to replicative research and that may help some to make up their minds about the relative value of early childhood curriculum approaches.

**Other Early Childhood
Curriculum Comparison Studies**

In drawing conclusions about early childhood curriculum differences, findings from three other projects should also be considered— two longitudinal studies of the effects of early childhood curriculum models (Karnes et al.,1983; Miller & Bizzell, 1983, 1984) and the Project Follow Through evaluations, the large federal study of early elementary curriculum models that began in 1968 and continues today. While none of these studies examined program effects on juvenile delinquency, they did consider a variety of other short- and long-term potential outcomes.

Karnes et al. (1983) compared five early childhood curriculum models—ranging from the Direct Instruction model (directed by its designers, Bereiter and Engelmann) to the traditional Nursery School model. The average IQ of the Direct Instruction group increased the most of the five groups during the two-year program—21 points as compared to 5 to 12 points for the other groups—but the difference disappeared in future years, just as in High/Scope's curriculum study. By the end of high school, the Direct Instruction group did relatively poorly on several measures of school success, though not to a statistically significant extent. For example, high school graduation was achieved by 70% of the Nursery School group, but only 48% of the Direct Instruction group, a rate no different from the 47% rate for the children who received no early childhood program (pp. 157–160). The High/Scope Perry Preschool study reported similar rates of 67% for the High/Scope curriculum group and 49% for the control group (Berrueta-Clement et al., 1984, pp. 30–32).

Miller and Bizzell (1983, 1984) compared four curriculum models in Head Start programs: Direct Instruction, DARCEE, Montessori, and traditional Nursery School. During their year in Head Start, the four groups averaged a 4-point IQ gain that disappeared a year later. Group differences during the preschool years in classroom behavior and program effects appeared related to curriculum objectives; for example, the Direct Instruction and DARCEE groups did relatively better on intellectual and academic measures. However, in subsequent years through tenth grade, curriculum models did not differ in their effects on school achievement and a variety of other measures. The one consistent finding was that the 12 males from the Montessori group who were contacted at follow-up significantly outperformed males from the other curriculum groups in IQ and school achievement.

Project Follow Through is another, much larger study comparing the effects of curriculum models on children. It differs from the three studies just described in that Follow Through programs serve elementary-school children rather than preschool children—in Piaget's terms, predominately concrete-operational children rather than pre-operational children. Stanford Research Institute (Stallings, 1975) and Abt Associates (Stebbins, St. Pierre, Proper, Anderson, & Cerva, 1977; Bock, Stebbins, & Proper, 1977) reported national evaluations of the short-term effects of Project Follow Through; six of the model sponsors have reported long-term evaluations as well (Olmsted & Szegda, 1987). In some communities but not in others, each curriculum model was successfully implemented; each contributed to children's immediate school achievement and success; and, of those with long-term data, each found some evidence of long-term educational effects. This variation by community is a persuasive argument for the tightly controlled, single-site curriculum comparison studies that have been conducted at the preschool level.

Keeping community variability in mind, some conclusions about the effects of Follow Through curriculum models can still be made. Stallings (1975), using classroom observational data, made a distinction between two types of Follow Through classrooms that resembles our distinction between child development programs and teacher-directed instruction programs. What we have called child development programs were flexible and open; children engaged in independent activities, chose their own groups part of the time, and had a wide variety of activities and materials. In what we have called teacher-directed instruction programs, children spent time on reading and math activities and experienced high rates of drill, practice and praise. Children who had been in teacher-directed instruction programs had better reading and mathematics scores. They also tended to take responsibility for their failures but not for their successes. Children who had been in child development programs had lower school absence rates and higher scores on a test of nonverbal reasoning and problem-solving. In short, the various curriculum models delivered on their objectives—teacher-directed instruction models on academic achievement, child development programs on other important aspects of child development.

The Limits of Direct Instruction

These studies show that direct instruction can lead to large, though probably temporary, improvements in the intellectual performance of preschool children and the school achievement of elementary-school children. However, there is some long-term evidence that direct instruction in the preschool years is not as effective as other preschool programs in preventing delinquent behavior and possibly high school dropout.

The explanation for these negative findings may be that the early childhood years are a developmental stage during which certain experiences help children develop the dispositions and skills by which they later avoid problematic behavior. The Direct Instruction preschool program may have failed to take full advantage of the opportunities that were available to influence positively the development of young children's social problem-solving skills. After all, its stated objectives were *academic*, while the other curricula in the comparison studies included *social* objectives, such as children learning to get along with other children. Kamii (1986), applying Piaget's (1970) theory of moral development to these findings, suggests that the Direct Instruction curriculum prevented children from developing autonomy because the teacher was authoritarian and used rewards and punishments whereas the other two curricula encouraged children's autonomy because they allowed teachers and children to discuss their points of view with one another.

Research on effective teaching has focused on teacher-directed instruction simply because it is the prevalent approach in the public schools. Rosenshine (1986) observed that research has found teacher-directed instruction more useful for teaching well-structured disciplines and skills and less useful for teaching less-structured, fuzzy domains such as creative writing. While academic skills may qualify as well-structured, surely the cognitive and social development and dispositions of preschoolers qualify as fuzzy domains. The skills developed during this time are essentially everyday-life skills of thinking, communicating, and problem-solving. Teacher-directed instruction that improves children's academic skills in the short run is clearly feasible. But these short-term gains may simply be an adult-satisfying diversion from the need to focus on conversational language, personal responsibility for learning, and other developmentally important skills and dispositions. Teacher-directed instruction is an essential means of teaching and learning for older children, adolescents, and adults. Rosenshine's (1986) well-structured disciplines and skills constitute a large part of the subject matter of education. The question is not whether teacher-directed instruction has a role in education, but rather the nature of this role.

The lessons learned by young children appear to come not only from curriculum content but also from the roles of the teacher and child. Young children are still learning what adults are like. In particular, young children living in poverty may have had little experience with the combination of expectations and nurturance that comes from teachers. Teacher-directed instruction emphasizes specific expectations and systematizes nurturance. A child development program establishes broad expectations and is more generous with unconditional nurturance.

Balancing Nurturance
and Accountability

Early childhood education is characterized by the need to find the middle way between extremes, the *match* between the learning activity and the child's emergent abilities and interests (Hunt, 1961). Young children will not just develop by themselves, but adults should not push them too hard. Young children are ready for appropriate education, but not for early academics. While this formulation seems simple enough, articles in popular magazines have sometimes oversimplified the three-way choice into a two-way choice, eliminating the middle way and suggesting that parents must either "let children be children" by leaving them alone or heap inappropriate academic pressures on them.

One example of the difficulty in finding this balance is the current state of U.S. kindergartens. As a result of recent educational reforms, expectations that students must demonstrate higher standards of academic performance have begun with high school graduation and been extended downward through the grade levels. Many states and school districts have adopted standard expectations about various academic skills that students are to master at each grade level (McNamara, 1987). Having expectations for 5-year-olds is not inappropriate in itself, but these expectations must be formed on the basis of their developmental status and the nature of young children's thinking (Egertson, 1987).

Early childhood education has engendered considerable enthusiasm because it has demonstrated the ability to affect subsequent life development. Surely, the ages of three to five are not uniquely powerful in this regard, but they may be uniquely variable. Maturational strides are greater during the first three years of life, but they are virtually universal. The years of schooling are more crucial in affecting the course of life, but there is little variation in school settings and their expectations for performance. Early childhood stands out because wide variations in experience can and do occur, and these variations affect how children first form the intellectual and social skills and dispositions that they will carry through schooling and adult life.

References

Bereiter, C. (1986). Does direct instruction cause delinquency? *Early Childhood Research Quarterly, 1*, 289–292.

Bereiter, C., & Engelmann, S. (1966). *Teaching the disadvantaged child in the preschool.* Englewood Cliffs, NJ: Prentice-Hall.

Berrueta-Clement, J. R., Schweinhart, L. J., Barnett, W. S., Epstein, A. S., & Weikart, D. P. (1984). *Changed lives: The effects of the Perry preschool program on youths through age 19* (Monographs of the High/Scope Educational Research Foundation, No. 8). Ypsilanti, MI: High/Scope Press.

Bock, G., Stebbins, L. B., & Proper, E. C. (1977). *Education as experimentation: A planned variation model*: Vol. 4B: *Effects of Follow Through models.* Cambridge, MA: Abt Associates.

Caplan, N., Whitmore, J. K., & Bui, Q. I. (1985, Third Quarter). Economic self-sufficiency among recently arrived refugees from Southeast Asia. *Economic Outlook USA*, pp. 60–63.

Caplan, N., Whitmore, J. K., Bui, Q. I., & Trautman, M. (1985). Study shows boat refugees' children achieve academic success. *Refugee Reports, 6*(10), 1–6.

Congressional Research Service & Congressional Budget Office. (1985). *Children in poverty.* Washington, DC: U.S. Government Printing Office.

Duncan, G. J., Coe, R. D., & Hill, M. S. (1984). The dynamics of poverty. In G. J. Duncan (with others), *Years of poverty, years of plenty: The changing economic fortunes of American workers and families* (pp. 33–70). Ann Arbor, MI: Institute for Social Research, University of Michigan.

Egertson, H. (1987, May 20). Reclaiming kindergarten for 5-year-olds, *Education Week,* pp. 28, 19.

Gersten, R. (1986). Response to "Consequences of three preschool curriculum models through age 15." *Early Childhood Research Quarterly, 1,* 293–302.

Gray, S. W., Ramsey, B. K., & Klaus, R. A. (1982). *From 3 to 20—The early training project.* Baltimore, MD: University Park Press.

Hill, M. S., & Ponza, M. (1983, Summer). Poverty and welfare dependence across generations, *Economic Outlook USA,* p. 61.

Hohmann, M., Banet, B., & Weikart, D. P. (1979). *Young children in action: A manual for preschool educators.* Ypsilanti, MI: High/Scope Press.

Hunt, J. M. (1961). *Intelligence and experience.* New York: Ronald Press.

Irvine, D. J. (1982). *Evaluation of the New York State experimental prekindergarten program.* Paper presented at the annual meeting of the American Educational Research Association, New York City.

Jencks, C., Bartlett, S., Corcoran, M., Crouse, J., Eaglesfield, D., Jackson, G., McClelland, K., Mueser, P., Olneck, M., Schwartz, J., Ward, S., & Williams, J. (1979). *Who gets ahead? The determinants of economic success in America.* New York: Basic Books.

Kamii, C. (1986). Autonomy vs. heteronomy. *Principal, 66*(1), 68–70.

Karnes, M. B., Schwedel, A. M., & Williams, M. B. (1983). A comparison of five approaches for educating young children from low-income homes. In Consortium for Longitudinal Studies, *As the twig is bent . . . Lasting effects of preschool programs* (pp. 133–170). Hillsdale, NJ: Lawrence Erlbaum Associates.

Lázar, I., Darlington, R., Murray, H., Royce, J., & Snipper, A. (1982). Lasting effects of early education. *Monographs of the Society for Research in Child Development, 47*(2–3, Serial No. 195).

Levenstein, P., O'Hara, J., & Madden, J. (1983). The mother-child home program of the verbal interaction project. In Consortium for Longitudinal Studies, *As the twig is bent . . . Lasting effects of preschool programs* (pp. 237–264). Hillsdale, NJ: Lawrence Erlbaum Associates.

Loeber R., & Dishion, T. (1983). Early predictors of male delinquency: A review, *Psychological Bulletin, 94,* 68–99.

McKey, R. H., Condelli, L., Ganson, H., Barrett, B., McConkey, C., & Plantz, M. (1985). *The impact of Head Start on children, families and communities.* (Final Report of the Head Start Evaluation, Synthesis and Utilization Project). Washington, DC: CSR, Inc.

McNamara, T. C. (1987, April). *A large school district's perspective on the structure controversy.* Paper presented at the annual meeting of the American Educational Research Association, Washington, DC.

Miller, L. B., & Bizzell, R. P. (1983). The Louisville experiment. In Consortium for Longitudinal Studies, *As the twig is bent . . . lasting effects of preschool programs* (pp. 171–200). Hillsdale, NJ: Lawrence Erlbaum Associates.

Miller, L. B., & Bizzell, R. P. (1984). Long-term effects of four preschool programs: 9th and 10th grade results. *Child Development, 55*, 1570–1587.

Monroe, E., & McDonald, M. S. (1981). *A follow-up study of the 1966 Head Start program, Rome City Schools, Rome, Georgia.* Unpublished paper.

Moore, K., Waite, L. J., Caldwell, S. B., & Hofferth, S. (1978). *The consequences of age at first childbirth: Educational attainment.* Washington, DC: Urban Institute.

National Assessment of Educational Progress, Education Commission of the States. (1983). *The third national mathematics assessment: Results, trends, and issues.* Denver: Author.

National Center for Education Statistics. (1982). *Preprimary enrollment 1980.* Washington, DC: Author.

National Center for Education Statistics. (1983). *Two years in high school: The status of 1980 sophomores in 1982.* Washington, DC: Author.

Olmsted, P. P., & Szegda, M. J. (1987). *Long-term effects of follow through participation.* Ypsilanti, MI: High/Scope Foundation.

Palmer, F. H. (1983). The Harlem Study: Effects by type of training, age of training, and social class. In Consortium for Longitudinal Studies, *As the twig is bent . . . lasting effects of preschool programs* (pp. 201–236). Hillsdale, NJ: Lawrence Erlbaum Associates.

Piaget, J. (1970). Piaget's theory. In P. H. Mussen (Ed.), *Carmichael's manual of child psychology* (3rd ed.). New York: John Wiley & Sons.

Piaget, J., & Inhelder, B. (1969). *The psychology of the child.* New York: Basic Books.

Pierson, D. E., Walker, D. K., & Tivnan, T. (1984). A school-based program from infancy to kindergarten for children and their parents. *The Personnel and Guidance Journal, 62*, 448–455.

Research and Policy Committee, Committee for Economic Development. (1985). *Investing in our children: Business and the public schools.* Washington, DC: Committee for Economic Development.

Rosenshine, B. V. (1986). Synthesis of research on explicit teaching. *Educational Leadership, 43*, 60–69.

Ruopp, R., Travers, J., Glantz, F., & Coelen, C. (1979). *Children at the center: Summary findings and policy implications of the National Day Care study.* Cambridge, MA: Abt Associates.

Schafer, W. E., & Olexa, C. (1971): *Tracking and opportunity: The locking out process and beyond.* Scranton, PA: Chandler Publications.

Schweinhart, L. J., Koshel, J. J., & Bridgman, A. (1987, March). Policy options for preschool programs, *Phi Delta Kappan, 68*, 524–529.

Schweinhart, L. J., & Weikart, D. P. (1980). *Young children grow up: The effects of the Perry preschool program on youths through age 15* (Monographs of the High/Scope Educational Research Foundation, No. 7) Ypsilanti, MI: High/Scope Press.

Schweinhart, L. J., Weikart, D. P., & Larner, M. B. (1986a). Consequences of three preschool curriculum models through age 15. *Early Childhood Research Quarterly, 1*, 15–35.

Schweinhart, L. J., Weikart, D. P., & Larner, M. B. (1986b). Child-initiated activities in early childhood programs may help prevent delinquency. *Early Childhood Research Quarterly, 1*, 303–312.

Stallings, J. (1975). Implementation and child effects of teaching practices in Follow Through classrooms. *Monographs of the Society for Research in Child Development, 40*(7–8, Serial No. 163).

Stebbins, L. B., St. Pierre, R. G., Proper, E. C., Anderson, R. B., & Cerva, T. R. (1977).

Education as experimentation: A planned variation model: Vol. 4A: *An evaluation of follow through*. Cambridge, MA: Abt Associates.

U.S. Bureau of the Census. (1983). *Child care arrangements of working mothers: June 1982* (Current Population Reports, Series P-23, No. 129). Washington, DC: U.S. Government Printing Office.

U.S. Bureau of the Census. (1986). *Money income and poverty status of families and persons in the United States: 1985 (Advance data from the March 1986 Current Population Survey)* (Current Population Reports, Series P-60, No. 154). Washington, DC: U.S. Government Printing Office.

Walsh, D. J. (1986). The trouble with program-directed curricula. *Principal, 66*(1), 68–70.

Weikart, D. P., Epstein A. S., Schweinhart, L. J., & Bond, J. T. (1978). *The Ypsilanti preschool curriculum demonstration project: Preschool years and longitudinal results* (Monographs of the High/Scope Educational Research Foundation, No.4). Ypsilanti, MI: High/Scope Press.

Westinghouse Learning Corporation. (1969). *The impact of Head Start: An evaluation of the effect of Head Start on children's cognitive and affective development* (Vols. 1–2). Athens, OH: Ohio University Press.

4

Prediction and Prevention of Learning Disabilities: Current State of the Art and Future Directions

Howard S. Adelman

In the following presentation, the primary focus is on learning disabilities. At the same time, many points discussed have relevance for efforts to understand the prediction and prevention of a wide range of learning and behavior problems.

The commonalities of concern are exemplified by decisions to implement widespread screening to identify children with learning disabilities. As has occurred with other mental health and educational problems, once learning disabilities achieved prominence, policy makers began calling for programs to prevent or at least intervene as early after onset as feasible. In turn, the desire to intervene early fueled widespread screening. Unfortunately, as with other learning and behavior problems, the substantial body of accrued research does not support the validity of large-scale screening programs. Indeed, findings indicate that available procedures are invalid predictors, do little to differentiate learning disabilities from other learning problems, and are rather insensitive in detecting mild to moderate problems. As a result, these assessment practices provide a poor foundation upon which to build prevention and early intervention programs for learning problems in general, never mind learning disabilities in particular.

One reason for the poor showing of screening procedures is that they are based on an inadequate model of the causes of learning and behavior problems. Along with understanding of this conceptual weakness have come calls for new paradigms and procedures.

In the interim, findings from relevant prevention and early intervention programs fortunately have indicated that effective steps can be taken even without satisfactory screening instruments. And even though outcome data on these ameliorative efforts are sparse, the value of such programs is evident, as are many implications for increasing their efficacy.

As the above points illustrate, then, awareness of concerns surrounding learning disabilities has significant implications for understanding problems and issues related to many other mental health and education problems. By highlighting the status of prediction and identification efforts and of prevention and early intervention programs relevant to learning disabilities, the following presentation is meant to clarify major implications for future work on learning and behavior problems in general. Before proceeding, however, it is essential to be clear about whom we are discussing.

Learning Disabilities:
Who Are We Talking About?

Many readers will be familiar with controversies about the difference between learning disabilities (LD) and other learning problems. For those who are not, a few comments are necessary.

Problems of Definition and Differentiation

There has been increasing frustration over the inadequacy of the prevailing LD definition and the failure to differentiate among those diagnosed as LD (Adelman & Taylor, 1985a, 1986a). Dissatisfaction with the definition is reflected in the degree to which individuals and organizations continue to argue for new definitions and the fact that practitioners and researchers continue to use a variety of definitions (Tucker, Stevens & Ysseldyke, 1983). The controversy has become so heated that, in 1984, the U.S. government established a task force to conduct a national survey and make recommendations (see Chalfant, 1985, for a summary of the group's report).

It is evident that any definition attempting to differentiate learning disabilities from underachievement runs into basic difficulties related to operationalizing and assessing specific criteria. This has been demonstrated by the problem of how to operationalize the idea of *severe academic underachievement* using discrepancy formulas. There is little agreement about what constitutes a severe discrepancy between aptitude and achievement or how the discrepancy can be measured validly. Thus, formulas and specific procedures and criteria for determining severe discrepancy vary from one locale to another (Forness, Sinclair, & Guthrie, 1983).

As definitions vary, so do criteria used in identifying individuals as LD. At present, many would agree with the 1984 National Task Force's conclusion that "a learning disability cannot be identified by any one criterion such as (a) a list of behavioral characteristics; (b) a test score(s); (c) evidence about a possible dysfunction in a psychological process; (d) the inability to identify other reasons for a student's failure in school; (e) identification of an etiological factor; or (f) a discrepancy between aptitude and achievement" (Chalfant, 1985, p. 12). However, less consensus is likely regarding the Task Force's view that, "By using all of these factors, . . . the probability of accurately identifying LD students will be increased" (Chalfant, 1985, p. 12).

The problem is not just the restricted focus on one or another of the above criteria. The problem is that the conceptual and empirical work required to evolve a valid differential diagnostic process has not been done (see Adelman, 1979; Senf, 1986). In particular, too little attention has been devoted to developing a classification scheme in which LD is first differentiated from other types of learning problems and then subtypes are conceived within each major category of learning problem (including LD). Without such a theory-based classification scheme, important areas in which diagnostic criteria, assessment procedures, and ameliorative strategies should be developed are ignored.

It is clear that the learning problems of youngsters currently diagnosed as LD differ not only in behavior manifested but also in etiology. Students in one LD program often differ from those in another in very important (but unidentified) ways. This is also true of those included in research samples. These differences are of considerable importance to prevention, remediation, research, and training programs, and to the policy decisions shaping them. The failure to account for this variability has undermined both research and practice. For example, because samples have differed from each other with respect to etiology, it has been difficult to arrive at valid conclusions about whether individuals with learning disabilities have unique intervention needs. In turn, this has hurt efforts to improve programs and evolve policy.

It is difficult to make sound public policy when learning disabilities are so poorly defined and differentiated and when prevalence and incidence estimates primarily reflect political motives. Because of this state of affairs, students diagnosed as LD have become the largest percentage of those in special education. As a result, current practices and policies have been called into question (Will, 1986). The reaction of policy makers provides another example of the type of political backlash to be expected when a field allows professional practices to get out of hand.

Classifying LD: Putting Learning Disabilities Back into Perspective

As a way of reducing the confusion caused by varying definitions and criteria, it has been recommended that specific marker variables, such as demographic, personality, and programmatic variables, be reported on every LD sample (e.g., Keogh, Major-Kingsley, Omori-Gordon, & Reid, 1982). However, this recommendation, along with efforts to identify "LD" subtypes (e.g., Lyon, 1983, 1985; McKinney, 1984; Rourke & Strang, 1983; Satz & Morris, 1981), overlooks the confusion caused by accepting the LD samples as validly diagnosed. That is, in starting with a group already diagnosed as LD, the researchers skip by the more fundamental problem of differentiating learning disabilities from other types of learning problems. Such activity works against conceptual clarity and does not deal with the most fundamental classification problem, namely, differentiating LD from other types of learning problems.

Lack of agreement about definition and about who should be diagnosed as LD has caused some people to question whether there is such a thing as a learning disability (e.g., Algozzine & Ysseldyke, 1986; Ysseldyke & Algozzine, 1983). The danger in this position is one of losing sight of learning problems caused by minor CNS dysfunction. The key to identifying these specific learning disabilities, of course, involves assessing minor neurological dysfunctioning. For the present, existing methodology precludes doing this in a valid manner, and thus, current diagnoses of LD are not an indication that an individual has such a dysfunction. Nevertheless, it remains scientifically valid to conceive of a subset of learning problems caused by neurological factors.

Think about a random sample of students with learning problems but no evident physical defects (e.g., no problems seeing or hearing, no *gross* brain damage). What makes it difficult for them to learn? Research on this question has been highly troublesome and relatively unproductive to date. Still, it is theoretically viable to suggest that some of these individuals have a relatively *minor* disorder, dysfunction, or maturational delay that affects their brain function and interferes with facets of their learning. To guide research, it continues to be essential to differentiate such individuals—first conceptually and as soon as possible empirically—from those whose learning problems stem from other causes. And, for now, it seems reasonable to reserve the term *learning disabilities* for them.

In our work with individuals whose learning problems are the *primary* concern (e.g., not due to severe emotional disturbance or mental retardation), my colleagues and I use the label *learning disabilities* for those whose learning difficulties, most conceivably, are caused by minor CNS dysfunctioning. Given this causal view and using a transactional paradigm for understanding human behavior (e.g., Bandura, 1978), we view these individuals as being at one end of a continuum and categorize them as Type III learning problems (Adelman, 1971; Adelman & Taylor, 1983a, 1986b). At the other end of the continuum, we put learning problems which are most attributable to causes outside individuals, namely, those that seem to result *primarily* from inadequacies in the environments in which learning takes place. We categorize these as Type I learning problems. To provide a mid-anchoring point, we designate a group consisting of those who do not learn and perform well in situations in which their individual differences and vulnerabilities are poorly accommodated or are responded to hostilely. The problems of an individual in this group can be seen as a relatively equal product of the person's characteristics and the failure of the learning environment to accommodate that individual. We categorize this group as Type II learning problems. To account for learning problems that are *secondary* to other personal disorders and handicapping conditions (such as sensory impairment, mental retardation, autism, or severe emotional disturbance), one can extend the continuum and add a group of Type IV learning problems. Figure 4.1 presents a hypothetical representation of (a) the relationship between the degree to which a student needs special accommodation in order to learn at school and (b) the proportions and types of subsequent learning problems.

I stress the above points because a literature review on the prediction and prevention of learning disabilities indicates a pervasive failure to differentiate LD from other types of learning problems. It is important to face up to the reality that, because of the inadequacies of current diagnostic procedures, practitioners assign the LD label inappropriately across the four types of learning problems designated above. That is, given current practices, any youngster with any type of learning problem stands a good chance of being diagnosed as LD. The result has been a tendency to equate most learning problems with learning disabilities and thus to trivialize the special concerns of those who are truly disabled. To highlight the problem of

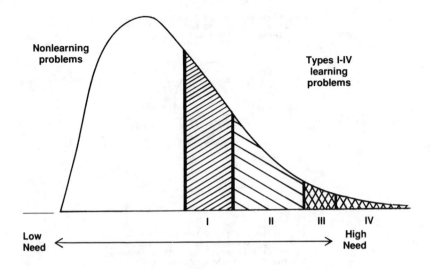

Degree to which student needs personalized instruction

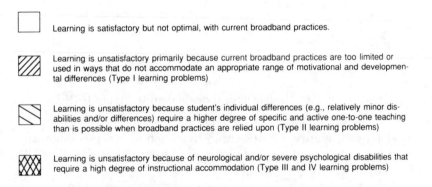

Learning is satisfactory but not optimal, with current broadband practices.

Learning is unsatisfactory primarily because current broadband practices are too limited or used in ways that do not accommodate an appropriate range of motivational and developmental differences (Type I learning problems)

Learning is unsatisfactory because student's individual differences (e.g., relatively minor disabilities and/or differences) require a higher degree of specific and active one-to-one teaching than is possible when broadband practices are relied upon (Type II learning problems)

Learning is unsatisfactory because of neurological and/or severe psychological disabilities that require a high degree of instructional accommodation (Type III and IV learning problems)

Figure 4.1 Types (and hypothesized proportions) of Learning Problems as a Function of the Degree to Which Instruction Is Personalized

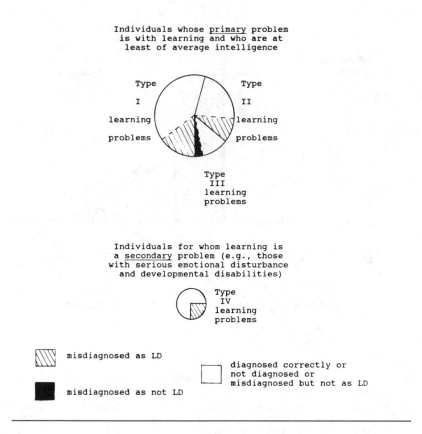

Individuals whose <u>primary</u> problem
is with learning and who are at
least of average intelligence

Type I learning problems

Type II learning problems

Type III learning problems

Individuals for whom learning is
a <u>secondary</u> problem (e.g., those
with serious emotional disturbance
and developmental disabilities)

Type IV learning problems

misdiagnosed as LD

misdiagnosed as not LD

diagnosed correctly or
not diagnosed or
misdiagnosed but not as LD

Figure 4.2 Degree of Misdiagnoses Hypothesized for Types I–IV Problems

misdiagnosis, Figure 4.2 presents a hypothetical representation suggesting the degree of misdiagnosis related to differences in Type I-IV learning problems.

Although the focus here is on learning disabilities, a comparable concern arises with respect to the diagnoses of a great deal of deviant and devious behavior. For example, the trend is for youngsters referred because of troublesome behavior to be diagnosed using labels such as conduct disorder and attention deficit disorder (with or without hyperactivity). And the tendency in interpreting these labels is to place the locus (cause) of the problem within the individual. Given the serious limitations of the diagnostic procedures used in assigning such labels, a considerable amount of misdiagnosis is inevitable, and given the pressure for making certain diagnoses, the proportion of false positive errors is likely to be far greater than false negatives. False positive errors lead to research samples that are heterogeneous with respect to cause (but which, unfortunately, tend to be treated and discussed as if this were not the case). False positive errors also lead to inappropriate decisions as to the proper focal point for intervention. Toward dealing with these problems, a classification typology such as that described above helps focus attention on the fact that any specific manifestation of deviant behavior might or might not be the result of internal pathology. That is, identical behaviors may stem from internal pathology (Type III and IV problems) or from circumstances where either the environment is the primary culprit (Type I problems) or the individual and the environment both significantly contribute to the problem (Type II problems). Current classification practices do not *adequately* account for this state of affairs and, thus, have a built-in bias not generally acknowledged.

The simple typology outlined above does not, of course, do justice to the complexities involved in differentiating among learning and behavior problems. It does demonstrate the value of using etiology as a classification principle. It also demonstrates the value of using a broad conception of causality to minimize the tendency to suggest all learning problems result from deficiencies or pathology within the individual. Thus, even this simple categorization avoids colluding with practices that "blame the victim" (Ryan, 1971) and perpetuate pathological biases in describing the causes of individuals' problems. It also helps to broaden the focus of intervention by emphasizing that prevention and remediation of some types of learning problems primarily involve altering learning environments rather than carrying out person-oriented treatments (see Adelman & Taylor, 1983a, 1986b).

Clearly, then, although a typology based solely on cause is insufficient for classifying learning and behavior problems, classifications that ignore causality are seriously flawed. (In general, besides cause, most researchers and practitioners find it desirable to describe and categorize psychological and educational problems in terms of such fundamental dimensions as severity, pervasiveness, and chronicity of problem manifestation—see Adelman & Taylor, 1986a). The point for emphasis here is simply that a comprehensive classification scheme is needed to differentiate LD from other types of primary learning problems. Without comprehensive class categories, it seems likely the debilitating trend toward learning disabilities becoming synonymous with all learning problems will remain unchecked.

The failure to differentiate LD from other types of learning problems represents a fundamental conceptual lapse that permeates the literature on the prediction and prevention of learning disabilities. To avoid this error, in the following discussion the term *learning disabilities* is used only to designate Type III learning problems as defined above. The distinction between Types I-IV learning problems also is used occasionally for purposes of clarifying certain points.

Prediction and Early Identification of Learning Problems and Disabilities

In various countries, there has been rapidly escalating interest in screening child problems, especially those that may result in young-sters not doing well at school (Frankenburg, Emde, & Sullivan, 1985). In the United States over the last 20 years, this interest has been reflected in federal legislation. For example, in 1967, Title XIX of the Social Security Act directed states with Medicaid programs to provide early and periodic screening, diagnosis, and treatment to all medicaid-eligible children; the Education of All Handicapped Children Act of 1975 (Public Law 94–142) called for educational and related services from preschool through age 21; and a primary emphasis in the 1983 Education of the Handicapped Amendments Act (PL 98–199) is on expanding and improving services to infants and preschoolers.

The desire to help children with special needs, reinforced by legisla-tive mandate, has made screening a large-scale and controversial enter-prise. In the early 1980s, a national survey by the Minnesota Depart-ment of Education (1982) found 24 states had some form of compre-hensive screening to find young children with problems. Surveys also indicate that specific practices vary greatly in their nature and quality across and within states (Gracey, Azzara, & Reinherz, 1984). Although well intentioned, it appears that the rush to establish screening pro-grams has resulted in a climate where consumers and suppliers are less critical than they should be in evaluating the validity of procedures.

Terminology

Before proceeding, let's get our terms straight. It is useful to differ-entiate the process of predicting *high risk* (or *at risk*) conditions from the process of identifying current problems. As the word *prediction* implies, the process of labeling a condition as *high risk* is a future judgment—an act of prophecy. Based on assessment of antecedent variables, future problems are hypothesized. In contrast, *identification* is the process by which current conditions are assessed to detect exist-ing problems. Addition of the adjective *early* to form the term *early identification,* although intuitively appealing and widely used, can be confusing. In effect, the term may denote identification at an early age or early after onset or both. (Too often, it is used as synonymous with prediction.)

It is also important to differentiate between screening and diagnosis. Research on prediction and identification of learning problems and disabilities has encompassed both screening and diagnostic procedures. Screening procedures usually are intended to survey large groups as a first stage in problem detection. These procedures are expected to have lower reliability and validity than those used for diagnostic classification or for generating a specific prescription. Indeed, the validity of most first-level screens is so low that they are expected to make a relatively large number of misidentifications. At best, such screening procedures are meant to provide a preliminary indication that something *may* be wrong and in need of correction. When diagnostic classification and specific prescriptions are wanted, assessment procedures of greater validity are required. Despite frequent warnings about the danger of blurring the distinction between screening and diagnosis, it is common for screening instruments to be misused.

Models Guiding Research

Three major models defining the focal point of intervention can be used in developing screening and diagnostic procedures. One focuses on the *person*, in terms of pathology (disorders and "illness") or lack of developmental readiness; another focuses on the *environment* (also emphasizing pathology or development deficiencies); and the third stresses the *interaction*/transaction of person and environment. Of the three models, only the first has been used extensively to guide prediction and identification research to early signs and symptoms of pathology, developmental deficits, or both. Although a large number of physiological and psychological signs and symptoms have been discussed in the literature, only a very delimited set of correlates of behavior and learning has been assessed validly and reported by researchers.

Because of dissatisfaction with the prevailing person-oriented model and findings related to it, the work of researchers who focus on the environment has taken on some prominence. This work is concerned with assessing home and school variables to clarify their contribution to learning problems. One result is a growing appreciation of factors in the environment that should be the focus of intervention.

Going a step further, interaction-oriented investigators hope to determine the degree to which learning problems stem not only from the person or environment, but also from the interplay of person and environmental variables. In particular, this research has been concerned with how well youngsters' response capabilities and motivation mesh with environmental factors such as differences in approaches to socialization (e.g., child-rearing practices, school instruction).

Research and Practice

Because of the trend toward widespread application, it should be stressed at the outset that evidence *does not* support the efficacy of any available psychometric or rating scale procedure for use in massive screening for mild to moderate learning problems among infants, preschoolers, or kindergartners. The fact is that few of the available procedures meet even the minimal standards set forth by the American Psychological Association and the American Educational Research Association (see "standards for Educational and Psychological Tests"). Such widespread application provides another example where pressure and enthusiasm for screening has led to inappropriate extrapolations of research findings and premature application of new procedures (Adelman, 1982).

The following brief discussion restricts its focus to research on screening of preschoolers and kindergartners. Moreover, my intent is only to highlight the state of the art, not to offer an exhaustive review.

Person screening. Screening specifically for LD has not differed in any substantive way from screening aimed at finding potential learning problems among that segment of prefirst-grade children who are of at least average intelligence. Thus, a reasonable sense of the state of the art can be found in data from two surveys of prekindergarten screening practices.

In Illinois, a statewide survey of preschool screening programs found 77% of the responding agencies used standardized but not well validated instruments; 23% used locally developed, largely unvalidated procedures (Van Duyne, Gargiulo, & Allen, 1980). Similar findings come from a 1984 survey in Minnesota, the first state (in 1977) to offer comprehensive, free screening to all prekindergarten children (Ysseldyke, Thurlow, O'Sullivan, & Bursaw, 1986). In this survey, the researchers found that the two most used instruments were the DIAL (Developmental Indicators for the Assessment of Learning) and the DDST (Denver Developmental Screening Test). The former has little empirical support for its reliability and validity (Lichtenstein & Ireton, 1984), and the latter was standardized in only one city and has overreferral rates as high as 44% (German, Williams, Herzfeld, & Marshall, 1982). Given this rate of overreferral, it is discomforting to note that the DDST is the screening instrument most often used by model early childhood education programs throughout the U.S. (Lehr, Ysseldyke, & Thurlow, 1986) and has even found its way to China (Chieh, Chu, Lu, Tang, & Wang, 1985).

The dedication to screening children for prospective learning problems, especially reading problems, is reflected in an extensive literature (e.g., see references in Adelman, 1982; Barnes, 1982; Lichtenstein & Ireton, 1984; Lipson & Wixson, 1986).[1] Hundreds of studies have been reported over the past decade, but many are so methodologically inadequate that their results defy valid interpretation.

The majority of studies have used psychometric tests to screen potential and current school problems. In this connection, narrow band tests have been found grossly inadequate; thus, the major focus has been on combinations of tests (test batteries) covering a moderate range of cognitive, language, and perceptual-motor functioning (e.g., see Badian, 1986; Eaves, Kendall, & Crichton 1974; Fletcher & Satz, 1980; Funk, Sturner & Green, 1986; Jansky & de Hirsch, 1973; Lyon & Smith, 1986; Silver & Hagin, 1981).

Validation of most psychometric screening procedures usually has been extremely limited. Poor test performance usually has been correlated with concurrent evidence of learning problems or with later, but relatively short-term, follow-up data. The consistent finding has been that the greater the time lapse between identifier and criteria of learning problems, the lower the correlation. It is not surprising, then, that current preschool and kindergarten screening procedures do not *predict* with satisfactory sensitivity. Such procedures can be used to detect individuals who manifest current difficulty with tasks and deportment. However, with the exception of the most severe and pervasive problems, most children identified will not have subsequent learning problems and will not be diagnosed as LD. In terms of Type I-IV learning problems, the screens are probably most accurate with regard to Types III and IV.

In contrast to psychometric approaches, efforts have been made to use teacher or parent ratings (Feshbach, Adelman, & Fuller, 1977; Glazzard, 1980; Pihl & Nagy, 1980). These too range in scope of areas assessed from narrow to moderately broad. The best rating scales have produced results as good as those found with psychometric procedures. That is, they accurately identify a moderate percentage of problems but also result in many errors. For example, Feshbach et al., (1977) found incorrect predictions about second grade reading performance in 23% of kindergartners screened for future reading problems by teacher ratings. Moreover, only 30% of the correct identifications were predictions of problems (i.e., accuracy was related mostly to predicting who would not have problems). Furthermore, the percentage of second graders designated as problems dropped considerably when an easier criterion measure of reading was used and when problem performance was defined by a higher cut-off score. This illustrates the likelihood that even the modest results reported in some research are inflated through use of inappropriately difficult criterion measures or excessively low cut-off scores. Thus, while it is true that the best available teacher rating scales are as good as the best available psychometric procedures, it should also be understood that being as good as the best is not to be equated with being very good or even good enough.

The incidence or base rate of the phenomenon under study, of course, also affects predictive accuracy. Base rates are lower for specific learning disabilities than for learning problems and underachievement in general. The relatively low incidence of LD means that anything other than a highly accurate screening instrument will make a large number of errors. Moreover, the only way such instruments can correctly identify a large proportion of individuals with learning disabilities is by making many more false positive than false negative identifications.

In general, then, the evidence shows that no currently available procedure intended for large-scale screening can uncover a large number of problems without making many false positive errors. The number of false positives can be reduced by altering the cut-off score. By doing this, however, the number of correct problem identifications is reduced and usually turns out to be that small percentage of youngsters with the most severe learning problems (e.g., Type III and IV). Ironically, most of these youngsters tend to be individuals who have already been identified by pediatricians, teachers, and parents without the use of costly screening programs.

The ease with which serious problems are detected through existing screens raises another important consideration in evaluating screening procedures. The appropriate standard for judging the utility of screening instruments should be their ability to identify individuals whose difficulties are not already recognized. If we use this standard, most procedures would be judged even less efficacious than has been the case. In poverty area schools, for example, the number of poor readers is so high that screening procedures would have to be much more effective than any that currently exist for there to be significant incremental validity beyond base rates.

In sum, there is considerable room for improvement with regard to person-oriented screening procedures. Available procedures assess only a very limited set of person variables and have been poorly validated. Beside design and sample deficiencies, the validation research is filled with flagrant examples of tester and rater bias and failure to control for fluctuations in children's performance due to motivation and the degree of assimilation of new skills. In addition, because of the current lack of standardized criteria and agreed upon norms and standards, varying cut-off points are applied in making decisions about normal functioning and problems. Thus, children with the same behaviors and levels of skill are seen as problems in one situation (e.g., one study, one school) and not in another. Finally, it must be stressed that none of the screening procedures has been systematically cross-validated to account for major sample differences or the leveling impact of routine use. Even if these deficiencies were corrected, however, it is unlikely that person-oriented screens could ever be sufficiently sensitive. The reason for this is that they restrict their focus to the individual.

Environment-focused screens. In the 1960s and 1970s, because of the modest results achieved by person-focused screens, some investigators turned their attention to assessing home and school environments. At the present, this type of research is still in its initial stages. A good sense of the work can be derived from reviews by Moos (1979) and Freund, Bradley, and Caldwell (1979).

The HOME Inventory (Home Observation for Measurement of the Environment) provides a representative and perhaps the most significant example of efforts to identify environment variables related to learning problems (Bradley & Rock, 1985; Caldwell & Bradley, 1979). A major objective of the inventory is to identify homes "likely to impede or foster cognitive development." Although a variety of studies have used the scales, findings indicate only moderate correlations with IQ and school achievement. Data do suggest the instrument may prove to be somewhat better in predicting mental development than infant measures (Elardo, Bradley & Caldwell, 1975; Van Doorninck, Caldwell, Wright, & Frankenburg, 1975; Wulbert, Inglis, Kriegsman, & Mills, 1975).

Not surprisingly, measures of classroom environments and specific program variables that may cause or contribute to learning problems are at an even earlier stage of development than home measures. Although the work of Walberg (1969), Barclay (1983), and Moos and his colleagues (Moos, 1979) has resulted in widely cited secondary school measures, only preliminary research has been done on comparable measures of prekindergarten (see Harms & Clifford, 1980) and elementary classrooms (see Toro, et al., 1985).

Future Directions

There is little doubt that research to develop measures of the classroom and home will continue. However, as with person-focused measures, used alone, the best environment scales probably will be most sensitive in identifying variables that contribute to *severe* problems. That is, they are likely to be most useful in detecting home factors associated with low IQ scores and classroom factors associated with high proportions of academic and deportment problems. Consequently, major increases in predictive accuracy should not be expected from person or environment screens.

Increasingly, researchers are coming to the conclusion that assessment strategies must measure "*both* the child *and* the processes within the child's environment" (Freund et al., 1979). Given this, progress in validating measures of person and environment is more than an end in itself; it becomes a necessary step in efforts to operationalize interaction oriented screens.

Toward interaction-focused screens. In a 1971 critique of person-focused screening, Adelman and Feshbach (1971) noted that prevailing models and screening strategies ignored key determinants of school success and failure. This critique reflects the view that an interactional paradigm offers the best model for understanding the causes of human problems (Adelman, 1971; Adelman & Taylor. 1983a, 1986b; Bandura, 1978; Sameroff, 1985). From this perspective, success or failure in school can be seen as a function of transactions between an individual's motivational and development status (e.g., interests, expectations, strengths, and limitations) and specific classroom situational factors encountered (e.g., individual differences among teachers and differing approaches to instruction). For instance, success in first grade depends not only on having the necessary skills and behaviors to learn, but also on the characteristics of the classroom situation to which a student is assigned. Students need greater capability and higher motivation to succeed in demanding programs; not accounting for this produces false negative predictions and identifications. At the same time, deficiencies may be accommodated and remedied in some classrooms; not accounting for this results in false positive errors.

It is reasonable to hypothesize, therefore, that the greater the congruity between a kindergartner's skills, deportment, and interests and those required in a specific first grade program, the greater the likelihood of success. Conversely, as suggested in Figure 4.1, the greater the discrepancy between a child's skills, deportment, and interests and those required, the greater the likelihood of failure. One way to test these hypotheses is to observe, under representative classroom conditions, a specific area of learning (such as the reading readiness program) to assess the degree to which a kindergartner is successful. This type of assessment can be accomplished by rating specific facets of the student and the environment and determining the discrepancy between the ratings. That is, one evaluates, in situ, a student's lack of relevant skills and interests, as well as the presence of interfering behaviors. Similarly, an evaluation is made of the first grade program to which the youngster is assigned to determine the skills, behaviors, and interests essential for coping with comparable tasks (e.g., reading). Then, an analysis is made of the discrepancy between what the youngster brings to the situation and what will be required for success in the classroom (e.g., in the reading program).

A close proximity between predictor and criterion variables, of course, is desirable to enhance predictive accuracy. The more closely predictor variables approximate criteria in time and content, the closer they are to being identification procedures and, as such, should produce fewer errors. Thus, in predicting who will have learning problems in the next grade, it is best to assess a student near the end of the school year. However, in assessing the classroom to which he or she will be assigned, it is best to observe the program as it functions during the first part of a school year. (This raises a number of practical, but eventually surmountable, problems.)

To date, efforts to develop interaction-focused screens have been frustrated primarily by the methodological difficulties involved in assessing instructional processes. However, progress on the problem should result from continued development of classroom measures and from increased research efforts based on interactional/transactional perspectives (Adelman & Feshbach, 1971; Feshbach et al., 1977; Lipson & Wixson, 1986).

Program improvement as a first step in screening. When learning problems are viewed as rooted in the environment or as reciprocally determined, another screening strategy that becomes apparent is program improvement. In this context, it is well to recall Hobb's (1975) views on screening: "Ideally, special screening programs to identify health problems and developmental difficulties of children should not be necessary. All children regardless of economic status should be able to participate in a comprehensive health maintenance program" (pp.

90–91). If this view of screening is correct, preventive and early-age programs should reduce the number of problems and thereby reduce and facilitate the task of finding those that remain.

Improving prevention and early interventive programs as the first step in a screening sequence for learning and behavior problems and disabilities represents an important, unresearched idea. The type of study needed is one in which a representative sample of preschool, kindergarten, and primary school programs (across socioeconomic groups) is upgraded to improve their capability for personalized and remedial instruction. The proportion of children subsequently found to manifest problems in these settings would then be compared with those identified in a matched control sample of standard programs. Data from this comparison would indicate the efficacy of the experimental settings in preventing some types of problems, primarily Type I and some Type II problems. Identification of learning problems in each classroom would only involve establishing criteria for daily performance and noting those who do not meet the criteria over a period of several weeks. Students in the experimental and control samples would be followed into the upper elementary grades to determine the degree to which false positive and false negative identifications were made. After this first study, a second could determine whether identification sensitivity and specificity are improved by adding formal assessment screening procedures to the experimental programs.

In conclusion, as the above discussion highlights, procedures currently used in screening learning disabilities produce too many errors. They are most successful in screening youngsters whose learning and behavior problems are so severe that they are readily identified by parents, pediatricians, and teachers. New approaches for research in this area clearly are needed. In this regard, assessment strategies accounting for learning as a reciprocally determined process are seen as promising. The upgrading of existing programs also is seen as an especially fruitful way to improve screening by both preventing problems and providing a more appropriate context for identifying moderate to serious functional problems.

Prevention and Early Intervention of Learning Problems and Disabilities

The extensive interest in screening children has colluded with the unfortunate tendency among clinicians and educators to assume the child is to be the object of change. Ironically, even some who stress the environment as the primary cause of many children's problems have continued to pursue interventions that focus mainly on changing the child.

Obviously, there are times when the proper focal point of intervention is the individual. However, it is equally obvious there are times when environments, such as home, school, and society, establish inappropriate standards and constrain choices in ways that cause children to experience learning problems and misbehave (e.g., Cowen, 1986; Goodwin, 1973; Hobbs, 1975; Kelly, Snowden, & Munoz, 1977; Kessler & Albee, 1975; Rhodes & Tracy, 1972). When the cause of the problem is the environment, the most appropriate intervention involves changing the enviroment to reduce hostile intrusiveness and accommodate a wider range of individual differences. For instance, the socialization agenda of the school often results in interventions that ignore and are even hostile to individual differences. When this happens, school practices themselves can be a primary cause of learning and behavior problems. Furthermore, efforts within schools to initiate helping interventions for those with learning and behavior problems often are undermined by the demands of the school's socialization agenda (Adelman & Taylor, 1983a, 1985b).

Problems of feasibility certainly arise when the environment is the culprit. It is seldom within the power of individual professionals to establish profound changes in the school or home. Many realities, therefore, collude with the trend toward making children assume not only the blame for the problem, but also the brunt of the intervention. Such realities, however, do not alter the fact that the object of change should be the environment or perhaps both the environment and the child, rather than the child alone. When the full scope of possibilities is ignored, the range of intervention strategies is inappropriately narrowed. The following overview of preventive and early-age programs tries to keep the entire range of intervention options in perspective.

Prevention

If one accepts that learning disabilities (Type III learning problems) are rooted in CNS dysfunctioning, then prevention is aimed at factors likely to produce mild-moderate neurological dysfunctions. Analysis of interventions designed for high risk infants suggests that preventive programs take two forms (Osofsky, 1986). One form is health care maintenance and problem prevention to provide pre, peri, and neonatal care, such as prenatal and well-child clinics and infant immunization outreach services. A second form is community education, such as parent programs to improve infant/child nutrition and physical safety and to increase cognitive stimulation.

The Yale Child Welfare Research Program provided an example of a promising, comprehensive preventive approach designed to offer medical, educational, and psychosocial benefits from birth to 2 1/2 years of age with follow-up assessment at 7 to 8 years of age (Rescorla & Zigler, 1981). Another example of the benefits to be gained through comprehensive infant intervention is found in Greenspan's (1981, 1986) work with multirisk families.

Health and safety maintenance and problem prevention programs have relevance for reducing learning disabilities among all segments of the population and are particulary important for those who live in poverty. For example, it has been reported that while the incidence of lead poisoning in the U.S. is 7%, it is over 15% in some poverty pockets (Berwick & Kamaroff, 1982). As Keogh, Wilcoxen, and Bernheimer (1986) note: "Based on the national figure of 7%, lead poisoning causes an additional 13 cases of learning disability and 1.4 cases of mental retardation in every thousand children. Lead-abatement and lead-screening programs reduce these figures to 7 cases of learning disability and 0.6 cases of mental retardation. Corresponding figures for inner-city areas would be approximately double, given the incidence of 15% for these areas" (p. 299). Thus, environmental protection programs designed to reduce lead toxicity clearly can make a significant contribution to the prevention of learning disabilities.

Early-Age Intervention

The most familiar early-age interventions are day care and early education programs. Examples of other early-age interventions include programs to educate parents about lead poisoning and about cognitive stimulation activities for babies who experience prenatal anoxia and for low birth weight and premature infants (Bromwich, 1981; Tjossem, 1976). In stopping a segment of youngsters from being diagnosed as LD and others from developing learning problems, these interventions are preventive; they are early interventive in that they begin a process of problem correction at an early age and usually very soon after onset. Most fall into what has been called secondary prevention.

For example, health programs and educational interventions designed for young children from low socioeconomic and other high risk populations and for mild to moderately handicapped children certainly contain some youngsters at risk for LD diagnosis. However, learning disabilities are widely diagnosed only after youngsters display major difficulties learning to read, write, spell, or do arithmetic. (Even then, many researchers and practitioners question the validity of the diagnoses.) Thus, it is rare to see anyone diagnosed LD prior to the latter part of the first grade. Prior to age 7, then, early intervention programs are for youngsters seen as at risk for a wide range of learning problems—not for learning disabilities per se.

For those with and without specific learning disabilities, the most widespread early-age intervention takes the form of early education programs. By enhancing individual capabilities, these programs can minimize the impact of current and subsequent environmental deficiencies and personal vulnerabilities. In the U.S., after passage of the Children's Early Assistance Act in 1968, a variety of handicapped children's early education programs (HCEEP's) were initiated (Swan, 1980, 1981). By the early 1980s, over 350 demonstration projects had been funded. Still, it should be noted that as of 1986 only about half the states had legislation mandating educational services for handicapped children age 5 and under. U.S. government statistics for the 1981–82 school year show that besides the 40,000 children age 3–5 in Head Start, 228,000 others received special education services under Public Law 94–142 (U.S. Administration for Children, Youth, and Families, 1983; U.S. Office of Special Education and Rehabilitation Services, 1983). These figures account for about half of all the estimated handicapped children in the 3–5 age group.

In general, data on early-age interventions for handicapped children support the benefits of such activity; they do not, however, clarify the types of intervention that are most effective (White, 1985–86; White, Bush & Casto, 1985–86). Casto and Mastropieri (1986) report a meta-analysis of 74 evaluation studies on programs for handicapped children through age 5. Although most of the studies sampled youngsters not seen as severely or profoundly handicapped, 73% of the studies did involve mentally retarded or multiply handicapped children. The findings suggest that the longer and more intense the program, the more positive the effects in terms of measures of intelligence, language, and academic achievement. Because of beliefs about the importance of age at start, parental involvement, and degree of structure, the analysis stressed data on these variables; the findings, however, were interpreted as unsupportive of the specific factors.

Additional models and supportive data for the overall value of preschool programs are readily found in general reviews (Consortium for Longitudinal Studies, 1983). In addition, a comparable body of promising data are being generated by studies on the impact of day care programs (Kilmer, 1983; McCartney, Scarr, Phillips, Grajek, & Schwartz, 1982; Travers & Ruopp, 1978).

Like the findings on early-age programs for the handicapped, the data on high quality early childhood education underscore the importance of such programs for ameliorating learning problems (e.g., Lazar, Darlington, Murray, Royce & Snipper, 1982). In terms of academic achievement, efficacy data comparing participants with nonparticipants show significant, lasting benefits. With specific regard to the need for special services, findings from the Perry Preschool follow-up study (at age 19) are noteworthy. Among samples of economically disadvantaged Blacks whose IQs ranged from 60 to 90, there was significantly less need for special education programs by those who had been in the preschool group (Berrueta-Clement, Schweinhart, Barnett, Epstein, & Weikart, 1984).

What constitutes a high quality early education program? In judging quality, the National Association for the Education of Young Children (1983) cites the following as essential elements to be evaluated: (1) physical environment; (2) health and safety; (3) nutrition and food service; (4) administration; (5) staff qualifications and development; (6) staff-parent interaction; (7) staff-child interaction; (8) child-child interaction; (9) curriculum; and (10) evaluation. Few would dismiss any of these elements, but some see the listing of components as insufficient. For instance, the Perry Preschool project staff state

> *Style of program operations* is the additional ingredient necessary to ensure high quality. The style . . . is manifested in the skillful blending of program elements. . . . Elements of particular importance are as follows: curriculum implementation, parent involvement, staff supervision, inservice training provision, teacher planning time, staff relationships, ongoing evaluation, and administrative leadership. These elements are not rigidly tied to a "right" way of doing things: for example, it is not as important which curriculum is chosen, as *that* a curriculum model is chosen to guide program operations. (Berrueta-Clement et al., 1984; pp. 109–110)

Although data on early childhood education are promising, generalizations of findings must be made cautiously. As Zigler (1987) stresses in arguing against formal schooling for 4-year-olds, (1) data widely cited about the success of preschool intervention programs primarily reflect benefits for economically disadvantaged children, and (2) the successful programs differ from "standard school fare in a number of important ways, providing primary health and social services, in addition to remedial academic programs" (p. 252). Thus, he questions the validity of using the data to justify formal schooling for all 4-year-olds and warns that current proposals for such compulsory schooling do not contain the elements that may have made preschool intervention programs beneficial. Zigler does favor providing early-age interventions as a universally available *option* but emphasizes they should primarily offer recreation and socialization with a secondary focus on developmentally appropriate educational curricula.

After Preschool

Once children arrive in kindergarten and the elementary grades, primary prevention and early intervention programs for learning problems are based in schools and have a twofold focus: (1) to enhance regular learning and instruction for all children and (2) to remedy problems that arise as soon as possible and with the least intervention needed. Accomplishment of these goals requires broadening the psychoeducational nature of regular school interventions and increasing the availability of support mechanisms for academic learning. Also needed are programs to train and provide consultation for teachers regarding what interventions to pursue prior to referring a student for special education.

Psychoeducational breadth. The status of education has been well scrutinized during the 1980s. There have been discussions of what constitutes effective schools, classrooms, and instruction (e.g., Berliner, 1984; Brophy & Good, 1986; Purkey & Smith, 1983; Rosenshine & Stevens, 1986), and there have been calls for educational reform (e.g., Boyer, 1983; Goodlad, 1984; National Commission on Excellence in Education, 1983; Sizer, 1984). Much has been made of deficiencies in leadership and training, order and management, and instructional procedures and supports for academic learning. I would suggest that a picture that also emerges is one of schools and classrooms operating with a rather narrow psychoeducational perspective.

Curriculum content, processes, and intended outcomes generally are designed to match a relatively narrow range of individual differences in development and motivation. Also, most school programs reflect a relatively narrow understanding of human psychology and mental health concepts and practices. Moreover, because a major focus in schools is on socialization, the tendency is to overrely on strategies designed to control behavior instead of using procedures more likely to foster positive attitudes toward learning and school. (Given the emphasis on socialization, it is ironic that schools are so ineffective in preventing, managing, and correcting deportment and adjustment problems.)

The narrow psychoeducational perspective reflected in school programs can be seen as both a cause of and contributor to the large number of school learning and behavior problems. It is also seen as an inhibitor of effective prevention and early intervention.

In partial reaction to this state of affairs, there has been a push to expand the school curricula to include mental health "basics." Recent examples are programs to enhance self-concept (Covington & Beery, 1976), develop skills in interpersonal and cognitive problem solving (Shure, 1979; Shure & Spivack, 1982; Spivack, Platt & Shure, 1976), train empathy (Feshbach, 1984), and increase cooperative behavior (Wright & Cowen, 1985). These efforts represent only a small part of decades of work aimed at improving the mental health climate in schools through curriculum change, teacher training, direct services, and consultation and collaboration (Zigler, Kagan, & Muenchow, 1982). Unfortunately, research has not established that this work has significantly influenced the mental health orientation of most principals and teachers or is of *direct* relevance to ameliorating learning problems.

A large-scale example of a mental health oriented school program which may have more direct relevance to learning problems is the Primary Mental Health Project (e.g., Cowen, 1980; Cowen, Gesten & Weissberg, 1980; Cowen, Trost, Lorion, Dorr, Izzo & Isaacson, 1975). The project represents a pioneering demonstration of how to add resources and broaden the remedial focus in kindergarten and early elementary grade classrooms. The emphasis is on prompt detection of early school adjustment problems, followed immediately by interventions aimed at specific objectives for a given youngster. The most recent follow-up data indicate that initial improvements in adjustment are maintained (Chandler, Weissberg, Cowen, & Guare, 1984). It remains for future research to clarify the impact of such improved adjustment on learning problems in general and learning disabilities in particular.

The most direct approaches for ameliorating learning problems try to improve individualization of instruction in regular classroom programs. The vast number of programs described as individualized attests to the concern over the narrow range of differences accounted for in classrooms and the desire to improve the situation (Joyce & Weil, 1986; Snow, 1986; Wang & Walberg, 1985; Will, 1986). Unfortunately, the term individualization is used indiscriminately, and modifications made to accommodate differences vary markedly. They range from simply enabling students to proceed at their own rate to allowing for major differences in what and how much is to be learned at a given time and in what standards are used in judging quality of performance. They also vary with regard to matters such as how time for learning is used, how learning and performance are evaluated and graded, and the degree to which classroom structure provides support and guidance toward autonomy as contrasted to overemphasizing control. In general, the term *individualization* is used to describe any approach designed to improve the match between instructional practices and a particular student's capabilities. In this respect, it overlaps the aptitude-treatment interaction model (Chronbach & Snow, 1976; Snow & Farr, in press).

Individualization usually is seen as an essential step in countering learning problems. The intent is to alter regular classroom practices to expand both the range of individual learning differences effectively accommodated and the scope of remedial instruction provided. Typically, the process tries to detect a student's deficiencies by monitoring daily performance on learning tasks and then modifying instruction to address the deficiencies. In addition, some programs attempt to assess the best teaching approach for a given child. A prominent example of the latter is Feuerstein's (1979) work focused on children at risk for learning problems. His Learning Potential Assessment Device (LPAD) emphasizes trial and appraisal teaching (involving a variety of teaching strategies) to determine how a child learns best. The data then are used to modify the instructional program to better accommodate the youngster's current learning capabilities.

Individualized instruction has been seen as especially important to the success of mainstreaming. One of the most cited examples of individualization is a program in which mildly handicapped children are integrated into regular elementary classes. Developed by the Learning Research Development Center in Pittsburgh, the program is called the Adapted Learning Environment Model (ALEM). It adapts the standard curriculum to emphasize exploratory learning and individualized instruction. Remediation and therapy, when needed, are provided by specialists and aides working in the classroom. The program clearly expands the range of individual differences accommodated in the regular classroom, and data suggest the process has a positive impact on basic skills and student self-concept (Wang & Walberg, 1985).

A major shortcoming of individualized instruction as widely practiced, however, is its overemphasis on differences in capability and its underemphasis on differences in *intrinsic* motivation. Neither educators nor mental health professionals have paid enough programmatic attention to the concept of intrinsic motivation as it relates to the causes and correction of learning and behavior problems. This oversight may account for the lack of maintenance and generalization of outcomes found in the majority of studies of training strategies designed to improve learning, problem solving, and social skills. New lines of work have been proposed to redress this oversight by suggesting direct strategies to ameliorate learning behavior problems by simultaneously reducing avoidance motivation and enhancing intrinsic motivation for immediate and ongoing learning (see Adelman, 1978; Adelman & Taylor, 1983b; Deci & Chandler, 1986; Deci & Ryan, 1985).

To broaden the scope of individualized classroom interventions, my colleagues and I have proposed and piloted a sequential and hierarchical model that includes a systematic focus on intrinsic motivation (Adelman, 1971; Adelman & Taylor, 1983a, 1986b). The model has implications for minimizing the impact of learning disabilities and for prevention of other types of learning problems. As illustrated in Figure 4.3, the first step focuses on changing the classroom environment. The intent is to improve learning for all students by making the program more responsive to learner differences in intrinsic motivation, as well as to differences in developmental capability. Moreover, in planning and implementing the program, primary consideration is given to the learner's perception of whether the program is appropriately responsive to his or her interests and abilities. We call this step personalization to differentiate it from individualized approaches that do not systematically accommodate differences in *both* motivation and development. Furthermore, we view personalization as a psychological construct because it is the learner's perception that is used to define whether the environment is appropriately responsive. When properly implemented, personalized instruction can reduce the need for remedial treatment and facilitate valid identification of remedial needs.

More specifically, step 1 involves installing a broad array of learning options in the classroom; then each student is assisted in sampling from the options. Decisions about which to pursue are heavily weighted in favor of the learner's view of what seems to be a good match. As the chosen options are pursued, learning efficacy is monitored and evaluated so that the student and teacher can modify initial decisions as appropriate.

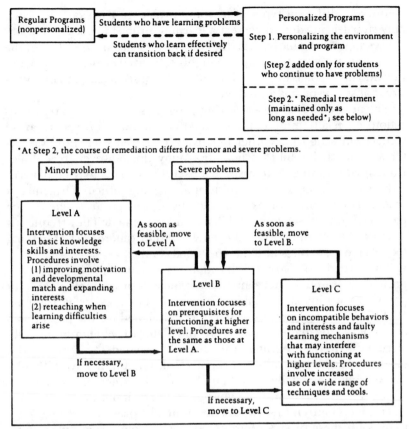

Figure 4.3 Sequences and Levels in Providing Personalized and Remedial Instruction

SOURCE: Adelman, H., & Taylor, L. (1986) An introduction to learning disabilities. Copyright ©. Reprinted by permission of Scott, Foresman and Company.

Step 2 is introduced only if a youngster has an ongoing learning problem. This remedial step focuses on one or more of three levels, i.e., Level A—stressing basic academics and everyday coping skills, Level B—emphasizing prerequisites needed for performing at Level A, and Level C—aimed first at reducing the impact of behaviors and interests incompatible with school learning and then at overcoming the impact of faulty learning mechanisms. The level(s) of remediation initially chosen depend on how severe the problem appears after step 1 has been implemented properly. Choice of subsequent level(s) is guided by remedial efficacy.

The sequential and hierarchical nature of the intervention also has made it a useful strategy for detecting errors in LD diagnoses and for identifying different types of learning problems. For example, when only step 1 is needed to correct a learning problem, it seems reasonable to suggest the individual does not have a learning *disability*. At the same time, when step 1 results in highly mobilized efforts to learn, but the individual still is extremely unsuccessful, it seems safer to hypothesize that she or he has a disability.

The advisability of personalizing programs extends to parent education, especially interventions aimed at parents who tend to avoid contact with school personnel. Relatively few parents are entirely disinterested in their child's schooling. Many do, however, feel disenfranchised and unable to assume a useful role. This may be particularly true of parents whose children are having difficulty learning at school. Homework, for example, looms as a major area where such parents find themselves immobilized and frustrated. They frequently can't do the assignments, and even when they can, the act of helping too often degenerates into interpersonal conflict.

The trend in parent education programs has been toward normative-oriented interventions in which a considerable degree of parent motivation and capability is presumed (see review by Topping, 1986). That is, few programs have been designed for the parent who does not readily manifest the desire and ability to help her or his child learn effectively. Programs are especially needed for parents who have poor academic skills or do not speak English or have difficulty relating interpersonally with their child or with school personnel. Intervention strategies must be developed to reach out to such parents when their children first experience academic problems. Primary objectives for these programs are to establish a point of positive contact and then to form an ongoing working relationship aimed at mutual problem solving. Accomplishment of these objectives will require resources and strategies for mobilizing, enhancing, and maintaining parent motivation. In particular, a program must be able to demonstrate credibility and immediate benefits to a parent (Sue & Zane, 1987). These objectives will also require establishment of mechanisms to aid parents in carrying out plans for helping their youngsters (e.g., schools will need to offer the type of added academic support discussed in the next section).

By this point, it should be clear there is a great deal of research to be done related to the problem of expanding the range of individual differences accommodated at school. It may not be evident, however, that the problem has been analyzed in cultural and sociopolitical, as well as psychoeducational terms. Those who view the problem in such terms argue that a satisfactory solution requires a fundamental transformation in the nature of public education. Minimally, the call has been for making schools truly pluralistic institutions. The achievement of such a goal, of course, requires development of sociopolitical strategies and a sociopolitical reform agenda. In this connection, it may be noted that a variety of advocacy steps have been proposed for developing the necessary strategies and accomplishing such an agenda (e.g., Biklen & Zollers, 1986).

Added academic support. In contrast to efforts to broaden the nature and scope of classroom interventions, there are programs designed mainly to supplement regular teaching for those who do not learn readily. Major examples are augmentation of classroom staff, computer assistance, and added outside instruction. The reality, however, is that there are very limited financial resources to meet the demand resulting from the growing number of students who require extra instruction. Thus, where increased staffing is needed, volunteers are often recruited, such as parents, students, senior citizens. In particular, tutoring by volunteers within and outside the classroom (including homework hotlines) continues to increase in popularity and warrants special attention here.

From a preventive and early intervention standpoint, volunteer tutoring programs make good sense. They provide a feasible way to offer the type of individual instruction most regular classroom teachers cannot find the time to give. Besides adult volunteers (Berger, 1981; Topping, 1986), such programs have made extensive use of classmates and older students (Allen, 1976; Cohen, 1986; Gartner, Kohler, & Riessman, 1971; Gerber & Kauffman, 1981).

One particularly ambitious example of a comprehensive approach to academic tutoring is reported by Melaragno (1976). Through a project called the "Tutorial Community," cross-age and same-age tutoring was introduced as a major component in an elementary school's instructional program. The approach stresses four types of tutoring: (1) intergrade tutoring, in which upper grade students tutor primary students; (2) interschool tutoring, in which junior high students teach upper grade elementary students; (3) interclass tutoring, in which students in the same class assist each other; and (4) informal tutoring, in which older students serve as playleaders for younger students on the playground, help with projects, and go along on school trips. The concept of a tutorial community conceives of tutoring as more than a supplement for instruction or remediation. Tutoring becomes a means by which the entire student body can aid and be aided and a sense of community can be established.

Although extensive evaluation data are lacking on volunteer tutoring programs, findings to date suggest positive benefits in terms of improved academic performance, social functioning, and attitudes toward school. Moreover, in the case of students tutoring other students, academic and attitudinal benefits are reported for the tutors as well (Allen, 1976; Gerber & Kauffman, 1981). In general, the quality of large-scale, tutoring programs seems dependent on the ability to recruit, train, and continuously guide volunteers (Harrison, 1976; Niedermeyer, 1976).

Teacher training/consultation for intervention prior to special education referral. The rapid increase in the number of youngsters diagnosed (and misdiagnosed) as learning disabled has raised the spectre of more students requiring special education services than can be served (Will, 1986). One positive aspect of this trend has been increased attention to working with regular classroom teachers to increase their instructional effectiveness with students who manifest learning and behavior problems (e.g., Chalfant, Pysh, & Moultrie, 1979). This work is bolstered by supportive, if limited, findings from research on the efficacy of consultation services (Curtis & Watson, 1980; Gutkin & Curtis, 1982; Medway, 1979).

A program model called a Prereferral Intervention System provides a recent example of a consultation program to improve regular classroom teachers' handling of learning problems (Graden, Casey & Christenson, 1985). In essence, the program is conceived of as a last ditch attempt to prevent the need for referral to special education programs. The intent is to intervene at the point of initial referral for special education assessment and work with the regular teacher to find a less disruptive and intrusive course of action. To this end, existing school resources are redirected from diagnostic and placement activity to problem solving with the teacher. The immediate objective is to find ways to alter the classroom program and improve instruction.

Analysis of the model's components indicates that much more is involved than consultation. Such an approach must also include mechanisms to (a) ensure the planned interventions are implemented in optimal ways and (b) analyze unsuccessful interventions to clarify why they were not effective and to specify next steps. Programs based on this model have been piloted, but evaluative data are too sparse to judge efficacy. Nevertheless, demonstration of the model itself performs an important function; it adds to the growing number of approaches that encourage investigation of the impact of enhancing regular classroom instruction prior to referral for special education.

Rehabilitation of school programs. In schools with extremely low academic test scores and high incidence of problem behavior, it is recognized that the entire school program requires rehabilitation. Interventions for this purpose rely heavily on a dynamic principal who is given additional resources and empowered to initiate major variations in school district policy. In some cases, the school is given a special status and identity, as has happened with magnet programs and other schools of choice.

The magnet approach in East Harlem has been cited by the media as a promising example of a dramatic metamorphosis of schools that were in extreme trouble. Schools with different specialties (e.g., science, the arts, sports) were created, and parents and children were offered a choice among them. This has allowed each school to portray itself as a special place of opportunity. As a result, the programs seem to be valued by an increasing segment of parents and students, and school personnel appear to be experiencing a sense of renewal. From a psychological perspective, the changes seem to be stimulating feelings of hope and a sense of community and commitment on the part of students, parents, and school personnel.

Perhaps more typical of future directions is a rehabilitative effort in the Los Angeles Unified School District called "Project Intervention" which was to begin in the fall of 1987. The project is described as a pilot organizational and instructional "plan of action designed to prove that all children can learn when the conditions of learning are at an optimum." New principals are being recruited for ten poverty area schools. Among the immediate changes to be made are a reduction in teacher-pupil ratio to 20 to 1 for the primary grades, establishment of formal planning and training periods for teachers, a mentor teacher program, an extended school year for students, teachers, and administrators, and parent education programs.

Whatever the approach to rehabilitating school programs, there is concern over whether changes will be long-lasting. Some critics warn that changes will simply produce temporary "Hawthorne" effects. In response, it has been suggested that, should this be the case, future efforts can be directed at institutionalizing valid changes to produce a lasting Hawthorne effect.

The Future: Needed—A Continuum of Programs

A review of the literature on predictive and early identification procedures relevant to learning disabilities suggests that widespread screening activity is premature and wasteful. Policy makers would do well to rethink their support of such programs.

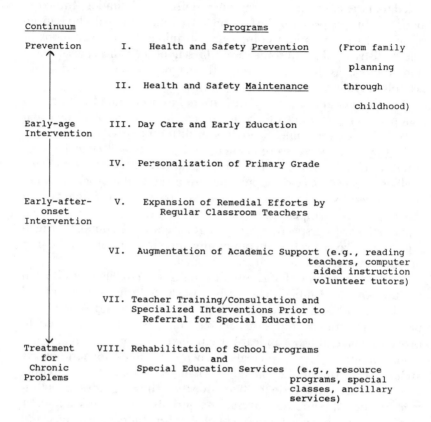

Figure 4.4 From Prevention to Treatment: A Continuum of Programs for Learning Problems

In contrast, a review of the range of preventive and early-age programs pertinent to learning disabilities clearly supports the value of these interventions. Analysis of the work in this area, however, indicates the lack of a comprehensive, coordinated thrust.

The types of programs that have been found useful are categorized and placed on a continuum ranging from prevention to treatment for chronic problems in Figure 4.4. The hope is (and available evidence seems to support the hope) that a more comprehensive set of preventive and early-age interventions will result in fewer referrals for extensive and intensive treatment. This would, of course, have major cost-benefit and policy implications and would lend support to proposals calling for a reversal of the current overemphasis on special education programs (Will, 1986).

The desirability of not overemphasizing special education does not, however, imply that such programs are unnecessary or less worthy of attention. As with other special populations, the assumption simply is that those with severe and pervasive learning and behavior problems will be better served once comprehensive prevention and early intervention programs are in place. They will be better served because such programs can eliminate or at least reduce the negative impact of experiencing learning and behavior problems. Moreover, specialized treatment (and related research) can be reserved for the small group with true disabilities. One benefit of this should be a considerable reduction in the resources required for special education programs. Any unspent money, including that saved by eliminating unnecessary screening programs, can be reallocated (e.g., to cover ongoing costs of prevention).

With the full continuum of learning and behavior problems in mind, a full range of services (and related professional training) is seen as necessary. In reaction to piecemeal approaches to service delivery, proposals have been made for comprehensive interventions. An example is seen in the notion of Schooling for Life (Zigler et al., 1982). Those who propose comprehensive programs recognize how much has already been learned about prevention and early-age intervention. They also recognize the important interrelationship that exists among certain intervention strategies, and they see the added impact to be gained from integrated and coordinated action. In this connection, the interventions outlined in Figure 4.4 should be viewed as integrally related; it seems likely that the impact of many of the programs will be exponentially improved by integrating and coordinating their implementation. Indeed, it seems probable that a major breakthrough in the battle against learning and behavior problems will only result from a comprehensive and coordinated implementation of all eight types of programs.

It is time to determine the efficacy of a comprehensive approach. The way to do this is with a demonstration project. I would like to see federal support generated for a consortium to develop and evaluate, in one catchment area, a coordinated program encompassing the entire continuum of interventions (outlined in Figure 4.4). The data from such a project would have preventive and ameliorative implications for a wide range of learning and behavior problems and would shed considerable light on cause and correction with respect to all psychoeducational problems, including learning disabilities.

Proposals are easy to make, and most are not seriously considered. The process of change is highly sociopolitical. If there is to be a significant change in the approach to ameliorating psychoeducational problems, steps must be taken to change society's perspectives, practices, priorities, and policies. To do any less is to continue to deal too narrowly with factors perpetuating the very unsatisfactory status quo.

Natural advocates for the type of project proposed are the various parent and professional groups who identify specifically with the field of learning disabilities and all others interested in prevention of educational and mental health problems. Thus, one step toward the proposed demonstration project involves stimulating a discussion among potential advocates regarding the nature and value of such a project. The research summary and the general proposal presented here provide a stimulus for the discussion and the foundation for an advocacy agenda. Subsequent discussion and research can further clarify specific details and courses of action. By the early 1990s the timing will be right for eliciting financial support for a comprehensive demonstration project—if enough organized advocacy and planning can be generated over the next few years.

Research accomplished over the past 25 years has taught us a great deal. We have learned about what is worth pursuing and what is not. And we have learned a lot about the sociopolitical hurdles that must be crossed for progress to be made. Given all we've learned, we can look forward to major breakthroughs during the next 25 years with reference to psychological and educational problems—assuming a sophisticated course is pursued to shape policy as a means to our ends.

Note

1. The list of screening and diagnostic procedures used in relation to LD is too great to present here. A representative list, categorized to clarify the specific nature of each procedure, is available in Adelman and Taylor (1986b).

References

Adelman, H. S. (1971). The not so specific learning disability population. *Exceptional Children, 8*, 114–120.

Adelman, H. S. (1978). The concept of intrinsic motivation: Implications for practice and research related to learning disabilities. *Learning Disability Quarterly, 1*, 43–54.

Adelman, H. S. (1979). Diagnostic classification of LD: A practical necessity and a procedural problem. *Learning Disability Quarterly, 2*, 56–62.

Adelman, H. S. (1982). Identifying learning problems at an early age: A critical appraisal. *Journal of Clinical Child Psychology, 11*, 255–261.

Adelman, H. S., & Feshbach, S. (1971). Predicting reading failure: Beyond the readiness model. *Exceptional Children, 37*, 349–354.

Adelman, H. S., & Taylor, L. (1983a). *Learning disabilities in perspective.* Glenview, IL: Scott, Foresman & Co.

Adelman, H. S. & Taylor, L. (1983b). Enhancing motivation for overcoming learning and behavior problems. *Journal of Learning Disabilities, 16*, 384–392.

Adelman, H. S., & Taylor, L. (1985a). The future of the LD field: A survey of fundamental concerns. *Journal of Learning Disabilities, 18*, 422–427.

Adelman, H. S., & Taylor, L. (1985b). Toward integrating intervention concepts, research, and practice. In S. I. Pfeiffer (Ed.), *Clinical child psychology: An introduction to theory, research, and practice* (pp. 57–92). New York: Grune & Stratton.

Adelman, H. S., & Taylor, L. (1986a). The problems of definition and differentiation and the need for a classification schema. *Journal of Learning Disabilities, 19*, 514–520.

Adelman, H. S., & Taylor, L. (1986b). *An introduction to learning disabilities.* Glenview, IL: Scott, Foresman & Co.

Algozzine, B., & Ysseldyke, J. E. (1986). The future of the LD field: Screening and diagnosis. *Journal of Learning Disabilities, 19*, 394–398.

Allen, V. L. (1976). *Children as teachers: Theory and research on tutoring.* New York: Academic Press.

Badian, N. A. (1986). Improving the prediction of reading for the individual child: A four-year follow-up. *Journal of Learning Disabilities, 19*, 262–269.

Bandura, A. (1978). The self system in reciprocal determinism. *American Psychologist, 33*, 344–358.

Barclay, J. R. (1983). *Barclay classroom assessment system.* Los Angeles: Western Psychological Services.

Barnes, K. E. (1982) *Preschool screening: The measurement and prediction of children at-risk.* Springfield, IL: C. C. Thomas.

Berger, E. H. (1981). *Parents as partners in education: The school and the home working together.* St. Louis, MO: C. V. Mosby.

Berliner, D. C. (1984). The half-full glass: A review of research on teaching. In P. L. Hosford (Ed.), *Using what we know about teaching* (pp. 51–77). Alexandria, VA: Association for Supervision and Curriculum Development.

Berrueta-Clement, J. R., Schweinhart, L. J., Barnett, W. S., Epstein, A. S., & Weikart, D. P. (1984). *Changed lives: The effects of the Perry preschool program on youths through age 19.* Ypsilanti, MI: High/Scope Press.

Berwick, D. M., & Kamaroff, A. L. (1982). Cost effectiveness of lead screening. *New England Journal of Medicine, 306*, 1392–1398.

Biklen, D., & Zollers, N. (1986). The focus of advocacy in the LD field. *Journal of Learning Disabilities, 19*, 579–586.

Boyer, E. L. (1983). *High School: A report on secondary education in America.* New York: Harper & Row.

Bradley, R. H., & Rock, S. L. (1985). The HOME Inventory: Its relation to school failure and development of an elementary-age version. In W. K. Frankenburg, R. N. Emde, & J. W. Sullivan (Eds.), *Early identification of children at risk: An international perspective* (pp. 159–173). New York: Plenum.

Bromwich, R. (1981). *Working with parents and infants: An interactional approach.* Baltimore: University Park Press.

Brophy, J., & Good, T. L. (1986). Teacher behavior and student achievement. In M. Wittrock (Ed.), *Third handbook of research on teaching* (pp. 328–375). New York: Macmillan.

Caldwell, B. M., & Bradley, R. H. (1979). *Home observation for measurement of the environment*. Little Rock: University of Arkansas at Little Rock, Center for Child Development and Education.

Casto, G., & Mastropieri, M. A. (1986). The efficacy of early intervention programs: A meta analysis. *Exceptional Children 52*, 417–424.

Chalfant, J. C. (1985). Identifying learning disabled students: A summary of the National Task Force Report. *Learning Disabilities Focus, 1*, 9–20.

Chalfant, J. C., Pysh, M. V., & Moultrie, R. (1979). Teacher assistance teams: A model for within-building problem solving. *Learning Disability Quarterly, 2* (3), 85–96.

Chandler, C., Weissberg, R. P., Cowen, E. L., & Guare, J. (1984). The long-term effects of a school-based secondary prevention program for young maladapting children. *Journal of Consulting and Clinical Psychology, 52*, 165–170.

Chieh, S., Chu, Y., Lu, S., Tang, T., & Wang, T. (1985). Application of the short DDST-R in urban districts of Shanghai: A preliminary report. In W. K. Frankenburg, R. N. Emde, & J. W. Sullivan (Eds.), *Early identification of children at risk: An international perspective* (pp. 329–332). New York: Plenum.

Chronbach, L. J., & Snow, R. E. (1976). *Aptitude and instructional methods*. New York: Irvington.

Cohen, J. (1986). Theoretical considerations of peer tutoring. *Psychology in the Schools, 23*, 175–186.

Consortium for Longitudinal Studies. (1983). *As the twig is bent . . . Lasting effects of preschool programs*. Hillsdale, NJ: Lawrence Erlbaum Associates.

Covington, M. V., & Beery, R. C. (1976). *Self-worth and school learning*. New York: Holt, Rinehart & Winston.

Cowen, E. L. (1980). The wooing of primary prevention. *American Journal of Community Psychology, 8*, 258–284.

Cowen, E. L. (1986). Primary prevention in mental health: Ten years of retrospect and ten years of prospect. In M. Kessler & S. E. Goldston (Eds.), *A decade of progress in primary prevention* (pp. 3–45). Hanover, NH: University Press of New England.

Cowen, E. L., Gesten, E. L. & Weissberg, R. P. (1980). An integrated network of preventively oriented school-based mental health approaches. In R. H. Price & P. Politzer (Eds.), *Evaluation and action in the social environment* (pp.173–210). New York: Academic Press.

Cowen, E. L., Trost, M. A., Lorion, R. P., Dorr, D., Izzo, L. D., & Isaacson, R. V. (1975). *New ways in school mental health: Early detection and prevention of school maladaption*. New York: Human Sciences Press, Inc.

Curtis, M. J., & Watson, K. (1980). Changes in consultee problem clarification skills following consultation. *Journal of School Psychology, 18*, 210–221.

Deci, E. L., & Chandler, C. L. (1986). The importance of motivation for the future of the LD field. *Journal of Learning Disabilities, 19*, 587–594.

Deci, E. L., & Ryan, R. (1985). *Intrinsic motivation and self-determination in human behavior*. New York: Plenum.

Eaves, L. C., Kendall, D. C., & Crichton, J. U. (1974). The early identification of learning disabilities: A follow-up report. *Journal of Learning Disabilities, 7*, 632–638.

Elardo, R., Bradley, R. H., & Caldwell, B. (1975). The relation of infants' home environments to mental test performance from six to thirty-six months: A longitudinal analysis. *Child Development, 46*, 71–76.

Feshbach, N. D. (1984). Empathy, empathy training and the regulation of aggression in elementary school children. In R. M. Kaplan, V. J. Konecni, & R. Novoco (Eds.),

Aggression in children and youth (pp. 192–208). The Hague, The Netherlands: Martinus Nijhoff.

Feshbach, S., Adelman, H. S., & Fuller, W. W. (1977). Prediction of reading and related academic problems. *Journal of Educational Psychology, 69*, 299–308.

Feuerstein, R. (1979). *The dynamic assessment of retarded performers: The learning potential assessment device, theory, instruments, and techniques.* Baltimore: University Park Press.

Fletcher, J. M., & Satz, P. (1980). Developmental changes in the neuropsychological correlates of reading achievement: A six-year longitudinal followup. *Journal of Clinical Neuropsychology, 2*, 23–37.

Forness, S. R., Sinclair, E., & Guthrie, D. (1983). Learning disability discrepancy formulas: Their use in actual practice. *Learning Disability Quarterly, 6*, 107–114.

Frankenburg, W. K., Emde, R. N., & Sullivan, J. W. (Eds.). (1985). *Early identification of children at risk: An international perspective.* New York: Plenum.

Freund, J. H., Bradley, R. H., & Caldwell, B. M. (1979). The home environment in the assessment of learning disabilities. *Learning Disability Quarterly, 2*, 39–51.

Funk, S. G., Sturner, R. A., & Green, J. A. (1986). Preschool prediction of early school performance: Relationship of McCarthy scales of children's abilities prior to school entry to achievement in kindergarten, first, and second grades. *Journal of School Psychology, 24*, 181–194.

Gartner, A., Kohler, M., & Riessman, F. (1971). *Children teach children.* New York: Harper.

Gerber, M. & Kauffman, J. M. (1981). Peer tutoring in academic settings. In P. S. Strain (Ed.), *The utilization of classroom peers as behavior change agents.* New York: Plenum Press.

German, M. L., Williams, E., Herzfeld, J., & Marshall, R. M. (1982). Utility of the revised Denver Developmental Screening Test and the Developmental Profile II in identifying preschool children with cognitive, language and motor problems, *Education and Training of the Mentally Retarded, 17*, 319–324.

Glazzard, M. (1980). The effectiveness of three kindergarten predictors for first-grade achievement. *Journal of Learning Disabilities, 10*, 95–99.

Goodlad, J. I. (1984). *A place called school: Prospects for the future.* New York: McGraw-Hill.

Goodwin, L. (1973). Bridging the gap between social research and public policy: We have a case in point. *Journal of Applied Social Behavioral Science, 9*, 85–114.

Gracey, C. A., Azzara, C. V., & Reinherz, H. (1984). Screening revisited: A survey of U.S. requirements. *Journal of Special Education, 18*, 101–107.

Graden, J. L., Casey, A., & Christenson, S. L. (1985). Implementing a prereferral intervention system: 1. The model. *Exceptional Children, 51*, 377–387.

Greenspan, S. I. (1981). *Psychopathology and adaptation in infancy and early childhood: Principles of clinical diagnosis and preventive intervention.* Clinical Infant Report No 1. New York: International Universities Press.

Greenspan, S. I. (1986). Psychopathology and preventive intervention in infancy: A clinical developmental research approach. In D. C. Farran & J. D. McKinney (Eds.), *Risk in intellectual and psychosocial development* (pp.129–167). Orlando: Academic Press.

Gutkin, T. B., & Curtis, M. J. (1982). School-based consultation: Theory and techniques. In C. R. Reynolds & T. B. Gutkin (Eds.), *The handbook of school psychology* (pp.796–828). New York: Wiley & Sons.

Harms, T., & Clifford, R. M. (1980). *Early Childhood Environment Rating Scale.* New York: Teachers College Press.

Harrison, G. V. (1976). Structured tutoring: Antidote for low achievement. In V. L. Allen (Ed.), *Children as teachers: Theory and research on tutoring* (pp. 169–176). New York: Academic Press.

Hobbs, N. (1975). *The futures of children: Categories, labels, and their consequence*. San Francisco: Jossey-Bass.

Jansky, J., & de Hirsch, K. (1973). *Preventing reading failure: Prediction, diagnosis, and intervention*. New York: Harper & Row.

Joyce, B., & Weil, M. (1986). *Models of teaching* (3nd ed.). New York: Prentice-Hall.

Kelly, J. G., Snowden, L. R., & Munoz, R. F. (1977). Social and community intervention. *Annual Review of Psychology, 28*, 323–361.

Keogh, B. K., Major-Kingsley, S., Omori-Gordon, H., & Reid, H. P. (1982). *A system of marker variables for the field of learning disabilities*. Syracuse, NY: Syracuse University Press.

Keogh, B. K., Wilcoxen, A. G., & Bernheimer, L. (1986). Prevention services for risk children: Evidence for policy and practice. In D. C. Farran & J. D. McKinney (Eds.), *Risk in intellectual and psychosocial development* (pp. 287–316). Orlando: Academic Press.

Kessler, M. & Albee, G. W. (1975). Primary prevention. *Annual review of psychology, 26*, 557–591.

Kilmer, S. (Ed.) (1983). *Advances in early education and daycare*. Greenwich, CT: JAI Press.

Lazar, I., Darlington, R., Murray, H., Royce, J., & Snipper, A. (1982). Lasting effects of early education. *Monographs of the Society for Research in Child Development, 47* (1–2, Serial No. 194).

Lehr, C. A., Ysseldyke, J. E., & Thurlow, M. L. (1986). *Assessment practices in model early childhood education programs*. (Research Report No. 7). Minneapolis, MN: University of Minnesota, Early Childhood Assessment Project.

Lichtenstein, R. & Ireton, H. (1984). *Preschool screening: Identifying young children with developmental and educational problems*. Orlando, FL: Grune & Stratton.

Lipson, M. Y., & Wixson, K. K. (1986). Reading disability research: An interactionist perspective. *Review of Educational Research, 56*, 111–136.

Lyon, G. R. (1983). Subgroups of learning disabled readers: Clinical and empirical identification. In H. R. Myklebust (Ed.), *Progress in learning disabilities Vol 5*. New York: Grune & Stratton.

Lyon, G. R. (1985). Identification and remediation of learning disability subtypes: Preliminary findings. *Learning Disabilities Focus, 1*, 21–35.

Lyon, M. A., & Smith, D. K. (1986). A comparison of at-risk preschool children's performance on the K-ABC, McCarthy scales, and Stanford-Binet. *Journal of Psychoeducational Assessment, 4*, 35–43.

McCartney, K., Scarr, S., Phillips, D., Grajek, S., & Schwartz, C. (1982). Environmental differences among day-care centers and their effects on children's development. In E. Zigler & E. Gordon (Eds.), *Day care: Scientific and social policy issues*. Boston: Auburn House.

McKinney, J. D. (1984). The search for subtypes of specific learning disability. *Journal of Learning Disabilities, 17*, 43–50.

Medway, F. J. (1979). How effective is school consultation: A review of recent literature. *Journal of School Psychology, 17*, 275–282.

Melaragno, R. J. (1976). The tutorial community. In V. L. Allen (Ed.), *Children as teachers: Theory and research on tutoring* (pp. 189–198). New York: Academic Press.

Minnesota Department of Education. (1982). *The third report for the Minnesota legislature on the preschool screening program. An executive summary of the 1980–81 statewide results.* St. Paul, MN: Author.

Moos, R. H. (1979). *Evaluating educational environments.* San Francisco: Jossey-Bass.

National Association for the Education of Young Children. (1983). Progress report on the Center Accreditation Project. *Young Children, 39,* 35–46.

National Commission on Excellence in Education (1983). *A nation at risk: The imperative for educational reform.* Washington, DC: U.S. Department of Education.

Niedermeyer, F. C. (1976). A model for the development or selection of school-based tutorial systems. In V. L. Allen (Ed.), *Children as teachers: Theory and research on tutoring* (pp. 179–188). New York: Academic Press.

Osofsky, J. D. (1986). Perspectives on infant mental health. In M. Kessler & S. E. Goldston (Eds.), *A decade of progress in primary prevention.* Hanover, NH: University Press of New England.

Pihl, R. O., & Nagy, K. A. (1980). The applicability of the Myklebust pupil rating scale. *Journal of Learning Disabilities, 13,* 109–113.

Purkey, S. C., & Smith, M. S. (1983). Effective schools: A review. *Elementary School Journal, 83,* 427–452.

Rescorla, L. A., & Zigler, E. (1981). The Yale child welfare research program: Implications for social policy. *Educational Evaluation and Policy Analysis, 3,* 5–14.

Rhodes, W. C., & Tracy, M. C. (1972). *A study of child variance: Intervention Vol. 2.* Ann Arbor: University of Michigan Press.

Rosenshine, B. V., & Stevens, R. (1986). Teaching functions. In M. Wittrock (Ed.), *Third handbook of research on teaching* (pp. 376–391). New York: Macmillan.

Rourke, B. P., & Strang, J. D. (1983). Subtypes of reading and arithmetic disabilities: A neurological analysis. In M. Rutter (Ed.), *Developmental neuropsychiatry* (pp. 473–488). New York: The Guilford Press.

Ryan, W. (1971). *Blaming the victim.* New York: Random House.

Sameroff, A. J. (1985). Environmental factors in the early screening of children at risk. In W. K. Frankenburg, R. N. Emde, & J. W. Sullivan (Eds.), *Early identification of children at risk: An international perspective* (pp. 21–44). New York: Plenum.

Satz, P., & Morris, R. (1981). Learning disability subtypes: A review. In F. J. Pirozzolo & M. C. Wittrock (Eds.), *Neuropsychological and cognitive processes in reading* (pp. 109–141). New York: Academic Press.

Senf, G. M. (1986). LD research in sociological and scientific perspective. In J. K. Torgesen & B. Y. L. Wong (Eds.), *Psychological and educational perspectives on learning disabilities* (pp. 27–53). Orlando FL: Academic Press.

Shure, M. B. (1979). Training children to solve interpersonal problems: A preventive approach. In R. F. Munoz, L. F. Snowden, & J. G. Kelly (Eds.), *Social and psychological research in community settings* (pp. 50–68). San Francisco: Jossey-Bass.

Shure, M. B., & Spivack, G. (1982). Interpersonal problem-solving in young children: A cognitive approach to prevention. *American Journal of Community Psychology, 10,* 341–356.

Silver, A. A., & Hagin, R. A. (1981). *SEARCH: A scanning instrument for identification of potential learning disability* (2nd ed.). New York: Walker Educational Book Corporation.

Sizer, T. R. (1984). *Horace's compromise: The dilemma of the American high school.* Boston: Houghton Mifflin.

Snow, R. E. (1986). Individual differences and the design of educational programs. *American Psychologist, 41*, 1029–1039.

Snow, R. E., & Farr, M. J. (Eds.). (in press). *Aptitude, learning, and instruction: Vol. 3. Conative and affective process analyses.* Hillsdale, NJ: Lawrence Earlbaum Associates

Spivack, G., Platt, J. J., & Shure, M. B. (1976). *The problem-solving approach to adjustment.* San Francisco: Jossey-Bass.

Sue, S., & Zane, N. (1987). The role of culture and cultural techniques in psychotherapy: A critique and reformulation. *American Psychologist, 42*, 37–45.

Swan, W. (1980). Handicapped children's early education program. *Exceptional Children, 47*, 12–14.

Swan, W. (1981). Efficacy studies in early childhood special education. *Journal of the Division for Early Childhood, 4*, 1–4.

Tjossem, T. J. (1976). *Intervention strategies for high risk infants and young children.* Baltimore: University Park Press.

Topping, K. J. (1986). *Parents as educators: Training parents to teach their children.* Cambridge, MA: Brookline Books.

Toro, P. A., Cowen, E. L., Gesten, E. L., Weissberg, R. P., Rapkin, B. D., & Davidson, E. (1985). Social environmental predictors of children's adjustment in elementary school classrooms. *American Journal of Community Psychology, 13*, 353–364.

Travers, J., & Ruopp, R. (1978). *National Day Care Study.* Cambridge, MA: ABT Associates.

Tucker, J., Stevens, L. J., & Ysseldyke, J. E. (1983). Learning disabilities: The experts speak out. *Journal of Learning Disabilities, 16*, 6–14.

U.S. Administration for Children, Youth, and Families. (1983). *Ninth annual report to Congress on Head Start services.* Washington, DC: Author.

U.S. Office of Special Education and Rehabilitation Services. (1983). *Fifth annual report to Congress on special education services.* Washington, DC: Author.

Van Doorninck, W., Caldwell, B., Wright, C., & Frankenburg, W. (1975). *The inventory of some stimulation as a predictor of school competence.* Paper presented at the Society for Research in Child Development. Denver, CO.

Van Duyne, H. J., Gargiulo, R., & Allen, J. A. (1980). A survey of Illinois preschool screening programs. *Illinois Council for Exceptional Children Quarterly, 29*, 11–16.

Walberg, H. J. (1969). Social environment as a mediator of classroom learning. *Journal of Educational Psychology, 60*, 443–448.

Wang, M., & Walberg, H. (Eds.). (1985). *Adapting instruction to individual differences.* Berkeley, CA: McCutchan.

White, K. R. (1985–86). Efficacy of early intervention. *Journal of Special Education, 19*, 401–416.

White, K. R., Bush, D. W., & Casto, G. C. (1985–86). Learning from reviews of early intervention. *Journal of Special Education, 19*, 417–428.

Will, M. (1986). *Educating students with learning problems: A shared responsibility.* Washington, DC: U.S. Department of Education.

Wright, S., & Cowen, E. L. (1985). The effects of peer-teaching on student perceptions of class environment, adjustment, and academic performance. *American Journal of Community Psychology, 13*, 417–431.

Wulbert, M., Inglis, S., Kriegsman, E., & Mills, B. (1975). Language delay and associated mother-child interactions. *Developmental Psychology, 11*, 61–70.

Ysseldyke, J. E., & Algozzine, B. (1983). LD or not LD: That's not the question! *Journal of Learning Disabilities, 16*, 29–31.

Ysseldyke, J. E., Thurlow, M. L., O'Sullivan, P., & Bursaw, R. A. (1986). Current screening and diagnostic practices in a state offering free preschool screening since 1977: Implications for the field. *Journal of Psychoeducational Assessment, 4*, 191–201.

Zigler, E. F. (1987). Formal schooling for four-year-olds? No. *American Psychologist, 42*, 254–260.

Zigler, E. F., Kagan, S. L., & Muenchow, S. (1982). Preventive intervention in the schools. In C. R. Reynolds & T. B. Gutkin (Eds.), *The handbook of school psychology* (pp. 774–795). New York: Wiley & Sons.

5

Substance Abuse Prevention and the Promotion of Competence

Gilbert J. Botvin
Linda Dusenbury

Introduction

Tobacco, alcohol, and drug abuse have been a source of concern to health professionals for at least the past 20 years. During that time, a concerted effort has been made by individuals and agencies in both the public and private sectors to reduce trends that began in the psychedelic 1960s and have continued, almost unabated, to the end of the 1970s and beginning of the 1980s. Although some evidence of a decline in substance use was observed in the early 1980s, use of a variety of psychoactive substances has continued at unacceptable levels.

There is also reason to believe that the decline observed in the use of most drugs in recent years may be leveling off (U.S. Public Health Service, 1986). The "Monitoring the Future" surveys of high school seniors, a major source of data concerning substance abuse trends among adolescents, found that use of 16 types of drugs was virtually unchanged or slightly increased in the class of 1985 compared with that of 1984. Furthermore, the use of cocaine significantly increased during the same time period. In addition to longstanding concerns over the deleterious health, legal, and pharmacological effects associated with substance abuse, new urgency now exists for the development of effective prevention strategies because of the role of intravenous drug use in the transmission of AIDS.

Over the years, a variety of approaches have been developed and tested to prevent or reduce substance use/abuse among adolescents. However, the development of effective prevention strategies has proven to be far more difficult than was initially imagined. School-based tobacco, alcohol, and drug education programs as well as public information programs have sought to deter substance use by increas-

146

ing adolescents' awareness of the adverse consequences of using these substances. Although this kind of strategy has proliferated for more than two decades, results indicate quite clearly that these approaches are not effective.

More recently, researchers have developed and tested substance abuse prevention programs that differ from conventional drug education programs in several important ways. First, these newer approaches are based on a more complete understanding of the causes of substance abuse among adolescents, with particular emphasis being placed on the importance of psychosocial factors. Second, these approaches are theory-based. Third, they utilize well-tested intervention techniques. And, fourth, evaluation studies testing these approaches have emphasized methodological rigor and have employed increasingly sophisticated research designs.

The purpose of this chapter is to describe a tobacco, alcohol, and drug abuse prevention program called Life Skills Training (LST). Unlike previous informational approaches, the prevention strategy on which this program is based is one that emphasizes the acquisition of skills for resisting social/environmental influences to smoke, drink, or use drugs. The teaching of these resistance skills is embedded within a larger program designed to promote individual competence. In this chapter, we will provide the background, theory, and rationale for this type of prevention program; provide a detailed description of the intervention strategy, including a discussion of issues relating to implementation; and summarize the results of our evaluation research. The final section will include information concerning conclusions to be drawn from this body of research and directions for future research.

Nature and Causes of Substance Abuse

Onset and Progression

Experimentation with one or more psychoactive substances and the subsequent development of regular patterns of use typically occur during the adolescent period. In contemporary American society some degree of experimentation with tobacco, alcohol, or drugs has become rather commonplace, particularly with respect to the so-called *gateway* substances of tobacco, alcohol, and marijuana. Although many individuals may discontinue substance use after a relatively brief period of experimentation, the initial period of use, for some individuals, results in the development of both psychological and physiological dependence.

Substance use experimentation generally occurs within the context of social situations. For this reason several researchers have speculated that substance use may serve as a major focus for social interaction and a sense of group identity (Becker, 1967; Jessor, 1976). As substance use increases in both frequency and amount, individuals also begin using these substances in a solitary fashion. This generally represents a transition to a more dependent pattern of use generally suggesting a shift from social use (e.g., social drinking) to greater substance use involvement. Although social and psychological factors appear to be primarily responsible for the initiation of substance use, pharmacological factors become increasingly important in reinforcing and maintaining regular patterns of use (Meyer & Mirin, 1979; Ray 1974).

In spite of warnings from parents, teachers and health professionals, adolescents exhibit a remarkable absence of concern about the adverse consequences related to the use of psychoactive substances. Adolescents also tend to overestimate their ability to avoid personally destructive patterns of use, frequently laboring under the illusion that they are in control and can discontinue use at any point, if they so desire. Adolescent cigarette smokers, for example, typically believe that they can quit smoking whenever they wish (Botvin, 1978). It is only after they have made a serious effort to quit smoking that they become aware of the extent to which they are dependent on tobacco.

Data from a number of sources also indicate that experimentation with one substance frequently leads to experimentation with others in a logical and generally predictable progression (Hamburg, Braemer, & Jahnke, 1975; Kandel, 1978). Most individuals typically begin by using alcohol and tobacco, progressing later on to the use of marijuana. For some individuals, this progression may eventuate in the use of depressants, stimulants, and psychedelics. The use of opiates and cocaine typically does not occur until the end of this progression.

Antecedents and Correlates

An extensive literature has developed concerning the antecedents and correlates of substance use/abuse. The earliest evidence comes from retrospective studies which, although suggestive, have generally been criticized by reviewers on methodological grounds. Additional data have been collected from a number of cross-sectional studies, as well as from a limited number of longitudinal investigations. Examination of the existing evidence indicates that the initiation and early stages of substance use are promoted by a complex mixture of cognitive, attitudinal, social, personality, pharmacological, and developmental factors (Blum & Richards, 1979; Braucht, Follingstadt, Brakarsh, & Berry, 1973; Jessor, 1976; Meyer & Mirin, 1979; Ray, 1974; Wechsler, 1976). Perhaps the strongest cluster of factors promoting substance use involves the substance use behavior of significant others such as parents, older siblings, and friends. Individuals who have family members or friends who are substance users have a significantly increased risk of becoming substance users themselves. Moreover, the portrayal in the popular media of substance use as something that is an integral part of popularity, sex appeal, sophistication, success, and good times appears to be both a subtle and powerful influence promoting substance use.

A variety of personal level variables have also been found to be associated with substance use (Millman & Botvin, 1983). These include psychological characteristics, health knowledge, and attitudes. A multitude of psychological characteristics have been associated with substance use/abuse including low self-esteem, low self-confidence, low self-satisfaction, greater need for social approval, low social-confidence, high anxiety, low assertiveness, greater impulsivity, rebelliousness, a low sense of personal control, and an impatience to acquire adult status. Furthermore, individuals who are aware of the adverse consequences of tobacco, alcohol, and drug use as well as those who have negative attitudes toward substance use have been found to be less likely to become substance users.

Substance use has also been found to be highly correlated with a variety of problem behaviors. Strong intercorrelations have been found with respect to the use of an array of psychoactive substances. Moreover, individuals who smoke, drink, or use drugs also tend to get lower grades in school, are not generally involved in adult sanctioned activities such as sports and clubs, and are also more likely than nonusers to exhibit antisocial patterns of behavior including lying, stealing, and cheating (Demone, 1973; Jessor, Collins, & Jessor, 1972; Wechsler & Thum, 1973). Finally, substance use has also been found to be related to premature sexual activity, truancy, and delinquency.

An important development, which is the outgrowth of a decade or more of research, is the recognition that there is an association between various types of problem behaviors. Correlations between behaviors have been found to be substantial and to be equally true for males and females. Furthermore, this association goes well beyond statistical correlations for groups of individuals; several types of problem behaviors are likely to occur within the same individual. Moreover, various types of behavior "correlate in a similar way with a large number of personality and environmental measures of psychosocial risk" (Jessor, 1982, p. 453). This finding suggests that a large number of problem behaviors may be caused by the same underlying factors. Thus, rather than viewing specific problem behaviors as separate or idiosyncratic behaviors, it may be more productive to view them as part of a general syndrome. The implication of this finding is that it may be possible to develop preventive interventions that can impact on the underlying determinants of several theoretically and empirically related problem behaviors at the same time, rather than developing separate interventions for each specific problem (Botvin, 1982; Swisher, 1979).

Adolescent Development and Substance Abuse Risk

Adolescence has been characterized as a time of storm and stress, a period of great physical and psychological change. During the adolescent years, individuals experiment with a wide range of behaviors and life-style patterns as part of a natural process of separating from parents, developing a sense of autonomy and independence, establishing an identity, and acquiring the skills necessary for functioning in an adult world.

Ironically, many of these developmental changes may substantially increase adolescents' risk of smoking, drinking, or using drugs. Some behaviors (e.g., smoking and drinking) are age-graded and, therefore, are proscribed for children and adolescents, while being widely viewed as acceptable for adults. Adolescents anxious to assume adult roles or appear more grown-up may engage in these behaviors as one way of laying claim to adult status. Moreover, since the use of illicit substances is legally proscribed for both adolescents and adults, engaging in the use of these substances may serve as a means of establishing solidarity with a particular reference group, rebelling against parental authority, or establishing a sense of identity.

A general by-product of normal psychosocial development is a shift in the relative influence of parents and peers. As individuals proceed from childhood to adolescence, there is a marked decline in parental influence accompanied by a corresponding increase in the influence of peers (Utech & Hoving, 1969). An increased reliance on the peer group may not only weaken parental influence with respect to substance use behavior, but may also facilitate the promotion of substance use in individuals who are members of peer groups that hold values supportive of substance use.

Another important developmental occurrence that may serve to increase an adolescent's risk of becoming a substance user relates to the rather profound cognitive changes taking place during this time. These changes ultimately affect how adolescents view the world, as well as the manner in which thinking occurs. In contrast to the preadolescent's *concrete-operational* mode of thinking, which is rigid, literal, and grounded in the here and now, adolescent thought is more relative, abstract, and hypothetical (Piaget, 1962). In general, this enables adolescents to conceive of a wide range of possibilities and logical alternatives, to accept deviations from established rules, and to recognize the frequently irrational and sometimes inconsistent nature of adult behavior. These changes in the manner in which adolescents think may serve to undermine previously acquired knowledge relating to the potential risks of smoking, drinking, or using drugs. For example, *formal-operational* thinking permits the discovery of inconsistencies or logical flaws in arguments being advanced by adults concerning the health risks associated with substance use. Similarly, this new mode of thinking may enable adolescents to formulate counterarguments to antidrug messages, permitting rationalizations for ignoring potential risks, particularly if substance use is perceived to have social or personal benefits. Thus, it is essential when developing a substance-abuse prevention program targeted at adolescents that consideration be given to the developmental tasks, issues, changes, and pressures affecting adolescent behavior.

Theoretical Perspectives

A consideration of the diversity of factors found to be associated with substance use leads to the inescapable conclusion that no single factor is both a necessary and sufficient condition for the initiation of substance use. Adolescent substance use/abuse appears to be the result of the complex interplay of many different factors. Several multivariate models have been posited in order to describe the interrelationships among an array of cognitive, attitudinal, social, personality, and behavioral factors (e.g., Jessor & Jessor, 1977).

Theories concerning the etiology of substance abuse are plentiful (see Lettieri, Sayers, & Pearson, 1980). However, most of these theories have limited heuristic value for generating strategies that might be effective approaches to prevention. Two theories that provide the basis for developing a useful conceptual framework for both understanding the etiology of substance abuse and developing potentially effective prevention strategies are social learning theory (Bandura, 1977) and problem behavior theory (Jessor & Jessor, 1977). The central features of each of these theories is summarized below, from the perspective of its importance for substance abuse prevention.

Social Learning Theory

According to social learning theory, individuals learn how to behave through a process of modeling and reinforcement, and through a vicarious process of observing models and the consequences models experience as a result of their behavior. Repeated exposure to successful, high-status role models who use substances, whether these role models are figures in the media, peers, or older siblings, are likely to influence adolescents. Similarly, the perception that smoking, drinking or drug use is standard practice among peers also serves to promote substance use through the establishment of normative beliefs supportive of substance use. These influences may suggest to adolescents that substance use is not only socially acceptable, but perhaps even necessary if one is to become popular, cool, sexy, grown-up, sophisticated, macho, or tough. This perceived social payoff for substance use is likely to increase adolescents' susceptibility to peer pressure.

Susceptibility or vulnerability to social influences that promote substance use is affected by knowledge, attitudes, and beliefs. Because individuals can establish goals for the future, social learning theory recognizes the importance of self-regulation and self-control. Individuals who have goals for the future that are inconsistent with substance use, and who are aware of the negative consequences of substance use, would be expected to be less likely to smoke, drink, or use drugs.

It appears that susceptibility to social influence generally (Bandura, 1969; Rotter, 1972) and to substance use in particular (Demone, 1973; Jessor et al., 1972; Wechsler & Thum, 1973) is related to low self-esteem, low self-satisfaction, low self-confidence, greater need for social approval, low sense of personal control, low assertiveness, greater impulsivity, and impatience to assume adult roles or appear grown-up. Based on this theoretical formulation and existing empirical evidence, some researchers (e.g., Botvin, 1982) have hypothesized that resistance to social influence could be promoted by fostering the development of characteristics associated with low susceptibility to such influence.

Problem Behavior Theory

Problem behavior theory focuses specifically on problems occurring during adolescence such as substance use, precocious sexual behavior, delinquency, and truancy. The theory derives from a social psychological framework, and recognizes the complex interaction of personal factors (i.e., cognitions, attitudes, beliefs), physiological/ genetic factors, and perceived environment factors (Jessor & Jessor, 1977).

A problem behavior is one that is identified by a group as a problem. It typically elicits a social response designed to control it. The social response may be informal and may merely involve disapproval. On the other hand, this response may be both formal and substantial, as in the case of incarceration. Many behaviors that are permissible for members of an older age group are viewed as problems for younger ones (e.g., smoking, drinking, sexual involvement); for these, age norms may serve as the defining characteristic.

According to problem behavior theory, the reason adolescents engage in problem behaviors such as substance use and premature sexual initiation is that these behaviors help the adolescent achieve personal goals; the behaviors are functional (i.e., they do something for the adolescents). Because these behaviors are functional, adolescents may be motivated to use them. For example, problem behaviors may serve as a way of coping with failure (real or anticipated), boredom, social anxiety, unhappiness, rejection, social isolation, low self-esteem, and a lack of self-efficacy. These behaviors may also serve as a way of achieving some personal goal—they may, for instance, facilitate admission to a particular peer group. For adolescents who are not achieving academically, the use of psychoactive substances may provide a way of achieving social status. Adolescents may believe that using substances will enhance their public image by making them look cool or by demonstrating independence from authority figures. Adolescents at the greatest risk of becoming substance users are those who perceive that alternative ways of achieving these same goals are unavailable.

According to problem-behavior theory, vulnerability to peer pressure to engage in the use of one or more substances is greater for adolescents who have fewer effective coping strategies in their repertoire, fewer skills for handling social situations, and greater anxiety about social situations. For these adolescents, the range of options for achieving personal goals is restricted at the same time that discomfort in interpersonal situations is high, motivating the adolescent to take some action in an effort to alleviate that discomfort.

Consistent with this, problem behavior would be extremely difficult to prevent if it were perceived as functional, unless alternative ways of achieving the same function or personal goals are available. The obvious and immediate way to delay substance use would be to make adolescents realize that it is a misperception to believe that the benefits of substance use outweigh the risks. But unless adolescents believe that there are alternative ways of coping with anxiety or alternative ways of establishing effective interpersonal relationships, they may be unwilling to forego the perceived benefits of substance use.

Implications for Substance Abuse Prevention

A prescription for the type of preventive intervention likely to be optimally effective flows naturally from a consideration of the factors promoting substance use/abuse within the framework of the theoretical perspectives described above. On one level, substance abuse prevention might proceed by eliminating, or at least reducing to the greatest extent possible, environmental influences promoting or facilitating the use of tobacco, alcohol, or drugs. This might be accomplished through measures that decrease the availability of these substances (either directly or indirectly), by decreasing the visibility of negative role models (i.e., substance users), by increasing the visibility of attractive, high-status positive role models, by altering attitudes and social norms concerning the acceptability of substance use/abuse, and by eliminating the promotion of substance use through the media (e.g., banning the advertisement of tobacco products and alcoholic beverages). Such changes, however, are extremely difficult, expensive, and may take years to achieve. Still, since substance abuse occurs as a result of both environmental and individual factors, it is unlikely that substance abuse could be entirely prevented using this strategy, even in the rare event that substantial environmental changes consistent with the goals delineated above were to be achieved.

Another logical approach to substance abuse prevention might involve the development of preventive interventions designed to reduce susceptibility or vulnerability to the various environmental factors promoting substance use on the one hand while, at the same time, attempting to reduce potential intrapsychic motivations to engage in substance use/abuse on the other. One strategy for decreasing susceptibility to prosubstance use environmental influences might involve the teaching of specific skills designed to resist various types of social influence to smoke, drink, or use drugs. One type of resistance skill would involve teaching adolescents techniques for effectively resisting peer pressure. Another would involve the teaching of skills designed to increase resistance to persuasive appeals from advertisers. Thus, adolescents' ability to deal with environmental influences promoting substance use might be increased by making them aware of these sources of influence and by teaching them specific skills designed to counter these influences.

Susceptibility to negative environmental influences might also be reduced by increasing self-esteem, a sense of personal control, self-confidence, self-satisfaction, and assertiveness. It would also be important to teach adolescents specific skills designed to increase the likelihood of achieving desired goals (e.g., interpersonal skills, goal-setting, self-directed behavior change techniques) as well as an array of general coping skills (e.g., anxiety reduction techniques, self-reinforcement techniques, positive thinking).

Limitations of Contemporary Prevention Strategies

Information Dissemination Approaches

The most common approach to substance-abuse prevention over the past 20 years has involved attempting to increase individuals' awareness of the adverse consequences of smoking, drinking, or using drugs. For example, smoking education programs typically provide students with factual information about the long-term consequences of smoking cigarettes, particularly in terms of lung cancer (Thompson, 1978). Similarly, alcohol and drug education programs provide students with factual information about the legal, pharmacological, and health effects of using these substances (Goodstadt, 1978). The implicit assumption of these approaches is that if individuals were sufficiently aware of the dangers of substance use, they would make a rational and logical decision not to use them. Closely akin to informational approaches to substance-abuse prevention are approaches that utilize fear-arousal messages designed to scare individuals into not smoking, drinking, or using drugs. Although implicit within informational approaches is the message that substance use is harmful, this message is made explicit in fear-arousal approaches. A final variation on the information-dissemination prevention strategy involves approaching the problem of drug use from a moral perspective. This prevention strategy generally involves lecturing to students about the evils of using drugs. While most prevention approaches rely heavily on information dissemination, many school-based education programs and public information campaigns have utilized messages with both moralistic and fear-arousal overtones.

Another substance-abuse prevention approach that has seen widespread application in schools has been referred to as *affective education*. This approach is based on a different set of assumptions than described above, with emphasis being placed on values clarification, teaching responsible decision making, increasing self-esteem and interpersonal skills, and promoting participation in alternatives (Swisher, 1979).

Efforts to demonstrate the effectiveness of prevention programs using these approaches have been hindered by the fact that many prevention programs have either failed to include an adequate evaluation component or have neglected to examine program effects with respect to substance use behavior. For example, Schaps, Bartolo, Moskowitz, Palley, and Churgin (1981) reviewed 127 evaluation studies of substance-abuse prevention programs, and found that only 4 had relatively well-designed evaluation components which also included an assessment of substance use behavior.

Reviews of the existing empirical evidence concerning the effectiveness of conventional approaches to tobacco, alcohol, and drug abuse prevention have consistently indicated that these approaches are not effective (Berberian, Gross, Lovejoy, & Paparella, 1976; Braucht et al., 1973; Dorn & Thompson, 1976; Richards, 1969; Schaps et al., 1981; Swisher & Hoffman, 1975). Evaluations of programs whose primary strategy was providing factual information indicate quite clearly that increased knowledge has virtually no impact on substance use or on intentions to engage in tobacco, alcohol or drugs at some point in the near future. Similarly, studies evaluating the effectiveness of affective education approaches indicate that they are equally ineffective.

Information-dissemination approaches appear to be inadequate because they are too narrow in their focus. Moreover, they are based on an incomplete understanding of the factors promoting substance use/abuse. Although knowledge about the negative consequences of substance use is important, it is only one of many factors considered to play a role in the initiation of substance use among adolescents. With respect to the affective education approaches, it has been hypothesized that they are not effective because they emphasize experiential classroom activities in an effort to teach decision making, increase self-esteem, and improve interpersonal skills, rather than using more appropriate techniques for facilitating skills acquisition (Botvin, 1984a). Thus, while the affective education strategy is more comprehensive than approaches based on the information-dissemination model, the lack of effectiveness evident in the research literature may be based, at least in part, on deficiencies relating to teaching method.

Psychological Inoculation
and Pressure-Resistance Skills

A major departure from the traditional approaches to tobacco, alcohol, and drug abuse prevention was triggered by the pioneering work of Evans and his colleagues at the University of Houston toward the end of 1970s. Unlike traditional information dissemination approaches, the strategy developed initially by Evans and his colleagues (Evans, 1976; Evans et al., 1978) focused on the social and psychological factors believed to be involved in the initiation of cigarette smoking. Evans' work was strongly influenced by persuasive communications theory, as formulated by McGuire (1964, 1968).

The prevention strategy developed by Evans showed adolescents films designed to increase their awareness of the various social pressures to smoke that they would be likely to encounter as they progressed through the critical junior high school period. The purpose of this was to "inoculate" them against such pressures. In addition, these films also included demonstrations of techniques for resisting these pressures to smoke. This prevention strategy also included a student feedback component, designed to correct the misperception that cigarette smoking is a highly normative behavior, and health-knowledge information concerning the immediate physiological effects of cigarette smoking.

Over the years, several variations on the model originally developed by Evans have been tested. A distinctive feature of these prevention models is that they have placed more emphasis on teaching students specific techniques for effectively dealing with both peer and media pressures to smoke, drink, or use drugs (Arkin, Roemhild, Johnson, Luepker, & Murray, 1981; Hurd et al., 1980; Luepker, Johnson, Murray, & Pechacek, 1983; McAlister, Perry, & Maccoby, 1979; Murray, Johnson, Leupker, Pechacek, & Jacobs, 1980; Perry, Killen, Slinkard, & McAlister, 1980; Telch, Killen, McAlister, Perry, & Maccoby, 1982). These programs were designed to increase students' awareness of the various social influences to engage in substance use along with specific resistance skills for effectively coping with these negative influences. Students are generally taught how to recognize high-risk situations in which they will be likely to experience peer pressure to smoke, drink, or use drugs so that those situations could be avoided. Moreover, students are taught how to handle situations in which they might experience peer pressure to engage in substance use. Typically, this includes teaching students not only what to say (i.e., the specific content of a refusal message), but also how to deliver it so that it will be maximally effective. Many of these programs have used either older or same age peer leaders to assist in the implementation of these prevention programs. Finally, students are generally provided with the opportunity to observe other students using these techniques as well as being provided with the opportunity to practice through the use of role playing.

Material has also generally been included in these programs to combat the perception that substance use is widespread (i.e,. "everybody's doing it"), since adolescents typically overestimate the prevalence of smoking, drinking, and the use of certain drugs. This has been accomplished by simply providing students with the prevalence rates of substance use among their age mates in terms of national survey data or conducting classroom or school-wide surveys organized and directed by students participating in the program. Finally, these programs typically include a component designed to increase students' awareness of the techniques used by advertisers in promoting the sale of tobacco products or alcoholic beverages, and to teach techniques for formulating counterarguments to the messages utilized by advertisers.

Considerable research has been conducted and published in recent years documenting the effectiveness of these kinds of psychosocial prevention strategies. Although variations exist across studies, a review of these preventive interventions indicates that they are able to reduce the rate of smoking by 35% to 45% after the initial intervention. Similar reductions have been reported for alcohol and marijuana use (e.g., McAlister, Perry, Killen, Slinkard, & Maccoby, 1980).

Follow-up studies indicate that the positive behavioral effects of these prevention approaches are evident for up to two years after the conclusion of these cigarette-smoking programs (Luepker et al., 1983; McAlister et al., 1980; Telch et al., 1982). Studies testing the application of these prevention strategies to substances such as alcohol and marijuana have only recently been conducted and, therefore, data concerning their long-term effectiveness are not yet available.

Toward a Comprehensive Prevention Strategy

Factual Information

While it is certainly the case that the provision of information concerning the negative consequences of tobacco, alcohol, and drug abuse is of only limited utility when used alone, this does not mean that factual information does not or cannot play an important role in substance-abuse prevention. Certain types of knowledge may be important, while other types of knowledge may actually be counterproductive. For example, it might be useful to correct the misperception that substance use is something that virtually everybody is engaged in, thereby reducing the perceived social support for engaging in these behaviors. On the other hand, information concerning specific pharmacological effects or technical information concerning substance use (e.g., modes of administration) may actually increase use by increasing curiosity.

The type of information provided must also be guided at least in part by a recognition of cognitive-developmental factors. Since adolescents tend to live in the here and now, information concerning the long-term adverse consequences of substance use is likely to be less salient than more immediate consequences. Furthermore, any discussion of consequences should take into account adolescents' basic concerns. Since a central concern of most adolescents relates to the development of interpersonal relationships, the perceived social benefits of smoking, drinking, or using drugs may override concerns for potential negative health consequences. However, negative consequences that adolescents might view as social liabilities (e.g., nicotine stains, bad breath, associating substance use with low social status) appear to be more meaningful and consequently may be more effective.

Personal and Social Competence

An essential aspect of psychosocial development and, ultimately of psychological adjustment, involves the acquisition of a repertoire of interpersonal skills and intrapersonal coping skills. Basic interpersonal skills are necessary for confident, responsive, and mutually beneficial relationships. If individuals either fail to develop these important skills or develop inadequate skills, it may adversely affect an individual's ability to develop mutually satisfying interpersonal relationships or may interfere with optimal functioning in school, work, or recreational situations (Coombs & Slaby, 1977). Furthermore, social-skills deficits may lead to rejection and social isolation, which may, in turn, result in poor psychological adjustment.

The development of social competence generally begins during early childhood, and as individuals progress through middle childhood and the early adolescent years they typically become socially proficient. In general, by the time individuals have become adolescents, they are expected to have acquired a repertoire of social skills including communication skills, conversational skills, complimenting skills, and assertive skills. Social skills are learned through a process involving modeling, behavior rehearsal, and reinforcement. The development of these skills is largely contingent upon having the opportunity to observe these skills being used by others as well as having sufficient opportunity to practice them.

Another important set of skills that appears to be a prerequisite for functioning effectively in an increasingly adult world are personal coping skills. One important personal skill is the ability to make logical and rational decisions without being unduly influenced by others. As individuals progress into childhood and early adolescence, they typically find themselves in situations that require increased independence, autonomy, and the ability to make informed decisions. Persuasive influences coming either from the media or from peers may lead an individual in a direction that is inconsistent with his or her own interests. Another important set of personal skills is the ability to cope with anxiety and stress, to elicit social support, to increase one's sense of personal control, and to emphasize the use of positive thinking and self-reinforcement techniques.

Recognizing the importance of individual competence, considerable research has been conducted in an effort to demonstrate the efficiency of various intervention approaches for the enhancement of competence. These studies have covered a broad range of domains and have focused on different target populations. For example, research has been conducted to test the efficacy of assertiveness training approaches (Pentz & Kazdin, 1982), interpersonal skills (Schinke, 1981), social problem solving (Elias, Gara, Ubriaco, Rothbaum, Clabby, & Schuyler, 1986; Spivack & Shure, 1982; Weissberg et al., 1981), study skills (Wise, Genshaft, & Byrley, 1987), and anxiety reduction (Deffenbacher & Suinn, 1982).

The LST Prevention Strategy

General Overview

The LST program was developed in an effort to increase adolescents' ability to deal with the various social influences to smoke, drink, and use drugs as well as to increase individual competence in an effort to attenuate intrapsychic motivations. Moreover, this approach was designed to be comprehensive, both in that it was designed to teach a broad range of personal and social skills and in that it was designed to prevent the development of several problems, conditions, and/or diseases. As such, the problem of substance abuse is addressed within the larger context of acquiring basic life skills and enhancing individual competence. The prevention program itself is in the form of a psychoeducational curriculum that focuses on the primary psychosocial determinants of substance abuse.

The LST approach has been designed to be implemented with junior high school students, since the junior high school period is viewed as a critical time during which students are likely to experience increasing pressure to engage in substance use and to begin experimenting with a wide range of new behaviors. Furthermore, the LST program has been designed to focus on the gateway substances of tobacco, alcohol, and marijuana. There is a dual rationale for focusing on these substances. First, these substances are the most widely used substances in our society. Second, they occur at the very beginning of the developmental sequence of substance abuse. Consequently, an intervention effectively impacting on these behaviors should prevent individuals from becoming abusers of other psychoactive substances which typically occur further along in the developmental progression.

Program Objectives

The specific objectives of the LST program are: (1) to provide students with the necessary skills for resisting direct social pressures to smoke, drink, or use drugs; (2) to decrease general susceptibility to the indirect social influences to engage in substance use by helping students to develop greater autonomy, self-esteem, self-mastery, and self-confidence; (3) to enable students to cope effectively with anxiety, particularly anxiety induced by social situations; (4) to increase students' knowledge of the immediate consequences of smoking and to provide accurate information concerning the prevalence rates of tobacco, alcohol, and marijuana use; and (5) to promote the development of attitudes and beliefs consistent with non-substance use.

Description of the LST Program

The LST program consists of a primary intervention, generally implemented in 15 to 20 class periods with seventh graders. A booster intervention has also been developed which is currently designed to be implemented in the eight and ninth grades.

Over the years, we have conceptualized the LST program components in two different ways. One way of conceptualizing the LST program involves seeing it in terms of the three broad areas covered: (1) information and social resistance skills targeted specifically at substance abuse prevention; (2) generic personal coping skills; and (3) generic social skills (Botvin & Wills, 1985). Conceptualizing the program in this manner facilitates the identification of program components and content areas which are either similar to or different from those incorporated into other recently developed psychosocial strategies for preventing substance abuse. However, a more detailed understanding of the basic content of the LST program can be more readily accomplished with a somewhat different conceptualization of program components. Thus, for the purposes of this chapter, the LST program is presented as a program consisting of five major components (Botvin, 1983). Each component contains two to six lessons designed to be taught in the sequence indicated in Table 5.1. A complete description of the content and activities of each session is contained in the LST teacher's manual (Botvin, 1983), which provides detailed step-by-step lesson plans.

Factual Information

The LST program contains four sessions that provide students with factual information concerning the negative consequences of use (with an emphasis on immediate consequences) and current prevalence rates among both adolescents and adults. The first session includes general health information about the adverse consequences of smoking cigarettes, with particular emphasis on consequences that are both relatively immediate and that might serve as social liabilities. The second session focuses on the immediate physiological effects of cigarette smoking. The third and fourth sessions are similar to the first, except that they focus on alcohol and marijuana, respectively.

Self-Directed Behavior Change

The second component of the LST program consists of two class periods and a self-improvement project. The class sessions focus on what self-image is, how it is formed, and how it can be improved through a self-improvement plan. Following this session, students begin a self-improvement project that generally lasts until the end of the semester. Each student selects a skill or behavior that he or she would like to change, and identifies a goal for a self-improvement project that is generally conducted over an eight- to ten-week period. The purpose of this component is to foster the development of self-esteem, teach the basic principles of self-directed behavior change, and increase a sense of personal control.

TABLE 5.1 Life Skills Training Program Description

Number of Sessions	Topic	Description
4	Substance Use: Myths and Realities	Common attitudes and beliefs about tobacco, alcohol, and marijuana use; current prevalence rates of adults and teenagers; the social acceptability of using these substances; the process of becoming a regular (habitual) user, and the difficulty of breaking these habits; the immediate physiological effects of smoking.
2.	Decision Making and Independent Thinking	Discussion of routine decision making; description of a general decision-making strategy; social influences affecting decisions; recognizing persuasive tactics; and the importance of independent thinking.
2	Media Influences and Advertising Techniques	Discussion of media influences on behavior; advertising techniques and the manipulation of consumer behavior; formulating counterarguments and other cognitive strategies for resisting advertising pressure; cigarette and alcohol advertising as case studies in the use of these techniques.
2	Self-Image and Self-Improvement	Discussion of self-image and how it is formed; the relationship between self-image and behavior; the importance of a positive self-image; alternative methods of improving one's self and self-image; beginning a self-improvement project.
2	Coping With Anxiety	Discussion of common anxiety-inducing situations; demonstration and practice of cognitive-behavioral techniques for coping with anxiety; instruction on the application of these techniques to everyday situations as active coping strategies.
2	Communication Skills	Discussion of the communication process; distinguishing between verbal and nonverbal communication; techniques for avoiding misunderstandings.
1	Social Skills (A)	Discussion on overcoming shyness; initiating social contacts, giving and receiving compliments; basic conversational skills: initiating, sustaining and ending conversations.
1	Social Skills (B)	Discussion of boy-girl relationships and the nature of attraction; conversing with the opposite sex; social activites and asking someone out for a date.
2	Assertiveness	Situations calling for assertiveness, reasons for not being assertive, verbal and nonverbal assertive skills; resisting peer pressures to smoke, drink, or use marijuana.

Decision Making

This component consists of four sessions designed to foster independent decision making. The first two sessions concern the decision-making process itself. A simple five-step decision-making strategy is demonstrated to students, and opportunities are provided for practice. The third and fourth sessions introduce students to the techniques used by advertisers to influence decisions made by consumers. Critical thinking skills as well as skills for formulating counterarguments to advertising appeals are demonstrated and practiced. Skills for analyzing advertisements, identifying ad appeals, and formulating counterarguments are then applied to cigarette ads and ads for alcoholic beverages.

Coping with Anxiety

The fourth component involves learning how to effectively cope with anxiety, with particular emphasis on the demonstration and practice of specific anxiety-reduction techniques. The component begins with a discussion of the phenomenology of anxiety, after a brief classroom exercise designed to produce a moderate degree of performance anxiety (e.g., with respect to taking an unexpected quiz or an oral presentation in front of the class). The common signs of anxiety are discussed along with the kinds of situations that produce anxiety. Three anxiety-reduction techniques are taught: self-directed relaxation using a 12-minute audiotape that includes the systematic relaxation of muscle groups combined with guided imagery, diaphragmatic (deep) breathing and the use of mental rehearsal.

Social Skills

The fifth and final component contains six sessions that deal with a variety of interpersonal skills. The first and second sessions cover basic communication skills. They define verbal and nonverbal communication and present specific guidelines for avoiding misunderstandings. The third session is designed to help students overcome shyness. Students are taught the skills necessary to initiate social contacts, give and receive compliments, and the fundamentals of conversational skills. The fourth session focuses on skills related to developing and maintaining relationships with the opposite sex. The final two sessions in this component deal with assertiveness. Students learn to identify and define assertive behavior, discuss why individuals may not act assertively, and discuss the benefits of being assertive in appropriate situations.

TABLE 5.2 Life Skills Training Program Description: Year 2 Booster Curriculum

Number of Sessions	Topic	Description
1	Cigarette Smoking: Causes and Effects	Factors promoting cigarette smoking; current prevalence rates of adults and teenagers; immediate physiologic effects of smoking.
1	Decision Making and Independent Thinking	Review of general decision-making strategy; clarifying values, practice making decisions based on values; review of persuasive tactics, and the importance of independent thinking.
1	Advertising	Identifying and analyzing advertising techniques and the manipulation of consumer behavior; cognitive strategies for resisting advertising pressure.
2	Coping With Anxiety	Discussion of common anxiety-inducing situations; review and practice of cognitive-behavioral techniques for coping with anxiety.
1	Communication Skills	Techniques for avoiding misunderstandings, verbal and nonverbal communication, listening skills and paraphrasing.
1	Social Skills	Review of basic conversational skills; demonstration and practice of initiating, sustaining, and ending a conversation.
2	Assertiveness (A)	Situations calling for assertiveness; review and practice of verbal and nonverbal skills.
1	Assertiveness (B)	Review and practice of resisting direct pressure to smoke, drink, or use marijuana; discussion and practice of asserting rights as a nonsmoker.

TABLE 5.3 Life Skills Training Program Description: Year 3 Booster Curriculum

Number of Sessions	Topic	Description
1	Decision Making and Problem Solving	Introduction to Year 3 Booster Curriculum; review and practice of decision-making strategy.
1	Coping With Anxiety	Review and practice of relaxation exercise, deep breathing, hand warming, controlling negative thoughts, mental rehearsal.
1	Social Skills	Review and practice of greetings and brief social exchanges; identification of skills for initiating, sustaining, and ending a conversation; practice of skills for initiating, sustaining, and ending a conversation.
1	Assertiveness	Discussion of situations calling for assertiveness; identification of verbal and nonverbal assertive skills; practice of verbal and nonverbal assertive skills.
1	Resisting Peer Pressure to Smoke, Drink, or Use Drugs	Identification of situations involving peer pressure to smoke, drink, or use drugs; guidelines on what to say and how to say it in situations involving peer pressure; practice of peer pressure resistance skills.

Booster Sessions

In addition to the primary LST program, which is generally taught in the seventh grade, a ten-session booster curriculum has been developed for the eighth grade and a five-session booster curriculum for the ninth grade. The booster sessions are designed to reinforce the material covered in the first year program, with an emphasis on the demonstration and practice of the personal coping skills and interpersonal skills, which form the foundation of this prevention approach. The content and structure of the booster program is presented in Tables 5.2 and 5.3, which briefly describe the units to be taught and the number of class sessions required for each.

LST Implementation Issues

Recruitment and Planning

The success of any school-based program depends on the approval and active support of a variety of individuals on the district and school levels. It is difficult to make a standard prescription for obtaining administrative clearance and support, since school districts vary considerably in structure and operating procedures (see Maher & Bennett, 1984, or Maher, Illback, & Zins, 1984, for detailed discussions of these issues). However, individuals within the system are often valuable sources of information about the power structure of the school district and the concerns of particular decision makers.

In our experience, it has been necessary to obtain permission and, most importantly, to gain the support of individuals on a variety of levels. During the early stages of this process, it is necessary to identify and communicate with those individuals or groups who have the power to make decisions concerning the adoption of new curricula. This decision-making group may include school superintendents and other district level administrators, school board members, principals, department heads, and classroom teachers. While they may not have the power to adopt curricula, concerned parents—particularly if organized into a cohesive group—can have an enormous influence on this decision-making group.

Since we have always approached the schools as outsiders, it has been more expeditious for us to contact district level individuals initially. Once we have obtained approval on the district level, we approached the schools directly with an introductory mailing describing the program, and this time we mention that we have the support of their school district. We emphasize that only a limited number of schools will be selected. Meetings are then arranged with the principals of interested schools, followed by meetings with department heads and teachers. In order to maximize the potential for having this type of prevention program successfully implemented, it is necessary that as much support as possible be obtained for the program at each level within the school system during the recruitment and planning stages. An absence of such support can create insurmountable obstacles to program implementation. Even when teachers acknowledge the importance of a program, they may undermine its implementation if they feel they have been coerced into teaching it. One of the lessons that we have learned in our research is that if preventive interventions are ever to be institutionalized, they must have the support of the individuals actually implementing them, as well as the individuals charged with the responsibility of adopting new programs.

The LST program is designed to be taught in its entirety each year and in the specified sequence, since skills covered in later sessions build on the ones covered earlier in the program. The LST program can be effectively implemented at a rate of once a week or several times a week on consecutive class days for several weeks. The program can be implemented through any subject area, although health and science classes appear to have been the most appropriate in our experience.

Selection and Training of Program Providers

In our own research, we have used three different types of program providers: project staff, older peer leaders, and regular classroom teachers. Regardless of the type of provider, it is important that individuals implementing the LST program feel that their participation is voluntary. It is also important, especially with peer leaders, that program providers be good role models—both with respect to substance use and the skills being taught. While it would be advantageous to have individuals who have experience teaching personal and social skills (e.g., health teachers, counselors) to teach the program, it does not appear to be necessary. Good teachers who have attended a training workshop can implement this program simply by following the detailed lesson plans in the LST Teacher's Manual.

Peer leaders of substance-abuse prevention programs have been the same age or older than the students receiving the intervention. In our studies, the peer leaders have had varying levels of responsibility for program implementation, ranging from being primarily responsible for program implementation to assisting teachers in leading small group discussions or organizing role-play scenarios. Peer leaders who are responsible for program implementation usually require a great deal of support and supervision, since they rarely have much experience in teaching and classroom management.

Program providers should have some training on how to implement the LST program, and the training should be tailored to the particular background and experience of the program providers. Peer leaders are generally provided with an initial four-hour orientation workshop, followed by weekly training sessions designed to prepare them to implement the specific program material of the upcoming session. For experienced teachers, we have found that a one-day orientation workshop, although clearly not ideal, is generally sufficient. The orientation workshop includes information on the background and rationale for the LST approach, the content of the curriculum, guidelines for scheduling and implementation, and practice conducting selected program components.

Quality Control

In an effort to standardize program implementation to the greatest extent possible, detailed curriculum materials have been developed for the LST approach to substance-abuse prevention. These materials include a teacher's manual with step-by-step lesson plans (Botvin, 1983), a student workbook (Botvin, 1979b), and a 12-minute relaxation tape (Botvin, 1979a) for the unit on coping with anxiety. In addition, a teacher's manual has been developed for both the eighth (Botvin, 1984b) and ninth grade (Botvin, 1980) booster sessions.

To foster high quality implementation, project staff conduct classroom observations of program implementation on a random basis. During these classroom observation sessions, observers assess fidelity of implementation by recording the percentage of session objectives and activities covered, and rate the quality of the implementation along several dimensions. Where appropriate, program providers are given feedback and consultation in an effort to fine tune the program during the early stages of implementation and prevent program "drift" during the later stages of implementation.

Evaluation Studies

Several evaluation studies have been conducted to determine the extent to which this type of prevention strategy is effective. In addition, these studies were designed to obtain information about the effectiveness of different types of providers, the effectiveness of booster sessions, effectiveness with different target populations, effectiveness on different gateway substances, and effectiveness with and without formal teacher training and ongoing consultation.

Throughout the course of our research, a concerted effort has been made to maximize internal and external validity. Considerable attention has been paid to research design and measurement issues, and numerous refinements have been made over the years in order to strengthen the methodological rigor of our research. As this research has evolved, our studies have progressed from small-scale pilot studies, involving just a few hundred students, to large-scale prevention trials involving several thousand students.

Study 1

The initial pilot study (Botvin, Eng, & Williams, 1980) was designed to determine the short-term efficacy of the LST program for preventing the onset of cigarette smoking among eighth, ninth, and tenth graders (N = 281) from two comparable suburban New York schools. After randomly assigning schools to experimental and control conditions, students were pretested by questionnaire. The LST program was implemented in the school assigned to the experimental condition by members of the project staff.

Posttest results indicated that there were 75% fewer new cigarette smokers in the experimental group compared with the controls. A three month follow-up study (Botvin & Eng, 1980) indicated that, although some erosion of the posttest effects was evident, there were still 67% fewer new smokers among the students who had participated in the LST program, compared with controls.

Study 2

A second study was conducted to determine the efficacy of the LST program when implemented by older peer leaders (Botvin & Eng, 1982). Once again, two comparable suburban New York schools were randomly assigned to experimental and control conditions (N = 426). Eleventh and twelfth grade peer leaders implemented the LST program with seventh graders in the experimental school. In addition to collecting self-report data by questionnaire concerning smoking behavior, saliva samples were collected from each student using the *bogus-pipeline* technique (Evans, Hansen, & Mittlemark, 1977).

Posttest results indicated that there were 58% fewer new smokers in the group receiving the LST program, compared with the students in the control group. These results were corroborated by the results of the saliva thiocyanate (SCN) analysis, which showed a significant increase in SCN levels among the students in the control group between the pretest and posttest—indicating increased cigarette smoking—and no significant change among the students who participated in the LST program. One year follow-up data indicated that there were 56% fewer students in the LST group who had become regular cigarette smokers since the pretest than in the control group.

Study 3

Our third study (Botvin, Renick, & Baker, 1983) was designed to determine the relative efficacy of the LST program when implemented by regular classroom teachers according to two different implementation schedules (one class per week versus multiple classes per week) as well as to determine the efficacy of booster sessions. Seventh grade students (N = 902) from seven suburban New York schools were involved in the study. Self report data were collected by questionnaire using the bogus-pipeline technique as in the previous study.

At the initial posttest, there were 50% fewer experimental smokers in the groups receiving the LST program when compared with controls; however, there were no differences between the groups receiving the LST program according to the two implementation schedules. At the one year follow-up, there were 55% fewer smokers among the students who received the LST program according to the more intensive implementation schedule. In addition, there were 87% fewer regular smokers among the students receiving the LST program in the seventh grade and booster sessions in the eight grade, compared with the students in the control group.

Study 4

In order to determine the potential for this type of intervention strategy with respect to other forms of substance use, a pilot study was conducted with 239 seventh graders from two New York City public schools (Botvin, Baker, Botvin, Filazzola, & Millman, 1984). Two comparable schools were randomly assigned to experimental and control conditions. Information was included in the LST program concerning the consequences of alcohol misuse and, where appropriate, the skills taught were applied to situations which might promote alcohol use.

All students were pretested and posttested by questionnaire during the seventh grade, and posttested again nine months after the pretest. No program effects were evident at the initial posttest. However, at the second posttest, 54% fewer LST students reported drinking during the past month in comparison to the controls, 73% fewer students reported heavy drinking, and 79% fewer students reported getting drunk one or more times per month.

Study 5

A study (Botvin, Baker, Renick, Filazzola, & Botvin, 1984) involving 1311 seventh graders from ten public schools in suburban New York was conducted to determine the efficacy of the LST approach for preventing marijuana use as well as the use of tobacco and alcohol. Within the context of this study, the relative efficacy of teachers and older peer leaders was assessed along with the efficacy of booster sessions conducted in both the eighth and ninth grades.

Program effects were evident at the initial posttest for tobacco, alcohol, and marijuana use; however, these effects were only evident for students in the peer-led condition. In general, these effects were of roughly the same magnitude as those obtained in our previous studies. For example, there were 40% fewer experimental smokers in the peer-led LST condition than in the control condition. The most interesting results were with respect to marijuana use; there were 71% fewer students in the peer-led LST condition reporting marijuana use, compared with controls.

One-year follow-up data indicate that significantly fewer students in the peer-led booster LST group were smoking and using marijuana, compared to the controls. Two-year follow-up data indicate that the strongest effects over time are with respect to cigarette smoking. Retrospective analysis of data concerning the quality of program implementation suggests considerably more variability among teachers than trained peer leaders. Some teachers implemented the LST program in a manner consistent with the intervention protocol, while others clearly did not. Analysis of a restricted sample of teachers who appear to have implemented the prevention program with a reasonable degree of fidelity approximated those obtained by peer leaders. While these results support the efficacy of this type of prevention program when implemented by both peer leaders and classroom teachers, they also suggest the need to identify and examine any potential barriers to successful implementation in order to ensure program effectiveness when conducted in the "real world."

Current Studies

In addition to the evaluation studies summarized above, we are in the process of conducting three large-scale prevention trials. One study involves two cohorts of approximately 10,000 students per cohort from 56 public schools in New York State. Using a randomized block design, schools were assigned to the following conditions: LST with a formal teacher training workshop, LST with packaged (written and video) teacher training, and a no-contact control. Teachers will implement the LST program with seventh graders. Booster sessions will be provided in both the eighth and ninth grades.

Two other studies are underway that will examine the extent to which this prevention strategy is suitable for urban minority students. One study is designed to determine the efficacy of the LST approach when implemented with predominantly black students ($N = 3000$) from 30 public schools in northern New Jersey. This study is currently in its developmental phase. The other study is being conducted with a predominantly Hispanic population in New York City. Approximately 3000 seventh graders from 47 schools are participating. Half of the students attend public schools, and half attend parochial schools. The prevention strategy used in this study is essentially the same as that used in our previous research; however, some modifications have been made in the curriculum materials in order to maximize cultural sensitivity and appropriateness to the target population. Evidence from both the pilot phase and first year of the full-scale prevention trial provides preliminary support for the efficacy of this approach when conducted with urban students in a multiracial environment.

Summary, Conclusions, and Future Directions

Substance abuse continues to be a major problem in this country, despite some recent evidence of decreases in the prevalence rates of several types of substance use among adolescents. The initiation and early stages of substance use/abuse appear to be the result of the complex interplay of a number of cognitive, attitudinal, social personality, pharmacological, and developmental factors. Traditional tobacco, alcohol, and drug abuse prevention approaches rely primarily on the provision of factual information about the adverse consequences of using these substances. Fear-arousal messages as well as messages with moral overtones are frequently incorporated into these approaches. Evaluation studies have indicated quite consistently that these approaches do not reduce substance use/abuse. Similarly, the evaluation literature has indicated that affective education approaches are not effective.

More recently, several new approaches to substance-abuse prevention have been developed. These approaches focus on the social and psychological factors that appear to play important roles in substance use initiation. A common feature of these prevention programs is that they include the teaching of a variety of resistance skills designed to assist adolescents in resisting social influences to engage in substance use, particularly those coming from the media and from peers. These approaches have yielded promising results, consistently demonstrating reductions in cigarette smoking and, in some cases, in alcohol and marijuana use.

A problem with these psychosocial approaches is that, although they provide adolescents with the skills necessary to resist substance use offers, they do little to affect changes in intrapersonal factors that may serve as powerful motivators. The LST approach described in this chapter is a more comprehensive prevention model. In addition to teaching adolescents important resistance skills related to the problem of substance abuse, it is designed to promote the development of generic personal and social competence. The results of evaluation studies testing the efficacy of this approach indicate that it can reduce tobacco, alcohol, and marijuana use by 50% or more. It also has been able to demonstrate an impact on several hypothesized mediating variables. Although most of the research with this approach has been conducted with white, middle-class populations, research currently underway also has provided preliminary data on its efficacy with urban minority adolescents.

The results obtained thus far with this type of prevention approach have been extremely encouraging. Still, considerably more research is needed. The current series of studies will help determine the longer-term effectiveness of this intervention strategy with both white, middle-class adolescents and urban minority adolescents. Future studies will need to focus on factors related to implementation which may serve as obstacles to dissemination. Moreover, future studies will need to be designed explicitly to determine the extent to which this type of prevention strategy can impact on a number of theoretically and empirically related problem behavior domains.

References

Arkin, R. M., Roemhild, H. J., Johnson, C. A., Luepker, R. V., & Murray, D. M. (1981). The Minnesota smoking prevention program: A seventh grade health curriculum supplement. *Journal of School Health, 51*, 611–616.

Bandura, A. (1969). *Principles of behavior modification.* New York: Holt, Rinehart and Winston.

Bandura, A. (1977). *Social learning theory.* Englewood Cliffs, NJ: Prentice-Hall.

Becker, H. S. (1967). History, culture and subjective experience: An exploration of the social basis of drug-induced experiences. *Journal of Health and Social Behavior, 8,* 163–176.

Berberian, R. M., Gross, C., Lovejoy, J., & Paparella, S. (1976). The effectiveness of drug education programs: A critical review. *Health Education Monographs, 4,* 377–398.

Blum, R., & Richards, L. (1979). Youthful drug use. In R. I. Dupont, A. Goldstein, & J. O'Donnell (Eds.), *Handbook on drug abuse* (Contract No. 271–77–6001, pp. 257–267). Washington, DC: National Institute on Drug Abuse.

Botvin, G. J. (1978, October). *The ethnography of teenage cigarette smoking.* Paper presented at the annual meeting of the American Public Health Association. Los Angeles.

Botvin, G. J. (speaker) (1979a). *Life skills training: Relaxation exercise.* Audio Cassette Tape (15 minutes). New York: Smithfield Press.

Botvin, G. J. (1979b). *Life skills training: Student guide.* New York: Smithfield Press.

Botvin, G. J. (1980). *Life skills training: Teacher's manual (ninth grade booster curriculum).* New York: Smithfield Press.

Botvin, G. J. (1982). Broadening the focus of smoking prevention strategies. In T. Coates, A. Peterson, & C. Perry (Eds.), *Promoting adolescent health: A dialog on research and practice* (pp. 137–148). New York: Academic Press.

Botvin, G. J. (1983). *Life skills training: Teacher's manual (seventh grade curriculum).* New York: Smithfield Press.

Botvin, G. J. (1984a). Improving personal competence: Toward a comprehensive approach to smoking prevention. In P. Lippert, A. L. McAlister, & H. Hoffmeister (Eds.), *Health promotion in youth: Problems and perspectives* (pp. 93–102). Berlin, Germany: Dietrich Reiner Verlag.

Botvin, G. J. (1984b). *Life skills training: Teacher's manual (eighth grade booster curriculum).* New York: Smithfield Press.

Botvin, G. J. Baker, E., Botvin, E. M., Filazzola, A. D., & Millman, R. B. (1984). Alcohol abuse prevention through the development of personal and social competence: A pilot study. *Journal of Studies on Alcohol, 45,* 550–552.

Botvin, G. J., Baker, E., Renick, N. L., Filazzola, A. D., & Botvin, E. M. (1984). A cognitive-behavioral approach to substance abuse prevention. *Addictive Behaviors, 9,* 137–147.

Botvin, G. J., & Eng, A. (1980). A comprehensive school-based smoking prevention program. *Journal of School Health, 50,* 209–213.

Botvin, G. J., & Eng, A. (1982). The efficacy of a multicomponent approach to the prevention of cigarette smoking. *Preventive Medicine, 11,* 199–211.

Botvin, G. J., Eng, A., & Williams, C. L. (1980). Preventing the onset of cigarette smoking through Life Skills Training. *Preventive Medicine, 9,* 135–143.

Botvin, G. J., Renick, N. L., & Baker, E. (1983). The effects of scheduling format and booster sessions on a broad-spectrum psychosocial approach to smoking prevention. *Journal of Behavioral Medicine, 6*, 359–379.

Botvin, G. J., & Wills, T. A. (1985). Personal and social skills training: Cognitive-behavioral approaches to substance abuse prevention. In C. Bell & R. Battjes (Eds.), *Prevention research: Deterring drug abuse among children and adolescents* (pp. 8–49). Washington, DC: NIDA Research Monograph.

Braucht, G. N., Follingstadt, D., Brakarsh, D., & Berry, K. L. (1973). Drug education: A review of goals, approaches and effectiveness, and a paradigm for evaluation. *Quarterly Journal of Studies on Alcohol, 34*, 1279–1292.

Coombs, M. L., & Slaby, D. A. (1977). Social skills training with children. In B. B. Lahey & A. E. Kazdin (Eds.), *Advances in clinical child psychology: Vol. 1.* (pp. 161–201). New York: Plenum Press.

Deffenbacher, J. L., & Suinn, R. M. (1982). The self-control of anxiety. In P. Karoly & F. H. Kanfer (Eds.), *Self management and behavior change: From theory to practice* (pp. 393–442). New York: Pergamon Press.

Demone, H. W. (1973). The nonuse and abuse of alcohol by male adolescents. In M. Chafetz (Ed.), *Proceedings on the second annual alcoholism conference* (DHEW Publication No. HSM 73–9083, pp. 24–32). Washington, DC: U.S. Government Printing Office.

Dorn, N., & Thompson, A. (1976). Evaluation of drug education in the longer term is not an optional extra. *Community Health, 7*, 154–161.

Elias, M., Gara, M., Ubriaco, M., Rothbaum, P. A., Clabby, J. F., & Schuyler, T. (1986). Impact of a preventive social problem-solving intervention on children's coping with middle school stress. *American Journal of Community Psychology, 14*, 259–275.

Evans, R. I. (1976). Smoking in children: Developing a social psychological strategy of deterrence. *Preventive Medicine, 5*, 122–127.

Evans, R. I., Hansen, W. B., & Mittlemark, M. B. (1977). Increasing the validity of self-reports of smoking behavior in children. *Journal of Applied Psychology, 62*, 521–523.

Evans, R. I., Rozelle, R. M., Mittlemark, M. B., Hansen, W. B., Bane, A. R., & Havis, J. (1978). Deterring the onset of smoking in children: Knowledge of immediate physiological effects and coping with peer pressure, media pressure, and parent modeling. *Journal of Applied Social Psychology, 8*, 126–135.

Goodstadt, M. S. (1978). Alcohol and drug education. *Health Education Monographs, 6*, 263–279.

Hamburg, B. A., Braemer, H. C., & Jahnke, W. A. (1975). Hierarchy of drug use in adolescence: Behavioral and attitudinal correlates of substantial drug use. *American Journal of Psychiatry, 132*, 1155–1167.

Hurd, P. D., Johnson, C. A., Pechacek, T., Best, L. P., Jacobs, D. R., & Luepker, R. V. (1980). Prevention of cigarette smoking in seventh grade students. *Journal of Behavioral Medicine, 3*, 15–28.

Jessor, R. (1976). Predicting time of onset of marijuana use: A developmental study of high school youth. In D. J. Lettieri, (Ed.), *Predicting adolescent drug abuse: A review of issues, methods and correlates* (DHEW Publication No. ADM 77–299). Washington, DC: U.S. Government Printing Office.

Jessor, R. (1982). Critical issues in research on adolescent health promotion. In T. Coates, A. Petersen, & C. Perry (Eds.), *Promoting adolescent health: A dialogue on research and practice* (pp. 447–465). New York: Academic Press.

Jessor, R., Collins, M. I., & Jessor, S. L. (1972). On becoming a drinker: Social psychological aspects of an adolescent transition. *Annals of the New York Academy of Sciences, 197*, 199–213.

Jessor, R., & Jessor, S. L. (1977). *Problem behavior and psychosocial development: a longitudinal study of youth.* New York: Academic Press.

Kandel, D. B. (1978). Convergences in prospective longitudinal surveys of drug use in normal populations. In D. B. Kandel (Ed.), *Longitudinal research on drug use: Empirical findings and methodological issues* (pp. 3–38). Washington, DC: Hemisphere-Willey.

Lettieri, D. J., Sayers, M., & Pearson, H. W. (1980). *Theories on drug abuse: Selected contemporary perspectives* (DHEW Publication No. ADM 80–967). Washington, DC: U.S. Government Printing Office.

Luepker, R. V., Johnson, C. A., Murray, D. M., & Pechacek, T. F. (1983). Prevention of cigarette smoking: Three year follow-up of an education program for youth. *Journal of Behavioral Medicine, 6,* 53–62.

Maher, C. A., & Bennett, R. E. (1984). *Planning and evaluating special education services.* Englewood Cliffs, NJ: Prentice-Hall.

Maher, C. A., Illback, R. J., & Zins, J. E. (Eds.). (1984). *Organizational psychology in the schools: A handbook for professionals.* Springfield, IL: Charles C. Thomas.

McAlister, A. L., Perry, C. L., Killen, J., Slinkard, L. A., & Maccoby, N. (1980). Pilot study of smoking, alcohol and drug abuse prevention. *American Journal of Public Health, 70,* 719–721.

McAlister, A. L., Perry, C. L., & Maccoby, N. (1979). Adolescent smoking: Onset and prevention. *Pediatrics, 63,* 650–658.

McGuire, W. J. (1964). Inducing resistance to persuasion: Some contemporary approaches. In L. Berkowitz (Ed.), *Advances in experimental social psychology: Vol. 1.* (pp. 192–227). New York: Academic Press.

McGuire, W. J. (1968). The nature of attitudes and attitude change. In G. Lindzey & E. Aronson (Eds.), *Handbook of social psychology* (pp. 136–314). Reading, MA: Addison-Wesley.

Meyer, R. E., & Mirin, S. M. (1979). *The heroin stimulus: Implications for a theory of addiction.* New York: Plenum Press.

Millman, R. B., & Botvin, G. J. (1983). Substance use, abuse and dependence. In M. Levine, W. B. Carey, A. C. Crocker, & R. T. Gross (Eds.), *Developmental behavioral pediatrics* (pp. 683–708). New York: W. B. Saunders Company.

Murray, D. M., Johnson, C. A., Leupker, R. V., Pechacek, T. F., & Jacobs, D. R. (1980). *Issues in smoking prevention research.* Paper presented at the meeting of the American Psychological Association. Montreal.

Pentz, M. A., & Kazdin, A. E. (1982). Assertion modeling and stimuli effects on assertive behavior and self-efficacy in adolescents. *Behavioral Research and Therapy, 20,* 365–371.

Perry, C., Killen, J., Slinkard, L. A., & McAlister, A. L. (1980). Peer teaching and smoking prevention among junior high students. *Adolescence, 9,* 277–281.

Piaget, J. (1962). *The moral judgment of the child.* New York: Collier.

Ray, O. S. (1974) *Drugs, society, and human behavior.* St. Louis: C.V. Mosby.

Richards, L. G. (1969, September). *Government programs and psychological principals in drug abuse education.* Paper presented at the annual convention of the American Psychological Association. Washington, DC.

Rotter, J. B. (1972). Generalized expectancies for internal versus external control of reinforcement. In J. B. Rotter, J. E. Chance, & E. J. Phares (Eds.), *Applications of a social learning theory of personality* (pp. 260–295). New York: Holt, Rinehart, and Winston.

Schaps, E., Bartolo, R. D., Moskowitz, J., Palley, C. S., & Churgin, S. (1981). A review of

127 drug abuse prevention program evaluations. *Journal of Drug Issues*, Winter, 17–43.

Schinke, S. P. (1981). Interpersonal skills training with adolescents. In M. Hersen, R. M. Eisler, & P. M. Miller (Eds.), *Progress in behavior modification: Vol. 2.* (pp. 65–115). New York: Academic Press.

Spivack, G., & Shure, M. D. (1982). The cognition of social adjustment: Interpersonal cognitive problem-solving thinking. In B. B. Lahey & A. E. Kazdin (Eds.), *Advances in child clinical psychology: Vol. 5.* (pp. 323–372). New York: Plenum Press.

Swisher, J. D. (1979). Prevention issues. In R. I. Dupont, A. Goldstein, & J. O'Donnell (Eds.), *Handbook on drug abuse* (Contract No. 271–77–6001, pp. 423–435). National Institute on Drug Abuse. Washington, DC: U.S. Government Printing Office.

Swisher, J. D., & Hoffman, A. (1975). Information: The irrelevant variable in drug education. In B. W. Corder, R. A. Smith, & J. D. Swisher (Eds.), *Drug abuse prevention: Perspectives for approaches for educators* (pp. 49–62). Dubuque, Iowa: William C. Brown.

Telch, M. J., Killen, J. D., McAlister, A. L., Perry, C. L., & Maccoby, N. (1982). Long-term follow-up of a pilot project on smoking prevention with adolescents. *Journal of Behavioral Medicine, 5*, 1–8.

Thompson, E. L. (1978). Smoking education programs. *American Journal of Public Health, 68*, 250–257.

U.S. Public Health Service (1986). *Drug abuse and drug abuse research: The second triennial report to congress from the secretary* (DHHS Publication No. ADM 87–1486). Washington, DC: U.S. Government Printing Office.

Utech, D., & Hoving, K. L. (1969). Parents and peers as competing influences in the decisions on children of differing ages. *Journal of Social Psychology, 78*, 267–274.

Wechsler, H. (1976). Alcohol intoxication and drug abuse among teenagers. *Quarterly Journal of Studies on Alcohol, 37*, 1672–1677.

Wechsler, H., & Thum D. (1973). Alcohol and drug abuse among teenagers. A questionnaire study. In M. Chafetz (Ed.), *Proceedings of the second annual alcoholism conference* (DHEW Publication No. HSM 73–9083). Washington, DC: U.S. Government Printing Office.

Weissberg, R. P., Gesten, E. L., Carnrike, C. L., Toro, P. A., Rapkin, B. D. Davidson, E., & Cowen, E. L. (1981). Social problem-solving skills training: A competence-building intervention with second- to fourth-grade children. *American Journal of Community Psychology, 9*, 411–423.

Wise, P.S., Genshaft, J. L., & Byrley, M. B. (1987). Study-skills training: A comprehensive approach. In C. A. Maher & J. E. Zins (Eds.), *Psycho-educational intervention in the schools* (pp. 66–80). New York: Pergamon Press.

6

The Use of Prediction Data in Understanding Delinquency

Magda Stouthamer-Loeber
Rolf Loeber

Predicting delinquency is valuable for understanding the course of crime, factors that influence its course, and the identification of markers that signal deviant processes. In addition, prediction data are relevant for judicial and clinical decision making. This article summarizes research findings on the prediction of delinquency. In the realm of early childhood behaviors, there is consensus that aggression (especially in conjunction with hyperactivity), drug use, truancy, lying, stealing, general problem behaviors, and poor educational achievement all predict later delinquency, albeit to varying degrees, with composite prediction scales yielding the highest degree of accuracy. In addition, studies show a reasonable consensus that the following family factors also predict delinquency: poor supervision, lack of involvement by parents, poor discipline, rejection by a parent, parental criminality and aggressiveness, marital problems, parental absence, and poor parental health. Variables reflecting socialization processes predicted later delinquency as well as children's early behavior. Although studied less frequently, youngsters' association with deviant peers is also predictive of delinquency.

Since the early work by the Gluecks (1940, 1950, 1959), efforts have been under way to predict delinquency based on data about behavior in children and the circumstances of their lives. The efforts to predict delinquency can serve several purposes, such as the formulation of theories about child development and the highlighting of early

Authors' Note: This chapter is reprinted from Stouthamer-Loeber, M., & Loeber, R. (1988). The use of prediction data in understanding delinquency. *Behavioral Science and the Law, 6* (3), 333-354. Copyright © 1988 by John Wiley and Sons, Inc. Reprinted by permission of John Wiley & Sons, Inc.

markers of deviancy that can be incorporated in prevention efforts for children at risk for delinquency. Additionally, prediction studies may influence judicial decision making. This chapter summarizes the results of a large number of studies linking earlier child behavior and circumstances in the child's environment with later delinquency. The material presented here combines information from three publications on the prediction of delinquency (Loeber & Stouthamer-Loeber, 1987), the influence of the family (Loeber & Stouthamer-Loeber, 1986a), and the stability of antisocial behavior (Loeber, 1982).

The Prediction of Delinquency
Based on Earlier Child Behavior

Several aspects of children's earlier behavior can be used to predict later delinquency. First, the form or content of early problem behaviors, such as aggression or lying, may be used to predict later delinquency. Second, certain configurations of these early problem behaviors and the circumstances under which they occur can be indicative of an increased risk for delinquency.

Early Problem Behaviors

The following is a summary of an extensive review of studies in which behavior during childhood and adolescence was linked to later delinquency (Loeber & Stouthamer-Loeber, 1987).

To compare the results of different studies that used a variety of statistical techniques for categorical data, a uniform measure of predictive power, called relative improvement over chance (RIOC), was applied. RIOC corrects the association between predictor and the outcome variables in a two-by-two table for chance and for maximum values due to discrepancies between the selection ratio applied to the predictor variable and the base rate of the outcome behavior.[1] The range is from 0 to 100%, with 100% indicating perfect predictability.

Summarizing a large number of studies has several drawbacks. Different studies use different kinds of populations and target behaviors, and assess these populations at different ages (from 4 to 20 years) and intervals (from 2 to 20 years). On the other hand, by pooling information from many sources, patterns may appear that single studies cannot show. Although some of the studies included females and Blacks, the majority of the studies were concerned with White males. Any conclusions, therefore, will primarily apply to this group. The reader is referred to the original paper for details on the studies that were included in the review.

The material is organized in Table 6.1 by predictors and by sex of the subjects. Studies are summarized by three categories of outcome: delinquency in general, serious delinquency, and recidivism. Delinquency in general includes any kind of offense regardless of seriousness, and may also contain status offenses (but excludes minor traffic offenses); serious delinquency refers to offenses listed in Part I of the FBI Crime Index, such as arson, robbery, rape, and homicide. The studies summarized in the tables are indicated by numbers in parenthesis, which correspond to the references in Appendix 1.

Aggression

The median RIOC for predicting delinquency on the basis of earlier aggression was 32.9% (range = 16.4–51.4%) for boys, and 25.2% (range = 17.0–30.3%) for studies with boys and girls. For studies predicting recidivism the median RIOC was slightly higher (38.3% with a range of 28.1–38.5%). It is important to note that in the studies summarized in Table 6.1 interpersonal aggression was measured by either teacher ratings, peer ratings, or self-reports. Studies in which parents reported on their children's aggression were lacking. Therefore, it is unclear how well early aggression as perceived by parents predicts later delinquency.

Drug Use

Only three studies were found in which drug use was linked to later delinquency. The median RIOC for general delinquency was 53.0% (range = 27.0–79.0%). Drug use also predicted continuing recidivism in multiple offenders (RIOC = 41.6%) (Osborn & West, 1980). Soft drug use is almost normative for certain age groups and, as such, is less useful as a predictor of delinquency than hard drug use; in only one study (Robins, Darvish, & Murphy, 1970), however, was type of drug taken into account.

Drug use was measured only in late adolescence for the obvious reason that very few young children engage in drug use. Therefore, drug use is best thought of as a predictor of a delinquent career rather than as an early predictor of onset of offending. For instance, there are several studies showing that many chronic offenders are poly-drug users, or drug and alcohol users (Petersilia, Greenwood, & Lavin, 1977; Tuchfeld, Clayton, & Logan, 1982). We need to learn more, however, about how substance abuse and delinquency are temporally related.

Truancy

Four studies were found relating truancy to later delinquency in general. The median RIOC was 25.5% (range = 20.4–26.3%). Serious

TABLE 6.1 Summary of Behavioral Predictors of Later Delinquency

Predictor (studies)	Sex	General Delinquency Median			Serious Delinquency Median			Recidivism Median		
		#(1)[c]	RIOC[d]	Range	#(1)	RIOC	Range	#(1)	RIOC	Range
Aggression (6,11,22,23,26,29,49)[a]	B	5	32.9[b]	16.4–51.4				3	38.3	28.1–38.5
(8,14)	B+G	3	25.2	17.0–30.3						
Drug use (6,29,32)	B	2	53.0	27.0–79.0				1	41.6	
Truancy (7,9,25,27,34)	B	4	25.5	20.4–26.3	2	46.5	27.8–65.1			
Lying (7,25)	B	2	22.4	22.0–22.7				1	31.0	
Stealing (25,27)	B	2	37.4	17.1–57.8	1	37.5		1	60.6	
General problem behavior (2,6,7,12,13,25,27,32,35,39,49)	B	12	26.6	4.0–64.2	3	66.3	9.1–91.8	3	52.5	26.0–89.0
(32)	G	1	82.9							
(53,14)	B+G	2	41.3	32.3–50.2						
Educational achievement (6,14,21,30,34,37,47,49,49,52)	B	11	22.9	11.1–46.1				1	42.9	
Prediction scales (4,38,41,42)	B	3	64.4	27.8–78.0				1	87.0	
Delinquency (15,16,17,28,30,35,51)	B							8	38.3	30.4–81.3
(35)	B+G							2	35.1	33.6–36.5

Source: From R. Loeber and M. Stouthamer-Loeber, "The Prediction of Delinquency," in H. C. Quay (Ed.), Handbook of Juvenile Delinquency, 1987. New York: Wiley. Copyright © 1987 John Wiley & Sons, Inc. Reprinted by permission of John Wiley & Sons, Inc. [a]The numbers refer to the references in Appendix 1. [b]Due to an error in the original table, this figure differs from the figure in the source. [c]#(1) Number of analyses. [d]RIOC = relative improvement over chance.

delinquency in children referred to a child guidance clinic was predicted with a RIOC of 27.8% (Nylander, 1979), and Glueck and Glueck (1940) reported that 77.2% of their delinquent subjects were truant (RIOC of 65.1%) compared to an average of 12.5% for all the subjects in the nondelinquent samples in the four studies summarized in the table. Nontruant delinquencies engaged mainly in minor offenses.

Lying

Delinquents often need to deny their criminal behavior verbally; therefore, lying is an almost necessary accompaniment to a delinquent career. Lying could be seen as a precursor of delinquency since it is one of the first concealing antisocial behaviors to develop (Stouthamer-Loeber, 1986). Lying in children however, has not often been related to later delinquency. The few summarized studies showed that in about a third of the delinquents, and in about 50% of the recidivists, lying was a precursor of later delinquency. Parent or peer reports of children's lying related to later official delinquency yielded a median RIOC of 22.4% (range = 22.0–22.7%). With regard to the identification of recidivists among delinquents, children's lying, as reported by parents and teachers, produced a RIOC of 31.0% (Mitchell & Rosa, 1981).

Stealing

The predictors in the summarized studies refer to unofficial reports by parents and teachers of children's stealing; that is, not by arrest or court records, although some of the acts reported may have come to the attention of the police. Since most official delinquency consists of property crime, one would expect that the similarity between predictor and outcome allows for the possibility of high RIOCs. Only two studies were found linking early stealing to later delinquency in general, yielding RIOCs of 57.8 and 17.1%. Early pilfering or theft in the latter study was predictive of serious crime, with a RIOC of 37.5%. Among delinquents, parent and teacher reports of stealing predicted recidivism with a RIOC of 60.5% (Mitchell & Rosa, 1981). Since the subjects in the summarized studies were already deviant (e.g., clinic populations or delinquents), it is not known how well early frequent stealing predicts later delinquency in normal populations.

General Problem Behaviors

Under this heading we have grouped a variety of predictors such as referral for antisocial behavior, poor socialization, and troublesomeness, including specific categories of behavior such as destructiveness, daring, and disruptive behaviors at school. RIOCs for male delinquency in general ranged from 4.0 to 64.2%, with most of them, however, in the range of 20 to 30%. The highest RIOC concerned youths referred for antisocial behavior to a clinic who had a much higher chance of having nontraffic arrests as adults than nonclinic controls (Robins, 1966) (RIOC = 64.2% for males and 82.9% for females). The lowest RIOC was found for the relationship of hyperactivity with later delinquency (RIOC = 4.0%) (Nylander, 1979). Male serious delinquency and recidivism were predicted by early problematic behavior with median RIOCs of 66.3% (range = 9.2–91.8%) and 52.5% (range 26.0–89.0%), respectively. Again, hyperactivity did not predict well (RIOC = 9.2%). We will return to this later.

Low Educational Achievement or IQ

The findings from longitudinal studies replicate those from cross-sectional studies in that low educational achievement is related to delinquency (Hirschi & Hindelang, 1977; Menard & Morse, 1984). In the studies reviewed here, the median RIOC of male delinquency in general (primarily measured as official delinquency) was 22.9% (range = 11.1–46.1%). With regard to self-reported delinquency, a low vocabulary score at age 8 to 10 and poor school learning results at age 11 were predictive of high self-reported delinquency at 14 to 16 years old (RIOCs = 27.4 and 18.3%, respectively) (Farrington, 1979). In one study (West & Farrington, 1973) IQ was related to recidivism, with a RIOC of 42.9%.

The exact mechanism by which educational achievement and delinquency are linked is very much in debate; the reader is referred to Hirschi and Hindelang (1977), Menard and Morse (1984), and Spivack (1983) for a sampling of different theories.

Prediction Indices

Teacher nominations of potentially delinquent children (Reckless & Dinitz, 1972; Scarpitti, 1964) have yielded high RIOCs (64.4 and 78.0%, respectively). Stott and Wilson (1968) used a teacher rating scale to predict delinquency, but the RIOC was only 27.8%. Spivack (1983; Spivack & Cianci, 1987) produced a high-risk profile for early elementary school children. The behaviors included in this profile were oversocially involved, impatience, disrespect/defiance, external blaming, and irrelevant responsiveness. Chronic offending was predicted with a RIOC of 87.0%. The score, however, predicted many more children to be delinquent than eventually became delinquent; that is, the index had a high false-positive rate.

A problem with nomination techniques such as the ones used by Reckless and Dinitz (1972) and Scarpitti (1964) is that which factors teachers based their nominations on is unclear. In addition to the children's own behavior, they may have included other factors such as socioeconomic status, sibling behavior, or parent behavior. This does not make the nomination technique less valuable as a prediction tool, but it is less helpful in specifying the factors involved in delinquency processes.

Early Delinquency

As discussed earlier in regard to stealing, the relationship between juvenile delinquency and later delinquency should be strong because of the similarity of predictor and criterion. The median RIOC for males was 34.5% (range = 30.4–41.2%). Self-reported delinquency, predicting self-reported chronic offending in boys and girls over a 2-year period, yielded a RIOC of 33.6% (Elliott, Dunford, & Huizinga, 1983). With regard to official delinquency as a predictor for later recidivism, the median RIOC was 45.5%, ranging from 32.0 to 81.3%.

Some researchers have found that seriousness of offending is a predictor of chronic offending (e.g., Knight & West, 1975; Shannon, 1978); however, all evidence does not point in the same direction. A number of researchers have reported findings suggesting that seriousness of offending is not related to chronicity (Elliott et al., 1983; Holland & McGarvey, 1984; Wolfgang, Figlio, & Sellin, 1972).

Summary of Predictors Based on Earlier Behavior

Serious delinquency and recidivism were almost always better predicted than delinquency in general. The median RIOC for all studies with delinquency in general as outcome was 27.0% (range = 4.0–79.0%), compared to 65.7% (range = 9.1–91.8%) and 38.5% (range = 26.0–89.0%) for serious delinquency and recidivism, respectively. For boys, aggression (median RIOC = 45.3%), stealing (median RIOC = 37.4%), and drug use (median RIOC = 53.0%) were the strongest predictors. Averaged over all the studies in Table 6.1, delinquency in girls is predicted as well as delinquency in boys.

Recidivism was equally well predicted by earlier offending, stealing, general problem behavior, drug use, or aggression. Composite scales, consisting of either teachers' judgments or a combination of variables, yielded higher predictions than those based on single variables.

**Particular Characteristics
of Early Problem Behaviors**

Loeber (1982) specified a number of conditions that increase the likelihood of continuity of antisocial behavior in children. These conditions were early onset, high frequency, variety of problem behaviors, and problem behaviors occurring in multiple settings.

Early Onset

Children who engage in problem behaviors at an early age, compared to their peers, are at an increased risk for continued problem behaviors. We will restrict our examples to early delinquency as a predictor of later delinquency. There is a fair amount of evidence, starting with Glueck and Glueck (1959), supporting the early onset hypothesis, but only a few examples will be highlighted here. Early onset seems to be related to several interconnected aspects of the later delinquent career, such as recidivism or chronic offending, higher delinquency rate per time interval, and the seriousness of the crimes committed. Farrington (1983) found that all of the 23 youths who had become chronic offenders by age 25 (i.e., those convicted six or more times) had been first convicted by their sixteenth birthday. To turn it around, 32.3% of those convicted before age 16 became chronic offenders, compared with none who were convicted after that age. Similarly, Robins and Ratcliff (1979) found that arrest before age 15 predicted adult offenses (RIOC = 36.5%). Other studies with similar results have been reported by Hamparian, Schuster, Dinitz, and Conrad (1978) and McCord (1981). The notion that an early start of a delinquent career has an effect on the rate of offending per time unit can be illustrated by data from the Cambridge Study in Delinquent Development (Farrington, 1982), which show that youths who committed their first crime between the ages of 10 to 12 averaged about twice as many convictions during ages 16 to 18 as those who committed their first crime between the ages of 13 and 15.

With regard to the seriousness of delinquent acts, Shannon (1978) found that age of first police contact strongly predicted seriousness of juvenile as well as adult crime. These findings are similar to those of Wolfgang and colleagues (1972), who reported that children with first police contact between the ages of 7 and 12 averaged more serious crimes than those who started their delinquent career later. Evidence that chronic offenders already exhibit nondelinquent problem behaviors early in life can be found in studies by Spivack (1983), Blumstein, Farrington, and Moitra (1985), Craig and Glick (1968), and Pulkkinen (1983).

High Frequency of Early Problem Behavior

Children who engage in very high rates of antisocial behavior are at an increased risk of continuing problem behaviors compared to those with lower rates of antisocial behaviors. Several studies have shown that children rated as very aggressive or troublesome in elementary school were more likely to continue to be aggressive or to have a delinquent record by the time they reached early adulthood (Osborn & West, 1978; Patterson, 1982; Pulkkinen, 1983). The same conclusion holds if rate of delinquency is used as a predictor of later delinquency. Loeber (1982) illustrated this principle with self-reported delinquency data from Elliot and Huizinga (1980) and showed that, the higher the rate of delinquency, the less the chance of remission a year later.

Variety of Problem Behavior

Children who engage in a wide variety of antisocial behaviors are more at risk for later antisocial careers than children who engage in fewer problem behaviors. An example of this can be found in the work by Robins and Ratcliff (1979), who reported in their retrospective study of Black men that only 6% of the children with no or only one type of antisocial behavior became delinquent compared to 39% of those with three or more categories of antisocial behavior.

Two potent combinations of problem behaviors have been identified. The first is the combination of aggressive and concealing antisocial behaviors, such as fighting and theft. Loeber and Stouthamer-Loeber (1986b) found in a follow-up of boys 9 to 16 years old after five years that those who had initially been rated as aggressive by their mothers and had engaged in high rates of self-reported theft scored significantly higher on a number of indices of delinquency than those boys who had been either high-rate thieves only or high-rate fighters only.

The second combination concerns conduct problems and hyperactivity. Many conduct problem children also exhibit symptoms of hyperactivity; that is, they are more restless and fidgety, have difficulty controlling their impulses, and have impairments in maintaining attention to tasks at hand. We will refer here to this syndrome as hyperactivity-impulsivity-attention deficits, or HIA. Several studies have pointed out that children who have both conduct problems and high HIA (on one or more of its components) are more at risk for delinquency than those with conduct problems only, or those with HIA only (e.g., Farrington, Loeber, & van Kammen, 1987; Magnusson, 1988). In addition, Farrington (1987) showed that both conduct problems and HIA, independently of each other, can contribute to the risk of chronic offending, that is, at least six convictions by the age of 24.

Problem Behavior in More Than One Setting

Children who show problem behavior in different settings, for example, school and home, appear more at risk for continued problem behavior than those who have problems in only one setting. Support for this can be found in the work of Mitchell and Rosa (1981) in which the chance of becoming a recidivist was 71% for children who had been identified by both teacher and parents as stealers, compared to 14% for parent-identified-only or 45% for teacher-identified-only stealers. Similar results were found when lying was used as the criterion. Other evidence can be found in McGee, Silva, and Williams (1983) and in Schachar, Rutter, and Smith (1981).

As mentioned earlier, the four characteristics discussed here are interrelated and form different facets that might profitably be taken into account when evaluating child problem behavior.

Environmental Predictors

Environmental variables refer to conditions in the child's environment, such as the child's family or peers, that may increase the likelihood of later delinquency. Longitudinal studies containing environmental predictors of delinquency have been reviewed recently by Loeber and Stouthamer-Loeber (1986a), and the following section is a summary of this review. The reader is referred to the Loeber and Stouthamer-Loeber (1986a) paper for details.

Family Variables

Table 6.2 summarizes studies relating environmental variables to later delinquency. The bulk of the environmental variables studied concern the family. For each family variable, the median RIOC and the number of analyses are reported. The findings should be interpreted with caution as the number of studies in each outcome category is often small. Loeber and Stouthamer-Loeber (1986a) chose four paradigms of family influence to organize the multitude of variables measured in the studies under review. These paradigms are not so much theoretical models as they are heuristic devices used to organize the material. The first two paradigms, Neglect and Conflict, concern socialization practices by parents directed at their children, and the last two paradigms, Parental Deviant Behavior and Attitudes and Disruption, concern background variables, that is, parent behaviors or circumstances that are not necessarily aimed at children, but might influence them nevertheless. The variables are not mutually exclusive; on the contrary, they may co-occur or follow each other over

TABLE 6.2 Summary of Environmental Variables as Predictors of Delinquency

Predictor (studies)	Sex	General Delinquency Median			Serious Delinquency Median			Recidivism Median		
		#(1)[b]	RIOC[c]	Range	#(1)	RIOC	Range	#(1)	RIOC	Range
Socialization Variables										
Neglect										
Poor supervision (5,6,50)[a]	B	2	51.0	21.2–80.8	1	29.2				
Parent uninvolvement (47)	B+G	1	31.0							
Conflict										
Poor discipline (18,49)	B	1	22.6		1	17.6				
Parent rejection (20)	B				2	38.7	33.7–43.8			
Background Variables										
Deviant Behavior and Attitudes										
Parent criminality and aggressiveness (6,20,28,36)	B	2	31.0	24.4–37.6	5	19.5	10.8–34.4	1	26.4	
Disruption										
Marital problems (20)	B				2	34.4	26.2–42.6			
Parent absence (10,19,34)	B	2	20.8	11.5–30.2	1	8.5				
(4,40,48)	B+G	3	18.6	7.4–25.1						
Poor parent health (49)	B	6	14.2	5.7–22.9						
Composite family handicap (1,2,17,28,43,44,46,49)	B	5	56.4	45.7–86.7				3	72.3	46.9–81.9
(43,45,47)	B+G	3	58.5	49.5–86.7						
Socioeconomic status (6,15,34,37,47,52)	B	6	17.7	10.5–30.9				3	14.0	11.7–49.3
Peers										
Deviant peers (6)	B	1	32.5							

Source: From R. Loeber and M. Stouthamer-Loeber, "The Prediction of Delinquency," in H. C. Quay (Ed.), *Handbook of Juvenile Delinquency*, 1987. New York: Wiley. Copyright © 1987 by John Wiley & Sons, Inc. Reprinted by permission of John Wiley & Sons, Inc. [a]The numbers refer to the references in Appendix 1. [b]#(1) Number of analyses. [c]RIOC = relative improvement over chance.

time. Often, several parenting skills or circumstances are less than optimal. Medium-level correlations between various parenting deficits have been noted by several investigators. We will first describe the paradigms and then present prediction data for their components.

Under Neglect, parent variables that concern the amount of time parents and children spend together and how much they know about the child's activities have been grouped. Parents' involvement with children can take the form of participating in activities or games together, going on outings, or just spending time talking to each other. Being actively involved with the child gives the parents an opportunity to teach the child socially acceptable skills and creates a possibility for mutual attachment and appreciation.

Parents who do not spend sufficient time with their children may not be in a position to supervise their children. When children are young, supervision takes place by personally being present or placing the child in the care of a responsible adult. As children grow older, supervision includes being informed as to where the child is and what his or her activities are when away from home. Lack of supervision makes it impossible to guide children's activities by advice, reinforcement, punishment, and the setting of rules. Apart from being informed about the child's activities, supervision presupposes that the parents have a set of standards that they find worthwhile to impose. Thus lack of supervision may have several different causes.

Whereas the Neglect paradigm is characterized by disengagement, the Conflict model contains variables related to active interactions and affect. Although actual conflict has rarely been measured in the survey studies under consideration, aspects of discipline and parental rejection have frequently been measured.

Parental Deviant Behavior and Attitudes can have their effect on children in several ways. First, parents may model deviant behavior that their children may adopt. Second, parents may not punish or discourage deviant behavior and, therefore, deprive their children of the consequences that might change children's behavior. For instance, parents with deviant values might protect children from the police, or not pay attention when goods of uncertain provenance are brought into the house. Parents might actively teach children to be aggressive or tough with the idea that real boys should be able to stand up for themselves. In contrast with the first two models in which children and parents are either not sufficiently in contact or too much in conflict, this model assumes a degree of concordance between parents and children, at least about some aspects of the child's behavior.

The Family Disruption paradigm contains a number of variables that have in common that the smooth functioning of a family may be interrupted by the stress created by certain circumstances such as marital problems, parental absence, and parental physical or mental ill health.

In general, all the variables listed in Table 6.2 produced an improvement over chance in classifying children as at risk for delinquency. Of the socialization variables (poor supervision, poor discipline, lack of parent involvement, and parents' rejection of the child) poor supervision was the best predictor of delinquency in general (median RIOC = 51.0%; range = 21.2–80.8%), but this was based on two studies. Parents' lack of involvement with and rejection of the child were the next best predictors, while poor discipline was the weakest predictor (RIOC = 17.6–22.6%). Discipline practices, however, are very difficult to measure (Patterson & Stouthamer-Loeber, 1984), and the results may reflect this.

The family background of the child is measured by the next five predictors in Table 6.2. Poor marital relations predicted serious delinquency relatively strongly (RIOC = 26.2–42.6%). In comparison, parental absence did not seem to have as strong a relationship with delinquency in general (median RIOCs 20.8 and 18.6%, respectively). Parental criminality and aggressiveness were more strongly related to general delinquency (median RIOC = 31.0%) than to serious delinquency (median RIOC = 19.5%). Poor parental health was least strongly related to delinquent outcome (median RIOC = 14.2%).

Composites of Family Variables

Predictors based on composites of family variables, like prediction indices based on composites of child behavior, usually yielded higher RIOCs than those based on single variables. The Gluecks' (1950) prediction table consisted mainly of parent-child interaction variables such as discipline, supervision, and affection, and has been modified by successive researchers. Although prediction indexes have been criticized (Prigmore, 1963; Reiss, 1951), the results show that parents' combined child-rearing practices are highly predictive of delinquency in children. Often prediction indices have used combinations of family *and* behavior variables (Farrington & Tarling, 1985; McCord, 1979; Osborn & West, 1978; Wadsworth, 1979; West & Farrington, 1973), with similar results. Median RIOCs for composite scores were 56.4% and 58.5% for the prediction of delinquency in general in male and mixed samples, respectively, and 72.3% for the prediction of recidivism.

Socioeconomic Status

The relationship of social class and delinquency has been a topic of intense study and, as with the relationship of academic achievement and delinquency, a number of extensive reviews have appeared to which the reader is referred (Braithwaite, 1981; Hindelang, Hirschi, & Weiss, 1979; Tittle, Villemez, & Smith, 1978). The longitudinal studies reporting on the relationship between socioeconomic status and delinquency have been reviewed in Loeber and Dishion (1983) and are summarized in Table 6.2. Socioeconomic status, like most of the other family background variables, was only weakly related to delinquency in general and to recidivism (median RIOCs were 17.7 and 14.0%, respectively).

Peers

Only one longitudinal study on the influence of deviant peers on later delinquency was found. Farrington (1979) reported that involvement with antisocial peers at the age of 18 was related to later delinquency with a RIOC of 32.5%. This area of possible influence on the delinquency process, although playing an important role in delinquency theories, has not yet been sufficiently studied (but see Elliott et al., 1983).

Comparisons Between Behavioral and Environmental Predictors

It has been the general concensus that the child's own behavior predicts later delinquency better than variables in the child's environment (Monahan, 1981). The material presented in Tables 6.1 and 6.2 is in agreement with this. Children's own behavior had a stronger predictive relationship with later delinquency than background variables such as parent absence, parent health, or socioeconomic status. Surprisingly, however, some of the socialization variables such as poor supervision and parental rejection predicted delinquency as strongly as children's own behavior.

Individual variables, such as children's problem behaviors or socialization variables, generally yielded RIOCs of about 25 to 35%. This is about half the value of RIOCs obtained with composite scores from prediction scales or combinations of family variables. This shows that, although individual variables can improve the prediction of delinquency considerably, the combination of several variables is much stronger, supporting Rutter's accumulative model of risk (1978).

Conclusion

The data presented earlier demonstrate a strong concensus about many factors predictive of later delinquency. Conclusions, however, need to be tempered for several reasons. The fact that a particular factor predicts delinquency always refers to a probabilistic relationship between predictor and outcome, with the inherent problem of sometimes high proportions of false-positive and false-negative errors. For that reason, risk data reflect the characteristics of populations of youngsters; such aggregated data should be applied to individual cases with caution. Individual youngsters may differ in crucial aspects (such as sex, race, or other characteristics) from those who formed the basis of the risk index used. Moreover, processes that led to delinquency or its desistance are still poorly understood, and may operate differently in some youngsters, and, therefore, not be recognized easily in risk indexes that apply the same criteria across all youngsters. Lastly, the fact that a particular factor predicts delinquency does not mean necessarily that such a factor is causal to delinquency. Given that there are a multitude of predictors and correlates of delinquency, it is not surprising that many of the factors are intercorrelated. For that reason, a particular risk factor may predict delinquency solely by virtue of its association with another, more causally relevant, factor. Prediction studies have, far too infrequently, sorted out which risk factors continue to predict later delinquency after other factors are partialed out. An even better test of the causal status of risk factors is systematically to manipulate the factor in an experimental group of subjects, but not in another control group of subjects, while allowing the randomized variation of other risk factors across the two groups. For obvious practical and ethical reasons, this is only possible for certain risk factors.

Our poor understanding of the causal status of risk factors in prediction studies has pressed home the need to describe more carefully the course of delinquency and intervening events during the interval between the times that a predictor and its later outcome are measured. Our study of prediction data has taught us to be hesitant about expecting that a single set of causal factors can explain the delinquent behavior of large populations of youngsters. Instead, it is much more likely that there are different groups of offenders whose behavior is influenced by unique as well as common causal factors. Loeber (in press) recently reinterpreted the results of a large number of studies, and concluded that a parsimonious description of delinquency would consist of at least two distinct trajectories that develop over time. One is called the versatile/aggressive path, and is characteristic of an early onset of problem behavior, often associated with hyperactivity and attention problems. Individuals in this trajectory have a high incidence of aggressive behavior, which leads to alienation by groups of peers and conflict with adults. Academic performance often deteriorates over time. There is also a gradual diversification of problem and delinquent behaviors over time, contributing to the versatile, unspecialized form of offending, often at a high rate. Remission is unlikely, at least prior to adulthood. A second likely path in the development of delinquency usually has a late onset and is characterized by mostly nonaggressive conduct problems in early life (such as truancy) and a preponderance of nonaggressive forms of crimes later (such as theft and fraud). Remission rate appears higher in this trajectory, partly because other handicapping conditions, such as attention problems and low intelligence, are often absent (for details, see Loeber, in press). There is little doubt that much needs to be learned about the course of delinquency and how this differs among youngsters.

It is to be hoped that improved knowledge of delinquent and predelinquent careers will provide better markers for use in distinguishing deviant from normal forms of development. The establishment of clearer markers than are now available will help to focus preventive approaches. Not only will a marker indicate that further deviancy is likely to develop over time, but it will also help us to pinpoint the type of deviancy that can be anticipated. In order to produce this kind of developmental knowledge, a large longitudinal study of 1500 boys, ages 6, 10 and 13, who are followed up each half-year is currently under way. Systematic assessments of the boys are complemented by assessments of their parents and their teachers, as well as school records and records of the juvenile court. In that way, a composite picture can be reconstructed of the pre- and the delinquent careers of the boys.

Rewards of such an investigation are also expected for the judicial and children's services systems, where court personnel often use formalized systems of risk factors in their decision making. Risk data, especially when representative of specific populations of youngsters, can be useful in many ways. First, such data can help officials to better gauge the risk of criminal career involvement of very young offenders, that is, those below the age of criminal responsibility, a relatively high proportion of whom become chronic offenders (Loeber, 1987). Second, even though many status offenders are less likely to reoffend later, it is likely that the behavioral profile of certain status offenders who continue to offend is different from those who desist. Third, diversion, parole, and probation decisions all can benefit from more precise information about different profiles of young offenders, and specific risks attached to each profile.

Decision making by police, court, and children's services personnel should not be seen as an instant appraisal, where one assessment of first offenders can forecast long-term outcomes many years hence. Instead, it is much more practical and economical to use stepwise screening methods, which have long been used effectively in personnel selection. Loeber, Dishion, and Patterson (1984) have demonstrated the use of such techniques (called multiple gating) in the identification of delinquents and multiple offenders. The procedure was cost-effective since it used a relatively inexpensive teacher rating as a first "gate," whereby a risk group was isolated. A second assessment, through a paper-and-pencil measure done by a parent, focused on this group, and led to a more densely packed risk group. The most expensive assessment, consisting of an interview with the parent about child-rearing practices, was reserved for the latter group and constituted the last "gate." Although Loeber and colleagues' (1984) gating procedure was applied concurrently, it lends itself to modifications, including one whereby the assessments are done with flexible intervals over time, depending on the emergence of new risk markers. Again, we anticipate that improved knowledge of pre- and delinquent careers will advanced these techniques considerably.

Appendix 1

1. Blumstein, Farrington, & Moitra, 1985
2. Craig & Glick, 1968
3. Elliott, Dunford, & Huizinga, 1983
4. Ensminger, Kellam, & Rubin, 1983
5. Farrington, 1978
6. Farrington, 1979
7. Farrington, 1981
8. Feldhusen, Thurston, & Benning, 1973
9. Glueck & Glueck, 1940
10. Gregory, 1965
11. Havighurst, Bowman, Liddle, Matthews, & Pierce, 1962
12. Huesmann, Eron, Lefkowitz, & Walder, 1984
13. Janes, Hesselbrock, Myers, & Penniman, 1979
14. Kirkegaard-Sorenson & Mednick, 1977
15. Knight & West, 1975
16. LeBlanc, 1980

17. McCord, 1979
18. McCord, 1981
19. McCord, 1982
20. McCord, 1984
21. McCord & McCord, 1959
22. Magnusson, 1984
23. Magnusson, Stottin, & Duner, 1983
24. Marsh, 1969
25. Mitchell & Rosa, 1981
26. Mulligan, Douglas, Hammond, & Tizard, 1963
27. Nylander, 1979
28. Osborn & West, 1978
29. Osborn & West, 1980
30. Polk, 1975
31. Reckless & Dinitz, 1972
32. Robins, 1966
33. Robins, Darvish, & Murphy, 1970
34. Robins & Hill, 1966
35. Robins & Ratcliff, 1979
36. Robins, West, & Herjanic, 1975
37. Rutter, Maugham, Mortimer, & Ouston, 1979
38. Scarpitti, 1964
39. Simcha-Fagan, 1979
40. Simcha-Fagan, Langner, Gersten, & Eisenberg, 1975
41. Spivack, 1983
42. Stott & Wilson, 1968
43. Tait & Hodges, 1972
44. Thompson, 1952
45. Trevett, 1972
46. Voss, 1963
47. Wadsworth, 1979
48. Wadsworth, 1980
49. West & Farrington, 1973
50. Wilson & Herbert, 1978
51. Wolfgang, 1977
52. Wolfgang, Figlio, & Sellin, 1972

Note

1. The formula for RIOC is: RIOC = Total correct − chance correct / Maximum correct − chance correct x 100 (see Loeber & Stouthamer-Loeber, 1987, for details)

References

Blumstein, A., Farrington, D. P., & Montra, S. (1985). Deliquency careers: Innocents, desisters, and persisters. In M. Tonry & N. Morris (Eds.). *Crime and justice* (Vol. 6). Chicago: University of Chicago Press

Braithwaite, J. (1981). The myth of social class and criminality reconsidered. *American Sociological Review, 46*, 36–57.

Craig, M. M., & Glick, S. J. (1968). School behavior related to later delinquency and non-delinquency. *Crimonologica, 5*, 17–27.

Elliott, D. S., Ageton, S. S., & Canter, R. J. (1979). An integrated theoretical perspective on delinquent behavior. *Journal of Research in Crime & Delinquency, 16*, 3–27.

Elliott, D. S., Dunford, F. W., & Huizinga, D. (1983). *The identification and prediction of career offenders utilizing self-reported and official data.* Unpublished manuscript, Behavioral Research Institute, Boulder, CO.

Elliott, D. S., & Huizinga, D. (1980). *Defining pattern delinquency: A conceptual typology of delinquent offenses.* Paper presented at the meeting of the American Society of Criminology, San Francisco, CA.

Ensminger, M. E., Kellam, S. G., & Rubin, B. R. (1983). School and family origins of delinquency: Comparisons by sex. In K. T. Van Dusen & S. A. Mednick (Eds.), *Antecedents of aggression and antisocial behavior.* Boston: Kluwer-Nijhoff.

Farrington, D. P. (1978). The family background of aggressive youths. In L. A. Hersov, M. Berger, & D. Schaffer (Eds.), *Aggression and antisocial behavior in childhood and adolescence* (pp. 73–93). Oxford: Pergamon.

Farrington, D. P. (1979). Environmental stress, delinquent behavior, and convictions. In I. G. Sarason & C. D. Spielberger (Eds.), *Stress and anxiety* (Vol. 6). Washington: Hemisphere.

Farrington, D. P. (1981). The prevalence of convictions. *The British Journal of Criminology, 21*, 173–175.

Farrington, D. P. (1982). Randomized experiments on crime and justice. In N. Morris & M. Tonry (Eds.), *Crime and justice* (Vol. 4). Chicago: University of Chicago Press.

Farrington, D. P. (1983). Offending from 10 to 25 years of age. In K. T. Van Dusen & S. A. Mednick (Eds.), *Antecedents of aggression and antisocial behavior.* Boston: Kluwer-Nijhoff.

Farrington, D. P., Loeber, R., & van Kammen, W. B. (1987). *Long-term criminal outcomes of hyperactivity-impulsivity-attention deficit and conduct problems in childhood.* Paper presented at the meeting of the Society for Life History Research, St. Louis.

Farrington, D. P., & Tarling, R. (Eds.). (1985). *Prediction in criminology.* Albany, NY: SUNY Press.

Feldhusen, J. F., Thurston, J. R., & Benning, J. J. (1973). A longitudinal study of delinquency and other aspects of children's behavior. *International Journal of Criminology & Penology, 1*, 341–351.

Glueck, S., & Glueck, E. T. (1940). *Juvenile delinquents grow up.* New York: Commonwealth Fund.

Glueck, S., & Glueck, E. T. (1950). *Unraveling juvenile delinquency.* Cambridge, MA: Harvard University Press.

Glueck, S., & Glueck, E. T. (1959). *Predicting delinquency and crime.* Cambridge, MA: Harvard University Press.

Gregory, I. (1965). Anterospective data following childhood loss of a parent: I. Delinquency and high school dropout. *Archives of General Psychiatry, 13*, 99–109.

Hamparian, D. M., Schuster, R., Dinitz, S., & Conrad, J. P. (1978). *Violent few—A study of dangerous juvenile offenders.* Lexington, MA: Heath Lexington.

Havighurst, R. J., Bowman, P., Liddle, G., Matthews, C., & Pierce, J. (1962). *Growing up in river city.* New York: Wiley.

Hindelang, M. J., Hirschi, T., & Weiss, J. G. (1979). Correlates of delinquency: The illusion of discrepancy between self-report and official measures. *American Sociological Review, 44,* 995–1014.

Hirschi, T., & Hindelang, M. J. (1977). Intelligence and delinquency: A revisionist review. *American Sociological Review, 42,* 571–587.

Holland, T. R., & McGarvey, B. (1984). Crime specialization, seriousness, progression, and Markov chains. *Journal of Consulting & Clinical Psychology, 52,* 837–840.

Huesmann, L. R., Eron, L. D., Lefkowitz, M. M. & Walder, L. O. (1984). The stability of aggression over time and generations. *Developmental Psychology, 20,* 1120–1134.

Janes, C. L., Hesselbrock, V. M., Myers, D. G., & Penniman, J. H. (1979). Problem boys in young adulthood—Teacher ratings and 12-year follow-up. *Journal of Youth & Adolescence, 8,* 453–472.

Kirkegaard-Sorensen, L., & Mednick, S. A. (1977). A prospective study of predictors of criminality. In S. A. Mednick & K. O. Christiansen (Eds.), *Biosocial bases of criminal behavior.* New York: Gardner.

Knight, B. J., & West, D. J. (1975). Temporary and continuing delinquency. *British Journal of Criminology, 15,* 43–50.

LeBlanc, M. (1980). *Developpement psycho-social et evolution de la deliquance au cours de l'adolescence.* Unpublished manuscript, University of Montreal, Groupe sur l'Inadeptation Juvenile, Montreal, Quebec.

Loeber, R. (1982). The stability of antisocial and delinquent child behavior: A review. *Child Development, 53,* 1431–1446.

Loeber, R. (1987). The prevalence, correlates, and continuity of serious conduct problems in elementary school children. *Criminology, 25,* 615–642.

Loeber, R. (in press). The natural histories of juvenile conduct problems, substance abuse, and delinquency: Evidence for developmental progressions. In B. B. Lahey & A. E. Kazdin (Eds.), *Advances in clinical psychology* (Vol. 10). New York: Plenum.

Loeber, R., & Dishion, T. J. (1983). Early predictors for male delinquency: A review. *Psychological Bulletin, 94,* 68–99.

Loeber, R., Dishion, T. J., & Patterson, G. R. (1984). Multiple gating: A multistage assessment procedure for identifying youths at risk for delinquency. *Journal of Research on Crime and Delinquency, 24,* 7–32.

Loeber, R., & Stouthamer-Loeber, M. (1986a). Family factors as correlates and predictors of juvenile conduct problems and delinquency. In N. Morris & M. Tonry (Eds.), *Crime and justice: An annual review of research* (Vol. 7, pp. 29–149). Chicago: University of Chicago Press.

Loeber, R., & Stouthamer-Loeber, M. (1986b). *Early childhood predictors of aggression and violence.* Paper presented at the meeting of the American Society of Criminologists, Atlanta.

Loeber, R., & Stouthamer-Loeber, M. (1987). The prediction of delinquency. In H. C. Quay (Ed.), *Handbook of juvenile delinquency.* New York: Wiley.

Magnusson, D. (1984). *Early conduct and biological factors in the developmental background of adult delinquency.* Paper presented at Henry Tajfel Memorial Lecture, Oxford.

Magnusson, D. (1988). *Individual development from an international perspective: A longitudinal study.* Hillsdale, NJ: Erlbaum.

Magnusson, D., Stottin, H., & Duner, A. (1983). Aggression and criminality in a longitudinal perspective. In K. T. Van Dusen & S. A. Mednick (Eds.), *Antecedents of aggression and antisocial behavior*. Boston: Kluwer-Nijhoff.

Marsh, R. W. (1969). The validity of the Bristol Social Adjustment Guides in delinquency prediction. *British Journal of Educational Psychology, 39*, 278–282.

McCord, J. (1979). Some child-rearing antecedents of criminal behavior in adult men. *Journal of Personality & Social Psychology, 37*, 1477–1486.

McCord, J. (1981). A longitudinal perspective on patterns of crime. *Criminology, 19*, 211–218.

McCord, J. (1982). A longitudinal study of the link between broken homes and criminality. In J. Gunn & D. P. Farrington (Eds.), *Abnormal offenders, delinquency and the criminal justice system*. London: Wiley.

McCord, J. (1984, July). *Family sources of crime*. Paper presented at the International Society for Research on Aggression, Turku, Finland.

McCord, W., & McCord, J. (1959). *Origins of crime*. Montclair, NJ: Patterson Smith.

McGee, R., Silva, P. A., & Williams, S. (1983). Parents' and teachers' perceptions of behavior problems in seven year old children. *The Exceptional Child, 30*, 151–161.

Menard, S., & Morse, B. J. (1984). A structuralist critique of the IQ-delinquency hypothesis: Theory and evidence. *American Journal of Sociology, 89*, 1347–1378.

Mitchell, S., & Rosa, P. (1981). Boyhood behavior problems as precursors of criminality: A fifteen year follow-up study. *Journal of Child Psychology & Psychiatry, 22*, 19–33.

Monahan, J. D. (1981). *Clinical prediction of violent behavior*. Washington, DC: Government Printing Office.

Mulligan, G., Douglas, J. W. B., Hammond, W. H., & Tizard, J. (1963). Delinquency and symptoms of maladjustment. *Proceedings of the Royal Society of Medicine, 56*, 1083–1086.

Nylander, I. (1979). A 20-year prospective follow-up study of 2164 cases at the child guidance clinics in Stockholm. *Acta Paediatrica Scandinavica, 68*, (Suppl. 276), 1–45.

Osborn, S. G., & West, D. J. (1978). The effectiveness of various predictors of criminal careers. *Journal of Adolescence, 1*, 101–117.

Osborn, S. G., & West, D. J. (1980). Do young delinquents really reform? *Journal of Adolescence, 3*, 99–114.

Patterson, G. R. (1982). *Coercive family interactions*. Eugene, OR: Castalia.

Patterson, G. R., & Stouthamer-Loeber, M. (1984). The correlation of family management practices and delinquency. *Child Development, 55*, 1299–1307.

Petersilia, J., Greenwood, P. W., & Lavin, M. (1977). *Criminal careers of habitual felons*. Santa Monica: Rand Corporation.

Pulkkinen, L. (1983). Search for alternatives to aggression in Finland. In A. P. Goldstein & M. Segall (Eds.), *Aggression in global perspective*. New York: Pergamon.

Polk, K. (1975). Schools and the delinquency experience. *Criminal Justice & Behavior, 2*, 315–338.

Prigmore, C. S. (1963). An analysis of rater reliability on the Glueck scale for the prediction of juvenile delinquency. *Journal of Criminal Law, Criminology, & Police Science, 54*, 30–41.

Reckless, W. C., & Dinitz, S. (1972). *The prevention of juvenile delinquency*. Columbus, OH: Ohio State University Press.

Reiss, A. J. (1951). The accuracy, efficiency, and validity of a prediction instrument. *American Journal of Sociology, 56*, 552–561.

Robins, L. N. (1966). *Deviant children grow up: A sociological and psychiatric study of sociopathic personality*. Baltimore: Williams & Wilkins.

Robins, L. N., Darvish, H. S., & Murphy, G. E. (1970). The long-term outcome for adolescent drug users: A follow-up study of 76 users and 146 nonusers. In J. Zubin & A. M. Freedman (Eds.), *The psychopathy of adolescence*. New York: Grune & Stratton.

Robins, L. N., & Hill, S. Y. (1966). Assessing the contribution of family structure, class and peer groups to juvenile delinquency. *Journal of Criminal Law, Criminology & Police Science, 57*, 325–334.

Robins, L. N., & Ratcliff, K. S. (1979). Risk factors in the continuation of childhood antisocial behavior into adulthood. *International Journal of Mental Health, 7*, 96–116.

Robins, L. N., West, P. A., & Herjanic, B. L. (1975). Arrests and delinquency in two generations: A study of Black urban families and their children. *Journal of Child Psychology & Psychiatry, 16*, 125–140.

Rutter, M. (1978). Family, area, and school influences in the genesis of conduct disorders. In L. A. Hersov, M. Berger, & D. Schaffer (Eds.), *Aggression and antisocial behavior in childhood and adolescence*. Oxford: Pergamon.

Rutter, M., Maugham, B., Mortimer, P., & Ouston, J. (1979). *15,000 hours—Secondary schools and their effects on children*. Cambridge, MA: Harvard University Press.

Scarpitti, F. R. (1964). Can teachers predict delinquency? *The Elementary School Journal, 65*, 130–136.

Schachar, R., Rutter, M., & Smith, A. (1981). The characteristics of situationally and pervasively hyperactive children: Implications for syndrome definition. *Journal of Child Psychology & Psychiatry, 22*, 375–392.

Shannon, L. W. (1978, August). *A cohort study of the relationship of adult criminal careers to juvenile careers*. Paper presented at the International Symposium on Selected Criminological Topics, University of Stockholm, Sweden.

Simcha-Fagan, O. (1979). The prediction of delinquent behavior over time: Sex-specific patterns related to official and survey reported delinquent behavior. In R. G. Simmons (Ed.), *Research in community and mental health: An annual compilation of research*. Greenwich, CT: JAI.

Simcha-Fagan, O., Langner, T. S., Gersten, J. C., & Eisenberg, J. G. (1975). *Violent and antisocial behavior: A longitudinal study of urban youth*. Unpublished Report of the Office of Child Development, (OCD-CB-480).

Spivack, G. (1983). *High risk early behaviors indicating vulnerability to delinquency in the community and school—A 15-year longitudinal study. Report to the Office of Juvenile Justice and Delinquency Prevention*. Philadelphia: Hahnemann University.

Spivack, G., & Cianci, N. (1987). High risk early behavior pattern and later delinquency. In J. D. Burchard & S. Burchard (Eds.), *Prevention of delinquent behavior*. Beverly Hills: Sage.

Stott, D. H., & Wilson, D. M. (1968). The prediction of early-adult criminality from school-age behaviors. *International Journal of Social Psychiatry, 14*, 5–8.

Stouthamer-Loeber, M. (1986). Lying as a problem behavior in children: A review. *Clinical Psychology Review, 6*, 267–289.

Tait, C. D., & Hodges, E. F. (1972). Follow-up study of Glueck table applied to a school population of problem boys and girls between the ages of five and fourteen. In S. Glueck & E. Glueck (Eds.), *Identification of predelinquents*. New York: Intercontinental Medical Book co.

Thompson, R. E. (1952). A validation of the Glueck social prediction scale for process to delinquency. *Journal of Criminal Law, Criminology, & Police Science, 43*, 451–470.

Tittle, C. R., Villemez, W. J., & Smith, D. A. (1978). The myth of social class and criminality: An empirical assessment of the empirical evidence. *American Sociological Review, 43*, 643–656.

Trevvett, N. B. (1972). Identifying delinquency-prone children. In S. Glueck & E.

Glueck (Eds.), *Identification of pre-delinquents*. New York: Intercontinental Medical Book Co.

Tuchfeld, B. S., Clayton, R. R., & Logan, J. A. (1982). Alcohol, drug use and delinquent and criminal behaviors. *Journal of Drug Issues, 12,* 185–198.

Voss, H. T. (1963). The predictive efficiency of the Glueck social prediction table. *Journal of Criminal Law & Criminology, 54,* 421–430.

Wadsworth, M. E. J. (1979). *Roots of delinquency, infancy, adolescence and crime.* Oxford: Robertson.

Wadsworth, M. E. J. (1980). Early life events and later behavioral outcomes in a British longitudinal study. In S. B. Sells, K. Crandell, M. Roff, J. S. Strauss, & W. Pollin (Eds.), *Human functioning in longitudinal perspective.* Baltimore: Williams & Wilkins.

West, D. J., & Farrington, D. P. (1973). *Who becomes delinquent.* London: Heinemann.

Wilson, H., & Herbert, G. W. (1978). *Parents and children of the inner city.* London: Routledge & Kegan Paul.

Wolfgang, M. E. (1977, September). *From boy to man—From delinquency to crime.* Paper presented at the National Symposium on the Serious Juvenile Offender, State of Minnesota, Minneapolis.

Wolfgang, M. E., Figlio, R. M., & Sellin, T. (1972). *Delinquency in a birth cohort.* Chicago: University of Chicago Press.

PART III

Promoting Social Competency and Coping Through the Schools

Social competency underlies effective functioning in many domains of human life and significantly influences life satisfaction, self-esteem, and psychological adjustment. It is within the context of early social relationships that these competencies emerge and mature. As children grow, they venture beyond their families and caregivers to function with greater autonomy amidst their peers. In this section we examine children's emerging social competency, and factors that promote its development and reduce the risk of subsequent interpersonal difficulties.

The school environment is one of the primary contexts for the development of social relationships during childhood. As such, the school setting represents a particularly important context for interventions designed to prevent the development of problematic interpersonal relationships. John Coie, Professor of Psychology at Duke University, David Rabiner, Assistant Professor of Psychology at the University of North Carolina at Greensboro, and John Lochman, Assistant Professor of Medical Psychology at Duke University Medical Center, discuss the importance of problematic peer relations for social development and examine the nature of peer rejection.

The work described in this chapter focuses upon youngsters who have been identified as in greatest need of help, an at-risk group, leading the authors to consider the complexities of defining risk populations. Coie and his colleagues present their ongoing work in the development and evaluation of programs designed to enhance children's social and academic competencies in order to prevent peer rejection and associated problems. They provide the reader with an intimate view of the successes, trade-offs, and limitations they have confronted in their own preventive interventions. In so doing, the authors enrich our appreciation of the necessary intricacies and evolution of preventive intervention designs.

An understanding of peer networks and the social support they provide would appear an obvious concern of those working in the schools. Yet, as Ana Mari Cauce and Debra Srebnik illustrate in the next chapter, little research has addressed these issues directly. Cauce, an Assistant Professor of Psychology at the University of Washington, and Srebnik, a doctoral candidate in clinical psychology at the University of Vermont, review research on youngsters' peer networks and social support systems and derive the implications of this work for school-based prevention efforts.

The authors demonstrate that an individual's social support network is not a unitary entity, but includes distinct groups of support providers. Different categories of providers (e.g., family members, friends, and formal school personnel) relate differentially to the youngsters' adjustment and competencies, a fact that is particularly important to the design and effectiveness of primary prevention programs. Cauce and Srebnik distinguish between peer support and peer group values, and consider the influence of each on social adjustment and competence. They argue that the degree to which interventionists address peer processes in their designs and evaluations may be critical in determining intervention effectiveness.

Social competency training has received particularly wide acclaim over the past decade, and has made its way into an ever increasing number of schools. Roger Weissberg, Associate Professor, Marlene Caplan, Associate Research Scientist, and Patricia Sivo, doctoral candidate, all of the Department of Psychology at Yale University, present a comprehensive overview and analysis of theoretical and practical issues in the conceptualization, design, implementation, evaluation, and dissemination of school-based preventive social competence promotion programs.

Weissberg and his colleagues offer an insightful critique of the conceptual model that currently guides most social competence promotion programs—the person-centered competence-enhancement approach. While its accomplishments have been many, its shortcomings present significant obstacles to reaping the full benefits of social competence training. The authors offer a new five-step conceptual framework to guide future endeavors, a model that focuses upon a number of significant developmental and ecological considerations for school-based social competence promotion programs.

Although social competency training has been integrated increasingly into the schools, little attention has been devoted to the ways in which such programs promote norms and values that may conflict with those of ethnically diverse communities. Mary Jane Rotheram-Borus, Associate Clinical Professor of Medical Psychology, Columbia University, and Sam Tsemberis, Assistant Clinical Professor of Psychiatry, New York University School of Medicine, address the complex issues related to the need to adapt social competency training programs to ethnically diverse populations.

Rotheram-Borus and Tsemberis examine the assumptions and implicit values of social competency training programs with regard to four dimensions: active versus passive manner of coping, group versus individual orientation, emotional expressiveness versus emotional restraint, and authoritarian versus egalitarian attitudes. They consider the fit between these implicit social values and those of various ethnic groups. The authors then turn to a series of strategies for improving social competency training programs in order to make them more effective for ethnically and developmentally diverse populations.

Moving beyond a specific focus on social competence and peer relations, Bruce Compas, Vicky Phares, and Normand Ledoux examine preventive interventions that have been developed to support children and adolescents in coping with life stress. Compas, an Associate Professor of Clinical Psychology at the University of Vermont, and Phares, a doctoral candidate in the same program, have been collaborating with Ledoux, a community psychologist of the Northeast Kingdom Mental Health Services, on such a program. In addition, Compas and his colleagues have been conducting a series of investigations of the processes involved in stress and coping in children and adolescents.

The authors present a cognitive-transactional model of stress and coping as it applies to children, adolescents, and their families. Within this context, they discuss variations in vulnerability to stress and the effectiveness of various patterns of coping, noting the developmental nature of these processes. Four dimensions of stress and coping preventive interventions are identified and used to analyze school-based programs and provide models for future research and program development. The case is made for the development of a comprehensive stress management program for children, parents, and teachers that focuses on the empowerment of participants.

7

Promoting Peer Relations in a School Setting

John D. Coie
David L. Rabiner
John E. Lochman

Identifying children at risk for various difficulties later in life, and then intervening with those children to reduce the likelihood that such difficulties will be experienced, is an important goal for psychologists and educators to pursue. This chapter will describe our efforts in pursuit of this goal over the past 12 years, including the factors contributing to the development of our intervention project, what that project has entailed, and what we have learned from the experience.

Intervention with a school-based population can follow two alternative models. First, one can institute a program on a school-wide basis designed to reduce the incidence of such negative events as dropping out or drug use. This approach assumes that all children can benefit from exposure to the intervention curriculum and makes no attempt to focus on individuals within the general population who are actually at greater risk for such outcomes. Classroom-based programs for training children in social problem-solving skills (e.g., Shure & Spivack, 1982; Weissberg, et al., 1981), are examples of this approach.

Alternatively, one can focus intervention efforts on a distinct segment of the population at special risk for future disorder. In other words, rather than spreading intervention resources over an entire group, which undoubtedly includes children who are likely to develop a particular disorder along with those who are not, an effort is made to identify those in greatest need of help and focus intervention efforts on them. This is the approach that we have taken in the work we will be describing.

The utility of this approach depends on being able to identify accurately an at-risk group. If one is going to intervene with a selective group, then one needs to be reasonably confident that the group is comprised of children who are more likely to make problematic adjustments in the absence of any intervention. After all, if children are going to develop adequately without help, then even though they may be experiencing some current difficulty, there is little basis for intervening with them in the interests of preventing the occurrence of some future disorder. One thus needs to be confident that the factors used to identify subjects for intervention truly have some predictive relation to later difficulty, and are not merely a marker of more transitory difficulty. It is also important, although not easy, to know whether the variables used to identify at-risk children are causally related to the consequences one is trying to prevent. This is particularly true since the variables by which subjects are identified frequently become the focus around which an intervention program is developed. In the intervention program we will be describing, we have chosen to intervene with socially rejected children (i.e., children who are disliked by their peers) because of the evidence that such children are at risk for various negative outcomes later in life. As we will later describe, our efforts have been directed toward improving the peer status of these youngsters, based on the assumption that being rejected is somehow causally related to subsequent difficulty. If this is not true, however, and social rejection is instead only correlated with some other variable that causally relates to poor adjustment, then we might succeed in improving the peer relationships of our intervention group and still do little to prevent their subsequent difficulty.

Identifying the Risk Population

Why have we chosen children rejected by their peers as an appropriate group for intervention? To date, considerable evidence has accumulated suggesting that childhood peer problems are predictive of various adjustment difficulties later in life. For example, Kohlberg, LaCrosse, and Ricks (1972) identified childhood peer relationships as one of few variables that were consistently related to subsequent maladjustment. More recently, additional evidence has emerged that supports this conclusion. This literature will be reviewed briefly.

There have been numerous retrospective studies suggesting that disturbed childhood peer relations are related to subsequent disorder. The basic methodology of those studies involves identifying a group of disturbed adults, and then searching for childhood characteristics that differentiate them from an adult group judged to have made satisfactory adjustments. A problem with such studies is that they may generate erroneous conclusions about the relation between life history and disordered outcomes because the question of how frequently individuals with similar backgrounds made adequate adjustments is not addressed. Nonetheless, they do provide suggestive evidence that can form the basis for methodologically superior longitudinal investigations.

In an early attempt to identify common childhood characteristics of adult schizophrenics (Kasanin & Veo, 1932), 50% were remembered by their elementary school teachers as being friendless and disliked. Similar conclusions of disturbed early peer relations in the background of adult schizophrenics were reported by Bower, Shellhamer, and Dailey (1960), Fleming and Ricks (1970), Friedlander (1945), Pollack, Woerner, Goodman, and Greenberg (1966), Ricks and Berry (1970), Stabenau and Pollin (1970), Watt (1972), and Watt, Stolorow, Lubensky, and McClelland (1970). Although several of these studies lack adequate control groups and are confounded by informants reporting on individuals they knew to be disturbed, the consistency of the findings is impressive.

While the preceding studies provide evidence of disturbed peer relations in the backgrounds of adult schizophrenics, a series of studies by Roff (1960, 1961, 1963) indicates the presence of early peer difficulties in a variety of adult "poor outcome" groups. Roff's work is based on large numbers of individuals seen at child guidance clinics who later entered some branch of military service. Patient groups consisted of individuals whose military service records indicated a particular undesirable outcome (i.e., psychotic, neurotic, or bad conduct). Control cases, in contrast, were child guidance clinic cases with a history of good military service. Peer-related information contained in clinic files was blindly abstracted for the different groups, and then rated as suggesting good, poor, or neutral peer relations. A global assessment of early peer relations as being "good," "poor," or "undecided" was then made based on these individually abstracted items.

The contrast in peer ratings between controls and the various poor outcome groups was striking. Members of the three bad outcome groups consistently had early peer relations that were judged to be poor, while the opposite was true for controls. Compared to the other childhood variables on which Roff assessed his good and poor outcome groups (i.e., information about parents, health and nervous habits, school performance, psychological test results, and psychiatric evaluations), the difference was greatest for the peer relations variable. It is also noteworthy, for reasons that will become apparent shortly, that the majority of bad outcome cases judged to have had poor early peer relations were regarded by their teachers and peers as an actively unpleasant group of youngsters.

Roff's work demonstrates that poor early peer relations are not restricted to the backgrounds of schizophrenics, but instead precede a variety of psychological problems. Similar conclusions were reached by Cowen, Pederson, Babigian, Izzo, and Trost (1973) who collected extensive information (psychological test data, parent and teacher interviews-behavior observations, and subjects' peer status) on third graders in a county school system. When subjects were 18, county psychiatric registers were searched to identify all psychiatric contacts by members of this cohort. Among subjects with a psychiatric history, the variable that most differentiated them from nonpsychiatric subjects was the presence of early peer difficulties. These studies suggest that intervening with children who have peer relationship problems may prevent them from experiencing a variety of difficulties as they develop.

In addition to the various retrospective investigations noted above, several longitudinal reports have documented the relationship between poor childhood peer relations and subsequent disorder. Such investigations are based on a *follow-forward* design in which children with known characteristics are tracked over the course of their development. These assessed characteristics can then be related to the occurrence of particular outcomes in a predictive fashion. This design avoids an important drawback associated with retrospective studies, in that the frequency with which children matched on particular variables attain different outcomes can be computed. This reduces the possibility of overestimating the importance of a particular childhood characteristic in the etiology of a subsequent disorder.

Based on the results of Roff's earlier retrospective studies, Roff, Sells, and Golden (1972) conducted a large-scale investigation of the relation between childhood peer difficulties and later delinquency. Peer status information was collected for approximately 38,000 third through sixth graders in schools throughout Minneapolis and Texas. Children were asked to indicate several classmates that they liked most and several others that they liked least. Children's overall social preference scores (i.e., liked-most nominations minus liked-least nominations) were used to classify them in low-, middle-, or high-status peer groups. Three to four years later, delinquency information was obtained for a selected number of male children in the sample. (Delinquency was defined as contact with juvenile authorities formal enough to result in the preparation of a case file.) The largest number of delinquents were from the lowest peer status group three to four years earlier, and approximately 20% of children from the lowest peer status group were delinquent at follow-up. Within a representative sample of school children, therefore, low peer status was predictive of delinquent behavior. It is interesting to note that boys in this low status group were again described to be an actively unpleasant group of youngsters, "complaining, quarrelsome, critical, touchy, domineering, and sometimes inclined to force themselves on others."

Although these studies clearly support the connection between childhood peer difficulties and adult disorder, important questions remain concerning the variety of early peer problems that are most worrisome. For example, children with peer relationship difficulties could have no friends and be actively disliked by their peer group, or could have no friends but be more or less ignored by their peer group. The former would be more likely to be aggressive, disruptive, obnoxious children (i.e., the kind that Roff appeared to be talking about), while the latter might be shy and withdrawn children who simply did not interact very much with peers. Although Roff's work suggests it is more likely to be an actively disliked group that is at greater long-term risk, none of the studies reported have addressed this question directly. One study that did directly compare the adult adjustment of children who were characterized as either aggressive or withdrawn (Havighurst, Bowman, Liddle, Matthews, & Pierce, 1962) indicates poor adult outcomes for both groups. Before implementing an intervention product that selected children based on difficulty in getting along with peers, it was important to differentiate what kind of early peer difficulties are most strongly associated with long-term risk.

Defining Peer Rejection

As we were especially interested in comparing the outcomes of actively disliked children with more passively ignored children, an initial task was to reliably identify these different groups. To do this required asking children about peers that they like (i.e., positive nominations) *and* peers that they dislike (i.e., negative nominations), because peer acceptance and peer rejection are only slightly negatively correlated, and the social status distinctions one can make using sociometric data depend on whether acceptance and rejection scores are combined to define status or whether status is defined by acceptance alone (Coie, Dodge, & Coppotelli, 1982). In the latter case, low acceptance scores (i.e., few nominations for being liked) would include children who are actively disliked (i.e., rejected) along with children who are neither liked nor disliked (i.e., neglected). Including a negative nomination item, however, permits these two groups to be distinguished.

A reason for not including a negative nomination procedure in past research reflected concerns about asking children to identify peers that they dislike. However, Hayvren and Hymel (1984) observed children both before and after administering sociometrics and found no differences in the negative treatment of most- or least-preferred peers. Our experience also supports the conclusion that, when administered with appropriate cautions about confidentiality, there are no adverse social consequences to using negative item sociometrics.

The sociometric procedure used in our project has, thus, included both positive and negative nomination items. Typically, the procedure is conducted in the classroom and is introduced to students as a study of childrens' friendships. Children are provided with a roster listing all other children in their grade, along with associated code numbers by which they are identified. They are then asked to write down the code numbers of the three people in their grade that they like the most, and the three grademates that they like the least. The importance of maintaining confidentiality about one's responses is emphasized, and the use of code numbers as a means for maintaining confidentiality is explained.

After this sociometric information is collected, the different peer status categories can be identified according to the combination of liked-most (LM) and liked-least (LL) nominations that each child receives. In the method we have adopted (Coie, Dodge, & Coppotelli, 1982), the number of LM and LL nominations for each child is transformed into standardized scores within grade level. The reliabilities for LM and LL scores was found to be 0.65 over a 12-week period. These scores are then used to derive two new sociometric variables—a social preference score (LM-LL), and a social impact score (LM + LL)—which are also standardized within grade. Popular children are defined as those with a standardized social preference score of greater than 1.0, an LM standardized score more than 0, and an LL standardized score less than 0. Popular children are youngsters who receive frequent nominations for being liked most and few or no nominations for being liked least, and the opposite is true for rejected children. Children are considered rejected if their standardized social preference score is less than -1.0, their LL (liked-least) standardized score is greater than 0 and their LM standardized score is less than 0. Neglected children are defined as being a low-visibility group. They have standardized social impact scores of less than -1 and receive no votes for being liked most. In contrast to the rejected group, however, they also receive few nominations for being liked least. Two other status groups, an average status group, and a group we have chosen to call *controversial*, are also identified by these sociometric variables. Average status children are those with standardized social preference scores between -.05 and .05, whereas controversial children are those with social impact scores greater than 1, and LM and LL scores both greater than 0. They are, in other words, a high-visibility group.

Although there is a history and a logic to this system for categorizing children into peer status groups, ultimately the value of the system depends on the usefulness of the distinctions that emerge from it. One way to approach this issue is to determine predictive validity of the different status categories. To this end, a cohort of 112 fifth graders on whom sociometric information had been collected was followed across their school years and various types of outcome information was collected when they were in 12th grade. The outcome measures collected included academic performance measures, contact with police or juvenile authorities, years truant, years retained in grade, and dropping out of school.

Compared to the other status groups, rejected children experienced a significantly greater number of negative outcomes than other children (Kupersmidt, 1983). Although rejected and neglected children were at approximately equal risk for truancy, rejected children were more likely than others either to be left back, drop out of school, or become delinquent. A second study in which outcomes were predicted from third-grade status found similar results (Rabiner, 1985). This suggests that rejected children are at greater long-term risk than neglected or other nonrejected children.

Stability of Peer Rejection

The results of two other studies, both focusing on the stability of rejected status, have also increased our confidence in targeting rejected children for intervention. As noted previously, the stability of the factors by which children are selected for intervention is important, since it makes little sense to intervene with children displaying a certain characteristic if that characteristic is unstable.

In the first study, Coie and Dodge (1983) examined the continuity of children's peer status over a five-year period. Two cohorts of children were included: a third-grade cohort and a fifth-grade cohort. Status was assessed in year 1 according to the sociometric procedure already described, and then again in each of four successive years. As can be seen from Table 7.1, for the fifth-grade sample rejected status was reasonably stable, as nearly half (42%) of children who were rejected in year 1 also were rejected in year 5. It is interesting to note that children who were rejected in year 1 also were significantly more likely to emerge as neglected in year 5. In sum, 60% of children rejected in grade five were part of a relatively friendless social status group (rejected or neglected) five years later. This suggests that rejected children who stayed involved with peers did so in a manner that perpetuated their being disliked, while others, perhaps as a consequence of being disliked, tended to gradually remove themselves from peer interaction. This contrasts sharply with the outcome of neglected fifth graders, the majority of whom (69%) were no longer part of a socially deviant status group (i.e., rejected or neglected) at the conclusion of the study.

While stability over the first year was quite similar for both the third- and fifth-grade cohorts, the third-grade cohort was much less stable as time went on. Rejected third graders were no more likely to be rejected five years later (in junior high school) than were members of any other status group. Since rejected status does not have especially good long-term stablity when assessed in a third-grade sample, it may be problematic to intervene based on peer status measured at this relatively young age. This factor has implications for the results of the intervention project that will be discussed shortly.

Coie and Kupersmidt (1983) next examined the stability of peer status across different peer situations. In this study, fourth-grade boys of different social status met in play groups once a week for six weeks. Five of the groups contained boys who already knew one another, while five were comprised of unfamiliar boys. After each meeting, the boys were asked to rate how much they liked the other children in their group. This procedure allowed us to assess the emergence of social status in newly formed groups and the extent to which a child's status is reestablished with a new group of peers.

In the familiar and, more importantly, the unfamiliar groups, the status of rejected children was quickly reestablished. The fact that status was reestablished when rejected children interacted with unfamiliar peers suggests that the social problems of these children transcend their immediate social situation and are not simply the result of unfortunate peer circumstances. This suggests that intervention is necessary to help rejected children develop more satisfying peer relationships. For neglected boys, the results were again different. They appeared to benefit from the opportunity to interact with new peers

TABLE 7.1 Percentage of Rejected Children Who Continue to Be Rejected
Across Successive Years

Cohort	Second Year	Third Year	Fourth Year	Fifth Year
Third Grade	47%	38%	23%	13%
Fifth Grade	52%	48%	50%	42%

and became considerably more outgoing in the unfamiliar peer situation. In contrast to rejected children, therefore, neglected children
may not require direct intervention to establish more satisfactory peer
relationships, and their status as neglected youngsters is not likely to
transcend different social situations.

Thus, there is considerable evidence that points toward socially
rejected children as a group appropriate for preventive intervention.
The timing of an intervention may be restricted to certain ages because of age differences in the stability of rejected status. Status in
third grade appears to be less stable than from fifth grade onward,
even though some data on the prediction of disorder (Rabiner, 1985)
suggest reasonable levels of predictability of disorder from third-
grade status.

Behavioral Bases for Peer Rejection

Given that rejected children are an appropriate group for intervention, the question becomes one of how to intervene. In our project,
which is consistent with the approach taken by others working in this
area, we have focused on aspects of rejected children's social behavior
that contributes to their being disliked. In focusing primarily on overt
behavior, we do not mean to deny or minimize the importance of less
obvious psychological factors or family factors that may play an
equally important role. Rather, we are trying to change the social
relationships of rejected children in the most direct way possible, and
we are also selecting an approach that is feasible to undertake in a
school-based setting.

In planning an intervention designed to alter the problematic social
behavior of rejected children and to improve their social relationships, it is important to know what aspects of their behavior lead to
their being disliked. Although the behavior associated with social rejection differs somewhat for boys and girls, and for children of different
ages, a remarkable degree of consistency has emerged in studies relating social behavior to social status. A brief review of research in this

area will be helpful in highlighting the consistencies that have emerged.

In a review of the behavioral bases for peer rejection, Coie, Dodge, and Kupersmidt (in press) point to several aversive behavior patterns that are consistently linked to rejection, as well as some evidence for the lack of certain social skills. Inappropriate aggression, disruptive and rule-violating activity, and off-task behavior in class have all been associated with peer rejection. While there is evidence for social withdrawal being related to rejection, it is not clear how much this is a consequence of peer rejection as opposed to being a cause of rejection. Rejected children also show deficiencies in critical social skills, such as knowing how to join others at group play. Likewise, they are described as less cooperative and helpful than other children. For example, Asarnow (1983), and Vosk, Forehand, Parker, and Rickard (1982) found that rejected children were more often off-task in the classroom and initiated aversive interactions with peers more often than popular children.

Evidence for behavioral differences between high- and low-status children does not necessarily provide conclusive evidence for identifying the focus of intervention for rejected children, since the contrast may say as much about the deviance of popular children from the norm as it does about the deficiencies of rejected children. For this reason, Dodge, Coie, and Brakke (1982) contrasted the behavior of average, popular, and rejected children in two related investigations. In an initial study, fifth-grade boys and girls were observed in both playground and classroom settings. As in the previously described studies, rejected children were more frequently observed to be off-task, less often found to be on-task, and were more aggressive than both the popular and average groups. In a second study of third- and fifth-grade boys in which a neglected group was also included, rejected boys differed from the other groups in ways similar to those just described. Neglected boys, in contrast, were more often alone but on-task than other children and also made fewer social approaches. This difference in the social behavior of rejected and neglected children underscores the importance of utilizing a sociometric procedure that combines positive and negative nominations to identify children in different status groups. When only a positive nomination procedure is used, the low-status group that results is likely to include both rejected and neglected children whose social behavior is actually quite distinct.

Putallaz and Wasserman (in press) have written an excellent review of research on the inability of rejected children to successfully join other children at play. The results of three different investigations of this process (Dodge, Schlundt, Schocken, & Delugach, 1983; Putallaz, 1983; Putallaz & Gottman, 1981) provide a consistent conclusion: Children who are rejected by peers fail in their efforts to join peers at play because they fail to consider the activities and purposes of the children they wish to join, and thus fail to adjust their behavior to match the group, as more socially successful children do. Sometimes, in groups where they are already established as rejected, rejected children react to entry situations either by hovering around the fringes of the group as though afraid they will be rebuffed or by making self-focused and self-aggrandizing statements that disrupt the group. These latter behaviors have been characterized by Putallaz and Wasserman as defensive reactions to the fear of not being allowed to join.

The studies just reviewed present a reasonably coherent picture of the links between behavior and rejected status among elementary school children. Rejected children are more frequently involved in negative interaction with peers, particularly aggressive and argumentative interactions. They are more frequently off-task and are involved in fewer positive peer interactions. Although this description is reasonably representative of rejected children overall, there are gender differences. For example, Ladd (1983) found gender differences in the social behavior of rejected children suggesting that while aggressive behavior is highly relevant to social status differences among boys, social participation may be more relevant to status among girls. A similar conclusion was reached by Coie and Whidby (1986), who noted that while aggression was linked to rejection in their sample of third graders, the effect was much stronger for boys than for girls. In contrast, teachers and peers described rejected girls to be more unhappy and socially isolated than other girls. This pattern was not indicated for boys.

A problem with the studies just reviewed is that by focusing on behavior differences among children whose peer group status was already defined, it is impossible to separate behavior responsible for the development of rejected status from behavior that may result from being rejected. This confound was first pointed out by Moore (1967) who noted that an awareness of how one is perceived may lead a child to behave in ways that are congruent with his social position. For example, a child who is aware of being rejected may expect others to treat him badly, and then misinterpret others' actions based on this expectation (Dodge, 1980). Alternatively, children who are disliked may adopt avoidant or competitive goals because they expect that prosocial initiatives will fail (Asher & Renshaw, 1981). The peer group may also act differently toward a child who is rejected. Dodge and Frame (1982) have demonstrated that peers develop biased perceptions of a child once that child has been identified by the peer group as disliked. The identical behavior of popular and rejected children may thus be evaluated differently by peers. In response to this "unfairness," an unpopular child may respond by becoming angry, or perhaps by giving up and pulling back from peer interaction. Such dynamics make it difficult to know whether the behavior that has been reported to characterize rejected children explains why they were rejected initially or is better understood as a consequence of being rejected. This has important implications for intervening with such children, since failing to alter behaviors that are actually responsible for the development of rejected status will reduce the likelihood of success.

Two recent investigations (Coie & Kupersmidt, 1983; Dodge, 1983) addressed this important question. The Coie and Kupersmidt study was discussed earlier, and involved bringing together unfamiliar children of known social status for six weekly one-hour play sessions. By interviewing boys about their preferences for other children in their group after each meeting and coding the behavior of boys during their interaction together, the relationship between social behavior and emerging social status was ascertained. The results of this study indicate that the aggressive characteristics of rejected children are not merely consequences of their rejected status. In the unfamiliar groups, rejected boys made more hostile and aversive comments than the other boys. They also engaged in more physical aggression than all but the average status boys. Although the incidence of physical aggression among average status boys is surprising, a subsequent analysis helps resolve this confusion. While average and rejected boys were judged by adult coders to be equally likely to become angry and aggressive when such behavior appeared justified, only the rejected boys displayed anger and aggression without apparent justification (Coie & Benenson, 1982). This suggests that the aggressive behavior of rejected children is more likely to be regarded as unprovoked and deviant by the peer group, and is consistent with their tendency to assume that others have acted toward them in hostile ways when available cues do not warrant this interpretation (Dodge & Frame, 1982). Another important finding was the increase in solitary inappropriate behavior observed to occur with rejected boys during the last two group sessions. This suggests that as boys came to be rejected in these new groups of peers, they responded by withdrawing from social interaction.

A second study employing a similar design (Dodge, 1983) brought together groups of eight unfamiliar boys, each unselected for prior status. The groups met daily for eight play sessions, and after the final session each boy was interviewed to find out whom he liked and disliked in his group. These nominations were then used to determine the social status of each boy within his particular play group. Boys' behavior during the eight play group sessions was then studied to determine behavior patterns associated with the development of different status types.

As in the previous study, Dodge found that boys who became rejected engaged in more inappropriate play, talked more, hit others more, and made more hostile comments than average status boys. Although rejected boys made frequent social approaches during the early sessions, these attempts tended to be unsuccessful, and they became increasingly isolated over the course of the eight-session groups. These results are consistent with the Coie and Kupersmidt findings and suggest that social withdrawal is likely to be a consistent consequence of rejection. This has important implications for intervention as it appears that merely trying to increase the social participation of rejected children, in the absence of providing them with more appropriate social skills, is unlikely to be effective.

These studies clearly indicate that aggressive and disruptive behavior is an important aspect of why children are rejected. It also suggests goals to pursue in intervening with rejected children: decreasing antisocial, aggressive behavior and increasing prosocial behavior. It is important to recognize that not all rejected children are aggressive. For example, in a sample of rejected third graders, approximately 50% were one standard deviation above the mean on peer descriptions of "starting fights" or "being disruptive" (Coie, 1985). While this supports the relation between aggressive, antisocial behavior and rejected status that has been discussed, it is also true that half of this rejected sample did not share these characteristics. What kinds of characteristics do these nonaggressive rejected children have? Rejected girls, as has been discussed, are likely to be seen as isolated and unhappy. Physical attractiveness has also been found to be correlated with social status, with unattractive children having a greater likelihood of being rejected (Langlois & Stephan, 1981). In working with these children, we have also found that a certain number present as rather strange or odd and are rejected primarily for this reason. The important point is that while clear behavioral correlates of social rejection have been demonstrated, rejected children should not be considered a homogeneous group. This diversity suggests that intervention focused on a particular cause of rejection is unlikely to be effective with all rejected children. An important goal for future research is to establish what kind of intervention works best with different types of rejected youngsters.

Methods for Improving Peer Status

Having discussed the reasons for intervening with rejected children and some of the reasons why children are rejected, we will briefly review previous intervention efforts with low-status children. Most early approaches to intervention (Allen, Hart, Buell, Harris, & Wolf, 1964) were based on the assumption that unpopular children lacked sufficient opportunities for peer interaction, and focused on increasing their rates of social participation. As already noted, this approach has obvious problems, as it fails to address the behavioral problems responsible for low social acceptance.

More recently, intervention efforts have focused on teaching unpopular children skills that will promote positive interaction with peers. Several investigators have tried to improve the social status of low-accepted children by this positive skills training approach (Bierman & Furman, 1984; Gresham & Nagle, 1980; Ladd, 1981; LaGreca & Santogrossi, 1980; Oden & Asher, 1977). Although the methods of instruction have differed, including both direct coaching of target skills and modeling by videotaped peers, the emphasis has been on promoting such behaviors as sharing, cooperation, communication, supportiveness, and complimenting others. Although each study has shown some effectiveness for the coaching procedure, the impact on actual peer status has been variable. In fact, only Ladd demonstrated significant gains in social acceptance that were evident both at posttesting and at follow-up (Oden and Asher also obtained significant improvement at follow-up). It should be noted that Ladd's method of selecting children for the intervention with low frequencies of the kinds of prosocial behavior taught in the program may have eliminated many socially active rejected children from his sample. In particular, many aggressive rejected children may have been eliminated since such children would tend to be of the more socially active type. The utility of a positive skills training approach for improving the social behavior *and* social acceptance of rejected children has thus not been conclusively demonstrated for the entire range of rejected children.

Although training rejected children in positive play skills has been a successful technique for improving the social relationships of some children, the mixed effectiveness of this approach has led to the search for other approaches. One line of inquiry that has just begun to be explored relates to the distinction between social skills, on the one hand, and social goals and expectations, on the other. For example, the behavior of some rejected children may be affected by expectations that they will fail (Asher & Renshaw, 1981). Putallaz and Wasserman (in press) note that some rejected children approach a group of classmates at play as though they expect to have difficulty joining. The morphology of their entry behavior reflects these expectations and is empirically related to failure at joining new groups. Rabiner (1987) has demonstrated that the social effectiveness of rejected boys can be enhanced by giving them positive expectations for encounters with new peers. Whether these results will translate into a treatment procedure with long-term effectiveness has yet to be explored.

Another approach to improving the successfulness of social skills intervention has been to focus more on the aversive behavior patterns that are related to peer rejection. While the positive skill training approach represents a strategy of substituting socially effective behaviors for socially ineffective and aversive behaviors, there is evidence that the impact of this strategy is limited (Bierman, Miller, & Stabb, 1987). Instead it may be necessary to combine positive social skills coaching with other social skills training focused on the management of anger and the use of goal-setting procedures to reduce the incidence of aggressive and disruptive behavior (Lochman, 1985).

Implementation Decisions

Before describing the intervention curriculum used in our project, a discussion of the pros and cons of intervening in the school setting is appropriate. There are several obvious advantages to intervening in the school. First, the school is the easiest place to identify a target population. It is difficult, in fact, to imagine conducting large-scale sociometric interviews in any other setting. Second, the school is also the location of most peer activity and is the place where much of rejected children's social difficulty occurs and where newly developed skills can be practiced. Third, school-based interventions provide the easiest access to the target population. Once the cooperation of school personnel has been enlisted, ready access to children in need of assistance can be obtained.

Despite these advantages, there are problems with a school-based intervention program that should be considered. Although many teachers are cooperative and supportive of intervention efforts (some, in fact, are quite happy to have a disruptive child temporarily removed from the class), others are not. Teachers are primarily interested in teaching academic skills and may fail to see the merit in removing a child from class for the purpose of improving his or her social relationships. When the cooperation and support of a child's teacher has not been obtained, it is extremely difficult to work effectively with that child. Cooperation from teachers is especially important since it is helpful and often necessary for a child's teacher to participate in monitoring his or her progress in targeted areas.

The space available for intervention at many schools is not likely to be optimal. When there is a private room available, it may be cramped and cluttered with extra school supplies. In other cases no private space may be available, and the corner of a library or multipurpose room may be the best the school can provide. Under these circumstances, when one may be working with a child in full view of other children, the child can become easily distracted or embarrassed. This latter possibility is especially important to consider, as it relates to the potential stigmatizing effects of removing rejected children from the classroom to work with them. Children are likely to be curious about why they were selected to be in a "special class," and if only unpopular children are included, they may become aware that it has something to do with their social status. There are ways to minimize this possibility, however, that we will subsequently discuss. We have also observed that being in a special activity often becomes a positive source of status for some children. Often the participants in our program were permitted to select classmates to join them in the a social skills training activities, and this gave them some status with peers, as well as providing them with positive play experiences with those who were chosen.

Another factor to consider before proceeding with a preventive intervention project in the schools concerns the age group to be targeted for intervention. The decision about when to intervene is subject to conflicting arguments based on the developmental principle that the younger the child is, the more readily change takes place. One argument is that it is easier to help younger children change their social behavior than the older children; younger children's habits are less well entrenched. Younger children may be less likely to be self-conscious about becoming involved in a curriculum of social skills training and, hence, less resistant to getting involved with it. The curriculum for younger children may be simpler because the social norms and patterns of interaction are less complicated than those of older children, and, thus, it is easier to get younger children in synchrony with their peers. Further, early intervention may spare the child more pain of rejection. All of these reasons would suggest that intervention should begin in the early grades, or even in kindergarten or preschool.

On the other hand, as we have intimated earlier, the timing of intervention should be related to the point in development that rejected status reliably predicts long-term disorder. The predictive validity of a variable for identifying risk for future disorder depends on the reliability and stability of that variable. An unreliable predictor will lead to the identification of unacceptable numbers of false positives and false negatives. Furthermore, if the initial measure of a successful intervention is the degree of change in criterion scores for the experimental and control groups, an unreliable or unstable criterion will make it difficult to evaluate the initial success of the intervention project because of regression to the mean in the postintervention scores of subjects selected because of their extreme scores. As we have seen, the stability of peer rejection increases with age, suggesting that it is better to wait to administer a preventive intervention program until the point when rejection is a more stable social phenomenon.

The choice of an age level for initiating preventive interventions with children at social risk for disorder involves a difficult trade-off between ease of intervention and stability of the criterion variable. In the case of the intervention study we will describe in the remainder of this chapter, we initially opted to compromise. We planned to identify our risk sample by means of sociometric data collected at the end of the fourth grade, intervene during the fifth grade, and conduct a follow-up assessment of the effectiveness of the intervention in the sixth grade. At this point members of the risk sample would be identified as stably improved or rejected and the long-term consequences of stable peer rejection would be assessed beginning in the first year of junior high school (seventh grade).

The fact that we were required to change these plans just prior to implementing them speaks to one additional aspect of the costs and benefits of conducting prevention projects in a school setting. During the year in which a pilot intervention was conducted with a group of fifth-grade rejected children, the school system switched over from a junior high school system to a middle school system. This meant that the transition year for children took place in sixth grade rather than seventh grade. As a result, it was necessary to screen children sociometrically in the third-grade year so that intervention could take place in the fourth grade and leave a year to follow-up the stability of status in the fifth grade in the same school setting. Otherwise, the stability of peer status at follow-up would have been assessed in a new peer setting under circumstances where social status is often disrupted, at least temporarily. The impact of this shift of plans for the research design was not to be realized until much later, but the experience of shifting a research design to meet the changing goals of the collaborating school systems was instructive.

The Intervention Program

Children were identified to participate in the intervention program based on the sociometric scoring procedure described previously. This screening took place in the spring of the third-grade year for three successive cohorts of students in 11 schools. The school population was predominantly black and from lower socioeconomic status families. Over the three years, more than 1600 children were screened. Each year approximately 100 rejected children were identified and parent permission was solicited from the subgroup that was randomly assigned to the intervention sample. On average, consent was obtained for about 90% of the children. However, given the low income level of many of the families in this school system, it was not unusual for children in the project to change schools in mid-year, sometimes more than once, resulting in attrition of subjects.

Based on the rejected childrens' academic achievements test scores and teacher reports, a poor achieving subgroup was identified as requiring academic tutoring in addition to social relations training. The inclusion of academic tutoring in the intervention curriculum was based on previous evidence that tutoring underachieving rejected children can increase both their academic skills and their social status among peers (Coie & Krehbiel, 1984). Rejected children not identified as having academic problems received only the social skills training portion of the curriculum.

The social relations training component of the intervention curriculum was provided by intervention staff members who worked on a part-time basis, typically graduate students in clinical and counseling psychology. In the first two years of the project, academic tutoring was also provided by this part-time staff. However, it became clear that they were not giving sufficient time to the tutoring because teachers were limiting their contract with the children. One reason for this was that teachers perceived the staff as persons dealing primarily with a social curriculum and were reluctant to have children spend more than two sessions per week with them. The staff themselves were, in fact, primarily invested in the social training curriculum, and given a restricted amount of time, devoted most of it to that curriculum. In the third year, academic tutoring was conducted by advanced undergraduates enrolled in a child clinical psychology course taught by the first author, as was the case with the earlier Coie and Krehbiel study. Teachers had no reluctance to allow this separate tutoring staff to take children for two sessions a week in addition to those taken up by the social skills training staff. Each session lasted approximately 45 minutes. Each staff person was assigned to work with children at one or two schools. In addition to reducing the amount of driving time between schools, having staff members concentrate on particular schools proved to be important in helping to develop cooperative relationships with school personnel. The staff attended weekly supervision meetings and staff meetings, discussing procedural issues and ongoing training issues.

The intervention program began in early October and continued through April, and spending this amount of time working in the schools requires a close and cooperative working relationship with the host schools. To achieve this, systematic efforts were made to understand teachers' perceptions of children's needs and difficulties, to obtain feedback from school personnel about their reactions to our assessment procedures and intervention efforts, and to increase their acceptance of the intervention staff and of the program. The intervention staff was available to consult with teachers about problems they might be having with any children in their classroom, not just those children in the project. This created the occasional dilemma of having teachers request assistance with rejected children who were part of our control group, but had not been identified to the teachers as such. Our policy was to minimize the issue of rejected status with teachers, and, thus, we did not identify control subjects to teachers.

Before making contact with children in the program, staff members reviewed preintervention assessment data on the children they were working with. These data included behavior observations taken during the previous spring, teacher checklist information on social behavior, self-concept information, and achievement test results for the low-achieving subjects. After meeting with a child's teacher to obtain his or her perspective, staff observed their subjects in the classroom and playground to get a first-hand view of them before being introduced to them.

When children were introduced to the staff they knew only that their parents had agreed to have them participate in a special set of classes on social relations training. They were not told they had been chosen because they were disliked by peers, since this would be intrusive and potentially destructive. They were told, instead, that their teachers had recommended them as someone who would be good to work with. Some children spontaneously described themselves as not having friends, while others persistently described themselves as having many friends. The latter often were not very motivated to try out ideas presented in the program, and staff had to develop additional techniques to motivate them.

Social skills program. The program was structured in terms of four major units spread across 36 sessions. One unit provided training in social problem-solving skills (Spivack & Shure, 1974). A second dealt with partner play skills and was derived from programs developed by Oden and Asher (1977) and Ladd (1981). A third unit provided training in group entry skills and was based on research by Putallaz (Putallaz, 1983; Putallaz & Gottman, 1981). The fourth unit focused on anger-coping skills (Lochman, Burch, Curry, & Lampron, 1984; Lochman, Lampron, Burch, & Curry, 1985; Lochman, Nelson, & Sims, 1981). Staff worked primarily with individuals for 26 sessions in which concepts were introduced, videotapes were observed for modeling effects and discussion, and some practice and goal setting was conducted. In some cases children who had trouble talking with an adult were worked with along with another child in the program. Group and paired play sessions comprised the remaining 10 sessions, allowing children to practice social skills and strategies they had been working on in individual sessions. Videotaping was sometimes used in these practice sessions.

The unit on social problem solving provided the basic framework for the total program, because it allowed the instructor to introduce other units as types of social situations in which the child may think of goals, problems, and best solutions. The seven scheduled problem-solving sessions focused on steps for problem identification, goal identification, inhibition of impulsive responses, generation of alternative solutions, and consideration of consequences to solutions. The more that children were able to consider varied alternative solutions to social problems, such as being left out of a game or being teased by peers, the more it was anticipated that they would be able to try out some of these alternatives in real social situations. However, as the importance of particular changes in social behavior became evident for a child, the child was encouraged to role play and practice the most adaptive behavioral solutions for these situations, and goals for change were sometimes established in the form of behavior contracts. Extensive use was made of a "problem-solving ladder" to make these steps concrete, and most of the students were able to help the staff member present the problem-solving process to their whole class.

The partner play unit consisted of nine sessions focusing on how to develop and maintain dyadic interactions with peers. This section initially emphasized use of nonverbal communication through eye contact, body language, and voice tone, and then proceeded to more complex interpersonal skills, such as negotiating, cooperating, and accepting rejection. Rehearsal and practice of these skills with peers was stressed in this section.

In the third unit, 14 sessions covered group entry skills. Skills included being able to recognize how "closed" or "open" the group was, what the group norms or rules were, who the group leader was, and the style of group interaction. Various strategies for joining different kinds of groups were then outlined and practiced in small group sessions.

Finally, the last four sessions focused on how to cope with strong emotional reactions such as anger and disappointment in interpersonal situations. Methods for inhibiting impulsive responses, reframing the ways in which one "wins" in an interpersonal conflict, and the use of coping self-statements were stressed.

The intervention program has been an evolving, flexible one, and the relative number of sessions directed at each unit has changed over the past two years. More importantly, flexibility has been stressed in applying this intervention to individual children, spending more time on units that are critical for a particular child, and less time on units that do not have impact on significant problems for the child. Thus, children who did not have problems with aggression might not spend as much time on the anger-coping unit, and children who had good partner play skills would spend less time on that unit.

After the completion of each unit, decisions about next steps were based on the children's needs. For children for whom anger control and aggression were especially salient issues, the anger-coping unit was often taken up second in their curriculum since it dealt with these areas. For the children for whom making friends and having fun with others was a greater problem, the group-entry and peer-play units came second. Most children were taught all four of the units over the course of the year.

Sometime during the month of November the training staff began to develop an intervention plan for each child. This plan focused on specific and general social needs of each child, since well-articulated goals for each child would give more direction to the intervention. These goals were reviewed during supervision sessions and once there was general agreement on the plans, decisions as to the order in which to teach the units could be made more easily.

Videotapes were used extensively to introduce the concepts, to present live illustrations of social problems and group behavior, to demonstrate alternative reactions to problem situations, and to portray graphically the consequences of these alternatives. Discussions with the children were used with the videotapes and these discussions were followed by role-playing behavior by the child, first with the staff member and later with peers. Later sessions in each unit placed increasing emphasis on role-playing and the observation and discussion of videotapes of this role-playing activity.

In the peer play and group sessions, a technique effectively employed by Bierman and Furman (1984) was introduced. Project children were allowed to invite other children from their classrooms to the role-play and practice sessions. The groups were asked to make films of themselves at play or handling difficult social situations. They were given Bierman's rationale that the films are needed to teach college students about the social activities of children their age. First the groups practiced situations in which the rejected children had received prior instruction and then role-playing activities were reviewed with the group. The group leaders singled out effective behavior that illustrated the training concepts. The groups then had film-making sessions, watched the films, and received performance feedback. The feedback was structured to reward and cue positive social behavior and give the group a feeling of successful task performance. The purpose of this strategy was to facilitate peer acceptance of the rejected children by classmates by providing them with the experience of working together successfully toward a superordinate group goal (Sherif, Harvey, White, Hood, & Sherif, 1961).

Intervention Results

The long-range goal of this project was to assess the consequences of the intervention by comparing the incidence of various forms of disorder among subjects who were no longer rejected with those who remained stably rejected. The immediate goal was to improve peer status among the intervention sample. The first level of evaluation for the project, therefore, was to compare intervention and control groups on measures of peer status. This can be done in two ways. One method is to compare numbers of subjects who are no longer rejected. The second way is to make group comparisons of mean social prefer-

TABLE 7.2 Mean Change in Social Preference Scores for Three Cohorts
(by intervention condition)

	Cohort						
Experimental	1984–85	(n)	1985–86	(n)	1986–87	(n)	Total
Social Skills Only	1.13	(14)	0.72	(17)	0.97	(15)	0.93
Tutoring & Social Skills Control	1.32	(17)	0.51	(20)	0.94	(16)	0.92
Social Skills Control	1.30	(6)	1.23	(7)	0.73	(14)	1.00
Tutoring Control	0.65	(15)	0.52	(12)	0.50	(16)	0.56

ence scores (liked-most votes minus liked-least votes), the primary sociometric dimension by which peer status is defined. The latter is the more rigorous approach to assessing the effectiveness of an intervention since covariate analyses can be used to control for preintervention differences in social preference scores, whereas the same thing can not be done for differences in the degree to which children are of rejected status.

Table 7.2 displays the mean changes in social preference scores, expressed in standard score terms, for each of the three intervention cohorts. The subjects for this analysis were only the black, rejected subjects in the study, since there were so few white children in the sample and social status for minority children tends to provide a less valid basis for predicting future disorder than for majority children (Kupersmidt, 1983). The analysis of covariance of postintervention means, with preintervention means serving as the covariate term, revealed only a nonsignificant trend ($p<.15$) for the comparison of the two low-achieving, experimental and control groups. Despite the substantial differences in mean change scores, the large, within-cell variance in scores worked against obtaining statistical significance. As the pattern of means in Table 7.2 indicates, the only apparent evidence for the effectiveness of the intervention was limited to those children who received both tutoring and social skills, since there were no differences in change for the two groups who were not in academic difficulty. The analysis of status change, from rejected to nonrejected, showed results parallel to those of the social preference score analyses, as can be seen in Table 7.3.

The results of the tutoring component of this intervention are strikingly similar to those of the Coie and Krehbiel (1984) study in which only low-achieving, rejected subjects were included in the intervention sample. In that earlier study, tutoring provided a positive

TABLE 7.3 Percentage of Subjects Changing From Rejected to Nonrejected
Social Status for Three Cohorts (by intervention condition)

	Cohort			
Experimental	1984–85	1985–86	1986–87	Total
Social Skills Only	56%	71%	73%	67%
Tutoring & Social Skills	76%	65%	69%	70%
Control				
Social Skills Control	83%	71%	71%	74%
Tutoring Control	67%	42%	50%	53%

enduring social consequence, whether paired with social skills training or not. Since tutoring was always paired with social skills training in the present study, it is not possible to determine whether tutoring alone would have been sufficient to improve peer social status. One important difference in the results of the two studies concerns the degree to which control subjects improved status without intervention. In the Coie and Krehbiel study, no improvements, even one year after the completion of the intervention, were seen in the control subjects, whereas in the present study there was a mean improvement in social preference scores of a half standard deviation. More than half of these low-achieving, rejected control subjects moved from rejected to nonrejected status after one year and three-fourths of the other rejected children improved their status. These results indicate much greater status instability than would have been expected from previous data.

When the amount of change that occurs within the two control conditions was compared, it was apparent that considerably more spontaneous improvement in social status was evident among previously rejected children who had better academic achievement than among the rejected children who also had academic difficulties. This finding highlights the importance of academic difficulties as an additional risk marker for rejected children, and when both risk factors are present, less spontaneous improvement is likely. The current results also suggest that many low-income, black children who are identified as rejected in third grade and who have adequate academic skills are actually quite resilient in their social status difficulties. It may not be effective to implement a preventive intervention with this group of rejected children, since many will show natural improvements during the following year. Instead, intervention for the rejected children with adequate academic skills should be deferred until later years when their social status difficulties become more stable.

The issue of status instability is one we broached earlier in the chapter, noting that the instability of the selection criterion would make it difficult to predict disorder from the risk criterion. The same is true for assessing change attributable to intervention, as can be seen from the present data. The degree of spontaneous improvement of the control groups is unusual in comparison to other social skills intervention studies (Bierman & Furman, 1984; Coie & Krehbiel, 1984; Gresham & Nagle, 1980; Ladd, 1981; LaGreca & Santogrossi, 1980; Oden & Asher, 1977). No change in status was found for the control groups in any of these studies. What accounts for the difference between the present samples and previous intervention samples is hard to document. The overall correlation of social preference scores from third to fourth grade was only $r = 0.49$, suggesting that there was low reliability in the original criterion scores. There are several possible explanations for this. The degree of literacy and the ability to focus on academic tasks may have been lower with this sample than with previous middle-class samples of similar ages. Related to this is the possibility that the relatively high mobility of our population (children frequently changed schools during the academic year, sometimes more than once) made it more difficult for children to keep track of peers. Many children were starting over socially from year to year, and even within the school year.

One conclusion that can be drawn from this work is that the decision to change the age level for screening the school population on the preintervention risk variable, a decision brought about by an organizational policy change of the host institution may have had significant consequences for the project by reducing the potential for program effectiveness. Similarly, this decision also may have had adverse implications for testing the prevention hypothesis. One lesson to be learned from this experience is the importance of knowing one's intervention population well before developing the intervention design. Particularly important for developmental interventions such as this are facts about the relative stability of criterion variables at different subject ages. As with so many things in life, timing is fundamental.

References

Allen, E., Hart, B., Buell, J., Harris, F., & Wolf, M. (1964). Effects of social reinforcement on isolate behavior of a nursery school child. *Child Development, 35,* 511–518.

Asarnow, J. R. (1983). Children with peer adjustment problems: Sequential and nonsequential analysis of school behaviors. *Journal of Consulting and Clinical Psychology, 51,* 709–717.

232   Coie et al.

Asher, S. R., & Renshaw, P. D. (1981). Children without friends: Social knowledge and social-skills training. In S. R. Asher & J. M. Gottman (Eds.), *The development of children's friendships* (pp. 273–296). Cambridge: Cambridge University Press.

Bierman, K. L., & Furman, W. (1984). The effects of social skills training and peer involvement on the social adjustment of preadolescents. *Child Development, 55,* 151–162.

Bierman, K. L., Miller, C. L., & Stabb, S. D. (1987). Improving the social behavior and peer acceptance of rejected boys: Effects of social skill training with instructions and prohibitions. *Journal of Consulting and Clinical Psychology, 55,* 194–200.

Bower, E. M., Shellhamer, T. A., & Dailey, J. M. (1960). School characteristics of male adolescents who later became schizophrenic. *American Journal of Orthopsychiatry, 30,* 712–729.

Coie, J. D. (1985). Fitting social skills intervention to the target group. In B. Schneider, K. H. Rubin, & J. E. Ledingham (Eds.), *Children's peer relations: Issues in assessment and intervention* (pp. 141–156). New York: Springer-Verlag.

Coie, J. D., & Benenson, J. F. (1982). *A qualitative analysis of the relationship between peer rejection and physically aggressive behavior.* Unpublished manuscript.

Coie, J. D., & Dodge, K. A. (1983). Continuity and changes in children's sociometric status: A five-year longitudinal study. *Merrill-Palmer Quarterly, 29,* 261–282.

Coie, J. D., Dodge, K. A., & Coppotelli, H. A. (1982). Dimensions and types of social status: A cross-age perspective. *Developmental Psychology, 18,* 557–569.

Coie, J. D., Dodge, K. A., & Kupersmidt, J. (in press). Peer group behavior and social status. In S. R. Asher & J. D., Coie (Eds.), *Peer rejection in childhood.* New York: Cambridge University Press.

Coie, J. D., & Krehbiel, G. (1984). Effects of academic tutoring on the social status of low-achieving, socially rejected children. *Child Development, 55,* 1465–1478.

Coie, J. D., & Kupersmidt, J. B. (1983). A behavioral analysis of emerging social status in boys' groups. *Child Development, 54,* 1400–1416.

Coie, J. D., & Whidby, J. M. (1986, April). *Gender differences in the basis for social rejection in childhood.* Paper presented at the annual meeting of the American Educational Research Association, San Francisco.

Cowen, E. L., Pederson, A., Babigian, H., Izzo, L. D., & Trost, M. A. (1973). Long-term follow-up of early detected vulnerable children. *Journal of Consulting and Clinical Psychology, 41,* 438–446.

Dodge, K. A. (1980). Social cognition and children's aggressive behavior. *Child Development, 51,* 162–170.

Dodge, K. A. (1983). Behavioral antecedents of peer social status. *Child Development, 54,* 1386–1399.

Dodge, K. A., Coie, J. D., & Brakke, N. P. (1982). Behavior patterns of socially rejected and neglected preadolescents: The roles of social approach and aggression. *Journal of Abnormal Child Psychology, 10,* 389–410.

Dodge, K. A., & Frame, C. L. (1982). Social cognition biases and deficits in aggressive boys. *Child Development, 53,* 620–635.

Dodge, K. A., Schlundt, D. G., Schocken, I., & Delugach, J. D. (1983). Social competence and children's sociometric status: The role of peer group entry strategies. *Merrill-Palmer Quarterly, 29,* 309–336.

Fleming, P., & Ricks, D. F. (1970). Emotions of children before schizophrenia and before character disorder. In M. Roff & D. F. Ricks (Eds.), *Life history studies in psychopathology* (pp. 240–264). Minneapolis: University of Minnesota Press.

Friedlander, D. (1945). Personality development of twenty-seven children who later became psychotic. *Journal of Abnormal and Social Psychology, 40*, 330–335.

Gresham, F. M., & Nagle, R. J. (1980). Social skills training with children: Responsiveness to modeling and coaching as a function of peer orientation. *Journal of Consulting and Clinical Psychology, 48*, 718–729.

Havighurst, R. J., Bowman, P. H., Liddle, G. P., Matthews, C. V., & Pierce, J. V. (1962). *Growing up in River City.* New York: Wiley.

Hayvren, M., & Hymel, S. (1984). Ethical issues in sociometric testing: Impact of sociometric measures on interaction behavior. *Developmental Psychology, 20*, 844–849.

Kasanin, J., & Veo, L. A. (1932). A study of the school adjustment of children who later became psychotic. *American Journal of Orthopsychiatry, 2*, 212–230.

Kohlberg, L., LaCrosse, J., & Ricks, D. (1972). The predictability of adult mental health from childhood behavior. In B. Wolman (Ed.), *Manual of child psychopathology* (pp. 1217–1284). New York: McGraw-Hill.

Kupersmidt, J. R. (1983, April). *Predicting delinquency and academic problems from childhood peer status.* Paper presented at the biennial meetings of the Society for Research in Child Development, Detroit.

Ladd, G. W. (1981). Effectiveness of a social learning method for enhancing children's social interaction and peer acceptance. *Child Development, 52*, 171–178.

Ladd, G. W. (1983). Social networks of popular, average, and rejected children in school settings. *Merrill-Palmer Quarterly, 29*, 283–308.

LaGreca, A., & Santogrossi, D. (1980). Social skills training with elementary school students: A behavioral group approach. *Journal of Consulting and Clinical Psychology, 48*, 220–227.

Langlois, J. H., & Stephan, C. W. (1981). Beauty and the beast: The role of physical attractiveness in the development of peer relations and social behavior. In S. S. Brehm, S. M. Kassin, & F. X. Gibbons (Eds.), *Developmental social psychology: Theory and research* (pp. 152–168). New York: Oxford University Press.

Lochman, J. E. (1985). Effects of different treatment lengths in cognitive behavioral interventions with aggressive boys. *Child Psychiatry and Human Development, 16*, 45–56.

Lochman, J. E., Burch, P. R., Curry, J. F., & Lampron, L. B. (1984). Treatment and generalization effects of cognitive behavioral and goal setting intervention with aggressive boys. *Journal of Consulting and Clinical Psychology, 52*, 915–916.

Lochman, J. E., Lampron, L. B., Burch, P. R., & Curry, J. F. (1985). Client characteristics associated with behavior change for treated and untreated aggressive boys. *Journal of Abnormal Child Psychology, 13*, 527–538.

Lochman, J. E., Nelson, W. M., & Sims, J. P. (1981). A cognitive behavioral program for use with aggressive children. *Journal of Clinical Child Psychology, 10*, 146–148.

Moore, S. G. (1967). Correlates of peer acceptance in nursery school children. In W. W. Hartup & N. L. Smothergill (Eds.), *The young child* (pp. 229–247). Washington, DC: National Association for the Education of Young Children.

Oden, S., & Asher, S. R. (1977). Coaching children in social skills for friendship-making. *Child Development, 48*, 495–506.

Pollack, M., Woerner, M., Goodman, W., & Greenberg, I. W. (1966). Childhood development patterns of hospitalized adult schizophrenic and nonschizophrenic patients and their siblings. *American Journal of Orthopsychiatry, 36*, 510–517.

Putallaz, M. (1983). Predicting children's sociometric status from their behavior. *Child Development, 54*, 1417–1426.

Putallaz, M., & Gottman, J. M. (1981). An interactional model of children's entry into peer groups. *Child Development, 52,* 986–994.

Putallaz, M., & Wasserman, A. (in press). Children's entry behavior. In S. R. Asher & J. D. Coie (Eds.), *Peer rejection in childhood.* New York: Cambridge University Press.

Rabiner, D. L. (1985). *Childhood peer relations as predictors of long-term adjustment.* Unpublished masters thesis, Duke University, Durham, NC.

Rabiner, D. L. (1987, April). *The role of expectations in the social problems of rejected children.* Paper presented at the biennial meetings of the Society for Research in Child Development, Baltimore.

Ricks, D. F., & Berry, J. C. (1970). Family and symptom patterns that precede schizophrenia. In M. Roff & D. F. Ricks (Eds.), *Life history research in psychopathology* (pp. 31–50). Minneapolis: University of Minnesota Press.

Roff, M. (1960). Relations between certain preservice factors and psychoneurosis during military duty. *Armed Forces Medical Journal, 11,* 152–160.

Roff, M. (1961). Childhood social interactions and young adult bad conduct. *Journal of Abnormal and Social Psychology, 63,* 333–337.

Roff, M. (1963). Childhood social interactions and young adult psychosis. *Journal of Clinical Psychology, 19,* 152–157.

Roff, M., Sells, S. B., & Golden, M. M. (1972). *Social adjustment and personality development in children.* Minneapolis: University of Minnesota Press.

Sherif, M., Harvey, O. J., White, B. J., Hood, W. R., & Sherif, C. W. (1961). *Intergroup conflict and cooperation: The robber's cave experiment.* Norman: University of Oklahoma.

Shure, M. B., & Spivack, G. (1982). Interpersonal problem-solving in young children: A cognitive approach to prevention. *American Journal of Community Psychology, 10,* 341–356.

Spivack, G., & Shure, M. B. (1974). *Social adjustment of young children: A cognitive approach to solving real-life problems.* San Francisco: Jossey-Bass.

Stabenau, J. R., & Pollin, W. (1970). Experiential differences for schizophrenics as compared with their non-schizophrenic siblings: Twin and family studies. In M. Roff & D. F. Ricks (Eds.), *Life history studies in psychopathology* (pp. 94–126). Minneapolis: University of Minnesota Press.

Vosk, B., Forehand, R., Parker, J. B., & Rickard, K. (1982). A multimethod comparison of popular and unpopular children. *Developmental Psychology, 18,* 571–575.

Watt, N. F. (1972). Longitudinal changes in the social behavior of children hospitalized for schizophrenia as adults. *Journal of Nervous and Mental Disease, 155,* 42–54.

Watt, N. F., Stolorow, R. D., Lubensky, A. W., & McClelland, D. C. (1970). School adjustment and the behavior of children hospitalized for schizophrenia as adults. *American Journal of Orthopsychiatry, 40,* 637–657.

Weissberg, R. P., Gesten, E. L., Carnrike, C. L., Toro, P. A., Rapkin, B. D., Davidson, E., & Cowen, E. L. (1981). Social problem-solving skill training: A competence building intervention with second-to-fourth grade children. *American Journal of Community Psychology, 9,* 411–423.

8

Peer Networks and Social Support: A Focus for Preventive Efforts with Youths

Ana Mari Cauce
Debra S. Srebnik

Reviewing the literature on peer networks and social support within youthful populations presents a task at once easy and difficult. This is because of the dearth of research directly dealing with the topic, on the one hand, and the many divergent bodies of literature that are relevant to it, on the other. This chapter concentrates primarily on research conducted within the social support/network paradigm, drawing upon developmental research and theory where appropriate.

The three major goals of this chapter correspond to its three main sections. First, we will attempt to demonstrate that peer support is a distinct component of children's social support networks. In this section we argue that differentiations between support providers have been understudied within the social support literature, although they may prove to be important and relevant distinctions. Second, we will discuss the effects of peer support and the role of peer group values in shaping these effects. Here we will present data suggesting that the peer group, by the support it provides and the values it promotes, influences youths' social adjustment and display of competence. The final section discusses implications for prevention efforts in a school context. In this section we argue for greater attention to peer processes and peer involvement in such efforts.

Structural Characteristics of Social
Support and Social Networks

Defining peer social support networks immediately raises a difficult question. What do we mean by "social-support networks," generally? The terms *social support* and *social networks* have become ubiqui-
tous in recent years, presently playing key roles in the theoretical,
research, and applied enterprises of prominent psychologists in the
areas of community psychology, social psychology, personality processes and individual differences, health psychology, social work, and
organizational psychology. Nonetheless, it has often been unclear
whether, despite the use of similar terminology, researchers in these
diverse areas are examining the same construct(s).

A preoccupation with the question of definition has become central
to the field and noteworthy attempts have been made to respond to it.
In the last few years alone, various literature reviews, theoretical articles, and empirical studies that address this question have been published (see recent reviews by Jacobson, 1986; Kessler, Price, & Wortman, 1985; Lin, Dean & Ensel, 1986; Peterson & Quadagno, 1985;
Sarason & Sarason, 1985; Tardy, 1985; Whittaker & Garbarino, 1983).
Barrera (1986), for example, has delineated three categories of social
support: (a) social embeddedness; (b) enacted support; and (c) perceived social support. *Embeddedness* refers to the strength of social ties
but does not specify which particular aspects of the ties are supportive. *Enacted support* assesses the occurrence of specific supportive actions, such as money lent or advice given. However, recall error is a
frequent problem in measurement and enacted support is highly variable and dependent on present life circumstances. As such, most research has been concerned with *perceived support,* that is, an individual's sense of having access to support from relationships if needed.
For the most part, we consider research pertaining to this construct.
Cohen and Wills (1985) have distinguished between four types of
perceived support: (a) esteem or emotional support; (b) informational
support or advice; (c) social companionship; and (d) instrumental or
material support. Although other researchers have presented different typologies of perceived support (e.g., Fiore, Becker, & Coppel,
1983; Gottlieb, 1978; House, 1981; Walker, MacBride, & Vachon,
1977), like Cohen and Wills, these attempts have been targeted primarily at identifying the various *functions* that might be served by
social ties rather than structural distinctions within social networks.

Considerations of these various typologies of support have led to
the development of a variety of social support measures, each of

which defines support in a slightly different manner. Nonetheless, there is some evidence that many, and perhaps most, social support instruments tap into the same support construct, which appears sufficiently robust to overcome the idiosyncratic nature of the measurement instruments. Sarason, Shearin, Pierce and Sarason (1987) compared the interrelationships and correlates of seven of the most frequently used pencil-and-paper or interview-format social support/ network scales. They found that these diverse measures of support appeared to relate to one construct—the "extent to which an individual is accepted, loved and involved in relationships with open communication" (p. 813). Furthermore, the authors stated that "subdividing the construct into discrete functions did not add to the sensitivity of the indices" (p. 813). This conclusion is remarkably similar to that of Sternberg and Grajeck (1984), who factor analyzed adults' responses to various measures of liking and loving in close relationships. They found that descriptions of these relationships were essentially unidimensional, yielding one general factor that they labeled "Interpersonal Communication, Sharing, and Support." Berndt and Perry (1986), in a study of second- to eighth-grade children, likewise found evidence that the positive features of supportive relationships (in this case friendships) formed one general factor. For children, this factor subsumed measures of play or association, prosocial behavior, intimacy, loyalty, and attachment or self-esteem enhancement. Thus, it appears that for both adults and children, social networks serve primarily an emotional support function.

Since much of our own work has utilized measures that tap only into the emotional support function, we welcome such findings. Yet, we are concerned that in reaching consensus about the holistic nature of social support, the field may close the door prematurely on other important distinctions that have remained largely unexplored. Here we refer specifically to distinctions between support providers that may form separable and distinct support systems.

The idea that individuals possess multiple support systems figured prominently in the work of Gerald Caplan (1974), a seminal theorist in the field. Yet, this construct has all but disappeared from the literature in the move toward the more overarching notion of social networks. While the tie between social-support and social-network research has undoubtedly been a productive one, it has become easy to forget that people do not really have one homogeneous social network. Rather, in most cases individuals are participants in various social networks that at times overlap each other while maintaining largely separable components or support systems.[1] According to Caplan, these systems might consist of "several supportive groups strategically situated in the community, at home, at work, in church, and in a series of recreational sites" and the individual might "move from one to the other throughout the day" (pp. 6–7). Caplan maintained that these systems were largely differentiated on a formal-informal dimension. Formal support systems, he believed, were "organized in a planned way by someone who is interested in promoting the health of the individual or population" (p. 7). Formal providers would include doctors, therapists, clergy, teachers, or guidance counselors. Informal support systems, by comparison, are less intentional and emerge "from the needs of the individual and the natural biosocial responses of people in his (sic) community" (p. 7). Friends and family members, for example, would be considered informal support providers.

Although few studies within the social support literature have distinguished between support from different providers (a notable exception is Procidiano and Heller, 1983), such a distinction may be especially crucial for children. In contrast to adults, children are more limited in their mobility. Our social institutions also serve to compartmentalize their relationships by setting and age.

Cauce, Felner, and Primavera (1982) were the first to examine empirically the distinctions between youngsters' systems of social support providers. They used factor analysis to examine the structural features of support systems in a sample of inner-city, mostly black, high school students. Based on Caplan's theoretical work, it was expected that two distinct support systems would be identified, one composed of informal support providers and the other of more formal providers.

Not surprisingly, a factor for formal support providers, composed primarily of school personnel, did emerge as distinct from informal support sources. However, the informal providers formed two distinct systems of their own—family and friends. Although this second distinction was not anticipated, the differentiation made by youths between relationships with adults (including family members) and friends was already well documented in the developmental literature.

Indeed, the unique role of peer friends, especially during late childhood through adolescence, has been fundamental to key developmental theorists. Most noteworthy, from a theoretical and historical perspective, are the works of Sullivan (1953) and Piaget (1932). Although a full description of their theories is well beyond the scope of this paper, both maintained that the egalitarian and/or intimate aspects of peer relations had important developmental implications for children.

The more recent American tradition of hard-nosed empiricism has served to document the unique role of peer relationships during childhood. Even infants and toddlers, it appears, more readily interact with unfamiliar children than unfamiliar adults (Lewis & Brooks, 1974) and their interactions with others like themselves become more friendly with continued contact (Eckerman, 1973; Mueller & Lucas, 1975; Vandell, Wilson, & Buchanan, 1979). An analysis of videotaped interactions between unacquainted pairs of one- and two-year-old toddlers revealed that explicitly positive social overtures between them were common (i.e., over 2000 such overtures in 13 hours of tape; Goldman & Ross, 1978; Ross & Goldman, 1977). Eckerman, Whatley, and Kutz (1975) studied the interactions of same-age toddlers and mother dyads in a laboratory playroom and found that toddlers (10 to 24 months old) preferred to interact with each other. Even in the presence of their mothers, 60% of their interactions were with peers. Furthermore, the nature of the children's interactions with each other were different in many respects from their interactions with their mothers or other adults. In contrast to their behavior with intimate adults, very young children rarely express affection for one another verbally or cling to each other (Eckerman et al., 1975). Yet, they follow one another around, engage one another in conversation, and, at times, offer help (Heathers, 1955). They also are more likely to engage in play with each other than with adults (Heathers, 1955).

This description of early peer interaction is strikingly similar to what is observed when teenagers are together. Indeed, the packlike behavior of teenagers has often been a cause for concern and alarm on the part of their parents. Adolescents' self-reports confirm not only that they spend most of their free time interacting with friends, but they enjoy this time more than that spent with adults. Adolescents also report engaging in intimate self-disclosure most often with same-age friends (Csikszentmihalyi, Larson, & Prescott, 1977). Furthermore, in an excellent review of peer relations, Hartup (1979) argued that bonds between peer friends are not merely secondary elaborations of the parental relationship but have a significant primary status. Thus, it appears that children's earliest experiences with other children have unique characteristics that are, at least in part, consistent through the childhood years.

As such, it was not surprising when the results of Cauce et al. (1982) were essentially replicated in a more recent study with white, upper-middle income, junior high school students in private schools (Cauce, Hannan, & Sargeant, 1987a). In this study, several new support sources were added to the original social support measure and, again, the family, friend, and formal/school systems were identified.

Distinctions between these three support systems appear robust and are best illustrated by the results of Srebnik and Cauce's (1988) study of the morphology of support systems. Given the sophisticated rating tasks involved, a college population (e.g. late adolescent) served as subjects. Various statistical techniques including factor analysis, multidimensional scaling, hierarchical cluster analysis, and multiple regression were used to analyze different subsets of the data yielding remarkably consistent results.

Results discussed here were obtained from two primary data sets. In the first set, subjects were asked to rate how similar various sources were in terms of support provided. In the second set, subjects rated these same support sources on a series of adjectives such as intimate, accessible, and warm. Figure 8.1 presents the plot obtained from the two dimensional multidimensional scaling analysis.[2] In order to aid the interpretation of dimensionality, a multiple regression analysis was also performed regressing adjective ratings for each source onto the multidimensional scaling solution.

As Figure 8.1 indicates, the first dimension appears to represent an "emotional closeness" or "intimacy" dimension, with boy/girlfriend, parents and siblings on the high end and boss, faculty advisor, and doctor/dentist on the low end. This interpretation was corroborated by the multiple regression analyses which suggest this dimension is highly related to the characteristics of intimate, warm, and loving. The second dimension consists of schoolmates and other friends on one end with doctor/dentist and aunt/uncle on the other. The adjectives *accessible* and *available* received the highest weightings in this dimension, providing support for the label "relevance to daily life."

In order to understand better the pattern of similarities, a hierarchical cluster analysis was also performed on the similarity ratings. Such an analysis helps to clarify the underlying structure of the data by focusing primarily on small distances (large similarities) in the ratings, while the multidimensional analysis focuses primarily on the large distances between ratings. In addition, this type of analysis seemed particularly appropriate since the two most commonly used approaches in measuring social support (i.e., analyzing the effects of each support source discretely and summing support across all sources) are analogous to the concept of moving from a weak to a strong cluster, the basis for the algorithm used in this clustering technique.

Results of the hierarchical cluster analysis are presented in Figure 8.2. As you move from the bottom to the top of this figure, the sources of support split successively into clusters. At the first step (the bottom of the figure), all of the sources are clustered together. At the second step, the formal sources become split from informal sources. At the

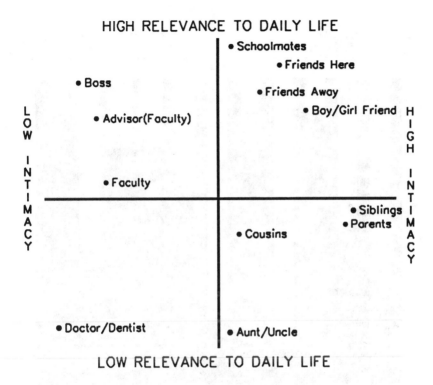

HIGH RELEVANCE TO DAILY LIFE

LOW RELEVANCE TO DAILY LIFE

Figure 8.1 Multidimensional Scaling Plot of Similarities Between Support Providers

third step the informal cluster becomes partitioned by splitting kin from peers and family. This procedure was allowed to continue until the point at which each source is in a class by itself.

As Figure 8.2 illustrates, separate clusters emerged forming formal, kin, friend, and nuclear family support systems. Of primary interest here, the friend system consisted of schoolmates, boy or girlfriend, friends here (i.e., friends residing in the same city), and friends away; all of which are most likely similar-age peers.

Thus it seems that, at least until late adolescence, peers form a distinct support system. According to the results presented in Figure 8.1, this peer system or network can be tentatively described as both highly intimate and highly accessible. The high level of intimacy dis-

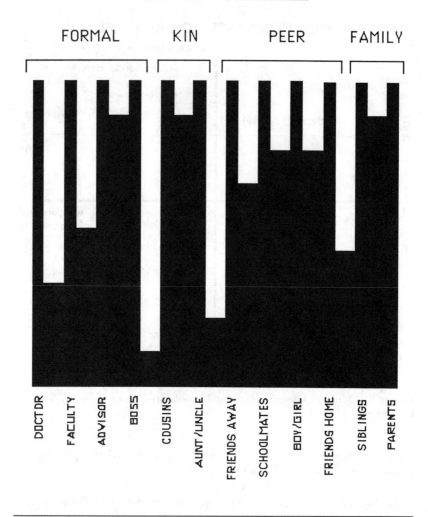

Figure 8.2 Hierarchical Clustering of Similarities Between Support Providers

tinguishes peer relationships from relationships with adults at school or work which are likewise influential in the course of daily life; a high level of accessibility and availability best distinguishes peer from family member systems.

Although this study was conducted with a college population, essential findings are remarkably consistent with recent developmental studies. For example, Furman and Bierman (1983) found that affection, support, common activities and propinquity were salient aspects in 4- to 7-year-olds' conceptions of friendship. In a study of fifth- and sixth-graders' relationships with mothers, fathers, siblings, grandparents, friends, and teachers, Furman and Buhrmester (1985) found that friends received the highest ratings for intimacy (together with mothers) and were rated the greatest source of companionship. In addition, children reported having more power in friendships than in relationships with adults. As such, we suspect that the egalitarian aspects of peer relations also distinguish them from those with family members; data are presently being collected to address this hypothesis further.

While there is consistency in support system delineations, it should be noted that the composition of each system also varies with an individual's developmental stage. For example, siblings were a part of the peer/friend system in early adolescence but part of the family system for the undergraduate sample of late adolescence (albeit, the family members closest to the friend/peer system, as illustrated in Figure 8.2). Furthermore, comparing the results of the current study with those of a pilot study conducted with graduate students (Cauce, 1983), boyfriend/girlfriend was part of the peer system for undergraduates and part of the family system for graduate students. Replications of these findings are still needed, yet their concordance with a developmental perspective and common sense are encouraging.

Differential Effects of
Peer Support/Peer Networks

Establishing that youths distinguish peer support providers from family members and more formal providers, such as school personnel, is of itself important from a theoretical viewpoint. However, in relation to prevention or intervention, such a distinction means little unless it relates to behavioral effects. That is, one must also demonstrate that separable support systems differentially affect functioning.

In this respect, the developmental literature on children's friendships and peer relations is again suggestive. Hartup (1979) argued that peer relations are especially important in the development of social competence, mastery of aggressive impulses, sexual socialization, empathy or role-taking, and more tentatively, school mastery. Evidence for these findings is drawn largely from studies that contrasted children rejected by their peers, or described as shy and reserved, with more accepted or sociable children (e.g. Bronson, 1966; Cowen, Pederson, Babijian, Izzo, & Trost, 1973; Roff, Sells, & Golden, 1972).

More recent and methodologically sophisticated studies suggest that children socially rejected and/or neglected by their peer group display more problem behaviors when compared to children liked by their peers (e.g., Coie & Dodge, 1983; Coie, Dodge, & Coppotelli, 1982). Indeed, elaborate classification schemes have been developed which group children in terms of their peer relations. In such schemes children are not only described as popular, rejected, neglected, and average, in terms of peer ratings, but also "controversial" (e.g., children whose visibility is high in the peer group, but who are often both liked and disliked by peers, Bukowski & Newcomb, 1985; Coie et al., 1982; Coie & Dodge, 1983; Dodge, 1983). Children in each of these categories display differential patterns of social behaviors with peers and in the classroom.

Previous research in the developmental literature also indicates that intimacy, affection, and support in friendships increase with age throughout childhood and into adolescence (Diaz & Berndt, 1982; Furman & Bierman, 1983; Hunter & Youniss, 1982). Together, such findings suggest that a child's relationships with peers affects adjustment and that accessing emotional support from peers is an important developmental accomplishment.

Nonetheless, these studies do not directly address whether there is a relationship between supportive peer networks and/or friendships and psychological adjustment. Indeed, as Berndt (1982) noted in his review of the effects of early adolescent friendships, although hypotheses about the effects of friendships have been proposed and suggestive evidence exists, few hypotheses have been tested directly. According to Berndt, "there is virtually no evidence for or against the hypothesis that friendships contribute to social adjustment during adolescence and later life" (p. 1458).

Research on social support was intended to examine specifically how close/supportive relationships influence adjustment. However, research on peer support as a unique construct is extremely rare. One exception is the work of Cauce and her colleagues, which attempted to examine more carefully the varying effects of distinct support providers.

Cauce et al. (1982) compared high school students above and below the median in reported support from each social system (e.g., family, peer, and formal/school) on a variety of adjustment indices. Although results varied somewhat by ethnicity and gender, in general, they suggested that children with high levels of family support reported higher levels of scholastic self-concept than those with low family support. Adolescents high in formal/school support reported higher levels of peer self-concept than those low in such support. And, adolescents high in peer support reported better peer self-concept while they evidenced lower grade-point-averages and more school absences than those low in peer support. Results of this study are somewhat compromised by statistical analyses that are now considered not particularly powerful or sensitive. Nevertheless, they do suggest differential effects for each support system.

Cauce, Hannan, and Sargeant (1987b) corroborated a pattern of differential effects using more sensitive regression analyses. Their analyses also addressed the role of each support system in buffering the consequences of negative life events. In this study, family support contributed to enhanced levels of perceived peer, physical, and general social competence. It also appeared to moderate the effects of stressful life events upon school competence.[3]

School support made a near-significant contribution to school competence and also buffered the effects of life stress upon school competence for those students with a more external locus of control for failure situations. Peer support, while contributing to enhanced levels of peer competence, was related to higher levels of anxiety and decreased school competence.

As such, these studies suggest that the effects of social support from adults (both family members and school personnel) are generally positive and in keeping with expectations. Family support, in particular, appears to demonstrate the most global effects upon adjustment, in keeping with Bogat's (1985) description of family members as "support generalists."

On the other hand, the effects of peer support are somewhat puzzling. Both studies revealed positive relationships between peer support and peer competence or self-concept, and both suggested that such support was negatively related to school competence. These consistent results are particulary noteworthy given the contrasting samples studied. The 1982 study involved a sample of mostly black, low SES, high school students in three inner-city schools, whereas the

1987b study involved a sample of all white, middle- to upper-SES, middle school students in two suburban private schools.

It is tempting to explain the negative relationship between peer support and school competence as consistent with the recent spate of literature on the so-called negative effects of social support. Yet, that literature is essentially unrelated to the findings discussed above. Most of the work on social supports' negative effects has dealt with the conflictual aspect of close and often otherwise supportive relationships; and it is the level of conflict (a facet not measured in the Cauce et al. studies) that relates to these negative effects (e.g., Fiore et al., 1983; Pagel, Erdly, & Becker, 1987; Rook, 1984).

In the studies by Cauce et al., peer support was simultaneously related to both better social adjustment within the peer group and indices of lowered school performance. Conversations with parents of adolescents and professionals working with adolescents have suggested that while adolescents may gain a great deal of support from their friends when dealing with personal problems and even social problems at school, their friends rarely openly express support for academic performance. As such, we prefer to think of peer support's seemingly paradoxical effects as side-effects of social support. These side-effects may emanate from the fact that social support is not context-free. More specifically, it is crucial to keep in mind that support from peers occurs within the context of peer group values.

An example may best illustrate this point. Let us imagine that Maria is having trouble with a complicated homework assignment and shares this problem with her best friend Wanda. Wanda might choose to help by lending Maria her class notes and reviewing them with her. However, Wanda may simply tell Maria that she worries too much about grades, acts like a grind, and suggest they go to the shopping mall to take Maria's mind off the difficult assignment. And, in fact, Maria may feel better following the afternoon at the mall. In both scenarios, Wanda is demonstrating caring and support for her friend and either interaction may buoy Maria's sense of peer competence or self concept. Yet one would expect the contrasting messages about school, each of which is tied to a gesture of social support, to affect Maria's school competence quite differently.

Zigler and Trickett's (1979) two-dimensional schema for conceptualizing social competence may be relevant in this respect. They suggest that one aspect of social competence reflects the success of the individual in meeting societal expectations; the other reflects the person's self-actualization, or personal development. Extrapolating from this schema, we believe that the drive for personal effectance in peer interactions represents an aspect of the more value-free or self-actualizing components of social competence. Humans, like other primates, are by nature social beings. As such, peer group values should not affect peer support's positive relationship to peer competence. Indeed, we expect this relationship to hold in all peer group cultures. On the other hand, a desire for mastery over school-related tasks appears to reflect societal expectations, and the context of peer group values should be quite important in determining how peer support will affect school competence.

In order to test this hypothesis, Cauce (1986) examined the contributions of both peer support and peer group values to peer and school competence. This study, which was conducted with a sample of black, low-SES, seventh-graders, employed multiple indicators of all constructs, including both a traditional self-report measure of peer support and a more objective measure of such support (i.e., number of *reciprocated* best friendships). Results confirmed the hypothesis; children's reports of their friends' attitudes toward school was a significant multivariate predictor of school competence as measured by self-perceptions, peer ratings, school grades, and achievement test scores. However, peer attitudes towards school were not related to peer competence, as measured by self-perceptions and peer-ratings. Thus, it appears that the context of social support is important in determining its impact on the more value-laden aspects of social competence but not on self-actualizing components.

It is also important to point out that, in this study, both the self-report and objective measures of peer support were positively related to school competence. In this vein, it is noteworthy that this study was conducted in a school that was part of the Yale Child Study Center Primary Prevention School Project developed by James Comer (for a full discussion of this program and its effects see Comer, 1980; and Cauce, Comer, & Schwartz, 1987). Although the full scale intervention had yet to begin at the time of the study, approximately 25% of the students sampled had attended an elementary school where the full intervention had been operant for over five years. An indication of the positive values held toward school in the general sample was the fact that 70% of the students said they would most like to be remembered in their school for being the "best student," as opposed to "most popular" (16%), "best athlete" (14%), or "most trouble" (0%). In addition, 96% of the sample reported that being a good student was at least somewhat important among their friends. Whether this favorable view of school achievement was a product of the prevention program or a sign of fertile ground for the program at its outset is unknown.

In all other respects examined, the students appeared typical for their age and SES: scores on all other measures were comparable to similar samples, school GPAs were at midrange, and mean achievement tests scores were approximately one year below grade level. Students also reported that the following values were at least somewhat important among their friends: (a) being a good dancer (35%), (b) having money (51%), (c) being good-looking (53%), (d) being a good athlete (72%), (e) and having nice clothes (78%).

Given the nature of this study, it is quite possible that the relationship between peer network and school performance is mediated by some third underlying variable. Social competence, in its global manifestations, is the most likely candidate (Heller, 1979; Heller & Swindle, 1983). Intelligence is another possible candidate. Yet, results indicated that peer network variables made a significant contribution to school grades after the effects of more global social competence[3] and intelligence (as indicated by achievement test scores) were held constant. This is quite remarkable since these two control variables alone accounted for almost 50% of the variance in grades.

While further work is needed before firm conclusions can be drawn, this series of studies does suggest that the peer network influences children's adjustment and display of competence. Such effects, while at times synergistic with those of family support and/or school support, seem particularly influential in terms of school and peer competence. Furthermore, the effects of the peer network are not simply a by-product of an underlying relationship between peer group status and individual levels of social competence and/or intelligence.

Peer Networks and Social Support:
Implications for Prevention

In light of the peer network's apparent effects upon youth's behavior, both in terms of the support it provides and the values it promotes, it would behoove us to pay closer attention to peer processes in designing and evaluating our preventive/interventive strategies within schools. In particular, the results of Cauce (1986) suggest that such processes may serve to support *naturally* (or undermine) the goals of prevention programs. Indeed, it may be that the peer group's support of program goals (such as increasing school competence) is a prerequisite for effective change. Or, it may be that such support is a concomitant outcome of effective programs. This is an empirical question that needs to be addressed, for its implications relevant to program design may be of great consequence. If some concordance between prevention program objectives and peer group values is necessary, it might be important for even those programs aimed at a subset of the student population (e.g., children at risk) to work simultaneously to influence and monitor the school-wide student and adult population.

Anecdotally, it is interesting to note that school-wide inoculation, so to speak, is the treatment of choice for schools in which pact suicides have occurred (Feron, 1987; Ravo, 1987). In the most recent instances, the affected schools have generally: (a) provided added counselors for those students who have actively sought help following the incidences (tertiary prevention); (b) recruited students who were close friends of the victims into discussion groups or counseling programs (secondary prevention); and, (c) held school-wide assemblies to heighten all students' awareness of indicators of depression and suicide intent (primary prevention). Both the assemblies and discussion groups have encouraged all students to support and take care of each other. The dire circumstances under which such programs have developed and the relatively low base rates for such incidences make it difficult to evaluate the success of these strategies. Yet, perhaps there is something to be learned from such tragedies; given appropriate guidance, peers may be each others' most sensitive supporters. Certainly the high degree of intimacy and accessibility among peers provides unique opportunities for this supportive role.

This does not mean that adults cannot exert beneficial influences on the lives of children and adolescents. To the contrary, research suggests that social support from adults—parents and school personnel—has uniformly positive effects. As such, Cauce et al. (1987b) called for policy makers to promote programs that encourage positive adult and child interactions.

Yet, it remains a fact that schools are populated primarily by youths, not adults. Age-based segregation is one of the few constants within American elementary, middle, and high schools (Sarason, 1971). This structure ensures the continuing prominence of the peer group in children's school lives and suggests that we must consider better ways to channel students' energies into activities that promote mutual help and support.

In this vein, Jason (1984) and his colleagues have developed a series of programs based on what he calls the "children helping children" approach. These range from programs for inner-city youth prone to recruitment by gangs to more traditional peer-tutoring programs. At the same time, the entire series of programs focuses on self-help and the involvement of youth as helpers as well as help recipients. As Jason notes, if youth are allowed input into and participation in preventive programs, they may have more commitment to the intervention goals and more investment in effecting behavioral, cognitive, and emotional change. As a consequence, program participants should be more likely to sustain accomplished gains over time (Jason, 1984).

The potential value of children helping children is clearly suggested by the large pool of potential helpers available within school contexts. Of course, one may wonder about the wisdom of such approaches in light of the fact that peer support has, in some cases, been related to poorer school performance. Yet, it seems quite likely that the children most apt to volunteer as helpers within any school program are those most invested in the school. This is an easily considered empirical question that might be assessed through early screening of child helpers. In any case, we do believe that careful monitoring and supervision of peer-based approaches to prevention are necessary and appropriate. The promise of these approaches make them too important to ignore.

Conclusions

In recent years, we have witnessed a rapid growth in research on children's friendships and peer relations. At the same time, research on adults' social networks and the support they provide has also expanded. In research with children, close attention has been paid to developmental processes, distinguishing between peer and adult influences. Yet, this work has been primarily descriptive in nature and has seldom addressed the effects of such relationships. Research on social support has focused on the effects of close relationships but it has not been sensitive to developmental issues, and the role of peer support providers rarely has been addressed. Indeed, these two bodies of related work have developed in marked isolation from each other and attempts at integration have only just begun.

We are not yet at a point where firm conclusions can be drawn regarding the role of peers in influencing children's adjustment and display of competence. Yet, the modest evidence we have suggests that the peer network is a powerful socializing agent that may become particularly important during late childhood and adolescence. We would do well to pay closer attention to peer group processes both in planning our interventions and in our research enterprises with youthful populations.

Notes

1. The "personal social network," where each individual is seen as maintaining *one* set of relationships is primarily a heuristic device. It allows one to map an individual's social world with him or her at the center (called the *anchor position*) with a link emanating out to each and all important relationships. Linkages are also drawn between other persons in the network who have relationships with each other. (These latter linkages are used to gauge the density or enmeshment within the network.) As a heuristic device, this technique has served its purpose well. It does not, however, realistically portray the intricacies of peoples' social lives. In particular, the inevitable tie between specific relationships and specific settings or contexts is absent from these maps and resulting measures.

2. The terms *school performance, school achievement,* and *school competence* are used interchangeably throughout this chapter. In Cauce et al. (1982) this construct was gauged by self-rated scholastic self-concept, school grades, and school absences; in Cauce (1986) it was measured by school grades, achievement test scores, peer-ratings for "best student," and self-rated school competence; in Cauce et al. (1987b) it was represented by self-rated school competence. Results reported in Cauce (1987), not discussed in this chapter, established via factor analysis and a multitrait-multimethod matrix that all these measures are highly intercorrelated and represent one underlying construct. Indeed the correlation between self-rated school competence and grade point average was .70. This same study suggested that various measures of peer competence, both self-rated peer competence and peer-ratings for "most popular," represented the same construct which was distinct from school competence.

3. In this study global social competence was measured using the *Social Competence Nomination Form* (Ford, 1982). This measure, based upon peer-ratings, is related to both a child's social cognition and interpersonal cognitive problem solving skills. Results of Cauce (1987) further suggested that this form tapped cognitive and social intelligence, relevant for both peer and school competence but not unique to either.

References

Barrera, M. (1986). Distinctions between social support concepts, measures, and models. *American Journal of Community Psychology, 14,* 413–445.

Berndt, T. J. (1982). The features and effects of friendship in early adolescence. *Child Development, 53,* 1447–1460.

Berndt, T. J., & Perry, T. B. (1986). Children's perceptions of friendships as supportive relationships. *Developmental Psychology, 22,* 640–648.

Bogat, G. A. (1985). Differentiating specialists and generalists within college students' social support network. *Journal of Youth and Adolescence, 14,* 23–35.

Bronson, W. C. (1966). Central orientations: A study of behavior organization from childhood to adolescence. *Child Development, 37,* 125–155.

Bukowski, W. M., & Newcomb, A. F. (1985). Variability in peer group perceptions: Support for the "controversial" sociometric classification group. *Developmental Psychology, 21,* 1032–1038.

Caplan, G. (1974). *Support systems and community mental health.* New York: Behavioral Publications.

Cauce, A. M. (1983). *Similarities between sources of social support: Delineating social support systems.* Unpublished manuscript, Yale University, New Haven, CT.

Cauce, A. M. (1986). Social networks and social competence: Exploring the effects of early adolescent friendships. *American Journal of Community Psychology, 14,* 607–628.

Cauce, A. M. (1987). School and peer competence in early adolescence: A test of domain-specific self-perceived competence. *Developmental Psychology, 23,* 287–291.

Cauce, A. M., Comer, J. P., & Schwartz, D. (1987). Long term effects of a systems-oriented school prevention program. *American Journal of Orthopsychiatry, 57,* 127–131.

Cauce, A. M., Felner, R. D., & Primavera, J. (1982). Social support in high-risk adolescents: Structural components and adaptive impact. *American Journal of Community Psychology, 10,* 417–428.

Cauce, A. M., Hannan, K., & Sargeant, M. (1987a). *Structural characteristics of early adolescents' social networks.* Unpublished manuscript, University of Delaware, Newark.

Cauce, A. M., Hannan, K., & Sargeant, M. (1987b, August). *Negative events, social support, and locus of control in early adolescence: Contributions to well-being.* Paper presented at the annual meeting of the American Psychological Association, New York City.

Cohen, S., & Wills, T. A. (1985). Stress, social support, and the buffering hypothesis. *Psychological Bulletin, 98,* 310–357.

Coie, J. D., & Dodge, K. A. (1983). Continuities and changes in children's social status: A 5-year longitudinal study. *Merrill-Palmer Quarterly, 29,* 261–282.

Coie, J. D., Dodge, K., & Coppotelli, H. (1982). Dimensions and types of social status: A cross-age perspective. *Developmental Psychology, 18,* 557–571.

Comer, J. P. (1980). *School power: implications of an intervention project.* New York: Free Press.

Cowen, E. L., Pederson, A., Babijian, H., Izzo, L. D., & Trost, M. A. (1973). Long-term follow-up of early detected vulnerable children. *Journal of Consulting and Clinical Psychology,* 438–446.

Csikszentmihalyi, M., Larson, R., & Prescott, S. (1977). The ecology of adolescent activity and experience. *Journal of Youth and Adolescence, 6,* 281–294.

Diaz, R. M., & Berndt, T. J. (1982). Children's knowledge of a best friend: Fact or fancy. *Developmental Psychology, 18,* 787–794.

Dodge, K. A. (1983). Behavioral antecedents of peer social status. *Child Development, 54,* 1386–1399.

Eckerman, C. O. (1973, August). *Competence in early social relations.* Paper presented at the annual meetings of the American Psychological Association, Montreal, Canada.

Eckerman, C. O., Whatley, J. L., & Kutz, S. L. (1975). The growth of play with peers during the second year of life. *Developmental Psychology, 11,* 42–49.

Feron, J. (1987, March 15). Suicide-prevention efforts gain acceptance in Westchester schools. *New York Times,* p. 30.

Fiore, J. Becker, J., & Coppel, D. (1983). Social network interactions: A buffer or a stress. *American Journal of Community Psychology, 11,* 423–439.

Ford, M. E. (1982). Social cognition and social competence in adolescence. *Developmental Psychology, 18,* 323–340.

Furman, W., & Bierman, K. L. (1983). Developmental changes in young children's conceptions of friendship. *Child Development, 54,* 549–556.

Furman, W., & Buhrmester, D. (1985). Children's perceptions of the personal relationships in their social networks. *Developmental Psychology, 21,* 1016–1024.

Goldman, B. D., & Ross, H. S. (1978). Social skills in action: An analysis of early peer games. In J. Glick & K. A. Clarke-Stewart (Eds.), *The development of social understanding* (pp. 401–407). New York: Gardner Press.

Gottlieb, B. H. (1978). The development and application of a classification scheme of informal helping behaviours. *Canadian Journal of Behavioral Science, 10,* 105–115.

Hartup, W. W. (1979). Peer relations and the growth of social competence. In M. H. Kent & J. E. Rolf (Eds.), *Primary prevention of psychopathology: Social competence in children* (pp. 150–170). Hanover, NH: University Press of New England.

Heathers, G. (1955). Emotional dependence and independence in nursery school play. *Journal of Genetic Psychology, 87,* 37–57.

Heller, K. (1979). The effects of social support: Prevention and treatment implications. In A. P. Goldstein & F. H. Kanfer (Eds.), *Maximizing treatment gains: Transfer enhancement in psychotheraphy* (pp. 353–387). New York: Academic Press.

Heller, K., & Swindle, R. (1983). Social networks, perceived social support, and coping with stress. In R. D. Felner, L. A. Jason, J. N. Moritsugu, & S. S. Farber (Eds.), *Preventive psychology: Theory, research, & practice* (pp. 87–103). New York: Pergamon Press.

House, J. S. (1981). *Work stress and social support.* Reading, MA: Addison-Wesley.

Hunter, F. T., & Youniss, J. (1982). Changes in functions of three relations during adolescence. *Developmental Psychology, 18,* 806–811.

Jacobson, D. (1986). Types and timing of social support. *Journal of Health and Social Behavior, 27,* 250–264.

Jason, L. A. (1984, November). Children helping children: Implications for prevention. In R. P. Lorion (Chair), *Behavioral treatment and prevention of disorders in disadvantaged children and adolescents.* Symposium at the annual meetings of the Association for the Advancement of Behavioral Therapy, Philadelphia.

Kessler, R. C., Price, R. H., & Wortman, C. B. (1985). Social factors in psychopathology: Stress, social support and coping processes. *Annual Review of Psychology, 36,* 531–572.

Lewis, M., & Brooks, J. (1974). Self, other and fear: Infants' reactions to people. In M. Lewis & L. A. Rosenblum (Eds.), *The origins of fear* (pp. 113–144). New York: Wiley.

Lin, N., Dean, A., & Ensel, W. M. (Eds.). (1986). *Social support, life events, and depression.* New York: Academic Press.

Mueller, E., & Lucas, T. (1975). A developmental analysis of peer interaction among toddlers. In M. Lewis & L. A. Rosenblum (Eds.), *Friendship and peer relations* (pp. 223–258). New York: Wiley.

Pagel, M., Erdly, W., & Becker, J. (1987). Social networks: We get by with (and in spite of) a little help from our friends. *Journal of Personality and Social Psychology, 53,* 793–804.

Peterson, W. H., & Quadagno, J. (Eds.). (1985). *Social bonds in later life.* Beverly Hills, CA: Sage publications.

Piaget, J. (1932). *The moral judgement of the child.* Glencoe, IL: Free Press.

Procidano, M. E., & Heller, K. (1983). Measures of perceived support from friends and from family: Three validation studies. *American Journal of Community Psychology, 11,* 1–24.

Ravo, N. (1987, March 13). A day after suicides, Bergenfield focuses on preventing more. *New York Times*, p. 2.

Roff, M., Sells, S. B., & Golden, M. M. (1972). *Social adjustment and personality development in children*. Minneapolis: University of Minnesota Press.

Rook, K. S. (1984). The negative side of social interaction: Impact on psychological well-being. *Journal of Personality and Social Psychology, 46*, 1097–1108.

Ross, H. S., & Goldman, B. D. (1977). Infants' sociability toward strangers. *Child Development, 48*, 638–642.

Sarason, S. B. (1971). *The culture of the school and the problem of change*. Boston: Allyn & Bacon.

Sarason, I. G., & Sarason, B. R. (Eds.). (1985). *Social support: Theory, research, and applications*. Boston, MA: Martinus Nijhoff.

Sarason, B. R., Shearin, E. N., Pierce, G. R. & Sarason, I. G. (1987). Interrelations of social support measures: Theoretical and practical implications. *Journal of Personality and Social Psychology, 52*, 813–832.

Srebnik, D. S., & Cauce, A. M. (1988, August). *Social support providers: A multidimensional analysis of network systems*. Paper presented at the annual meetings of the American Psychological Association, Atlanta, GA.

Sternberg, R. J., & Grajeck, S. (1984). The nature of love. *Journal of Personality and Social Psychology, 47*, 312–329.

Sullivan, H. S. (1953). *Interpersonal theory of psychiatry*. New York: Norton.

Tardy, C. H. (1985). Social support measurement. *American Journal of Community Psychology, 13*, 187–202.

Vandell, D. L., Wilson, K. S., & Buchanan, N. R. (1979, March). *Peer interaction in the first year: An examination of its structure, content, and sensitivity to toys*. Paper presented at the biennial meetings of the Society for Research in Child Development, San Francisco, CA.

Walker, K., MacBride, A., & Vachon, M. (1977). Social support networks and the crisis of bereavement. *Social Science and Medicine, 11*, 34–41.

Whittaker, J. K., & Garbarino, J. (1983). *Social support networks*. New York: Aldine.

Zigler, E., & Trickett, E. K. (1979). The role of national social policy in promoting social competence in children. In M. W. Kent & J. E. Rolf (Eds.), *Primary prevention of psychopathology: Social competence in children* (pp. 280–296). Hanover, NH: University Press of New England.

9

A New Conceptual Framework for Establishing School-Based Social Competence Promotion Programs

Roger P. Weissberg
Marlene Zelek Caplan
Patricia J. Sivo

The National Mental Health Association (NMHA) Commission on the Prevention of Mental-Emotional Disabilities recently recommended that "programs should be developed in schools (preschool through high school) that incorporate validated mental health strategies and competence building as an integral part of the curriculum" (Long, 1986, p. 828). We believe that this recommendation is very important, and we are actively involved in research to design and evaluate school-based social competence promotion (SCP) programs.[1] However, although there have been some promising advances in developing brief SCP demonstration projects, progress in the area of establishing comprehensive, enduring school-based SCP programs has been slow. Apparently, this work has been easier to endorse with enthusiasm than to accomplish with effectiveness.

This chapter discusses key theoretical and practical issues in the conceptualization, design, implementation, evaluation, and dissemination of school-based preventive SCP programs. We suggest that these programs should employ a systematic, integrated combination of in-

Authors' Note: The authors gratefully acknowledge the support provided by the William T. Grant Foundation Faculty Scholars Program in Mental Health of Children and the Justice Planning Division of the Connecticut Office of Policy and Management (Grant Number 86JJ4240573). We also express our appreciation to Superintendent John Dow, Deputy Superintendent Rosa Quezada, and the many New Haven administrators, staff, and students who have collaborated with us to develop school-based social competence promotion programs. Finally, we thank Loisa Bennetto for her helpful editorial comments on an earlier draft of this chapter.

tervention approaches to: (a) enhance the capacities of children and adolescents to coordinate cognition, affect, and behavior so that they may effectively handle developmentally relevant social tasks; and (b) create environmental settings and resources that support the promotion of adaptive behavior and good developmental outcomes. The primary objectives of SCP programs are to foster the behavioral effectiveness and the positive self-perceptions of students regarding their functioning in the domains of school, work, interpersonal relationships, and leisure activities (Ford, 1985). Beyond these beneficial outcomes, promoting social competence may also serve as a protective factor to prevent the development of psychopathology (Garmezy, 1987; Rutter, 1987).

This chapter begins with a rationale for why preventive SCP programming should become a central mission of the American school system. Then, we describe and critique the current conceptual model that guides most SCP program development and evaluation efforts (i.e., the person-centered competence-enhancement approach), suggesting that it makes school-based SCP training appear deceptively simple. Next, we present a new five-step conceptual framework (see Table 9.1) that emphasizes several critical developmental and ecological considerations when establishing school-based SCP programs. We cite programmatic issues and empirical findings from our research to highlight how the new model is influencing our efforts. We also offer several recommendations for future SCP research and practice.

The Need for School-Based Preventive Mental Health Programs

Albee (1982, 1985) cited several National Institute of Mental Health statistics to document the inadequacy of the American mental health system's response to people experiencing emotional problems. There are more than 35 million American adults, 15% to 20% of the population, who suffer from severe emotional and behavioral disturbances. A large additional segment of our population, perhaps as many as 50 million people, also experience serious psychological distress. Yet the entire mental health system provides services to only 7 million people annually.

The discrepancy between the need for services and available resources for children and youth may be even larger. Recent estimates suggest that 7.5 to 9.5 million youngsters, i.e., 12% to 15% of all individuals under the age of 18, experience emotional or behavioral problems that warrant treatment (Office of Technology Assessment,

1986). In addition, several prevalence surveys indicate that approximately 30% of American children have school adjustment problems (Glidewell & Swallow, 1969; Rubin & Balow, 1978), and that this figure runs considerably higher in some urban school systems (Kellam, Branch, Agrawal, & Ensminger, 1975). Unfortunately, estimates suggest that 70% to 90% of youngsters who need mental health services do not receive them (Hobbs, 1982; Office of Technology Assessment, 1986).

One major reason for this country's inadequate response to people with adjustment problems is that our mental health system is dominated by a passive-receptive stance to treatment (Cowen, Gesten, & Weissberg, 1980). Currently, most of our professional resources focus on assessing and treating people suffering from severe disturbances in the context of hospitals, outpatient clinics, and private practice settings (Albee, 1982). Interventions generally begin after an individual seeks or is encouraged to get help for a serious dysfunction that has developed over several years. Such treatment is typically very expensive, requiring a great deal of expertise and sustained involvement. Ironically, since the prognosis for a positive outcome to treatment is less favorable with severely disturbed people, one could argue that a major proportion of our scarce mental health resources is being directed in a cost-ineffective manner toward a small segment of people who will benefit least from them.

Clearly, difficult choices must be made about the most humane and cost-effective ways to allocate our limited mental health resources. Primary prevention represents a network of strategies that differ from traditional treatment approaches with respect to the nature, timing, and targeting of their intervention practices. Such interventions engineer environmental systems and/or strengthen people's personal and social resources to promote adaptive behavior and prevent psychopathology in large groups of people. During the past 25 years, many promising prevention approaches have been developed (see Buckner, Trickett, & Corse, 1985; Cowen, 1982, 1988; Felner, Jason, Moritsugu, & Farber, 1983; Joffe, Albee, & Kelly, 1984; Roberts & Peterson, 1984). Of all these strategies, many investigators are most optimistic about the potentially widespread positive effects that SCP efforts can have. Kornberg and Caplan (1980), who reviewed 650 papers on bio-psycho-social risk factors and preventive interventions, concluded that "research emphasis on methods for fostering mental health through the promotion of competence is probably the most significant development in recent primary prevention programming" (p. 105). Bloom (1979) suggested that much human suffering results from a lack of competence and effective coping strategies, and the diminished self-esteem that accompanies these deficiencies. He argued that a substantial body of research indicates that competence building may be the most persuasive way to help people deal with individual and social problems.

Because of the large number of children whose current and future psychosocial functioning is of concern, it seems both logical and critical to establish effective SCP prevention programs in the schools. Schools are compulsory institutions that have significant and sustained contact (i.e., 15,000 hours over a child's school career) with most children during their formative years of personality development (Rutter, Maughan, Mortimore, & Ouston, 1979). Furthermore, they have the potential to be especially well-suited sites for SCP programs to promote life skills and to prevent social maladaptation. Under the right circumstances, learning activities may be introduced and environments can be created that afford multiple opportunities for children, their parents, and school personnel to use adaptive interpersonal skills and to receive feedback about their application. In addition, many related community-based educational experiences can be structured to enhance the effects of school-based instruction (Sarason, 1983; Zigler, Kagan, & Muenchow, 1982).

At this point in time, society's concern about such problems as drug abuse, teenage pregnancy, delinquency, school dropout, suicide, and AIDS has created greater receptivity to implementing school-based prevention programs. Recent federal, state, and local funding increases are leading to the implementation of many new interventions. Given the current climate, investigators are faced with an exciting opportunity and a difficult challenge: Can we help schools to establish effective, enduring, ecologically valid prevention programs?

Unfortunately, the history of introducing and disseminating programmatic innovations in the schools indicates that these tasks are difficult to accomplish successfully (Berman & McLaughlin, 1978; Elias, 1987; Sarason, 1982). Furthermore, although preparing children to function adaptively in society is typically cited as a critical goal of schooling, the educational system traditionally has not taken responsibility for directly promoting children's positive social development and life skills through formal, systematic programming. Before schools are willing or able to implement comprehensive SCP programs, proponents must clearly articulate the objectives and instructional models for such interventions, their benefits for children and school personnel, and methods for effectively integrating them into the system. However, the framework that currently guides most SCP research, the person-centered model, is not comprehensive enough to provide this information. The next two sections describe the person-centered SCP model and its limitations.

The Current Prevailing Model for SCP Intervention and Evaluation: The Person-Centered, Competence-Enhancement Approach

Cowen (1985) suggested that the three key tasks of person-centered SCP investigators were to: "(a) Identify skills or competencies with generative bases linking their presence to adjustment or absence to maladjustment; (b) Develop age and situationally appropriate programs to impart those skills; (c) Demonstrate that the targeted skills were acquired, adjustment enhanced, and that those two sets of gains were linked" (p. 40). To illustrate how investigators typically operationalize this model, we briefly describe how it has been applied to the most frequently cited exemplar of a successful primary prevention SCP program: interpersonal cognitive problem-solving (ICPS) training (Shure & Spivack, 1982; Spivack & Shure, 1974).

Many generative research studies across different age and sociodemograhic samples indicate that well-adjusted individuals fare better than maladjusted peers on tests evaluating component ICPS skills such as: sensing problems, recognizing feelings, generating alternative solutions, anticipating consequences, and using means-ends thinking to reach specified goals (Spivack, Platt, & Shure, 1976; Spivack & Shure, 1982). These data prompted Spivack et al. (1976) to hypothesize that enhancing people's ICPS skills would improve their behavioral adjustment. Based on a series of studies demonstrating that aggressive and inhibited 4- and 5-year-olds were more deficient than adjusted peers in generating alternative solutions and consequences, Spivack and Shure (1974) designed a 46-lesson program to teach these skills to inner-city preschoolers and kindergartners. In replicating studies, they found that ICPS-trained children improved, relative to nonprogram controls, in alternative-solution and consequential thinking and in teacher-rated behavioral adjustment. These improvements remained stable one year after training ended. Spivack and Shure also reported that gains in alternative solution thinking and adjustment were related, and suggested that the acquisition of this ICPS skill mediated improved behavior.[2]

The Report of the Task Panel on Prevention (1978) highlighted the findings of Spivack and Shure (1974) and other problem-solving training researchers as instructive and exciting. In fact, the Report maintained that competence training is "unquestionably a powerful tool for primary prevention" (p. 1843), and devoted more space to describing problem-solving interventions than any other prevention strategy. Since then, there has been a dramatic increase in problem-solving training studies (see reviews by Denham & Almeida, 1987; Durlak, 1983; Kirschenbaum & Ordman, 1984; Pellegrini & Urbain, 1985; Spivack & Shure, 1982; Tisdelle & St. Lawrence, 1986; Weissberg & Allen, 1986) and, more generally, in SCP research (see reviews by Cowen, 1985; Durlak & Jason, 1984; Kent & Rolf, 1979; Ladd & Mize, 1983).

Evaluations of these programs typically address three key questions: (a) Does training improve children's cognitive or behavioral skills? (b) Does training enhance children's adjustment as rated by teachers, peers, and/or self-report measures? and (c) Are skill acquisition and adjustment gains related? With respect to these questions, reviewers indicate that most SCP interventions significantly improve children's targeted skills; however, only some interventions successfully promote their adjustment; and few, if any, investigators find that specific skill acquisition directly mediates gains in adjustment (e.g., see reviews by Denham & Almeida, 1987; Durlak, 1983; Kirschenbaum & Ordman, 1984; Pellegrini & Urbain, 1985; Weissberg & Allen, 1986). Thus, in spite of the initial enthusiasm about the potential of person-centered preventive SCP programs, recent reviews are more reserved in their assessments of the field's current level of actual accomplishment.

In theory, school-based SCP is an attractive pathway to primary prevention in mental health (Report of the Task Panel on Prevention, 1978). However, based on the studies conducted to date, there is insufficient scientific evidence to comment definitively on its actual value. Levine and Perkins (1980) contended that it is a mistake to place excessive emphasis on person-centered SCP interventions with children in the absence of strong evidence of long-term preventive effects. They suggested that preventive interventions will only produce lasting effects when they are structured to focus on a variety of problems that are encountered over time at different developmental milestones and across various settings. They criticized the Report of the Task Panel on Prevention (1978) for describing competence training as an approach that promotes individual's adjustment independent of actual environmental settings.

To improve the effectiveness of future SCP interventions, investigators must critically examine the factors that have limited advances in this field. One reason for the mixed findings may have its roots in the very framework used to guide SCP program development and evaluation. Therefore, it may be valuable to scrutinize the person-centered SCP model and identify ways that this apparently straightforward formulation may compromise the success of SCP program and evaluation efforts.

Critique of the Person-Centered Model for School-Based SCP Training

In certain respects, the person-centered, preventive SCP model resembles the 200-year-old medical paradigm that has structured research to prevent a broad array of communicable diseases (e.g., polio) and nutritional diseases (e.g., rickets). The three-step medical paradigm involves: identifying reliably diagnosable diseases that are important enough to justify the development of prevention programs; conducting laboratory and epidemiological research to generate hypotheses about how such diseases develop; and designing and assessing experimental prevention programs based on the results of these studies (Bloom, 1985). This approach has been successful when applied to diseases that have a single cause or necessary precondition, but with multi-determined medical conditions, it is often inadequate. It has been even less effective when applied to psychosocial dysfunctions where multifactorial causation is typically the rule, and interventions must influence a diverse array of both person-centered and environmental variables to prevent or treat such problems.

In order to develop and evaluate SCP programs effectively, one must have a clear view about how social competence and psychosocial problem behaviors develop. The best current research and theory present compelling evidence that they develop from multiple influences rather than a single cause (e.g., Dodge, Pettit, McClaskey, & Brown, 1986; Hawkins & Weis, 1985; Jessor, 1984; Rutter, 1982, 1987).

For example, Rutter (1982) proposed that socially maladaptive problem behaviors develop through a complex interaction of four causative influences: individual predisposition, ecological predisposition, current circumstances, and prevailing opportunities or situations. Individual predispositional factors affecting one's behavior include genetic (e.g., temperament), physical (e.g., perinatal complications, serious illness), and environmental influences (e.g., the quality of parental love, discipline, and modeling). Ecological predispositions—such as the social environments provided by schools, peer groups, the community, and media—affect the acceptability of particular forms of behavior. Thus, the specific behaviors that youngsters engage in are influenced by the values of their peer group and the social expectations of the settings in which they interact.

Current circumstances, such as the stresses and supports people experience, also influence whether or not problem behaviors develop. Acute stressors, such as failing a final exam or losing a close friend, may precipitate depression or a suicide attempt. On the other hand, protective factors (e.g., positive communicative relationships with parents or peers; high perceived competence due to scholastic or athletic achievements) may help one to cope more effectively with stressful events. Finally, prevailing opportunities or situations interact with the previous causative influences to affect behavioral outcomes for individuals. For example, someone may feel depressed or anxious because of a genetic predisposition, attendance at a competitive or impersonal school, or the acute stress of parental divorce. Whether this results in substance abuse, a suicide attempt, or some other negative end state may depend on whether one has consistent access to cocaine, a gun, or some other problem-promoting stimulus. On the other hand, easy access to an understanding teacher or other support systems that encourage and reinforce a child's coping efforts may promote more adaptive development in spite of these risk variables (Masten & Garmezy, 1985).

These views regarding the multifactorial causation of behavior may help to explain two common negative findings identified by reviewers of brief person-centered SCP programs. First, very few investigators find that specific skill gains directly mediate improved adjustment in the children who benefit from training. Second, most attempts to evaluate the long-term effects of SCP programs yield equivocal findings. As we identify reasons for these negative findings, we highlight some limitations of the person-centered SCP model and present constructive ways to modify it.

Should we try to demonstrate that skill acquisition mediates adjustment gains? Most reviewers argue that it is theoretically important for SCP researchers to document linkages between skill acquisition and improved adjustment. In contrast, we believe that linkage analyses, as they have been conducted in most studies of large-scale prevention programs, are neither sensible nor informative. In fact, the person-centered perspective may cause some investigators to focus on the wrong mediating variables as they design and evaluate SCP programs.

The Report of the Task Panel on Prevention (1978) stated that Spivack and Shure "demonstrated direct linkages between the amount of gain in ICPS skills—particularly in the ability to generate alternative solutions—and improvement in subsequent adjustment" (p. 1841). Most reviewers indicate that there have been no compelling demonstrations of linkage since that time. Certain critics argue that the inability to identify specific ICPS mediators indicates that it may be incorrect to hypothesize that training ICPS skills promotes adjustment (e.g., Durlak, 1983). Others, who take a more moderate position, suggest that investigators must use more reliable and valid measures that assess: more developmentally and culturally appropriate ICPS skills; problem-solving processes rather than discrete skills; or domain-specific rather than assumed cross-situational abilities (e.g., Dodge et al., 1986; Rubin & Krasnor, 1986). In contrast, we contend that these suggestions will not significantly improve efforts to identify which intervention variables promote behavior change, as long as they are carried out in the context of a person-centered perspective.

We believe that no primary prevention researchers, including Spivack and Shure, have provided confirming evidence that skill acquisition *directly* mediates improved adjustment. Recently, Shure and Spivack (1982) presented new analyses of their 1974 data. Although they reported that the average alternative-solution gain score for program children who improved in adjustment was significantly higher than the mean gain score for those who remained maladjusted, it is important to note that the latter group also improved significantly in generating alternatives. Indeed, if there is any linkage between ICPS skill acquisition and subsequent adjustment gains, the nature of this complex relationship remains unclear. Given the repeated failure of other investigators to replicate Spivack and Shure's (1974) linkage finding, it seems plausible that their result may have occurred due to chance or because of other undetected, correlated variables. It may be more fruitful to replace linear searches for mediators with new strategies that realistically acknowledge the multivariate complexity of factors that contribute to children's behavioral improvement.

Furthermore, we are concerned about treating a measure of alternative solution thinking as if it adequately reflects the array of potential mediators of positive adjustment that problem-solving training offers. For example, such interventions may also: improve other cognitive, affective, or behavioral skills (e.g., consequential thinking, recognizing or expressing feelings, behaving assertively); enhance expectations about resolving most conflicts effectively; create opportunities to observe and practice effective solutions to a wide variety of problems; and introduce a common language that fosters improved social support and communication with teachers and peers when real-life problems occur. Given this variety of potential mediators, it is unlikely that one circumscribed cognitive skill could realistically account for much of the variance in the improved behavior.

In addition, Elias et al. (1986) commented that SCP interventions differ considerably in the nature of training offered and that variability in the quality of program implementation greatly affects intervention outcomes. For example, Rotheram (1982b) and Thompson-Roundtree and Musun-Baskett (1984) reported that relationships between the styles and performance of teachers and adjustment outcomes of students may be stronger than linkages between skill acquisition and adjustment gains. Spivack and Shure (1982) contended that teachers should use problem-solving dialoguing throughout the day in order to foster the maintenance and generalization of children's improved social behavior. Thus, it appears that *how* teachers convey material may be as important as *what* they convey in terms of promoting social competence.

In conclusion, the search for one direct, person-centered, mediating variable seems misguided when theory and clinical experience indicate that many factors play important mediating roles in behavioral improvement. Analyzing data from large heterogeneous samples may mask linkages that do exist in individual children or groups of children with similar skill levels or behavior patterns. Furthermore, variables such as teacher behavior and other environmental supports often play critical roles in promoting improved behavior. We are not suggesting that identifying mediating variables is unimportant. Instead, we argue that the issue is far more complicated than the person-centered SCP model suggests, and that new conceptualizations and approaches are needed to identify valid SCP mediators. In the meantime, it seems appropriate to consider SCP programs that consistently promote children's skills and adjustment to be effective, independent of the results of their linkage analyses. Evidently, some beneficial things are occuring even if research has not yet identified the contributing factors.

Is it realisitic to expect brief SCP programs to produce long-term benefits? There are several prevention advocates who caution that it is unrealistic to believe that short-term SCP programs can inoculate people against psychopathology for life in the same way that a polio vaccine protects people from that disease. For example, Zigler and Berman (1983) argued that "development is a continuous process; experiences at any given age are affected by and build on experiences that have come before. Thus, intervention at later stages of life can no more wipe out a history of disadvantage than can a brief early intervention inoculate a child against continuing disadvantage" (p. 88). They believe that the concept of critical periods is not useful for directing childhood intervention strategies and suggest that it is necessary to dovetail developmentally appropriate intervention programs from the prenatal stage through adolescence. Bloom (1985) also contended that developing competence training efforts to help people deal with stressful transitional life-events across the life span (e.g., school entrance, puberty, parenting, retirement) is more reasonable than providing a brief one-shot intervention during a critical period.

The multifactorial causative model of behavior suggests that precipitating crisis events and noxious environmental settings often play important roles in causing psychosocial dysfunction. Consequently, it seems doubtful that the effects of a beneficial psychosocial intervention, conducted at an early age, will endure without continued reinforcement or subsequent developmentally appropriate supports. In addition, when confronted with stressors, the availability of environmental resources may be critical to successful coping, even for well-adjusted individuals. These perspectives support the NMHA Commission's position regarding the need to develop preschool through high school SCP training (Long, 1986).

Finally, Elias (1987) argued that prevention efforts require changes in both persons and their settings in order to be efficacious and endure beyond one-time demonstration projects. However, most investigators do not examine the effects of their interventions on the system in which they occur, nor do they examine the process by which prevention programs become a part of the structure and routine of relevant settings (Kelly, 1987; Trickett, 1984). Until SCP researchers broaden their intervention perspective beyond a person-centered orientation, we believe that they will make only minor contributions to the effort of creating school-based programs that have enduring beneficial effects on large numbers of people and systems.

A New Conceptual Framework for Establishing School-Based SCP Programs

Table 9.1 outlines five phases that we view as critical to the establishment of effective school-based SCP efforts: (a) *Conceptualization* stresses the importance of explicity articulating the learning objectives of SCP programs and the theoretical considerations that guide the

TABLE 9.1 A New Framework for Conceptualizing, Designing, Implementing, Evaluating, and Disseminating School-Based SCP Programs

1 *Conceptualization.* Use theory, research findings, and intervention experience to identify combinations of personal resources (e.g., skills, beliefs, and knowledge) and environmental supports that promote social competence in specified domains and/or prevent psychopathology.

2. *Design.* Create replicable curricula that explicitly describe how to: (a) teach targeted personal resources to students; and (b) structure real-life opportunities where they can be practiced and reinforced. Ensure that the training program is developmentally and culturally appropriate, and based on effective classroom teaching principles.

3. *Implementation.* Adapt the program to the ecology of the school setting. Then provide proficient instruction, supervision, and on-site monitoring and coaching to ensure that training agents implement the program with integrity.

4. *Evaluation.* Conduct a comprehensive evaluation to: (a) document that the program has been carried out effectively; (b) assess whether the program improves students' personal resources, their social environments, and specified domains of social competence and adjustment; and (c) identify combinations of critical program learnings and environmental factors that contribute to social-competence and adjustment changes in selected groups of children.

5. *Maintenance and Dissemination.* Determine which program practices and system-level supports enable a successful program to sustain its beneficial impact over time and to be disseminated effectively to new sites.

selection and structuring of intervention strategies; (b) *Design* involves the creation of developmentally and culturally appropriate training materials and activities with clearly specified, replicable guidelines for implementation; (c) *Implementation* highlights issues related to adapting intervention programs to fit the ecological realities of school settings and identifies methods to ensure that training agents convey program concepts with integrity; (d) *Evaluation* focuses on ways to assess the quality of program implementation, the effects of training on target students, and the program variables that contribute to students' behavioral improvement; and (e) *Maintenance and Dissemination* identifies program practices and system-level policies or structures that allow beneficial SCP programs to endure and be replicated successfully in new sites.

In the following subsections, we present our views regarding the critical tasks for each phase. We also cite program issues and evaluation findings from our research to show how our new framework and SCP program efforts influence each other (Weissberg & Caplan, 1988; Weissberg, Caplan, & Bennetto, 1988; Weissberg & Gesten, 1982).

Conceptual Considerations

Currently, there is considerable debate about how to define social competence (Greenspan, 1981; Zigler & Trickett, 1978). It is critical that SCP investigators describe what they mean by social competence or incompetence and that they distinguish these terms from related concepts such as social skills or psychopathology. Our conceptualization of SCP has been influenced by several theorists (e.g., Dodge, 1986; Ford, 1982, 1985; Hawkins & Weis, 1985; Waters & Sroufe, 1983).

Waters and Sroufe (1983) defined the competent individual as "one who is able to make use of environmental and personal resources to achieve a good developmental outcome" (p. 81). Educable or modifiable personal resources include: cognitive, affective, and behavioral skills; personal beliefs and social attitudes; acquired information and tacit knowledge about relevant social issues and situations; and self-perceptions of performance efficacy in specific social domains or tasks. Environmental resources refer to important people (e.g., parents, teachers, peers), organizational policies and rules, formal and informal activities, and other setting-related variables that facilitate the development of one's capacity to coordinate affect, cognition, and behavior.

The ability to benefit from one's environment and achieve good developmental outcomes often depends on utilizing personal resources to recognize and generate the competence-enhancing opportunities that a setting has to offer. Good developmental outcomes emphasize both proximate and ultimate criteria. Proximate criteria, which focus on the critical tasks of one's developmental level and the requirements of the settings in which one functions, involve behavior that is adaptive in the present and also lays the foundation for positive developmental change. Good ultimate outcomes during adulthood involve: the ability to interact effectively at work, during leisure activities, and in interpersonal relationships; having positive expectations about one's performance in these domains; and the absence of psychopathology.

Several investigators view social competence as a summary term that reflects personal or social judgments about the general quality of an individual's performance in a given situation (Dodge, 1986; Ford, 1982; Hops, 1983; McFall, 1982; Waters & Sroufe, 1983). It is helpful to distinguish between the molar superordinate construct of social competence and the specific personal resources (e.g., skills, beliefs) that one coordinates synergistically to deal with social situations. The flexible coordination of these resources contributes to the performance of socially competent behavior, and adjustment problems may occur when one has difficulties in one or more resource areas. It is also important to emphasize that diverse skills and beliefs differentially mediate social competence for individuals at different ages and from varying social, economic, and ethnic contexts (Laosa, 1984; McFall, 1982).

The task of identifying which personal resources predict social competence is more complex than initially hypothesized. Historically, most studies of these relationships focused on individual component skills (e.g., alternative solution thinking) and personality traits or behavior independent of situation contexts. They typically found significant, but weak correlations (Rubin & Krasnor, 1986). Several investigators have recently begun to examine relations between children's social information processing patterns and behavioral competence within a situational context (Dodge et al., 1986; Rubin & Krasnor, 1986).

Dodge et al. (1986) proposed that five sequential processing steps are necessary for socially competent responding: encoding relevant social cues in the environment; interpreting them accurately; accessing or generating potential behavioral responses to the interpreted cues; evaluating the consequences of alternative responses and selecting an optimal choice; and effectively enacting the chosen response, self-monitoring its effects. Evaluating all five processing steps yields a far more accurate predictor of behavioral competence than assessing one or two discrete skills (Dodge, 1986). Since multiple processes are involved in behavioral responding, training children to use a processing framework may have stronger effects than focusing on only one or two component skills—especially since deficits at one stage of processing may negatively affect one's performance at a later stage.

Recent research also supports the value of employing a domain specific model to explain relations between social information-processing patterns and social behavior. Dodge et al. (1986) examined the reactions of children to situations involving peer group entry and peer provocation. Only children's group entry processing variables predicted their competence at actual group entry, whereas children's provocation processing variables predicted how aggressively they reacted in actual provocation situations. This suggests that children will not automatically and adaptively apply generic processing skills to every social task they face.

Slaby and Guerra (1988), who contend that SCP interventions should emphasize both process and content, point out that people's beliefs about specific behaviors significantly influence how they respond to particular situations. For example, some children who are challenged to fight may be adept social information processors. However, if they have been socialized to believe that people should fight when challenged, they may set a goal of beating up the aggressor and apply their processing skills to winning rather than generating options to achieve a potentially more adaptive goal. Thus, if one's primary training objective is to reduce aggression, focusing on students' information processing skills and beliefs about aggression may be more effective than teaching information processing strategies independent of specific situational contexts or students' beliefs. Similarly, attempts to promote students' competence at making friends may be most beneficial when they address students' skills, beliefs, and knowledge relevant to friendship-making situations. The domain-specific intervention model is supported by Durlak's (1983) review which indicates that targeted task-specific SCP programs typically have stronger and more beneficial effects than general cognitive or developmental SCP interventions.

Ford (1985) identified two central areas of competence that have important theoretical significance for intervention efforts: (a) the behavioral effectiveness of one's transactions with the environment (i.e., attaining adaptive personal and social goals in school, at work, during leisure activities, or in interpersonal relationships); and (b) the extent to which one has positive self-perceptions and a sense of efficacy when encountering social situations in these domains. Behavioral effectiveness and a sense of personal well-being are two key characteristics of mental health, and the objective of mental health interventions, whether preventive or treatment-oriented, should be to enhance or restore them.

It is also important to distinguish between social competence and psychopathology in order to achieve more conceptual clarity as the objectives of SCP programs are operationalized. We consider efforts to promote competence in major social domains to be important activities in and of themselves. Beyond these positive effects, enhancing social competence may also serve as a protective factor to prevent the development of psychopathology or maladjustment by helping one to cope more adaptively with stress (Garmezy, 1987; Rutter, 1982, 1987). We believe that certain critics of SCP programs, such as Lamb and Zusman (1982), have overemphasized the importance of preventing psychopathology (e.g., psychiatric disorders) and underestimated the value of promoting social competence. This perspective may cause reviewers to assess incorrectly the beneficial effects of an intervention. A program may enhance social competence in several domains, but fail to prevent more distal forms of psychopathology (e.g., conduct disorders, substance abuse) which have lower base rates and may occur later in development. In addition, these programs may improve the behavioral effectiveness and self-esteem of some people with diagnosable psychiatric disorders. Consequently, it seems most desirable to evaluate the effects of SCP programs on both social competence and psychopathology.

In summary, the broad conceptual task of SCP investigators is to identify combinations of processing skills, beliefs, and knowledge as well as environmental resources that promote social competence in specified domains and/or prevent psychopathology. Obtaining this information helps to shape decisions about what personal resources to teach in SCP programs, and how to enhance and reinforce them most effectively. This perspective, which expands upon the person-centered SCP model, has numerous implications for program design and evaluation.

Program Design Issues

Hawkins and Weis (1985) asserted that three conditions are critical for children to develop socially competent behavior: (a) they must have the cognitive, affective, and behavioral skills to succeed in a setting; (b) they must have multiple opportunities for meaningful positive involvements to apply these skills; and (c) those with whom they interact must consistently reinforce competent behavioral performance. According to this model, interventions that teach social skills must also be directed at environmental settings to create resources to reinforce children's real-life application, generalization, and maintenance of those skills. Person-centered SCP programs that focus on improving children's skills without also concentrating on the social tasks they face or the environmental settings in which they function will have limited effect on a select group at best (Elias, 1987; Levine & Perkins, 1980).

Hawkins and Weis's (1985) model suggests that the key task for SCP program designers is to create replicable curricula that describe how to: (a) teach targeted skills, beliefs, and information to students; and (b) structure meaningful real-life opportunities where they can be practiced and reinforced. The content of these training materials should be developmentally and culturally sensitive, and based on sound principles of effective classroom instruction (Hunter, 1987). Realistically, it takes several years of piloting and revising before general SCP objectives are effectively translated into a curriculum that is both interesting and beneficial to students. Our efforts to design curricula have benefited greatly through interactive collaboration with teachers. Initially, we develop lesson objectives, try out some of our ideas in the classroom, and then write the first draft of a lesson plan. Next, teachers critique the lesson plans and suggest modifications and/or additions before piloting them. After observing several teachers in action, we incorporate the best of their strategies into structured, detailed scripts.

Designing programs that effectively teach skills, beliefs, and information to students. Theoretically, there is a vast array of personal resources that one might teach to promote social competence. Among the integrated set of resources possessed by individuals who behave competently in a particular context are the abilities to: perceive the nature of the task and the feelings and perspectives of the people involved; feel motivated to establish an adaptive goal to address the situation; have confidence that they can successfully achieve their objective; access or generate goal-directed alternatives and link them with realistic consequences; decide on the optimal strategy, and when necessary, develop elaborated implementation plans that anticipate potential obstacles; carry out the chosen strategy with behavioral skill; self-monitor behavioral performance with the capacity to abandon ineffective plans, try back-up strategies, or reformulate goals as needed; and engage in emotion-focused coping when a desired goal cannot be reached or provide self-reinforcement for successful goal attainment (Dodge et al., 1986; D'Zurilla, 1986; Elias et al., 1986; Lazarus, 1980; Moos & Schaefer, 1986; Rubin & Krasnor, 1986; Weissberg & Allen, 1986).

Attempting to teach all of these resources in one program would be overwhelming. The specific personal resources that one teaches, how they are taught, and the situations for which they are used vary considerably depending on the age and the sociodemographic characteristics of the target population (Furman, 1980). In order to establish effective preschool to high-school SCP curricula, program designers must address fundamental questions such as: What combination of processing skills, beliefs, and information are appropriate to teach to children from different age, SES, and ethnic groups? In what sequence should these personal resources be taught to maximize their adaptive use in daily interactions? What social tasks are critical to master at what grade levels? What classroom teaching methods (e.g., verbal instruction, modeling, coaching, role play, self-instruction, positive reinforcement, peer instruction, cooperative learning) are most conducive to promoting skill and social-competence improvements that are generalized and maintained?

Weissberg et al.'s (1988) effort to design a middle-school SCP curriculum has been guided by the social information processing models of Rubin and Krasnor (1986) and Dodge (1986). Students use the following six-step, sequential model to cope with social problems: (a) stop, calm down, and think before you act; (b) say the problem and how you feel; (c) set a positive goal; (d) think of lots of solutions; (e) think ahead to the consequences; and (f) go ahead and try the best plan. In an initial evaluation, this SCP approach significantly improved middle-school students' information processing skills and social competence (Weissberg & Caplan, 1988).

In spite of these positive findings, some investigators might question whether the program employs too few or too many SCP steps and if they are sequenced properly. There is considerable debate about how many steps are beneficial to teach children at different age levels. For example, other SCP researchers have developed 4-step (Bash & Camp, 1980), 8-step (Elias et al., 1986), and 11-step models (Greenberg, 1987). At a more basic level, one might also challenge the desirability of teaching an explicit, directed, problem-solving approach. Other beneficial interventions employ an alternative Piagetian-influenced discovery teaching strategy that exposes children to a variety of problems, and guides them to discuss and practice ways to handle them (e.g., Elardo & Cooper, 1977; Spivack & Shure, 1974). Research is needed to clarify the effects that directed- and discovery-oriented interventions have on children with different sociodemographic characteristics, learning styles, and levels of adjustment. Other related unresolved debates concern the extent to which programs should focus on: (a) the promotion of cognitive, affective, and/or behavioral skills; and (b) the establishment of prosocial goals and behaviors by program trainers rather than the students themselves.

Well-designed programs are also sensitive to developmental and cultural issues in terms of the social situations that they emphasize. For example, Weissberg et al. (1988) focused on stressful problems and social tasks that a sample of inner-city adolescents reported experiencing frequently. The writings of Hill (1980) and Lipsitz (1984) have also prompted us to highlight important domains of social competence for young adolescents such as: communicating with parents and other adults; managing a new school structure with varied responsibilities; meeting new peers; coping with peer and media pressure to take dangerous risks; and establishing adaptive realistic goals for health, education, leisure activities, and future careers.

Among these competence domains, program teachers and students should prioritize the topics they wish to emphasize. It is doubtful that generic skill training will promote competence or prevent negative outcomes in multiple domains without first addressing students' beliefs and knowledge about those areas. Consequently, programs to prevent specific problem behaviors (e.g., substance use or teen pregnancy) might include a common processing framework, but the program content addressing students' beliefs and knowledge within these domains would differ considerably.

Theory should also influence the selection and sequencing of the SCP training approaches (e.g., modeling, role play). All too often, SCP training methods are applied haphazardly rather than systematically. Recently, Ladd and Mize (1983) presented a theoretical model for social-skills training based on Bandura's (1977) cognitive social-learning model of skill acquisition and behavior change. They articulated specific, sequential steps to: introduce skills, beliefs, and information to children; promote their ability to translate these concepts into competent social behavior; and foster skill maintenance and generalization to diverse situations. Ladd and Mize's (1983) structured training methodology offers a standard for other SCP program designers. While their approach is not the only way to enhance social competence, they have drawn attention to the importance of using theory to guide the inclusion and ordering of specific training methods and program lessons. Hunter's (1987) organized sequence of effective classroom instructional techniques also provides helpful direction about how to structure curriculum lessons.

If program lessons and teaching formats are not developmentally and culturally appropriate, they will not be effective. Students become frustrated when the skills being conveyed are too complex; they become bored when the concepts are too simple. In addition, curriculum content must be relevant to students' life experiences, yet not too personal or threatening. In many instances, the way that students respond to SCP training may be affected more by the style in which information is conveyed than by the content. Video is a valuable instructional tool to introduce controversial subject matter for discussion and to model the adaptive integration of cognition, affect, and behavior (Harwood & Weissberg, 1987). Cooperative learning exercises, during which students teach each other about SCP concepts, are powerful motivators to involve students as active program participants (Johnson, Johnson, Holubec, & Roy, 1984). It is critical to determine the best way to integrate these approaches systematically to capitalize on their potential for positively affecting students.

Finally, SCP training manuals should be written for, at least, four different audiences: researchers, teachers, parents, and students. SCP researchers are concerned that the intervention is theory-based in terms of its program content, the sequencing of concepts, and the training methods employed. Teachers desire clear and specific lesson plans that explain what to teach and how to convey it in an effective educational fashion. Parents require that these interventions focus on content and promote values that conform to the community standards and are sensitive to cultural norms. And students demand interesting, relevant, and informative lessons to motivate them to acquire and utilize the skills being taught.

Designing programs that create opportunities for students to practice skills and receive reinforcement. It is not uncommon for school administrators to receive the following tempting, well-intentioned offer from university researchers: "Let *our* graduate students or staff implement *our* SCP program in *your* schools. We won't require any work of your overburdened teachers. In fact, teachers do not even have to be present when the lessons are taught. If the program has positive impact, we will offer a workshop about it to interested teachers." From our perspective, this represents an operationalization of the person-centered SCP model at its worst. We recommend that school officials reject this proposal for a better deal!

If school-based SCP programs are ever going to produce lasting effects, classroom teachers, full-time support staff (e.g., school mental health professionals), and students (i.e., peer leaders) will have to be the primary training agents. This strategy allows schools to assume program ownership and to implement training on a regularly scheduled year-to-year basis, rather than being dependent on outside agencies to provide the service. In addition, school personnel and peers are more available and appropriate than outside training agents to establish school-based opportunities and resources that allow students to practice their newly acquired learnings and receive rewards for their efforts.

Weissberg et al. (1988) emphasized that teaching classroom lessons is only part of their total intervention. Teachers also learn to model to students the means by which they apply program concepts to handle classroom situations more adaptively. Most importantly, teachers also use the six-step social information processing framework to "dialogue" with students to prompt their adaptive application of newly acquired skills and to reinforce their effective efforts. Several investigators contend that most students will not benefit significantly from an SCP intervention unless their teachers consistently and competently use dialoguing when real-life social tasks and problems occur during the day (Spivack & Shure, 1982; Weissberg, 1985).

Weissberg et al. (1988) also proposed several different ways to create environmental resources, both in and out of the classroom, that support the development of socially competent behavior. For example, the curriculum introduces a class project, "101 Ways to Make the World a Better Place," in which students use their personal resources to benefit others in their class, school, home, or community. Teachers set up "good news" and "problem" boxes in the classroom to encourage students to share some of their latest achievements and to promote continued use of the problem-solving model for dealing with interpersonal concerns. Teachers are asked to conduct regularly scheduled class problem-solving meetings and use worksheets that provide students with a structured approach for reviewing the ways in which they handled various social tasks. In certain instances, students may have personal problems that require more involvement or expertise than a classroom teacher may be able to provide. The program emphasizes that, while some issues are suitable for classroom discussion, others are more appropriate to handle privately. In order to make it easier for students to approach various helping resources, there are opportunities in the curriculum for school staff and community service providers to participate in class lessons to explain their function and how they can be helpful to students. We also provide training to other school staff (e.g., counselors, in-house suspension teachers, and principals). This enables additional school personnel to work from, reinforce, and extend SCP concepts introduced by the teacher.

Recent research suggests that same-age or older students who serve as facilitators in middle-school and high-school SCP programs often promote adaptive behavior as much as or more than classroom teachers (e.g., Botvin, Baker, Renick, Filazolla, & Botvin, 1984). Designing interventions in which teachers collaborate with peer leaders appears to be a very promising approach (Perry & Jessor, 1985), and should be further developed as an important feature of SCP programs.

In theory, a school-based systems approach that promotes personal and environmental resources should be more powerful than a strictly person-centered effort. However, as SCP programs become an integral part of the school curriculum, there are many ecological and implementation concerns to address. No matter how well a curriculum is designed, it will not positively affect children if a school system fails to implement it effectively.

Implementing Interventions with Integrity

There are many SCP interventions that improve children's performance in targeted skill areas, but fail to enhance their social competence (Durlak, 1983; Kirschenbaum & Ordman, 1984). While some
critics interpret these results as the failure of the particular intervention strategy, others contend that these findings may reflect shortcomings in the program's design or implementation. We illustrate this
debate by briefly describing some of our earlier SCP efforts.

Weissberg and Gesten (1982) reviewed three consecutive prevention studies in which they trained classroom teachers to teach
problem-solving skills to second- to fourth-grade students. In all three
interventions, program children improved significantly more than
controls on several tests of cognitive and behavioral problem-solving
skills. In contrast, competence findings were mixed. In the first year
suburban children, who received a 9-week, 17-lesson training program, showed no competence gains at post assessment (Gesten et al.,
1982). Next, Weissberg, Gesten, Rapkin et al. (1981) strengthened the
pilot program by increasing the number of lessons from 17 to 52, the
frequency of training from 2 to 4 times a week, and the length of the
intervention from 9 weeks to 4 months. They reported that suburban,
but not inner-city youngsters improved on several measures of
teacher-rated competence and problem behavior. In the third intervention, Weissberg, Gesten, Carnrike et al. (1981) found that both
suburban and inner-city children who received an improved 42-lesson
program gained more than controls in self-reported confidence about
resolving interpersonal problems and teacher ratings of problem and
competence behaviors.

Viewed as three independent studies, these findings suggest that
problem-solving training does not consistently enhance children's adjustment. However, Weissberg and Gesten (1982) gave greater cre-
dence to their more recent findings since each program built on and
benefited from earlier ones. Although aspects of the third intervention were similar to the initial version, several important modifications were made in curriculum content, program structure, instructional strategies, and the training and on-site supervision of
teachers who implemented the program. Weissberg and Gesten
(1982) contended that it is unrealistic to expect that a newly developed SCP program, taught for the first time by classroom teachers
being trained by consultants without extensive program experience,
will promote students' competence. Instead they argued that well-
designed SCP programs will be more beneficial when they are imple-

mented by experienced SCP teachers who are trained by knowledgeable consultants.

Yeaton and Sechrest (1981) defined integrity of treatment as "the degree to which treatment is delivered as intended" (p. 160). Well-designed programs that are implemented with low integrity typically appear ineffective. Thus, investigators must specify ways to ensure the proper teaching of SCP programs. Effective implementation practices include: developing a structured detailed curriculum; offering teacher training before, during, and after the intervention; providing classroom assistance and on-site coaching as training agents deliver the program; and organizing system policies and supports that encourage teachers to convey the program effectively.

Providing proficient instruction, supervision, and on-site coaching to training agents. Ideally, effective SCP teachers should master a variety of instructional responsibilities. At the most basic level, they should understand program concepts and be able to convey them in ways that motivate students to learn. They should also be able to: (a) model socially competent cognition, affect, and behavior; (b) use dialoguing flexibly to prompt and reinforce student attempts to problem solve and behave adaptively; (c) create real-life opportunities that encourage students to practice their newly acquired learnings; and (d) identify and remediate specific resource deficits in children with varying skill levels or behavior problems. Realistically speaking, it typically requires consultative support and teaching a program at least once before teachers begin to master these areas.

There are several training/supervision procedures that facilitate the development of SCP instructional competence. Prior to the classroom intervention, several training sessions should be devoted to overviewing the entire training manual, learning program concepts, and demonstrating how the skills being taught can help teachers to resolve commonly encountered problems. Teachers who experience the value of SCP training firsthand and internalize the process tend to become more knowledgeable, enthusiastic instructors. After classroom instruction begins, it is beneficial to conduct frequent (e.g., bimonthly) meetings to discuss teacher reactions to previous lessons and to role play upcoming lessons. During these sessions, experienced SCP teachers or consultants can provide videotaped and live modeling demonstrations of effective SCP training strategies and dialoguing. Then teachers can role play lessons and receive feedback. The opportunities to share reactions about teaching and classroom management techniques, and to watch others present lessons to students have been characterized by teachers as valuable learning experiences.

The most important training/supervision practice is on-site coaching. In the context of a group meeting, teachers may have difficulty summarizing how they implement SCP lessons and how their students respond to them. On-site coaching, which involves observing teachers conducting actual classroom lessons, enables consultants to monitor the integrity of classroom training efforts and to provide corrective feedback, as needed, about the best ways to promote student competence.

Even with detailed curriculum and good teacher training, many variables may interfere with effective program delivery. For example, some students are physically or mentally absent while lessons are being taught. Classroom management problems may create an environment that is not conducive to SCP concept mastery. Changes in the school schedule or other instructional demands often result in teachers having inadequate time to teach a lesson. On other occassions, teachers may focus on one interesting part of a lesson for longer than is intended, and then have to rush through the rest of the lesson. In summary, although trainers may meet teaching objectives by mentioning all the key points a lesson plan emphasizes, this does not guarantee that students will meet program learning objectives. Clearly, there is a need to specify criteria that will enable researchers to document that teachers are properly implementing the program and that students are mastering key concepts.

Adapting SCP programs to the ecology of the school setting. Our initial SCP efforts were conducted in elementary schools (Weissberg, 1985). More recently, we have worked at the secondary-school level (Weissberg & Caplan, 1988). The differences between the cultures of the two school settings are enormous (Sarason, 1982). Experiencing this contrast has underscored the powerful impact that ecological variables have on how effective or enduring an SCP program can be.

It is easier to introduce SCP programming in elementary schools than in secondary schools. Most elementary-school teachers and administrators are strongly committed to students' academic and social development. In addition, classes are typically self-contained so students remain with the same teacher for the most if not all of the day. Thus, teachers have more flexibility about when to teach the program during the course of the day or week. Finally, in most instances, elementary-school teachers are directly responsible to their building principal. Thus, if the principal supports a program, teachers feel more comfortable treating it as a priority.

This set of circumstances may seem ideal to person-centered SCP researchers implementing a one-time demonstration project. While they come to the schools with a clear understanding of their program and experimental needs, they may pay little attention to how their program fits in with the curricula that are taught in previous or subsequent grades or at other points during the school year. When teachers ask if this program should be incorporated as part of the social studies, science, or health curriculum, the investigator may tell them to decide what is best given their needs. This response may be adequate in the short term as teachers decide what they will replace or streamline to fit the program into their schedule. However, without more thoughtful planning, it is doubtful that the program will be taught in a systematic, effective way after the researcher leaves the setting (Berman & McLaughlin, 1978).

Secondary schools differ from elementary schools in many ways. For example, most secondary schools are departmentalized. Students who had one teacher in elementary school may now have five. Teachers may see students for five periods rather than for five days a week, and may teach 150 rather than 25 students a year. In addition, teachers specializing in one subject area must often seek approval from a department supervisor (as well as the building principal) before they introduce a new program in their class. These factors make it more confusing and usually more difficult to implement SCP programs at the secondary-school level.

There is nothing like departmentalization to sensitize an SCP investigator to the ecological realities of a school! When teachers have less time with each class of students, the resulting perception of having too much to teach in too little time prompts them to be more concerned about structural program issues such as: How many lessons are in the overall program? How many lessons are taught per week? How long does each lesson last? There is often a discrepancy between the number of SCP lessons investigators believe it requires to affect students' behavior and how many lessons teachers are willing to sacrifice from their usual teaching responsibilities. There may also be conflicts about the ideal number of times per week that lessons should be taught. In our early SCP efforts at the middle-school level, teachers taught SCP lessons twice a week. Several teachers expressed concern that teaching SCP and traditional subjects on alternate days detracted from the capacity of some students to master both curricula. From the school perspective, it is more common to teach a new unit for five days a week from start to finish. Teachers also raise issues about making SCP training more similar to other subjects by assigning homework and grading students' performance. Experience suggests that students and teachers take the lessons more seriously when homework and grades are incorporated into the program.

It is also difficult to determine which department (e.g., social studies, science, health, or language arts) should provide SCP training. Unless SCP investigators work closely with school personnel to make an informed choice about this decision, it is unlikely that the SCP program will become a permanent part of the school's curriculum. Before recommending how SCP training could be best integrated into a district's instructional activities, it is advisable to examine current curricular requirements across all departments. When a department adopts SCP programming, it is critical that it replace a unit of comparable length in the existing curriculum. Otherwise, teachers will have to abbreviate what they ordinarily teach as well as SCP training, and student learning in both areas will suffer. In certain school systems, it may be preferable to include SCP during morning or afternoon home-room periods or in specialized courses devoted to life skills training.

Additional problems in training and scheduling often arise when a district initiates several SCP-related efforts concurrently. For example, a school may introduce independent programs to prevent substance abuse or teen pregnancy and other initiatives to promote employment skills or good health habits. Unless these efforts are coordinated, teachers and students will feel confused and burdened—especially if different processing skills and content areas are emphasized by each program.

Finally, although there are many virtues to having classroom teachers serve as primary trainers, there are also limitations. First, some teachers lack the interpersonal skills or desire to be SCP trainers. Consequently, mandating that all teachers in a certain department provide SCP instruction may create negative experiences for such teachers and their students. Second, specialized health educators, rather than classroom teachers, may be needed to work with older students in order to address questions about certain sensitive topics such as drugs and sex. In fact, in certain health education programs dealing with issues such as substance abuse, positive effects were greater when peers rather than teachers served as the primary training agents (Botvin et al., 1984). Finally, many communities object to classroom discussions about personal family matters. For example, while it may be appropriate to discuss strategies for dealing with teasing or fighting, discussions about personal experiences of child abuse and parental alcoholism are better dealt with elsewhere. Therefore, schools require back-up supports that allow students to discuss issues that are too personal to raise in class.

In conclusion, experience working in different school settings (e.g., elementary and secondary) and diverse school districts with varying priorities show us that there is no single best way to implement an SCP program. Clearly, however, knowledge of the priorities and ecological realities of systems in which interventions are placed will increase the likelihood that a beneficial program may become an integral part of the system's curriculum.

Program Evaluation

Evaluation of SCP interventions have typically followed the person-centered approach. Researchers assess targeted skill acquisition and improvements in behavioral adjustment, and search for linkages between skill and adjustment gains (Cowen, 1985). This section identifies the limitations of this evaluation framework and suggests ways to modify it. We emphasize the importance of: (a) documenting that the intervention has been implemented with integrity; (b) assessing program effects on a broader array of dependent variables (e.g., personal resources, social environments, specified domains of social competence, and adjustment); and (c) identifying combinations of critical program learnings and environmental supports that foster improved social competence and adjustment in selected groups of children.

Document that the program was implemented with integrity. When an SCP intervention fails to enhance targeted skills or adjustment, there are two equally plausible conclusions: either the intervention was ineffective or the program was not delivered in a fashion likely to be beneficial. A conceptual framework for evaluating interventions is useful only if it allows for a clear interpretation of outcome results. Unfortunately, many person-centered SCP program evaluators can not compellingly explain negative outcome findings because they do not attempt to document how well their programs are implemented. For example, when Weissberg and Gesten (1982) followed the person-centered model of evaluation in their early research, they could offer only *post hoc* explanations for why their initial interventions failed to promote the adjustment of their subjects.

From a scientific standpoint, it would be preferable to design SCP evaluations to collect both process and outcome data, and to report results in two stages. First, researchers should document the integrity of program implementation by evaluating process variables presumed to mediate learning. Prior to analyzing outcome data, researchers would assess the extent to which teachers met established criteria with respect to conveying program concepts and creating opportunities to use skills. The decision to conduct outcome analyses would hinge on the documented effectiveness of program implementation. For the field to advance, future SCP evaluations must examine treatment integrity as well as outcomes (Yeaton & Sechrest, 1981).

Common implementation problems that lead to negative outcome results include situations when: (a) teachers convey classroom SCP lessons ineffectively; or (b) teachers present lessons adequately, but do not create meaningful opportunities to prompt and reinforce students for applying SCP learnings in daily interactions. In an effort to gather information on the integrity of program implementation, Weissberg and Caplan (1988) devised a checklist to assess teacher effectiveness in the classroom. Two observers independently rated all program teachers on two dimensions: (a) mastery and conveyance of program concepts, and (b) modeling and encouragement of targeted skills. The raters achieved high inter-rater agreement. Interestingly, positive relationships were found between the quality of teacher implementation and improvements in students' problem-solving thinking and social competence. Although preliminary, these findings suggest the importance of taking into account program integrity when assessing the impact of SCP interventions.

It also seems worthwhile to investigate features that might contribute to instructional performance. For example, training agents should rate the training manual they use in terms of the quality of its detail, clarity, content, structure, and instructional approaches used to convey skills and information. SCP program evaluators should describe clearly the structure and content of teacher training meetings and on-site coaching since inadequate or insufficient teacher training/supervision may negatively affect implementation integrity. The consultants and training agents should also rate the quality of the teacher training/supervision being offered. It is also worth noting whether building principals, other school personnel, and parents are involved in training, and if so, how. We suspect that better and more extensive staff training will contribute to more proficient instruction.

It is critical for SCP programs to specify plans for quality control, including on-site monitoring to detect implementation lapses and coaching to help teachers improve the quality of their training efforts. In addition, investigators must document which aspects of implementation are central for facilitating students' competencies and develop assessment strategies for reliably rating trainer performance in those areas. Until this is done, our proposal to evaluate implementation integrity before assessing program outcome will remain an interesting theoritical notion rather than a common expectation of acceptable research practice.

Assess whether the program improves students' personal resources, their social environments, and specified domains of social competence and adjustment. Many reviewers (e.g., Krasnor & Rubin, 1981) express the common concern that evaluations of SCP interventions rely primarily on cognitive variables, often to the neglect of affective (e.g., empathy, emotion-focused coping, impulse control) and behavioral skills (e.g., interactions with peers, assertiveness). The conceptualization of target skills should also be broadened to include children's beliefs, social values, and expectations about behavioral outcomes. As noted earlier, we prefer the term *personal resources* to *skills* as a way of emphasizing the array of variables that meaningfully contribute to competent behavioral responding.

Even when only cognitive skills are assessed, researchers primarily emphasize evaluations of discrete skills rather than processes. This is problematic given the fact that many social developmentalists contend that measuring separate units of cognition, affect, or behavior accounts for only a small proportion of variance in explaining social competence (Waters & Sroufe, 1983). Our thinking in this area has been influenced by the sequential assessment techniques of Dodge et al. (1986) who have articulated a five-step information-processing model of competence. We are currently applying Dodge's processing framework to an assessment of the problem-solving skills of young adolescents. Dodge et al.'s (1986) perspectives on domain specificity have also affected our strategies of cognitive skill evaluation. For example, the primary cognitive assessment instrument to evaluate our middle-school SCP program presents students with a series of provocation situations rather than an array of disparate social tasks (Weissberg & Caplan, 1988). This decision reflects the priority our intervention places on teaching alternatives to aggressive behavior.

It has been argued that change in both individuals and their settings is required for enduring program effects (Elias, 1987). Others have emphasized the importance of providing opportunities for guided applications of skills outside of training classes (Hawkins & Weis, 1985). Assessment of program effects needs to be broadened to include not only personal resources, but also an evaluation of social environmental change (Trickett, 1984). In the schools, such environmental effects might include: the extent to which training agents encourage use of newly acquired skills during and after program implementation; consistency among various school personnel (e.g., teachers, guidance counselors, in-house suspension teachers) in the use of dialoguing and socialization techniques; and the development of new policies or activities that structure opportunities and rewards for the competent student behavior.

Finally, in SCP outcome studies, it is important to evaluate specific domains of social competence as well as psychosocial problem behaviors and maladjustment. While the latter variables may serve as distal goals for interventions, it is equally important to promote more proximal, developmentally appropriate, basic competencies. Examples of key domains of competence emphasized in our middle-school SCP program include: communicating effectively with parents and adults; meeting new peers; adaptively handling situations that provoke aggression; and coping with peer pressure to take dangerous or unhealthy risks (Weissberg et al., 1988). Student competence in these domains can be assessed by ratings provided by teachers, parents, peers, and self-reports (Hops, 1983). One critical endeavor for SCP researchers is to identify developmentally and culturally sensitive assessment techniques to measure domains of competence for children at all grade levels.

Jessor (1984) and Garmezy (1987) pointed out that the promotion of social competence may serve as a protective factor against the development of psychosocial problem behaviors (e.g., substance abuse, teen pregnancy, school dropout) and psychopathology (e.g., conduct disorder, depression, anxiety). Periodic follow-up assessments conducted as children progress through school will enable a careful tracking of both early risk behaviors and psychiatric symptoms as they emerge and change over time (Kellam, Dolan, Crockett, Carran, & Edelsohn, 1986). Employing longitudinal assessment strategies that evaluate multiple indicators of social competence and maladaptation may clarify relationships between social competence and psychopathology as well as the long-term effects and limitations of SCP training.

Identify combinations of critical program learnings and environmental factors that contribute to social competence and adjustment improvements in selected groups of children. When a child benefits from SCP training, it may be due to a combination of factors. SCP training may promote a child's capacity to: manage stress or anger more effectively; perceive problem situations more accurately; set positive, prosocial goals; generate more adaptive alternative solutions; anticipate consequences more realistically; enact solutions with more behavioral effectiveness, planfulness, and persistence. It may also enhance children's beliefs that they are capable of handling certain social tasks effectively or provide them with information about the actual risks of engaging in various dangerous behaviors. Finally, SCP training may also improve communication between students and their teachers, or clarify how to seek help from friends, family members, or other resources when faced with difficult situations.

Given this array of potential mediators, the assumption of a one-to-one correspondence between specific skills and competence/ maladjustment would appear to underestimate the complexity of how social competence or problem behaviors develop (Rutter, 1982). At the very least, it appears theoritically sensible to expect that combinations of diverse personal and environmental resources would contribute to adjustment changes. The picture is further complicated by the findings of Rotheram (1982a) who suggested that building on children's strengths rather than targeting their deficits may be a more beneficial approach for promoting social competence. These perspectives cause one to question whether it is possible to identify variables that mediate improved adjustment in children involved in a primary prevention program, especially when a group is heterogeneous in terms of their sociodemographic characteristics and their initial skill and adjustment levels.

The task of identifying mediators is extremely difficult. It seems unlikely that useful information will be gleaned by the commonly employed data-analytic strategy of assessing linkage relationships for an entire sample of trained subjects. We recommend that SCP investigators explore alternative approaches to address this issue. One promising strategy may involve using a replicated single-case experimental design methodology to study selected subjects intensively across multiple domains at multiple time points (Barlow & Hersen, 1984). Certain factors should inform decisions about the best way to identify subjects for participation in such research. Most important, one must be confident that the subjects will be exposed to effective classroom training. Consequently, it may be best to select students enrolled in classes taught by experienced SCP teachers with documented histories of implementing programs with integrity. It is also essential to identify the qualities of students that one wants to assess, and the personal and environmental variables that are most likely to mediate social competence and adjustment improvements. Finally, it will be informative to assess children's functioning on multiple occasions in multiple contexts. One priority is to assess competence at both school and home. In spite of the suggested benefits that SCP training has on children's behavior at school, there is still very little information about whether this training produces similarly positive effects in the homes of sociodemographically diverse students. Clearly, there are a multitude of important questions and issues that this methodology, seldom used in the context of assessing primary prevention SCP program outcomes, could address.

Maintenance and Dissemination of Beneficial SCP Programs

When the senior author moved to New Haven in 1982, he met with the Director of Research for the New Haven Schools to exchange views about SCP programming. Before endorsing the proposed projects, the Director requested answers to two questions: (a) How would the SCP programs benefit students, school personnel, and the community? and (b) If the programs were beneficial, what steps could be taken to ensure that they would endure in the school system after funding ended or if the researcher left the area? Most university researchers easily provide acceptable responses to the first question. In contrast, many are less concerned and less informed about the second issue. We contend that reseachers must respond knowledgeably to both questions before they can develop enduring, ecologically valid, school-based SCP interventions. If researchers addressed both issues satisfactorily before beginning their work in the schools, the ecological validity of most programs would improve.

This recommendation stems from our concern that educational innovators and school personnel have a weak track record concerning the development of lasting, effective programs. Berman and Mc-Laughlin's (1978) comprehensive review of federal efforts to support the implementation and maintenance of educational innovations in local school districts indicates that: (a) no group of existing educational treatments has consistently improved student outcomes; (b) successful demonstration projects generally have difficulty sustaining their success for several years; and (c) successful programs are not easily disseminated, and attempts to replicate them in new sites are generally less beneficial than the original effort.

In spite of this pessimistic assessment about the history of implementing, maintaining, and disseminating beneficial educational innovations, several strategies have been identified that increase the likelihood of institutionalizing successful programs (Blakely et al., 1987; Commins, 1987). We briefly summarize some of these suggestions and the strategies we employ for collaborating with school systems to create maximally beneficial programs by highlighting three areas: (a) system entry with the goals of assessing system resources/needs and establishing close collaborative working relationships; (b) instituting first-rate staff and organizational development training efforts; and (c) creating system structures and policies to support effective SCP programming.

System entry. Before implementing new programs it is important that program developers: (a) obtain information from the school system and local community about potential resources and supports as well as barriers and resistance to a proposed innovation; (b) interact with potential program users and recipients to assess their receptivity to and concerns about involvement with the effort; (c) ensure that top-level district officials in the system are aware of and support the innovation and its goals; and (d) identify personnel in the system to serve as within-system advocates of the innovation (Commins, 1987).

Prior to our implementation in the New Haven school system, we met with many school administrators, teachers, parents, and students to gain a better sense of the system's resources, needs, and current programming efforts.[3] Our systems-entry effort was more comprehensive than the approach commonly employed by person-centered researchers, who pay little attention to the larger organizational structure in which their targeted group is involved. We believe that more reconnaissance and relationship development is desirable at the outset if one wishes to establish a solid, long-term collaboration with the system. We learned a great deal about the system's operating procedures, and also developed supportive contacts with several individuals who have played key roles in advocating for and improving our SCP efforts.

Discussions with several Yale faculty members (e.g., Dr. Seymour Sarason and Dr. James Comer), who have collaborated with the New Haven schools for many years, have also proved invaluable. The most important objectives for these conversations were to: (a) learn more about their experiences working with the system; (b) obtain their reactions to and suggestions about our proposed plan of SCP research; and (c) ensure that our efforts would complement rather than clash with their longstanding programs. Finally, our staff also met with several officials from key state agencies that establish policy and provide funding for innovative school-based programming efforts. Our efforts to create lasting SCP programs have been aided tremendously by awareness of potential state-level supports and barriers to such efforts.

Establishing staff and organizational development training. Although it is difficult to maintain and disseminate successful demonstration programs, Berman and McLaughlin (1978) identified several factors that facilitate these efforts. These include: offering concrete, extended staff development and training that is teacher-specific; using experienced SCP teachers as co-trainers of other teachers; involving building principals in training; providing systematic on-site consultation and classroom assistance from training consultants and experienced program teachers; creating opportunities for teachers to observe similar programs in other classes or schools; regularly scheduling project meetings that address practical problems; and involving teachers in project decision-making. In New Haven, the Director of Staff and Organizational Development has supported our efforts, programmatically and financially, to adhere to these practices.

It requires considerable effort to lay the foundation for effective program dissemination. Commins (1987) recommended working with appropriate school officials to identify two settings where the innovation is likely to succeed for initial implementation. It may take several years of close collaboration between SCP program developers and school personnel to firmly establish the effort. Once that objective is achieved, careful collaborative planning for expanding to other schools may begin. There are several advantages to establishing programs in a few local settings before attempting wider dissemination: (a) staff from those schools can help to train teachers from other settings; (b) personnel from new schools can site-visit the first setting to observe the program in action; (c) positive reactions by the administrative and teaching staffs at the initial program schools often enhance receptivity and enthusiasm for implementation at new sites; and (d) there is adequate time to adapt the program to the ecological realities of the system planfully, rather in a crisis-oriented fashion (Blakely et al., 1987).

Developing system structures and policies to support SCP programming. With problems such as substance abuse, teen pregnancy, and AIDS, our society is becoming increasingly receptive to incorporating SCP programming as an integral part of the school curriculum. However, unless formal structures and policies are established to help achieve this goal, we fear that SCP will be a fad that comes and goes, just like many other educational innovations (Sarason, 1983). We have several recommendations to solidify SCP's foundations and increase its staying power.

One priority is to articulate the sequencing of preschool through high-school SCP curricula so that each year builds on the preceding ones, but varies sufficiently so that students find lessons understandable, informative, and novel. In New Haven, we are collaborating with a committee of administrators, teachers, and parents to develop a comprehensive social development curriculum. The Deputy Superintendent has asked us to detail the scope and sequence of the program at each grade level (i.e., the same requirement of curriculum committees for math, social studies, science, etc.). We are focusing on theory, research findings, and available curricula as we attempt to specify the processing skills, beliefs, social tasks, domains of competence, and training methods that should be emphasized at each grade level. Although there have been a few initial efforts to develop comprehensive mental health education (Nerad, 1986) and substance abuse prevention programs (Roberts & Fitzmahan, 1986), we are not aware of any outstanding program models. Until schools have several excellent packages from which to choose, it is not likely that they will choose any.

Second, school systems need to identify an explicit place in the curriculum for these programs to exist. Some districts may choose to incorporate it as part of the health, science, or social studies curriculum. This could be effective as long as such programming becomes an integral part of the curriculum rather than an add-on that teachers must infuse or squeeze into their normal teaching requirements. Another possibility would be to establish an independent SCP or life-skills area of instruction. Third, there must be some accountability to document that children are meeting SCP learning objectives. For these programs to last, it is crucial to develop easy-to-administer, valid assessment measures to evaluate students' levels of performance and growth.

Finally, someone in the system should be assigned the responsibility of monitoring the implementation and impact of SCP training. With no one accountable, it is far too easy for a program to fall through the cracks. In New Haven, we have proposed that the system establish a position for a Supervisor of Social Development. This individual would have responsibility for comprehensive SCP programming in the same way that supervisors of traditional academic subjects are responsible for their areas of instruction. While some people look askance at us when we make this recommendation, there is consensus that new structures and policies are needed to support the development of a viable SCP program in the district. The challenge that lies ahead is to determine a cost-efficient, effective way to achieve this objective.

Concluding Remarks

There is an old joke about a nearsighted man who has misplaced his keys late at night and is looking for them by the light of a street lamp. Another man comes along and offers to join the search. After looking for a considerable period of time, the second man asks, "Are you sure this is where you lost them?" The first replies, "No, but this is where the light is!"

We contend that university researchers and school personnel who employ person-centered SCP models to develop school-based prevention programs suffer from the same myopia as the first man. Although person-centered intervention strategies often yield short-term benefits, they will produce limited results, at best, if they fail to attend to the environmental systems in which these interventions occur. Investigators who persist in using the person-centered model may never find the "keys" to developing enduring prevention programs that benefit large numbers of children. More energy and resources should be devoted to designing comprehensive, ecologically oriented, multi-year interventions which are more likely to produce positive developmental outcomes.

The major objective of this chapter has been to propose a new conceptual model that identifies places where additional light is needed. We believe that attention to all five phases of school-based SCP programming—conceptualization, design, implementation, evaluation, and dissemination—will enhance future efforts. Realistically speaking, it may require decades of effective collaboration between university researchers and school personnel to develop enduring preschool through high-school SCP programming. It will be necessary to create new initiatives and to increase funding that supports the development and long-term maintenance of these collaborations. The investment is essential if we are to establish effective schools with beneficial SCP programs to develop educated, socially competent citizens.

Notes

1. In fact, ten years ago the senior author of this chapter was a co-author on a paper presented at the Third Vermont Conference for the Primary Prevention of Psychopathology (Gesten, Flores de Apodaca, Rains, Weissberg, & Cowen, 1979). That paper describes the first effort of the Rochester Social Problem-Solving (SPS) Group to develop, implement, and evaluate a classroom-based, teacher-taught SPS program to second and third graders. We recommend that interested readers review that paper to identify, first-hand, how some perspectives on school-based SCP program and evaluation efforts have evolved during the past decade.

2. We disagree with Spivack and Shure's interpretation of this result. Finding relationships between gains in skills and adjustment does not necessarily suggest that skill acquisition directly mediates adjustment improvements. We will detail our perspective

about this finding later. For now, we report Spivack and Shure's position uncritically to illustrate parsimoniously the person-centered SCP model.

3. Some of our key New Haven contacts during system entry included the following: Superintendent of Schools; several members of the Board of Education; Assistant Superintendents of Administration, Curriculum, and Finance; Director of Pupil Personnel Services; Chairpersons of the Departments of Social Work, Psychology, Guidance/Counseling, and Special Education; Supervisors of Science, Social Studies, Math, and Reading/Language Arts; the President of the Teachers' Union; the Director of Staff and Organizational Development; the President of the city-wide Parent-Teachers' Organization; and the Director of Research and Special Programs.

References

Albee, G. W. (1982). Preventing psychopathology and promoting human potential. *American Psychologist, 37*, 1043–1051.

Albee, G. W. (1985). The argument for primary prevention. *The Journal of Primary Prevention, 5*, 213–219.

Bandura, A. (1977). *Social learning theory.* Englewood Cliffs, NJ: Prentice-Hall.

Barlow, D. H., & Hersen, M. (1984). *Single case experimental designs: Strategies for assessing behavior change* (2nd ed.). New York: Pergamon Press.

Bash, M. S., & Camp, B. W. (1980). Teacher training in the Think Aloud classroom program. In G. Cartledge & J. F. Milburn (Eds.), *Teaching social skills to children: Innovative approaches* (pp. 143–178). New York: Pergamon Press.

Berman, P., & McLaughlin, M. W. (1978). *Federal programs supporting educational change: Vol. 8. Implementing and sustaining innovations.* Santa Monica, CA: The Rand Corporation.

Blakely, C. H., Mayer, J. P., Gottschalk, R. G., Schmitt, N., Davidson, W. S., Roitman, D. B., & Emshoff, J. G. (1987). The fidelity-adaptation debate: Implications for the implementation of public sector social programs. *American Journal of Community Psychology, 13*, 253–268.

Bloom, B. L. (1979). Prevention of mental disorders: Recent advances in theory and practice. *Community Mental Health Journal, 15*, 179–191.

Bloom, B. L. (1985). New possibilities in prevention. In R. L. Hough, P. A. Gongla, V. B. Brown, & S. E. Goldston (Eds.), *Psychiatric epidemiology and prevention: The possibilities* (pp. 31–52). Los Angeles, CA: NIMH.

Botvin, G. J., Baker, E., Renick, N. L., Filazzola, A. D., & Botvin, E. (1984). A cognitive-behavioral approach to substance abuse prevention. *Addictive Behaviors, 9*, 137–147.

Buckner, J. C., Trickett, E. J., & Corse, S. J. (1985). *Primary prevention in mental health: An annotated bibliography* (DHHS Publication No. 85–1405). Washington, DC: U.S. Government Printing Office.

Commins, W. (1987, May). *Institutionalization of mental health innovations: The case of elementary schools.* Paper presented at the Biennial Conference on Community Research and Action, Columbia, SC.

Cowen, E. L. (1982). Research in primary prevention in mental health. *American Journal of Community Psychology, 10*, 239–367.

Cowen, E. L. (1985). Person-centered approaches to primary prevention in mental health: Situation-focused and competence-enhancement. *American Journal of Community Psychology, 13*, 31–48.

Cowen, E. L. (1988). Primary prevention in mental health: Ten years of retrospect and ten years of prospect. In M. Kessler & S. E. Goldston (Eds.), *A decade of progress in primary prevention* (pp. 3–45). Hanover, NH: University Press of New England.

Cowen, E. L., Gesten, E. L., & Weissberg, R. P. (1980). An integrated network of preventively oriented school-based mental health approaches. In R. H. Price & P. Politzer (Eds.), *Evaluation and action in the community context* (pp. 173–210). New York: Academic Press.

Denham, S. A., & Almeida, M. C. (1987). Children's social problem-solving skills, behavioral adjustment, and interventions: A meta-analysis evaluating theory and practice. *Journal of Applied Developmental Psychology, 8*, 391–409.

Dodge, K. A. (1986). A social information processing model of social competence in children. In M. Perlmutter (Ed.), *Cognitive perspectives on children's social and behavioral development* (pp. 77–125). Hillsdale, NJ: Lawrence Erlbaum Associates.

Dodge, K. A., Pettit, G. S., McClaskey, C. L., & Brown, M. M. (1986). Social competence in children. *Monographs of the Society for Research in Child Development, 51*(2, Serial No. 213).

Durlak, J. A. (1983). Social problem solving as a primary prevention strategy. In R. D. Felner, L. A. Jason, J. N. Moritsugu, & S. S. Farber (Eds.), *Preventive psychology: theory, research, and practice* (pp. 31–48). New York: Pergamon Press.

Durlak, J. A., & Jason, L. A. (1984). Preventive programs for school-aged children and adolescents. In M. C. Roberts & L. Peterson (Eds.), *Prevention of problems in childhood: Psychological research and applications* (pp. 103–132). New York: John Wiley.

D'Zurilla, T. J. (1986). *Problem-solving therapy: A social competence approach to clinical intervention.* New York: Springer.

Elardo, P. T., & Cooper, M. (1977). *AWARE: Activities for social development.* Menlo Park, CA: Addison-Wesley.

Elias, M. J. (1987). Establishing enduring prevention programs: Advancing the legacy of Swampscott. *American Journal of Community Psychology, 15*, 539–554.

Elias, M. J., Gara, M., Ubriaco, M., Rothbaum, P. A., Clabby, J. F., & Schuyler, T. (1986). Impact of a preventive social problem-solving intervention on children's coping with middle-school stressors. *American Journal of Community Psychology, 14*, 259–275.

Felner, R. D., Jason, L. A., Moritsugu, J. N., & Farber, S. S. (Eds.). (1983). *Preventive psychology: Theory, research, and practice.* New York: Pergamon Press.

Ford, M. E. (1982). Social cognition and social competence in adolescence. *Developmental Psychology, 18*, 323–340.

Ford, M. E. (1985). Primary prevention: Key issues and a competence perspective. *The Journal of Primary Prevention, 5*, 264–266.

Furman, W. (1980). Promoting social development: Developmental implications for treatment. In B. B. Lahey & A. E. Kazdin (Eds.), *Advances in clinical child psychology: Vol. 3.* (pp. 1–40). New York: Plenum Press.

Garmezy, N. (1987). Stress, competence, and development: Continuities in the study of schizophrenic adults, children vulnerable to psychopathology, and the search for stress-resistant children. *American Journal of Orthopsychiatry, 57*, 159–174.

Gesten, E. L., Flores de Apodaca, R., Rains, M., Weissberg, R. P., & Cowen, E. L. (1979). Promoting peer-related social competence in schools. In M. W. Kent & J. E. Rolf (Eds.), *Social competence in children* (pp. 220–247). Hanover, NH: University Press of New England.

Gesten, E. L., Rains, M., Rapkin, B. D., Weissberg, R. P., Flores de Apodaca, R., Cowen, E. L., & Bowen, R. (1982). Training children in social problem-solving skills: A competence building approach, first and second look. *American Journal of Community Psychology, 10*, 95–115.

Glidewell, J. C., & Swallow, C. S. (1969). *The prevalence of maladjustment in elementary schools. Report prepared for the Joint Commission on Mental Illness and Health of Children.* Chicago: University of Chicago Press.

Greenberg, M. T. (1987). *The PATHS Project: Preventive intervention for children.* Unpublished manuscript, University of Washington, Seattle.

Greenspan, S. (1981). Social competence and handicapped individuals: Practical implications for a proposed model. *Advances in Special Education, 3*, 41–82.

Harwood, R., & Weissberg, R. P. (1987). The potential of video in the promotion of social competence in children and adolescents. *Journal of Early Adolescence, 7*, 345–363.

Hawkins, J. D., & Weis, J. G. (1985). The social development model: An integrated approach to delinquency prevention. *Journal of Primary Prevention, 6*, 73–97.

Hill, J. P. (1980). *Understanding early adolescence: A framework.* Carrboro, NC: The Center for Early Adolescence.

Hobbs, H. (1982). *The troubled and troubling child.* San Francisco: Jossey-Bass.

Hops, H. (1983). Children's social competence and skills: Current research practices and future directions. *Behavior Therapy, 14*, 3–18.

Hunter, M. (1987). *Mastery teaching.* El Segundo, CA: TIP Publications.

Jessor, R. (1984). Adolescent development and behavioral health. In J. D. Matarazzo, Sharlene M. Weiss, J. A. Herd, N. E. Miller, & Steven M. Weiss (Eds.), *Behavioral health: A handbook of health enhancement and disease prevention* (pp. 69–90). New York: John Wiley.

Joffe, J. M., Albee, G. W., & Kelly, L. D. (1984). *Readings in primary prevention of psychopathology: Basic concepts.* Hanover, NH: University Press of New England.

Johnson, D. W., Johnson, R. T., Holubec, E. J., & Roy, P. (1984). *Circles of learning.* Alexandria, VA: Association for Supervision and Curriculum Development.

Kellam, S. G., Branch, J. D., Agrawal, K. C., & Ensminger, M. E. (1975). *Mental health and going to school: The Woodlawn program of assessment, early intervention, and evaluation.* Chicago: University of Chicago Press.

Kellam, S. G., Dolan, L., Crockett, L., Carran, D., & Edelsohn, G. (1986, December). *Prevention research on early risk behaviors.* Paper presented at the meeting on Early Brain Development, Environment, and Mental Health, Moscow.

Kelly, J. G. (1987). Seven criteria when conducting community-based prevention research: A research agenda and commentary. In J. A. Steinberg & M. M. Silverman (Eds.), *Preventing mental disorders* (pp. 57–71). Rockville, MD: NIMH.

Kent, M. W., & Rolf, J. E. (1979). *Social competence in children.* Hanover, NH: University Press of New England.

Kirschenbaum, D. S., & Ordman, A. H. (1984). Preventive interventions for children: Cognitive behavioral perspectives. In A. W. Meyers & W. E. Craighead (Eds.), *Cognitive behavior therapy with children* (pp. 377–409). New York: Plenum Press.

Kornberg, M. S., & Caplan, G. (1980). Risk factors and preventive intervention in child psychotherapy: A review. *The Journal of Primary Prevention, 1*, 71–133.

Krasnor, L., & Rubin, K. H. (1981). Assessment of social problem solving in young children. In T. Merluzzi, C. Glass, & M. Genest (Eds.), *Cognitive assessment* (pp. 452–478). New York: Guilford Press.

Ladd, G. W., & Mize, J. (1983). A cognitive-social learning model of social-skills training. *Psychological Review, 90*, 127–157.

Lamb, H. R., & Zusman, J. (1982). The seductiveness of primary prevention. In F. D. Perlmutter (Ed.), *Mental health promotion and primary prevention* (pp. 19–30). San Francisco: Jossey-Bass.

Laosa, L. M. (1984). Social competence in childhood: Toward a developmental, socioculturally relativistic paradigm. In J. M. Joffe, G. W. Albee, & L. D. Kelly (Eds.), *Readings in primary prevention of psychopathology* (pp. 261–285). Hanover, NH: University Press of New England.

Lazarus, R. S. (1980). The stress and coping paradigm. In L. A. Bond & J. C. Rosen (Eds.), *Competence and coping during adulthood* (pp. 28–74). Hanover, NH: University Press of New England.

Levine, M., & Perkins, D. V. (1980). Social setting interventions and primary prevention: Comments on the Report of the Task Panel on Prevention to the President's Commission on Mental Health. *American Journal of Community Psychology, 8,* 147–157.

Lipsitz, J. (1984). *Successful schools for young adolescents.* New Brunswick, NJ: Transaction Books.

Long, B. B. (1986). The prevention of mental-emotional disabilities: A report from a National Mental Health Association Commission. *American Psychologist, 41,* 825–829.

Masten, A. S., & Garmezy, N. (1985). Risk, vulnerability, and protective factors in developmental psychopathology. In B. B. Lahey & A. E. Kazdin (Eds.), *Advances in clinical child psychology: Vol. 8* (pp. 1–52). New York: Plenum Press.

McFall, R. M. (1982). A review and reformulation of the concept of social skills. *Behavioral Assessment, 4,* 1–33.

Moos, R. H., & Schaefer, J. A. (1986). Life transitions and crises: A conceptual overview. In R. H. Moos (Ed.), *Coping with life crises: An integrated approach* (pp. 3–28). New York: Plenum Press.

Nerad, A. S. (1986). Mental health education in schools. *Resource papers to the report of the National Mental Health Association Commission on the prevention of mental-emotional disabilities* (pp. 191–196). Washington DC: National Mental Health Association.

Office of Technology Assessment (1986). *Children's mental health: problems and services.* Washington, DC: U.S. Government Printing Office.

Pellegrini, D., & Urbain, E. S. (1985). An evaluation of interpersonal cognitive problem-solving training efforts with children. *Journal of Child Psychology and Psychiatry, 26,* 17–41.

Perry, C. L., & Jessor, R. (1985). The concept of health promotion and the prevention of adolescent drug abuse. *Health Education Quarterly, 12,* 169–184.

Report of the Task Panel on Prevention. (1978). *Task panel reports submitted to the President's Commission on Mental Health: Vol. 4* (pp. 1822–1863). Washington, DC: U.S. Government Printing Office.

Roberts, C., & Fitzmahan, L. (1986). *Here's Looking at you, 2000: A teacher's guide for drug education.* Seattle, WA: Comprehensive Health Education Foundation.

Roberts, M. C., & Peterson, L. (Eds.). (1984). *Prevention of problems in childhood: Psychological research and applications.* New York: John Wiley.

Rotheram, M. J. (1982a). Social skills training with underachievers, disruptive, and exceptional children. *Psychology in the Schools, 19,* 532–539.

Rotheram, M. J. (1982b). Variations in children's assertiveness due to trainer assertion level. *Journal of Community Psychology, 10,* 228–236.

Rubin, K. H., & Krasnor, L. R. (1986). Social-cognitive and social behavioral perspectives on problem solving. In M. Perlmutter (Ed.), *Cognitive perspectives on children's social and behavioral-development* (pp. 1–68). Hillsdale, NJ: Lawrence Erlbaum Associates.

Rubin, R. A., & Balow, B. (1978). Prevalence of teacher identified behavior problems: A longitudinal study. *Exceptional Children, 45*, 102–111.

Rutter, M. (1982). Prevention of children's psychosocial disrorders: Myth and substance. *Pediatrics, 70*, 883–894.

Rutter, M. (1987). Psychosocial resilience and protective mechanisms. *American Journal of Orthopsychiatry, 57*, 316–331.

Rutter, M., Maughan, B., Mortimore, P., & Ouston, J. (1979). *Fifteen thousand hours: Secondary schools and their effects on children.* Cambridge, MA: Harvard University Press.

Sarason, S. B. (1982). *The culture of the school and the problem of change* (2nd ed.). Boston, MA: Allyn & Bacon.

Sarason, S. B. (1983). *Schooling in America: Scapegoat and salvation.* New York: The Free Press.

Shure, M. B., & Spivack, G. (1982). Interpersonal problem-solving in young children: A cognitive approach to prevention. *American Journal of Community Psychology, 10*, 341–356.

Slaby, R. G., & Guerra, N. G. (1988). Cognitive mediators of aggression in adolescent offenders: 1. Assessment. *Developmental Psychology, 24*, 580–588.

Spivack, G., Platt, J. J., & Shure, M. B. (1976). *The problem-solving approach to adjustment.* San Francisco: Jossey-Bass.

Spivack, G., & Shure, M. B. (1974). *Social adjustment of young children.* San Francisco: Jossey-Bass.

Spivack, G., & Shure, M. B. (1982). The cognition of social adjustment: Interpersonal cognitive problem-solving thinking. In B. B. Lahey & A. E. Kazdin (Eds.), *Advances in clinical child psychology*: Vol. 5 (pp. 323–372). New York: Plenum Press.

Thompson-Roundtree, P., & Musun-Baskett, L. (1984). A further examination of Project AWARE: The relationship between teacher behaviors and changes in student behavior. *Journal of School Psychology, 19*, 260–266.

Tisdelle, D. A., & St. Lawrence, J. S. (1986). Interpersonal problem-solving competency: Review and critique of the literature. *Clinical Psychology Review, 6*, 337–356.

Trickett, E. J. (1984). Toward a distinctive community psychology: An ecological metaphor for the conduct of community research and the nature of training. *American Journal of Community Psychology, 12*, 261–280.

Waters, E., & Sroufe, L. A. (1983). Social competence as a developmental construct. *Developmental Review, 3*, 79–97.

Weissberg, R. P. (1985). Designing effective social problem-solving programs for the classroom. In B. H. Schneider, K. H. Rubin, & J. E. Ledingham (Eds.), *Children's peer relations: Issues in assessment and intervention* (pp. 225–242). New York: Springer-Verlag.

Weissberg, R. P., & Allen, J. P. (1986). Promoting children's social skills and adaptive interpersonal behavior. In L. Michelson & B. Edelstein (Eds.), *Handbook of Prevention* (pp. 153–175). New York: Plenum Press.

Weissberg, R. P., & Caplan, M. Z. (1988). *The evaluation of a social competence promotion program with young, urban adolescents.* Manuscript submitted for publication.

Weissberg, R. P., Caplan, M. Z., & Bennetto, L. (1988). *The Yale-New Haven Social Problem-Solving (SPS) Program for Young Adolescents.* New Haven, CT: Yale University.

Weissberg, R. P., & Gesten, E. L. (1982). Considerations for developing effective school-based social problem-solving training programs. *School Psychology Review, 11*, 56–63.

Weissberg, R. P., Gesten, E. L., Carnrike, C. L., Toro, P. A., Rapkin, B. D., Davidson, E.,

& Cowen, E. L. (1981). Social problem-solving skills training: A competence-building intervention with second- to fourth-grade children. *American Journal of Community Psychology, 9*, 411–423.

Weissberg, R. P., Gesten, E. L., Rapkin, B. D., Cowen, E. L., Davidson, E., Flores de Apodaca, R., & McKim, B. J. (1981). The evaluation of a social-problem-solving training program for suburban and inner-city third-grade children. *Journal of Consulting and Clinical Psychology, 49*, 251–261.

Yeaton, W. H., & Sechrest, L. (1981). Critical dimensions in the choice and maintenance of successful treatments: Strength, integrity, and effectiveness. *Journal of Consulting and Clinical Psychology, 49*, 156–167.

Zigler, E., & Berman, W. (1983). Discerning the future of early childhood intervention. *American Psychologist, 38*, 894–906.

Zigler, E., Kagan, S. L. & Muenchow, S. (1982). Preventive intervention in the schools. In C. R. Reynolds & T. B. Gutkin (Eds.), *The Handbook of School Psychology* (pp. 774–795). New York: John Wiley & Sons.

Zigler, E., & Trickett, P. (1978). IQ, social competence, and evaluation of early childhood education programs. *American Psychologist, 33*, 789–798.

10

Social Competency Training Programs in Ethnically Diverse Communities

Mary Jane Rotheram-Borus
Sam J. Tsemberis

The importance of social competence has been well established over the past 20 years. It is regarded as a highly desirable quality, inversely related to psychopathology in later life (Cowen, Pederson, Babigian, Izzo, & Trost, 1973) and positively related to I.Q. and healthy adjustment in the classroom (Cartledge & Milburn, 1980; Deluty, 1985; Dorman, 1973). Social competence in children and adolescents is defined by an ability to successfully achieve social goals in a manner that is mutually rewarding to the child and to others in his/her environment (O'Malley, 1977). Social competence is usually assessed by peers' and teachers' ratings (Ladd & Asher, 1985). Its evaluation is often difficult because it is inevitably tied to sociocultural norms and personal characteristics such as age, gender, and ethnicity (Conger & Conger, 1982).

Numerous clinicians and researchers have developed skill-building approaches to enhance children's social competence. A recent search of the literature on this topic yielded 172 articles published in educational and psychological journals during the last ten years. The influence of these programs is expanding as each successive cohort of children is successfully trained (Weissberg, 1985), leading researchers to advocate widescale adoption of social competency building (Argyle, 1984; Cowen, 1985; Elias & Clabby, 1984). As these intervention programs proliferate, they are applied to a wider variety of populations differing in age, gender, socioeconomic status, religion, and ethnicity.

The ethnic context of each community provides a unique framework in which SCT researchers must adapt their programs in an innovative manner, because the norms and values of the ethnic community present constraints that demand changes in existing programs. SCT programs have implicit values defining socially appropriate normative behaviors, values that may be compatible or conflicting with the values of the children, teachers, and parents of a culturally diverse community. Efforts to train children to be socially competent may lead to socialization in accordance with only one standard of competence, a standard that may well be at odds with the norms of minority children.

Ethnic families and children share the same superordinate goals as the mainstream culture (e.g., a good education and a good job), and the children need to develop the social skills and understanding of mainstream culture that enable them to successfully realize these goals (Martinez, 1977). However, implementing traditional SCT among minority children raises a number of serious questions. Are there negative consequences for minority children who acquire a set of sociocultural behaviors and norms that differ from those of their parents or extended family? How will SCT programs affect ethnic children's distinct and idiosyncratic ways of expressing their ethnic identity? How might SCT programs affect the social psychology of the classroom in order to enhance children's positive cross-ethnic interaction and reduce prejudice? These are some of the issues that will be addressed in this chapter.

Before discussing the interplay of ethnicity and SCT, it is important to define certain key terms: race, ethnicity, minority, majority, and mainstream. *Race* refers to a genetically determined set of physical characteristics. *Ethnicity* is a broader concept referring to people who conceive of themselves as alike by virtue of their common ancestry, real or fictitious, and who are so regarded by others (Shibutani & Kwan, 1965). This chapter focuses on ethnicity rather than race. There is substantial evidence that ethnicity shapes social perceptions, expectations, attitudes, and behaviors.

Minority group membership may be defined in relative terms. A group may be considered a minority because it is a smaller group numerically. In the United States at the present time, 12% of the population is Black American. Therefore, in the U.S., Black Americans are a minority group. In any one school or community Black Americans may be a *majority* in number. Yet these students remain the minority in the context of the larger community. The more important implication of minority membership is having less status and power. Majority, mainstream, or dominant status typically refers to being a member of the group with the most power.

While minority children are exposed to the norms, values, and behavior patterns of the majority group through school, media, and personal contact, *mainstream* children often are not exposed to those aspects of minority cultures (Goodman, 1964). Cultural exposure can lead to three different processes occurring: (a) assimilation—the ethnic group loses its distinctiveness and becomes part of the mainstream culture, (b) acculturation—acceptance of one's own and another's group with the norms of both groups being modified by the contact, and (c) pluralism—maintenance of separate norms, values and customs (Padilla, 1980). SCT will affect each of these processes.

To make explicit the implicit social values of person-centered SCT programs, we will review the common features of these programs. We will then discuss ethnic differences that may relate to the effectiveness of these programs and consider how SCT programs may be tailored to serve the needs of children from ethnically diverse communities.

SCT Programs: Common Features and Assumptions

Some preventive intervention programs address the educational, economic, legal, and political systems at a macro-level (Argyle, 1984; Rappaport, 1977, 1981). However, the SCT programs that are the focus of this chapter are person-centered (Cowen, 1985) and have seven common features.

1. *A set of specific skills is taught.* Programs focus on the degree to which children's affective, behavioral, and cognitive skills are integrated. The interaction of one's thoughts, actions, and feelings is emphasized (Rotheram, 1982a; Rotheram, in press; Rotheram, Armstrong, & Booraem, 1982).

2. *Members participate in structured activities, usually in a group setting.* Each program outlines specific concepts or skills to be acquired, usually in an ordered sequence with one skill building upon the acquisition of more basic skills.

3. *Peers and/or adults provide social support.* Each program stipulates that trainers should create a supportive and rewarding experience in which children's strengths are recognized and emphasized. Spivack and Shure (1974) specified that training should be fun.

4. *The social skills to be acquired are practiced in the group setting.* Many programs include rehearsal during the training (e.g., Oden & Asher, 1977), while others highlight the importance of practicing skills throughout the school day. For example, Spivack and Shure (1974)

trained teachers to "dialogue" with children whenever interpersonal problems occurred, not only during training sessions, but during recess and academic class time.

5. *An active style of coping with problem situations is encouraged.* Each program promotes the view that the individual can actively and consciously think new thoughts, behave in alternative ways, or increase awareness of feelings. Children learn that they can be effective in changing problematic situations.

6. *A language or vocabulary for understanding one's affective, behavioral, and cognitive responses to problems is provided.* Each program has its own concrete symbols, acronyms, or mnemonic devices to help participants remember the skills taught. For example, Meichenbaum (1977) uses the "Think Aloud" program, Gilbert (1988) teaches "GUTSS" (group understanding and training in social skills), and Hazel, Sherman, Schumaker, and Sheldon (1985) teach "ASSET," a social skills program for adolescents.

7. *Programs aim to make the skills that are acquired relevant and useful to children and adolescents at various stages of development.* For example, Spivack and Shure (1974) initially trained kindergarten children. Later, the interpersonal problem solving program was adapted to third and fourth graders (e.g., Weissberg, Gesten, Carnrike, Toro, Rapkin, Davidson, & Cowen, 1981; Weissberg, Gesten, Rapkin, Cowen, Davidson, Flores de Apodaca, & McKim, 1981), fifth and sixth graders (Cohen, Brennan, & Sexton, 1984; Gersick, Grady, & Snow, 1988), seventh and eighth graders (Weissberg, this book), and adolescents (Curran, 1977), as well as to children with a variety of presenting problems (see Urbain & Kendall, 1980, for a review).

Ethnic Variation in Sociocultural Norms and Values

Ethnicity shapes people's patterns of thinking, feeling, and behaving in both obvious and subtle ways (McGoldrick, Pearce, & Giordano, 1982). It also influences values, social customs, perceptions, social roles, language usage, expression of emotion, and rules of social interactions (Ogbu, 1981). There is substantial evidence to document ethnic differences in attitudes, expression of affect, and behavior across cultures (Hofstede, 1980; Stewart, 1972; Triandis, 1972; Whiting & Whiting, 1975) and within cultures (Forgas, 1979). These differences are not random, but are organized and interdependent within the gestalt of a particular culture (Ogbu, 1982).

At the same time, people in every culture have fundamental human needs that are universal, but the particular manner in which they are expressed and met accounts for the cultural differences and variations. For example, parents care a great deal about the physical and psychological well-being of their children and want them to succeed in school. The challenge that is posed to SCT programs is whether they can help ethnic groups achieve mainstream goals successfully without damaging the integrity of the ethnic group's expression of its norms and values.

When we examine the seven features common to social competency programs, we find embedded in them a number of underlying assumptions and value orientations that relate to at least four dimensions along which ethnic groups have been found to differ.

1. *Active versus passive manner of coping.* An active coping style is associated with "doing" and "getting things done" rather than being or becoming, a future time orientation in which time moves quickly, and a perception that we control our environment (Burger, 1973; Diaz-Guerrero, 1967, 1979; Stewart, 1972). SCT programs typically emphasize an active, precise, assertive, achievement-oriented style that teaches children to address problems directly and assume in internal locus of control. There is an implicit assumption that actively coping with one's environment is both useful and positive. These assumptions stand in contrast to cultural values that emphasize the natural order of the universe and the unfolding nature of problem resolution (Spiegel, 1982). To a Mohawk Indian an active problem-solving style expresses mistrust in God's plan for harmony between individual and nature (Glood & Elm, in press). Likewise, in Mexican-American culture, time is present- rather than future-oriented, leading to a deemphasis on active structuring and planning in one's style of coping (Boney, 1971; Diaz-Guerrero, 1973, 1979; Holtzman, Diaz-Guerrero, & Schwartz, 1975; Kagan & Carlson, 1975; Kagan & Madsen, 1971; Nevius, 1982).

2. *Group versus individual orientation.* This dimension is related conceptually and empirically to that of cooperation versus competition. SCT programs teach children an affiliative approach with an emphasis on autonomy and an inner-directed approach to solving social problems. This is combined with an emphasis on competition and a personal orientation toward group activities, illustrated, for example, by assertiveness training programs (Huey & Rank, 1984). However, some cultures, particularly the Japanese and Asian (Doi, 1973), focus on group cooperation, decision making, and group needs rather than those of the individual. A tie score at the end of a major league

baseball game between two national teams is the outcome most preferred by Japanese fans (ABC News, April, 1988). Children in group-oriented cultures tend to be more cooperative and to function better in classrooms that deemphasize individual competition by having children work in small interdependent groups (MacDonald & Gallimore, 1971). Therefore, the emphasis on individual-competitive norms and achievement encourages, for example, Asian children to adopt a stance that is at odds with that of their parents and culture.

3. *Emotional expressiveness versus emotional restraint.* This dimension relates to the content and boundaries of interpersonal exchanges. SCT programs usually encourage children to identify correctly and express their positive and negative emotions without ambiguity (Baskin & Hess, 1980). Americans, according to Stewart (1972), see themselves as direct and open in social interactions, particularly in contrast to the polite, ritualistic manner typical of the Japanese and other Oriental cultures (Burger, 1973). Asian Americans are cautious in expressing feelings and thus appear more socially introverted in comparison to Whites (Sue & Wagner, 1973). In Hispanic cultures, maintaining a positive relationship is an important social rule, even if it requires than one refrain from directly expressing negative feelings (Diaz-Guerrero, 1982). For example, if a Mexican-American child were invited to a party of a peer that she/he did not like, it is unlikely that the invitation would be refused in a direct manner. The child would likely smile and respond pleasantly to the invitation, and then simply not attend, thus signalling his/her negative feelings. In addition, the dimensions of openness, privacy, intimate social space, and public space, and the norms or "proxemic rules" that govern appropriate behavior vary across cultures (Hall, 1966).

4. *Authoritarian versus egalitarian attitudes.* This dimension has been identified by many writers as important in structuring the power hierarchy in social interactions. With children, this dimension translates into whether they regard parents and teachers as clear authority figures who are to be respected and obeyed without question or, instead, as more nearly equal figures with whom they may raise questions and/or disagree. The SCT programs generally teach children respectful and polite self-assertion. Yet even the behaviors that are considered a show of respect among Anglo-Americans (e.g., a child making eye contact with an adult) may be regarded as disrepectful by members of other ethnic groups.

There is a growing body of empirical evidence that these dimensions of ethnic differences emerge early in childhood within heterogeneous populations such as those found in the United States. For example:

(a) Native American children have been found to be more cooperative, social and intimate (Batchold, 1982; Miller, 1973), less achievement oriented, independent, and authoritarian (Batchold, 1982;
1984), more likely to initiate nonphysical play (Platz, 1977), and likely
to perceive greater internal locus of control (Echohawk, 1978) than
their White American peers.

(b) Mexican-American children have been found to be less competitive (Kagan, Knight, Martinez, & Santa, 1981; de la Serna, 1982),
less motivated academically (Argulewicz, Elliot, & Hall, 1982), usually less active and more avoidant of conflict situations (Boney, 1971;
Kagan & Madsen, 1971), more group oriented and cooperative with
greater skills at conflict resolution (Knight & Kagan, 1982; Knudson,
1979), less assertive (Kagan & Carlson, 1975), and likely to perceive
greater external locus of control (Kagan & Ender, 1975) than White
Americans.

(c) Black children have been found to use different norms for
entering and cooperating in groups, be more group oriented (Shade,
1982), and to be perceived as more aggressive in ambiguous situations
(Sagar & Schofield, 1980) than their White peers.

(d) White, middle-class children in the United States were rated as
more individualistic and deferential to authority, and less emotionally
expressive than their Black peers (Kochman, 1981; Sagar & Schofield,
1980).

(e) In a comparison of Hawaiian-American and Japanese-American
children, the former were found to use problem-solving strategies
that included greater family input and immediate solutions (Gallimore, Boggs, & Jordan, 1974).

(f) Less verbal interaction was found among Native-American as
compared to Black-American children (Ainsworth, 1984).

(g) White-Americans, particularly males, have been shown to use
greater interpersonal distance than either Puerto-Rican or Black-
American children (Aiello & Jones, 1971).

Ethnic differences often result in two kinds of difficulties: (1) minority children misinterpret the behavior of majority group members
or of other ethnic groups because of differences in ethnic socialization; and (2) patterns of behavior displayed by minority children are
perceived and labelled as socially incompetent by a majority group
member although they may be consistent with the expectations of the
ethnic group.

What happens when, through SCT, a minority child acquires new
norms about how to behave or interpret social cues in a manner that is

determined by the mainstream to be more socially competent? Particularly in relation to parents and extended family, are the new behaviors likely to elicit happy, rewarding responses or are they likely to be greeted with consternation? For example, how is a Mexican-American father likely to respond to his daughter when she looks him in the eye when being scolded, as her teachers taught her, rather than looking toward the ground as her culture has taught her?

Conversely, when children do not share social norms because of differences in ethnic background, how may SCT programs promote greater cross-ethnic understanding and positive relations among peers? For example, Phinney and Rotheram (1985) found that Mexican-American and Black children had different social expectations in response to a disliked peer requesting to borrow a quarter to buy lunch. Black children reported that they would be more likely to refuse the request than Mexican-American children. There were differences in social rules about sharing behaviors between Black and Mexican-American children. If teachers and children were to receive information regarding differences in social rules across groups, would they have fewer misunderstandings?

SCT programs are likely to increase the congruence between teachers' and children's academic and social expectations, norms, and values, reducing the likelihood of conflict between teachers and students. For example, in the case of the Mexican-American girl whose family taught her to look downward when being chastised, mainstream teachers may learn to reinterpret her behavior as showing respect or the child may learn that eye contact is a positive social behavior at school but not at home. As peers participate jointly in SCT groups, they may develop a fuller understanding of one another's behaviors. If the implicit social rules of different ethnic groups are made explicit, mutual understanding, and positive interactions would increase.

Thus, SCT programs can have both positive and negative effects on children's social relationships. The critical question becomes "what particular influences will arise with whom, and in what setting?" While these issues are no different from those that have plagued all program evaluations for the last 30 years, they have not been addressed by SCT planners, especially those who have focused upon minority children.

Improving SCT Programs

There are at least three implications that must be addressed by researchers who implement social competency programs in ethnically diverse communities: (1) trainers need to examine and make explicit the underlying values and assumptions of SCT; (2) ethnic differences in sociocultural norms need to be considered in the design and delivery of the programs; and (3) researchers need to evaluate the effects of SCT programs across different domains of the child's life, at different developmental stages, and in different interpersonal settings including the family's home and among cross-ethnic and same-ethnic peers.

Making the Norms and Values of SCT Programs Explicit

We have discussed common implicit values of SCT programs in terms of four dimensions that differentiate certain American ethnic groups. Overall, SCT programs are more likely to encourage children to be active, oriented to individual goals, emotionally expressive, and respectful of authority figures. At the same time, despite their commonalities, SCT programs vary considerably from one another. Therefore, both developers and consumers of SCT programs must identify and articulate these variations, with particular attention to the fit between the implicit norms and values of the program and the target population and program goals.

Interpersonal problem solving training (e.g., Spivack & Shure, 1974) targets thinking skills. The teaching of goal clarity and generation of alternatives is more likely to affect the dimensions of activity and individual versus group orientation than the other dimensions we described. In contrast, the Magic Circle (Baskin & Hess, 1980) is more focused upon children's feelings and will affect the dimension of emotional expressiveness. Similarly, Cantor and Helfat's (1976) program places more emphasis upon emotional expressiveness than does the assertiveness training program of Rotheram, et al. (1982). Those programs with a behavioral focus (e.g., Ladd, 1981; Ladd & Asher, 1985) are likely to address each of these dimensions; however, they are also the most likely to teach mainstream norms regarding verbal and nonverbal behaviors and, thereby, violate ethnic-specific social norms.

When these different programs are delivered to children of diverse ethnic backgrounds, the fit between program and family values will vary. For example, when Spivack and Shure's (1974) interpersonal problem solving is delivered to Black or White children, family norms are more likely to coincide with the active and individual orientation of the training values. However, when interpersonal problem solving is implemented with Mexican-American or Japanese children, it may be more likely to violate family values and create conflicts for the

children. Similarly, Rotheram et al.'s (1982; Rotheram, 1982b) assertiveness training program is more likely to be problematic for
Mexican-American children than for Black-American children, since
assertiveness is less consistent with the values of Mexican-American
culture.

Adapting Design and Delivery of SCT Programs

It is clear that the norms and values of communities must be considered when designing SCT programs for their use. Within this context,
we need to address several questions. How much involvement from
school staff, parents, and the local community is necessary in order to
tailor a program to reflect the community's values and norms? Should
the ethnic composition of the training groups be homogeneous or
heterogeneous? Which language should be used to deliver the program?

Community involvement. Community psychologists consistently emphasize the importance of community involvement and investment in
school-based programs (Heller & Monahan, 1977). While SCT trainers
emphasize the the importance of involving teachers, administrators,
and parents, these groups characteristically are not full participants in
either program design or implementation. Program implementation
typically evolves slowly over a period of several years. Teachers who
ultimately deliver the programs are selected based upon their interest
rather than their skills, training, or the needs of their students. Only
after a long period of time do these teachers become proficient at
implementing the program. SCT training does not become an ongoing
part of the school curriculum until several years after its initial implementation in that setting, and rarely is it employed to identify and
triage youngsters who may need other academic or clinical services
(Rotheram, 1987). Typically SCT is not integrated into the community
within or beyond the school. In particular, parents are viewed by SCT
trainers as inaccessible, and it is expected that only a few parents will
attend meetings for these intervention programs. Only Gersick, Grady,
and Snow's (1988) program involved parents as an integral part of SCT
drug prevention program. In general, the reality of establishing an
effective SCT intervention program is very different from the ideal
design of such programs.

The implementation of SCT in an ethnically diverse community
presents an opportunity for community involvement in the program
development. This may occur both among school personnel and at
the interface of the school and the broader community. SCT pro-

grams create the opportunity for cross-ethnic involvement among students, teachers, parents and school administrators as well as among members from various school related agencies. Such contact is increasingly important since prejudice continues on a very wide scale in our ethnically diverse society. A recent violent incident in New York City's Howard Beach section became the focal point for the expression of White and Black prejudice (Aboud, 1987). SCT programs provide members of a school community with a forum for working cooperatively on a common goal, thus creating a powerful intervention with the potential to decrease prejudice (Miller & Brewer, 1984).

There has been one outstanding example of how SCT created a school atmosphere that facilitated successful learning and positive cross-ethnic interactions. The Kahmehameha school project tailored classroom environments to the norms of the children's ethnic group (Gallimore, Boggs, & Jordan, 1974). For example, the Hawaiian children were given group rather than individual projects, consistent with the emphasis on group orientation in their culture, and teachers were recruited and trained to recognize positive contributions of Hawaiian culture. Children received special training in social competence skills that involved children with various ethnic backgrounds.

Successful programs such as the Kahmehameha project are rare, considering the magnitude and importance of ethnic prejudice. We have not yet solved the problems of how to increase community involvement, how to increase parent involvement in school-based programs, or how to change teachers' attitudes about their involvement with parents. While SCT programs do not provide solutions to these problems, they provide an opportunity to address very important social issues at the school level. For example, it may be important to design programs that use a problem-solving approach to discover differences in ethnic norms and values, rather than use a didactic or lecture approach to teach ethnic differences. Rotheram (1982b) found that when children had less assertive, directive leaders, they gained more in problem-solving skills. Since socially competent behaviors are defined differently by each ethnic group, SCT trainers need to be on a fact-finding mission, rather than deliver a prescribed set of norms. With such an approach, SCT becomes an opportunity for understanding cross-ethnic differences and increasing skills for behaving in a socially competent manner with other ethnic groups. While the primary goal of SCT is not multicultural education, delivery of programs in culturally diverse communities demands attention to ethnic differences. Those SCT programs that use a dynamic fact-finding approach have the potential to increase teachers' and students' awareness of the problem-solving style, social norms, and values of their ethnically diverse students and peers.

Composition of training groups. What is the optimal ethnic composition of training groups? There are advantages and disadvantages to structuring groups with same- or cross-ethnic peers. In ethnically homogeneous groups, children have the opportunity to build cohesion and exchange positive feelings and experiences regarding their ethnic heritage. In cross-ethnic groups, there is increased opportunity for learning about the norms and values of other groups; however, although articulated as ethnic differences, these variations often are perceived and maintained as negative evaluations of the social competence of cross-ethnic peers.

In our own work, it has been valuable to conduct SCT in groups of children of mixed ethnic background. Sessions then are planned in which children are asked to identify social situations in which the norms of the two groups differ. Children break into teams of same-ethnic peers to rehearse and to present the "correct" social behavior of their group to the total group. Their presentations help to heighten the sensitivity of cross-ethnic peers to ethnic variations. The use of "break-out" exercises with same-ethnic peers maintains the cohesion of the training groups and increases the potential for positive cross-ethnic understanding and attitudes. Children have an opportunity to interact with cross-ethnic peers in a cooperative setting (Rogers, Hennigan, Bowman, & Miller, 1984) and to acquire a pluralistic understanding of others' values and goals.

Language. What language should be employed when conducting SCT programs with minority children? Several issues appear relevant to the choice of language instruction. First, many minority children *choose* not to speak English, particularly in situations of free play with peers, as a signal of their chosen ethnic identity. Heller (1982; 1984) described the behavior of children who were Francophone and Anglophone speakers in Canada. At a French-speaking school where all children were fluent in French and English, the natural groupings children formed during recess and other free play segregated the students by language choice and by extension, by their ethnic identity. Are French Canadian children who *choose* to speak English less socially competent? Since the English speaking group was smaller and ascribed less status by those speaking French, the English-speaking children were rated as less popular by peers, often the central index of social competence assessments. Clearly, in this case, language is a choice reflecting other features of a child's identity and, also, is primary in shaping others' evaluations of an individual's social competence. Evaluations of social competence may be confounded by the individual's *choices* of an ethnic identity.

A second consideration is that minority children report that they value the language of the majority group more than their own (Lambert, 1972). This may lead the child to view his or her native language as inferior and form a negative attitude toward and only a partial fluency in the second language (Lambert, 1980). To use English or any mainstream language exclusively in SCT programs for ethnically diverse groups may implicitly support this bias.

Third, to compete successfully in the mainstream, children may need to be competent in the mainstream language—both in writing and speaking. Educators still debate whether there is a transfer of learned skills from the first to the second language because of a "common underlying proficiency," which implies that experience with either language can promote development and proficiency in both languages (Cummins, 1984). Linguists have suggested that children *code switch,* that is, they have a register of the language of the dominant group, as well as of their own. L. Jason (personal communication, March 25, 1988) gave an account of a student who "could not" speak Black English in the presence of a White professor. However, when working with Black children in a community agency, the student found it comfortable and easy to speak Black English. Children's competence will often be context-bound. Minority children may have an extensive repertoire of affective, behavioral, and cognitive skills that are not accessible in a school context.

SCT Research and Program Evaluation and the Development of Ethnic Identity

Researchers need to assess the effects of SCT programs across different domains of the child's life, at different developmental stages, and in different interpersonal settings including in the family and among cross-ethnic and same-ethnic peers. To understand the ways in which SCT may affect children's ethnic identity differentially as a function developmental stage, it is useful to review briefly the literature on the development of children's ethnic identity.

Ethnic identity is a broad concept and includes several components: ethnic awareness (the awareness of one's own and other's groups), self-identification (the label used for one's own group), attitudes (feelings and thoughts about one's own and other ethnic groups), and behavior (behavior patterns specific to an ethnic group). The term *ethnic identity* has been used to refer to all of these components, alone or in combination. The salience of each of these components varies with developmental phase. Aboud and Skerry (1984), Katz (1976), and Porter (1971) each propose a stage model to explain children's acquisition of ethnic identity. They specify an age-related progression in the ability to perceive, process, and interpret racial or ethnic stimuli, which leads to the evolution of one's ethnic identity.

The relevant developmental models generally describe children's growth through 8 or 9 years old. There are only limited empirical data regarding the development of ethnic identity during middle childhood, adolescence, and adulthood (e.g., Cross, 1971; Banks, 1976). However, there is evidence that ethnically related psychological processes are affecting youngsters' adjustment, particularly peer relationships during middle childhood and adolescence. The acquisition of ethnic labels and identifying characteristics associated with those labels, particularly for minority children, continues beyond the childhood years. Recent studies indicate that there is a decrease in children's prejudicial feelings from about seven years of age continuing into adolescence (Aboud & Skerry, 1984). The number of cross-ethnic friends decreases during middle childhood (Singleton & Asher, 1977) and ethnic differences become pronounced with the onset of puberty and dating (Schofield, 1982). Several researchers (Giles, Llado, McKirnan, & Taylor, 1979: Rosenthal, 1987; Rosenthal & Hrynevich, 1985; Taylor, Simard, & Aboud, 1972) found subtle developmental changes in the boundaries of group membership among adolescents. These boundaries significantly affect cross-ethnic interaction.

The interplay between the development of ethnic identity and children's social and academic competence has been considered within the context of the effects of biculturalism. Biculturalism refers to the process by which minority children must acquire the norms of mainstream culture in order to succeed in school and later in the work force (Stonequist, 1935). Prior to 1974, it was assumed that minority children would be at a disadvantage because they experience acculturative stress when forced to adjust to the mainstream group (Stonequist, 1935; McFee, 1968). In the 1930s to 1950s a series of studies reported that Black American children preferred White dolls to Black dolls (e.g., Clark & Clark, 1947), findings that were replicated with minority children in other cultures (e.g., Vaughan, 1978). Acculturative stress was thought to be associated with insecurity, anxiety, increased emotionality, distrust, hostility, and defensiveness (e.g., Goodman, 1964; Paz, 1961; Stevenson & Stewart, 1958). While the interpretations and methodologies of these studies were criticized repeatedly, the findings emerged consistently throughout this period.

With the increasing ethnic pride that characterized the 1960s and

1970s, biculturalism became defined as a positive process (Ramirez, 1977; Ramirez & Casteneda, 1974; Ramirez & Price-Williams, 1974). Minority children were presumed to be exposed to the norms of their own group as well as to the norms of the dominant group. This dual exposure was hypothesized to result in cognitive flexibility and enhanced adaptiveness. Biculturalism was reframed as a valued experience and was expected to be associated with higher self-esteem, greater understanding, and higher achievement than for previous cohorts of minorities (Ramirez, 1983).

There is little empirical data on issues pertaining to biculturalism, particularly with children. In studies conducted with fourth and fifth graders, those who shared the social expectations of their own group had higher self-esteem than those who did not (Phinney & Rotheram, 1985). Further, the children with positive identification with their own group showed positive same- and across-ethnic attitudes, as well as positive adjustment (Rotheram, 1987). Rotheram (1988) found that positive adjustment for adolescents was related to having a strongly cohesive sense of self-identity, regardless of whether it was an ethnic or a mainstream identity. That is, minority adolescents, who were consistent in identifying themselves as strongly ethnic in their self-labels, attitudes, friendship patterns, social expectations, and in maintaining traditional values, were well-adjusted on the Achenbach Youth Self-Report Inventory. Similarly, minority adolescents who identified strongly as mainstream in their self-labels, attitudes, behaviors, and social expectations, scored well on the same measure. Those youngsters who were less consistent in their self-reports were less well adjusted.

What are the implications of these developmental processes for the delivery of SCT? First, training children to be socially competent is aimed at affecting the ethnically defined ways children perceive, act, and feel. SCT is likely to encourage adoption of mainstream patterns. We know little about how this affects the child's ethnic identity. There is a great need for research addressing this issue. Will SCT lead children to be increasingly bicultural or increasingly mainstream? Since ethnicity appears to be independent of social competence, the answer to this question needs to be studied.

From the developmental literature, we can predict that SCT is likely to affect ethnic identity in different ways at different ages. However, we can generate only crude hypotheses regarding the specific nature of these relationships. SCT is not likely to have immediate consequences for young children's sense of ethnic identity because they have only general affective responses to ethnic differences and have not acquired cognitive labels for, nor a clear and consistent understanding of characteristics that mark ethnic differences. For young children SCT is a more systematized approach to socializing children to adaptive ways of succeeding at school. For children in middle childhood and adolescence who are acutely aware of ethnic differences, SCT may have both positive and negative consequences. Presented sensitively, training can emphasize and articulate ethnic differences among youngsters. Helping them to perceive and value ethnic differences among their peers rather than view them as deficits or social incompetence, may help to increase cross-ethnic understanding and foster cross-ethnic friendships.

The potential of helping minority children identify the effects of using behavior patterns or codes different from those of their ethnic group is another potentially positive contribution of SCT programs. If ethnic differences are simply ignored by SCT, it seems likely that minority children will be taught implicitly that they must adopt mainstream patterns and identification. The potential negative consequences of such a communication is evident.

Ethnic differences in definitions of social competencies also suggest that SCT may be judged as differentially effective depending upon the specific outcomes evaluated. SCT may lead minority children to improved adjustment in school, an environment that reflects mainstream norms. However, these same children may become less successful at home and with neighborhood friends following training. There has been no evaluation of SCT across domains of children's lives. Such evaluations are needed.

Summary and Conclusions

Ethnic differences in sociocultural norms present both opportunities to increase the benefits of training, as well as potential limitations. SCT programs may increase children's and teachers' cross-ethnic understanding by identifying ways in which ethnic differences in sociocultural norms and values are influencing perceptions. Since minority children may not share the norms and values of the mainstream group, SCT may provide the possibility for minority children to learn to "code switch" in social interaction repertoires as bilingual children do in their choice of languages. That is, children may become able to switch social registers and rules regarding appropriate social behaviors as they appear most appropriate or useful in the home, school, and community.

Including discussions of children's various social expectations, problem solutions, and behavioral patterns offers the opportunity for SCT to increase minority and mainstream children's awareness of the United States as a pluralistic society, rather than as a melting pot. Pluralistic norms for socially competent behavior are more likely to result in positive self concepts, particularly for minority children. And a review of the implicit values and norm assumptions characterizing a number of SCT programs suggests that children experiencing SCT will increase their skills at responding in an active, deferent, individually goal-focused manner, with a fair degree of emotional restraint—a demeanor valued in U.S. mainstream culture.

The delivery format of SCT offers additional opportunities for children from different ethnic groups to work collaboratively to achieve common goals. This is likely to have secondary benefits of reducing cross-ethnic conflict and increasing positive cross-ethnic attitudes. Designing and evaluating the school-based program also provides a forum in which parents, teachers, and community leaders can collaborate to develop a program congruent with the range of norms and values of their community.

Within these contexts, the limitations of SCT for minority children also need to be considered. Exposing children to the norms and values of other groups and explicitly labeling ethnic differences may antagonize parents and create confusion for children. For children from strongly traditional ethnic families, in particular, SCT may create, rather than reduce, problems in nonschool settings. The need for data on the effects of SCT across different domains of a child's life is critical.

References

Aboud, F. E. (1987). The development of the ethnic self-identification and attitudes. In J. Phinney & M. Rotheram (Eds.), *Children's ethnic socialization: Pluralism and development* (pp. 32–55). Beverly Hills, CA: Sage.

Aboud, F. E., & Skerry, S. (1984). The development of ethnic attitudes. *Journal of Cross Cultural Psychology, 15,* 3–34.

Aiello, M., Jr., & Jones, C. (1971). Field study of the proxemic behavior of young school children in 3 subcultural groups. *Journal of Personality and Social Psychology, 19,* 351–356.

Ainsworth, N. (1984). The cultural shaping of oral discourse. *Theory into Practice, 23,* 2, 132–137.

Argulewicz, E. N., Elliot, S. N., & Hall, R. (1982). Comparison of behavioral ratings of Anglo-American and Mexican-American gifted children. *Psychology in the Schools, 19,* 4, 469–472.

Argyle, M. (1984). Some new developments in social skill training. *Bulletin of the British Psychological Society, 37*, 405–410.

Banks, W. C. (1976). White preference in Blacks: A paradigm in search of a phenomenon. *Psychological Bulletin, 83*, 1179–1186.

Baskin, E. J., & Hess, R. D. (1980). Does affective education work? A review of seven programs. *Journal of School Psychology, 18*, 40–50.

Batchold, L. (1982). Children's social interactions and parental attitudes among Hupa Indians and Anglo-Americans. *Journal of Social Psychology, 116*, 9–17.

Batchold, L. (1984). Antecedents of caregiver attitudes and social behavior of Hupa Indians and Anglo-Americans preschoolers in California. *Child Study Journal, 13*, 217–233.

Boney, J. (1971). An analysis of the participation of racially integrated guidance groups. *Journal of Negro Education, 40*, 390–393.

Burger, H. (1973). Cultural pluralism and the schools. In C. Brembeck & W. Hill (Eds.). *Cultural challenges to education* (pp. 88–116). Lexington, MA: D.C. Heath.

Cantor, C. L., & Helfat, L. (1976). Training for affective education: A model for change in the schools. *Journal of Clinical Child Psychology, 5*, 5–8.

Cartledge, G., & Milburn, J. (Eds.). (1980). *Teaching social skills to children: Innovative approaches.* New York: Pergamon.

Clark, K. B., & Clark, M. P. (1947). Racial identification and preference in Negro children. In T. M. Newcomb & E. L. Hartley (Eds.), *Reading in social psychology* (pp. 169–178). New York: Holt, Rinehart & Winston.

Cohen, J. A., Brennan, C. D., & Sexton, B. (1984). *A social cognitive approach to the prevention of adolescent substance abuse. Intervention I: Sixth grade.* (A manual). New Haven, CT: Yale University School of Medicine, The Consultation Center.

Conger, J. C., & Conger, A. J. (1982). Components of heterosocial competence. In J. P. Curran & P. M. Monti (Eds.), *Social Skills training: A practical handbook for assessment and treatment* (pp. 313–347). New York: Guilford.

Cowen, E. L. (1985). Person-centered approaches to primary prevention in mental health: Situation-focused and competence-enhancement. *American Journal of Community Psychology, 13*, 31–48.

Cowen, E. L., Pederson, A., Babigian, H., Izzo, L. D., & Trost, M. A. (1973). Long-term follow-up of early detected vulnerable children. *Journal of Consulting and Clinical Psychology, 41*, 438–446.

Cross, W. (1971). The Negro to Black conversion experience. *Black World, 20*, 13–27.

Cummins, J. (1984). *Bilingualism and special education: Issues in assessment and pedagogy.* San Diego: College Hill Press.

Curran, J. (1977). Skills training as an approach to the treatment of heterosexual-social anxiety: A review. *Psychological Bulletin, 84*, 140–157.

de la Serna, M. (1982). Competitive behaviors among urban Mexican-Americans and Anglo-American children. *Revista Interamericana de Psicologia, 16*, 70–76.

Deluty, R. H. (1985). Consistency of assertive, aggressive, and submissive behavior for children. *Journal of Personality and Social Psychology, 49*, 1054–1065.

Diaz-Guerrero, R. (1967). The active and passive syndrome. *Revista Interamericana de Psicologia, 1*, 263–272.

Diaz-Guerrero, R. (1973). Interpreting coping styles across nations from sex and social class differences. *International Journal of Psychology, 8*, 191–203.

Diaz-Guerrero, R. (1979). Origines de la personnalite humaine et des systemes sociaux. *Revue de Psychologie Appliquee, 29*, 383–410.

Diaz-Guerrero, R. (1982). The psychology of the historic-sociocultural premise. *Spanish Language Psychology, 2*, 383–410.

Doi, T. (1973). *Anatomy of dependence.* New York: Harper & Row.

Dorman, L. (1973). Assertive behavior and cognitive performance in preschool children. *Journal of Genetic Psychology, 123*, 155–162.

Echohawk, L. (1978). Locus of control among American Indian youth. *Dissertation Abstracts International, 38*, (9-B), 4450–4451.

Elias, M. J., & Clabby, J. F. (1984). Integrating social and affective education into public school curriculum and instruction. In C. Maher, R. Illback, & J. Zins (Eds.), *Organizational psychology in the schools: A handbook for professionals* (pp. 143–172). Springfield, IL: CC Thomas.

Forgas, J. (1979). *Social episodes.* New York: Academic Press.

Gallimore, R., Boggs, J., & Jordan, C. (1974). *Culture, behavior and education.* Beverly Hills, CA: Sage.

Gersick, K., Grady, K., & Snow, D. (1988). Social cognitive skill development with sixth graders and its initial impact on substance use. *Journal of Drug Education* (pp. 215–237), *summer issue.*

Gilbert, M. (1988). Group understanding and training in social skills. Unpublished manuscript, Vancouver General Hospital, Department of Psychology, Vancouver.

Giles, H., Llado, N., McKirnan, D. H., & Taylor, D. M. (1979). Social identity in Puerto Rico. *International Journal of Psychology, 14*, 185–201.

Glood, E., & Elm, L. (in press). Suicidal behavior among Native-American youth. In M. Rotheram, J. Bradley, & N. Obolensky (Eds.), *Evaluation of suicide within community settings.* Tulsa, OK: University of Oklahoma Press.

Goodman, M. E. (1964). *Race awareness in young children.* New York: Collier. (Original work published 1952).

Hall, E. T. (1966). *The hidden dimension.* Garden City, NY: Anchor Books.

Hazel, J. S., Sherman, J. A., Schumaker, J. B., & Sheldon, J. (1985). Group social skill training with adolescents: critical review. In D. Upper & S. M. Ross (Eds.), *Handbook of behavioral group therapy* (pp. 203–246). New York: Plenum.

Heller, M. (1982). Negotiations of language choice in Montreal. In J. Gumperz (Ed.), *Language and social identity* (pp. 381–386). Cambridge: Cambridge University Press.

Heller, M. (1984). Language and ethnic identity in a Toronto French language school. *Canadian Ethnic Studies, 16*, 1–14.

Heller, K., & Monahan, J. (1977). *Psychology and community change.* Homewood, IL: Dorsey Press.

Hofstede, G. (1980). *Culture's consequences: International differences in work-related values.* Beverly Hills, CA: Sage.

Holtzman, W. H., Diaz-Guerrero, R., & Schwartz, J. D. (1975). *Personality development into two cultures.* Austin: University of Texas Press.

Huey, W., & Rank, R. (1984). Effects of counselor and peer led assertiveness training groups for Black adolescents who are aggressive. *Journal of Counseling Psychology, 31*, 193–203.

Kagan, S., & Carlson, J. (1975). Development of adaptive assertiveness in Mexican and United States children. *Developmental Psychology, 11*, 71–78.

Kagan, S., & Ender, P. B. (1975). Maternal response to success and failure of Anglo-American, Mexican-American, and Mexican children. *Child Development, 46*, 452–458.

Kagan, S., Knight, G., Martinez, S., & Santa, P. (1981). Conflict resolution style among Mexican children. *Journal of Cross-Cultural Psychology, 12*, 222–232.

Kagan, S., & Madsen, M. C. (1971). Cooperation and competition of Mexican, Mexican-American and Anglo-American children of two ages under four instructional sets. *Developmental Psychology, 5*, 32–39.

Katz, P. A. (1976). The acquisition of racial attitudes in children. In P. A. Katz (Ed.), *Towards the elimination of racism* (pp. 125–154). New York: Pergamon.

Knight, G., & Kagan, S. (1982). Siblings, birth order and cooperative-competitive social behavior: A comparison of Anglo-American and Mexican-American children. *Journal of Cross-Cultural Psychology, 13*, 239–249.

Knudson, K. (1979). The relationships among affective role-taking, empathy, and prosocial behavior in a sample of Mexican-American and Anglo-American children of two ages. *Dissertation Abstracts International, 39*, (8)B, 1042.

Kochman, T. (1981). *Black and white styles in conflict.* Chicago: University of Chicago Press.

Ladd, G. W. (1981). Effectiveness of a social learning method for enhancing children's social interaction and peer acceptance. *Child Development, 52*, 171–178.

Ladd, G. W., & Asher, S. R. (1985). Social skills training and children's peer relations: Current issues in research and practice. In L. L' Abate & M. A. Milan (Eds.), *Handbook of social skill training* (pp. 219–244). New York: Wiley.

Lambert, W. (1972). *Language, psychology and culture.* Stanford, CA: Stanford University Press.

Lambert, W. (1980). The social psychology of language: A perspective for the 1980's. In H. Giles, W. P. Robinson, & P. A. Smith (Eds.), *Language: social psychological perspectives* (pp. 415–424). Oxford: Pergamon Press.

MacDonald, S., & Gallimore, R. (1971). *Battle in the classroom: Innovations in classroom techniques.* Scranton: Intext.

Martinez, J. (1977). *Chicano psychology.* New York: Academic Press.

McFee, M. (1968). The 150% man, a product of Blackfeet acculturation. *American Anthropologist, 70*, 1096–1103.

McGoldrick, M., Pearce, J., & Giordano, J. (Eds.). (1982). *Ethnicity and family therapy.* New York: Guilford.

Meichenbaum, D. (1977). *Cognitive-behavior modification: An integrative approach.* New York: Plenum.

Miller, A. (1973). Integration and acculturation of cooperative behavior among Blackfoot Indian and non-Indian Canadian children. *Journal of Cross-Cultural Psychology, 4*, 374–380.

Miller, N., & Brewer, M. (Eds.). (1984). *Groups in contact: The psychology of desegregation.* New York: Academic Press.

Nevius, J. (1982). School participation and culture in play groups of young children. *Journal of Social Psychology, 116*, 291–292.

Oden, S. L., & Asher, S. R. (1977). Coaching children in social skills for friendship making. *Child Development, 48*, 495–506.

Ogbu, J. (1981). Origins of human competence: A cultural ecological perspective. *Child Development, 52*, 413–429.

Ogbu, J. (1982). Socialization: A cultural ecological approach. In K. Borman (Ed.), *The social life of children in a changing society* (pp. 253–271). Hillsdale, NJ: Erlbaum.

O'Malley, M. (1977). Research perspective on social competence. *Merrill-Palmer Quarterly, 23*, 29–44.

Padilla, A. (Ed.). (1980). *Acculturation: Theory, models, and some new findings*. Boulder, CO: Westview Press.

Paz, Q. (1961). *The labyrinth of solitude*. New York: Grove.

Phinney, J., & Rotheram, M. J. (1985, August). *Ethnic behavior patterns among Black and Mexican-American children*. Paper presented at the annual meetings of the American Psychological Association, Los Angeles.

Platz, D. L. (1977). Fantasy predisposition, play preference and early home experiences of White and Navajo kindergarten children. *Dissertation Abstracts International, 38*, (1-A), 105.

Porter, J. D. R. (1971). *Black child, white child: The development of racial attitudes*. Cambridge, MA: Harvard University Press.

Ramirez, M., III (1977). Recognizing and understanding diversity, multiculturalism and the Chicano movement in psychology. In J. Martinez (Ed.), *Chicano Psychology* (pp. 343–353). New York: Academic Press.

Ramirez, M., III (1983). *Psychology of the Americas: Mestizo perspectives on personality and mental health*. New York: Academic Press.

Ramirez, M., III, & Casteneda, A. (1974). *Cultural democracy, bicognitive development, and education*. New York: Academic Press.

Ramirez, M., III, & Price-Williams, D. (1974). Cognitive styles of children of three ethnic groups in the United States. *Journal of Cross-Cultural Psychology, 5*, 212–219.

Rappaport, J. (1977). *Community psychology: Values, research and action*. New York: Holt, Rinehart & Winston.

Rappaport, J. (1981). In praise of paradox. *American Journal of Community Psychology, 9*, 1–25.

Rogers, M., Hennigan, K., Bowman, C., & Miller, N. (1984). Intergroup acceptance in classroom and playground settings. In N. Miller & M. Brewer (Eds.), *Groups in contact: The psychology of desegregation* (pp. 214–229). New York: Academic Press.

Rosenthal, D. A. (1987). Ethnic identity development in adolescence. In J. Phinney & M. J. Rotheram (Eds.), *Children's ethnic socialization: Pluralism and development* (pp. 156–180). Beverly Hills: Sage.

Rosenthal, D. A., & Hrynevich, C. (1985). Ethnicity and ethnic identity: A comparative study of Greek-, Italian-, and Anglo-Australian adolescents. *International Journal of Psychology, 20*, 723–742.

Rotheram, M. J. (1982a). Assertiveness training with under-achievers, disruptive and exceptional children. *Psychology in the Schools, 19*, 532–539.

Rotheram, M. J. (1982b). Variations in children's assertiveness due to trainer assertiveness level. *Journal of Community Psychology, 10*, 228–236.

Rotheram, M. J. (1987). Evaluation of imminent danger of suicide in children. *American Journal of Orthopsychiatry, 47*(1), 59–67.

Rotheram, M. J. (1988). The child and the school. In L. Combrinck-Graham (Ed.), *The child in family therapy* (pp. 295–331). New York: Guilford Press.

Rotheram, M. J. (in press). Fourteen ounces of prevention. In R. Price, E. Cowen, R. Lorion, & V. Ramos-McKay (Eds.), *Assertivess training for children*. Washington, DC: APA Press.

Rotheram, M. J., Armstrong, M., & Booraem, C. (1982). Assertiveness training in fourth- and fifth-grade children. *American Journal of Community Psychology, 10*, 567–582.

Sagar, H. A., & Schofield, J. W., (1980). Racial and behavioral cues in Black and White children's perceptions of ambiguously aggressive acts. *Journal of Personality and Social Psychology, 39*, 590–598.

Schofield, J. W. (1982). *Black and white in school: Trust, tension or tolerance?* New York: Praeger.

Shade, B. (1982). Afro-American cognitive style: A variable in school success? *Review of Educational Research, 52,* 219–244.

Shibutani, T., & Kwan, K. (1965). *Ethnic stratification.* New York: MacMillan.

Singleton, L. C., & Asher, S. R. (1977). Peer preferences and interaction among third-grade children in an integrated school district. *Journal of Educational Psychology, 69,* 330–336.

Spiegel, J. (1982). An ecological model of ethnic families. In M. McGoldrick, J. Pearce, & J. Giordano (Eds.), *Ethnicity and family therapy* (pp. 31–51). New York: Guilford.

Spivack, G., Platt, J., & Shure, M. (1976). *The problem-solving approach to adjustment.* San Francisco: Jossey-Bass.

Spivack, G., & Shure, M. B. (1974). *Social adjustment of young children: A cognitive approach to solving real-life problems.* San Francisco: Jossey-Bass.

Stevenson, H. W., & Stewart, E. C. (1958). A developmental study of racial awareness in young children. *Child Development, 29,* 399–409.

Stewart, E. (1972). *American cultural patterns: A cross-cultural perspective.* Chicago: Intercultural Press.

Stonequist, E. V. (1935). The problem of a marginal man. *American Journal of Sociology, 41,* 1–12.

Sue, S., & Wagner, N. (Eds). (1973). *Asian-Americans: psychological perspectives.* Ben Lomond, CA: Science and Behavior Books.

Taylor, D. M., Simard, L. M., & Aboud, F. E. (1972). Ethnic identification in Canada: A cross-cultural investigation. *Canadian Journal of Behavioural Science, 4,* 13–20.

Triandis, H. (1972). *The analysis of subjective culture.* New York: John Wiley.

Urbain, E. S., & Kendall, P. C. (1980). Review of social-cognitive problem-solving interventions with children. *Psychological Bulletin, 88,* 109–143.

Vaughan, G. M. (1978). Social categorization and intergroup behavior in children. In H. Tajfel (Ed.), *Differentiation between social groups: Studies in the social psychology of intergroup relations* (pp. 339–360). London: Academic Press.

Weissberg, R. P. (1985). Developing effective social problem-solving programs for the classroom. In B. Schneider, K. H. Rubin & J. Ledingham (Eds.), *Peer relationships and social skills in childhood,* (Vol. 2) (pp.252–242). New York: Springer-Verlag.

Weissberg, R. P, Gesten, E. L., Carnrike, C. L., Toro, P. A., Rapkin, B. D., Davidson, E., & Cowen, E. L. (1981). Social problem-solving skills training: A competence building intervention with second to fourth-grade children. *American Journal of Community Psychology, 9,* 411–423.

Weissberg, R. P., Gesten, E. L., Rapkin, B. D., Cowen, E. L., Davidson, E., Flores de Apodaca, R., & McKim, B. J. (1981). The evaluation of social problem-solving training program for suburban and inner-city third-grade children. *Journal of Consulting and Clinical Psychology, 49,* 251–261.

Whiting, B. B., & Whiting, J. W. (1975). *Children of six cultures: A psycho-cultural analysis.* Cambridge, MA: Harvard University Press.

11

Stress and Coping Preventive Interventions for Children and Adolescents

Bruce E. Compas, Vicky Phares
Normand Ledoux

Some say it was Mark Twain, speaking at the very first Vermont Conference on the Primary Prevention of Psychopathology who said, "Everybody talks about stress but no one does anything about it." Regardless of the truth of this rumor, things have improved considerably since Twain's time and a number of promising school-based programs have been developed to assist children and adolescents in coping with life stress. The purpose of this chapter is to review examples of such programs, place them in the broader context of stress and coping theory, and identify directions for future research. The first portion briefly describes a cognitive-transactional model of stress and coping as it applies to children, adolescents, and their families. Emphasis is placed on recent work by our research group, the Vermont Stress, Coping, and Development Project. Next, the key issues facing the field are outlined. The third section of the paper reviews empirical studies evaluating school-based stress and coping preventive interventions. Finally, future directions for this area of research are described with an emphasis on the development of comprehensive programs for children, adolescents, and their families.

Stress and Coping

Given the wide use of the terms *stress* and *coping* in both the professional literature and our culture as a whole, it is important to clarify what is meant by these concepts. In this regard, we have drawn extensively on the work of Richard Lazarus and Susan Folkman, who define psychological stress as "a particular relationship between the person and the environment that is appraised by the person as taxing or exceeding his or her resources and endangering his or her well being" (1984, p. 19). Sources of stress in the environment include both major life events (e.g., death of a loved one) and chronic stressors or daily hassles (e.g., problems with finances or traffic problems). Further, the impact of a stressor on a person depends on the appraised meaning that the event holds for that individual. That is, the degree to which an event is experienced as stressful by an individual depends on the importance that the event holds in that person's priorities, values, and commitments. With regard to coping, Lazarus and Folkman have defined it as "constantly changing cognitive and behavioral efforts to manage specific external and/or internal demands that are appraised as taxing or exceeding the resources of the person" (1984, p. 141). Coping is further delineated into problem-focused coping (efforts to act on the source of the stressful relationship between the person and the environment) and emotion-focused coping (efforts to regulate the emotional distress associated with the stressful encounter).

These definitions highlight several important considerations for the development of stress and coping preventive interventions for children and adolescents. First, stress is a function of both the person and the environment and preventive interventions will need to address both of these factors if they are to represent comprehensive efforts in assisting youngsters in managing life stress. Second, stressors of both major and minor magnitude can serve as targets of preventive interventions for children. Third, individuals may vary in their vulnerability to different types of stress as a function of their cognitive appraisals, values, goals, and commitments. Preventive interventions will need to enable individuals to identify the types of stress to which they are most vulnerable. Fourth, a comprehensive intervention will need to include components to enhance both problem- and emotion-focused coping in order improve youngsters' coping skills. Each of these points will be dealt with in more detail below.

Vulnerability to Stress

Evidence has accumulated to indicate that stressful life events of both major and minor magnitude are related to psychological and behavioral problems in children and adolescents (Compas, 1987b; Johnson, 1986). However, there are considerable differences between individuals in their vulnerability to different types of stress. A series of investigations by our research group has identified five sources of individual differences in vulnerability to stress among children and adolescents: (a) developmental factors; (b) gender related factors; (c) the proximal nature of daily as opposed to major stressful events; (d) stress and symptoms in the lives of significant others; and (e) individual differences in self-perceptions of competence and the importance of different domains of functioning.

With regard to developmental differences, a cross-sectional study (Wagner & Compas, 1988) indicated that the relation between stressful events and symptoms varied across three age groups of adolescents. The association between six subtypes of stressful events and psychological symptoms was analyzed in young adolescents (12–14 years old), middle adolescents (15–17 years old), and older adolescents who were attending college (18–20 years old). The subtypes of events included family stressors (e.g., pressures or expectations by parents), peer stressors (e.g., fights with or problems with friends), academic stressors (e.g., doing poorly on an exam or paper), autonomy stressors (e.g., moving away from parents' home), intimacy stressors (e.g., breaking up with boyfriend or girlfriend), and network stressors (e.g., friend having emotional problems). Using stepwise multiple regression analyses to predict psychological symptoms, only family stressors were predictive of psychological symptoms for young adolescents, only peer stressors were predictive of symptoms for middle adolescents, and only academic stressors were predictive for older adolescents attending college. Although there may be substantial individual differences within each of these age groups, we believe that these findings highlight an important point for preventive interventions with children and adolescents; sources of stress change with development. If prevention programs are to be effective in helping youngsters manage stress, they will need to account for the types of stress that are significant for the age group targeted by the program.

Studies of stress during adolescence have by and large indicated that adolescent girls report more stressful events and are more affected by stressful events than are adolescent boys (e.g., Burke & Weir, 1978; Compas, Davis, & Forsythe, 1985; Compas, Slavin Wagner, & Vanatta, 1986; Newcomb, Huba, & Bentler, 1981). Wagner and Compas (1988) expanded on these earlier studies by comparing females and males on the occurrence, perceived stressfulness, and association with psychological symptoms for the subtypes of stressful events described above. The most striking and consistent pattern of differences between males and females involved network events, that is, stressors that affect others in one's social network without directly influencing the individual (Kessler & McLeod, 1984). Both young and middle adolescent girls reported more network stressors than boys, and female college students rated network events as more stressful than males (Wagner & Compas, 1988). These findings, along with the general trend for female adolescents to report more stressful events than males, indicate boys and girls may be struggling with different types of stress and may have somewhat different needs in terms of interventions designed to aid them in coping.

A third issue in sources of vulnerability to stress revolves around the role of major life events as compared to chronic, daily stressors in the development and maintenance of emotional/behavior problems. Studies with adult populations have attempted to pit these two sources of stress against one another in an effort to determine which is the more potent predictor of psychological symptoms (e.g., Kanner, Coyne, Schaefer, & Lazarus, 1981; Monroe, 1983). However, two studies by our research group have indicated that major and daily stressors play different but complementary roles in relation to symptoms. In a prospective study of major life events, daily stressors, and psychological symptoms in a sample of older adolescents during the transition from high school to college, Wagner, Compas, and Howell (1988) found that daily stressors mediated the association between major events and symptoms. That is, major events were related to daily stressors and daily stressors were related to symptoms, but major events were not directly associated with symptoms. Compas, Howell, Phares, Williams, and Ledoux (1989) found a similar pattern in the association of major and daily stress with emotional/behavioral problems in a sample of young adolescents and their parents. We take these findings to mean that major life events (e.g., divorce of parents, moving to a new school) affect emotional well-being through the stream of minor stresses and hassles they create in daily living (cf. Felner, Farber, & Primavera, 1983). Thus, preventive interventions may need to facilitate coping with daily stressors rather than with major life events per se.

A fourth source of vulnerability to stress involves the level of stress and symptoms experienced by significant others in children's lives. An unfortunate characteristic of stress research has been to examine stressful events and symptoms experienced by individuals independent of the context in which they experience these events. Most importantly, little attention has been paid to the importance of close interpersonal relationships and the ways in which stress and symptoms might be "transmitted" between individuals. Compas, Howell et al. (1989) and Compas, Howell, Phares, Williams, and Giunta (in press) found that there were significant associations between the stressful events and symptoms reported by young adolescents and their parents. Psychological symptoms experienced by parents in association with stress in their own lives had adverse consequences for the well-being of their children, and parents' symptoms were related to stressful events experienced by their children. Although the findings of other studies of parent and child stress and symptoms have varied (e.g., Cohen, Burt, & Bjork, 1987; Holahan & Moos, 1987; Thomson & Vaux, 1986), research indicates generally that another important target for prevention efforts may be to enhance the coping skills of family members as well as targeted children and adolescents. If parents are more effective in managing their own stress, they may present less risk to the well-being of their children.

Finally, a number of social cognitive factors may influence individuals' vulnerability to different types of stressful events. In a study of college students' vulnerabilty to depression, Hammen, Marks, Mayol, and deMayo (1985) found that individuals with "dependent" cognitive schemas were vulnerable to the effects of interpersonal loss events, whereas individuals with "self-critical" schemas were vulnerable to achievement related stressors. Recent findings (Compas & Banez, 1988) reveal a similar pattern of vulnerability to social/interpersonal stressors in 11- to 14-year-olds. Children with low levels of self-perceived social competence were more vulnerable to the effects of stressful events involving social or interpersonal relationships than children with high levels of perceived social competence; and children with low levels of self-perceived scholastic competence were more vulnerable to academic achievement stress than children with high perceived competence in this domain. Thus, social cognitive factors may predispose individuals to be vulnerable to specific kinds of stressful events.

Coping with Stress

A substantial body of literature exists to indicate that the ways in which children and adolescents cope with stress influence the relation between stress and adjustment (Compas, 1987a; Compas, Malcarne, & Banez, in press). It appears that youngsters use both problem- and emotion-focused coping strategies in response to stressful events and the effectiveness of these two types of coping depends on a number of situational and individual factors. For example, Forsythe and Compas (1987) found the psychological symptoms of college students varied as a function of the interaction between the amount of problem- and emotion-focused coping used by subjects and their appraisals of control over stress. Specifically, psychological symptoms were high when subjects mismatched their coping and perceptions of control, that is, using more problem-focused coping when perceived control was low and using more emotion-focused coping when perceived control was high. Conversely, symptoms were lower when coping and appraisals were matched, that is, using more problem-focused coping when perceived control was high and using more emotion-focused coping when perceived control was low. A similar pattern of results has been found with a sample of 11- to 14-year-old youngsters (Compas, Malcarne, & Fondacaro, 1988). These results highlight the importance of teaching both types of coping and the usefulness of each for different stressful circumstances as a part of a comprehensive stress and coping intervention.

The varying utility of problem- and emotion-focused coping described above suggests that an individual must be flexible in her or his responses to the changing demands of stressful situations encountered in everyday life. In contrast, individuals who are rigid and unchanging in the ways they cope are unlikely to be effective in managing different types of stress. Findings reported by Compas, Forsythe, and Wagner (1988) support this view; higher levels of consistency in coping with chronic stressors over a four-week period were associated with higher levels of psychological symptoms. Although the causal direction of this relationship warrants further investigation (i.e., symptoms predicted greater subsequent consistency in coping but consistency in coping did not predict later symptoms), these data further underscore the need to teach a variety of coping strategies to enhance successful mastery of daily stressful experiences.

Characteristics of Stress and Coping Preventive Interventions

The research discussed above suggests several dimensions on which stress and coping preventive interventions can be distinguished: (a) the degree to which the intervention focuses on changing individual youngsters by enhancing their coping skills and competencies, versus changing features of the environment to reduce sources of stress; (b) the degree to which the program focuses on specific sources of stress or more general stressors faced by youngsters; (c) if coping skills are taught, the extent to which problem-focused strategies, emotion-focused strategies, or both are emphasized; and (d) the degree to which the desired outcome of the program is competency enhancement (promotion) or problem prevention.

The distinction between person-centered and environment-centered interventions is a long-standing one in prevention and community psychology (e.g., Cowen, 1980, 1985; Felner & Felner, this volume; Glenwick & Jason, 1984; Rappaport, 1981). As these authors and others have noted, person- and environment-centered approaches to prevention are not incompatible with each other and may actually serve complementary functions. That is, there are a number of identifiable stressors that have predictable adverse effects on child and adolescent development (e.g., high levels of conflict between parents, high levels of change in the psychosocial environment associated with certain major life transitions), and efforts can be made to alter features of the environment associated with these stressors. Further, to the extent that stress and symptoms can be transmitted between individuals, deficiencies in the coping skills of significant others may represent a source of stress for children/adolescents and serve as an appropriate target for intervention in the social environment. On the other hand, a number of sources of both major and daily stress (e.g., unexpected loss of a family member through death) are more difficult to predict and control. These latter problems may lend themselves more to interventions designed to help children/adolescents ward off their adverse consequences.

A similar distinction is often made in choosing between specific or general sources of stress in children's lives as the target for prevention efforts. Because certain stressors such as loss of a parent through death or divorce are known risk factors for emotional/behavior problems, preventive interventions can be developed to target children exposed to these specific risk factors. On the other hand, research has shown that the cumulative effects of a wide variety of major and daily stressors are related to psychological distress (Compas, 1987b; Johnson, 1986). The majority of children and adolescents may not have experienced specific events that can be singled out as risk factors, but they may nevertheless be at risk because of the variety of stressors they have encountered. As such, both broadly and narrowly focused programs may be viable.

With regard to the types of coping skills taught in preventive interventions, both problem- and emotion-focused coping skills will be important. A large number of interventions have been developed under the general title of "stress management" programs that emphasize the use of relaxation techniques as a primary method of coping with stress (e.g., Woolfolk & Lehrer, 1984). In contrast, numerous programs have been developed which emphasize "problem-solving" skills to actively confront sources of stress (e.g., Pedro-Carroll & Cowen, 1985). These different emphases may be appropriate for programs that test different objectives and address different types of stress.

Finally, a distinction can be made between programs designed to enhance personal competencies as opposed to preventing emotional/behavioral problems. Stress and coping preventive interventions designed to enhance competencies are those that facilitate effective coping in whole populations, regardless of their exposure to sources of increased risk for disorder. Programs designed to prevent emotional/behavior problems are those which address populations previously exposed to sources of risk and who may already evidence disorder associated with these risks. Although programs often have one or the other of these objectives, it is possible and even desirable to integrate both into a single program (Rolf, 1985).

School-Based Stress and Coping Preventive Interventions for Children and Adolescents

The four characteristics of stress and coping preventive interventions described above will now be used to evaluate programs for children and adolescents. Consistent with the focus of this book, emphasis will be given to school-based stress and coping preventive interventions. Representative school-based programs are presented in Table 11.1. Each program is described in terms of the population served, the focus on person or environment factors, whether the program addresses a specific type of stress or sources of stress in general, the types of coping skills taught, the desired outcome (competence enhancement vs. problem reduction), and the results of controlled outcome studies of the program that have been reported in the literature. We have not included a large number of outstanding programs that teach coping skills because they do not do so in the context of how these coping skills can be used to manage stressful life experiences. These include interventions designed to enhance problem-solving skills (e.g., Spivack & Shure, 1982, 1985; Weissberg, Caplan, & Sivo, this volume), and programs designed to prevent specific disorders or problems (e.g., the work of Botvin & Dusenbury, this volume, on the prevention of substance abuse).

A number of themes can be identified in the eight studies summarized in Table 11.1. First, the majority of programs (six) were designed to address a specific stressor (e.g., parental divorce) rather than general sources of stress in youngsters' lives. As such, they tend to reflect secondary prevention efforts designed to aid populations already exposed to increased risk for emotional/behavior problems and often already displaying such problems. Second, six of the eight programs were child-focused; efforts to reduce sources of stress in youngsters' social environments have been rare. Third, when coping skills were taught as a component of the intervention, instruction has focused on both problem- and emotion-focused coping skills (six programs) or emotion-focused coping skills were taught alone (one program). No interventions reported teaching exclusively problem-focused coping.

Outcome data on these preventive interventions have been quite promising in general, with some positive effects reported for every program. Beneficial outcomes have included increases in the use of various coping skills (e.g., Elias, Gara, Ubriaco, Rothbaum, Clabby, & Schuyler, 1986), reduced emotional/behavioral problems (e.g., Pedro-Carroll & Cowen, 1985), increased school attendance and enhanced academic performance (e.g., Felner, Ginter, & Primavera, 1982), and improvements in self-esteem (e.g., Stolberg & Garrison, 1985). Positive effects have resulted from both person- and environment-focused programs, from programs teaching both problem- and emotion-focused coping as well as those teaching only emotion-focused coping, from programs addressing both general and specific sources of stress, and from programs serving populations previously exposed to a significant stressor and already displaying emotional/behavioral problems as well as those serving youngsters who are not exhibiting significant problems prior to their participation in the program. The findings do not provide clear support for the superiority of one approach over another. Rather, as one would expect, the effectiveness of each approach must be defined in terms of one's goals and objectives. Further, some programs have produced unexpected and mixed results.

Four programs summarized in Table 11.1 have been selected for more detailed discussion: the Divorce Adjustment Project (Stolberg & Garrison, 1985), the Children of Divorce Intervention Program (Pedro-Carroll & Cowen, 1985; Pedro-Carroll, Cowen, Hightower, & Guare, 1986), the Transition Project (Felner et al., 1982), and the Improving Social Awareness-Social Problem Solving Project (Elias, Clabby, Corr, Ubriaco, & Schuyler, 1982). These programs were selected because they vary along a number of the dimensions represented in Table 11.1, including focusing on children versus environments, teaching different types of coping skills, focusing on a specific stressor versus sources of stress in general, and reflecting primary or secondary prevention.

TABLE 11.1 Stress and Coping Preventive Intervention Programs for Children and Adolescents

Study	Sample	Source of Stress	Focus on Child vs. Environment	Type of Coping Taught	Desired Outcome	Evaluation
Bogat, Jones, & Jason (1980)	1st through 7th grade students (n = 56)	Transition to new school	Child	Social support and information	Promotion of knowledge and self-esteem	Increased social self-esteem, increased knowledge about school setting, improved school conduct
Elias et al. (1986)	5th grade students (n = 158)	Transition to middle school	Child	Problem-focused and emotion-focused	Prevention of stress and promotion of coping skills	Fewer and less intense stressful events, enhanced coping skills
Felner, Ginter, & Primavera (1982)	9th grade students (n = 172)	Transition to high school	Environment	None	Prevention of absenteeism, promotion of self-esteem and academic performance	Maintenance of self-esteem, grades, school attendance, and positive perceptions of school environment
Felner, Norton, Cowen & Farber (1981)	School age children (unspecified)	Major life events	Child	Problem-focused and emotion-focused	Prevention of behavior problems and enhancement of school adjustment	No controlled evaluation data

Pedro-Carroll & Cowen (1985)	3rd through 6th grade students (n = 75)	Parental divorce	Child	Problem-focused and emotion-focused	Prevention of behavior problems and enhancement of self-esteem and school adjustment	Reduction in behavior problems and improved school adjustment
Pedro-Carroll et al. (1986)	4th through 6th grade students (n = 132)	Parental divorce	Child	Problem-focused and emotion-focused	Prevention of behavior problems and enhancement of perceived control and school adjustment	Reduction in behavior problems and improved school adjustment
Stolberg & Garrison (1985)	7–13 year olds and their mothers (n = 82)	Parental divorce	Child and environment	Problem-focused and emotion-focused	Reduced behavior problems and stress, enhanced self-esteem	Children and mothers showed improvement, varying with type of intervention
Zaichkowsky & Zaichkowsky (1984)	4th grade students (n = 43)	Multiple stressors, unspecified	Child	Emotion-focused	Reduced anxiety	Improved control over anxiety

Divorce Adjustment Project

The Divorce Adjustment Project (DAP) is a preventive intervention addressing the problems and needs of children whose parents have recently divorced (Stolberg & Garrison, 1985). The intervention consists of the "Children's Support Group" (CSG), a 12-session psychoeducational program to help 7- to 13-year-olds meet the behavioral and emotional demands associated with parental divorce, and the "Single Parents' Support Group" (SPSG), a 12-session program to provide support and skill development to divorced, custodial mothers.

Although the overall focus of the DAP is the major life event of divorce, the intervention actually targets a number of discrete stressors or hassles associated with divorce. For example, the CSG includes discussion of problems such as "what to say when father does not make his Saturday date" and "what to do about vacations" (see Stolberg, Cullen, Garrison, & Brophy, 1981). Similarly parents' groups focus on topics including sexuality, work, and child discipline (see Garrison, Stolberg, Mallonnee, Carpenter, & Antrim, 1984). A wide range of problem- and emotion-focused coping skills are taught to both children and parents. For example, children are taught problem-solving skills, anger-control skills, communication skills, and relaxation skills. In summary, the DAP represents a comprehensive program for children at risk for emotional/behavior problems related to their exposure to a stressor of significant magnitude. The program addresses both a major life event and an array of hassles associated with that event, focuses on both children and an aspect of their social environment (i.e., their parents), and teaches both problem- and emotion-focused coping skills.

The initial evaluation of the program compared four groups: children in the CSG only, parents in the SPSG only, concurrent participation by parents and children in these groups, and a no-treatment control. Results of the evaluation (Stolberg & Garrison, 1985) indicated that children in the CSG-alone condition showed significant increases in self-esteem and social skills, parents in the SPSG-alone group improved more on a measure of adjustment to divorce, and parents in the combined intervention group reported an increase in positive life events. In general, however, the combined CSG and SPSG intervention did not produce the expected effects. The researchers noted that the failure of this more comprehensive intervention to produce incrementally more powerful effects may have been the result of pretreatment differences between this group and the other treatment groups (e.g., mothers in this group had lower employment status, had been separated longer than others, and reported less time spent by noncustodial fathers with their children; Stolberg & Garrison, 1985).

Children of Divorce Intervention Program

The Children of Divorce Intervention Program (CODIP) shares the same target population as the DAP and many similar methods, but differs in some fundamental ways (Pedro-Carroll & Cowen, 1985; Pedro-Carroll et al., 1986). CODIP is a ten-week school-based prevention program for fourth-grade through sixth-grade children of divorce. Similar to the Children's Support Group in the DAP, CODIP maintains an emphasis on support and skill building for children. In addition, CODIP added a component focusing on divorce-related feelings and experiences early in the program, supplemented the cognitive skill building component by using discussion, filmstrips, and role plays of divorce-related experiences, and reduced the number of sessions devoted to anger control (Pedro-Carroll & Cowen, 1985). Thus, CODIP teaches youngsters both problem- and emotion-focused coping in reference to a specific stressor, i.e., divorce. Similar to DAP, coping with the hassles and chronic stressors related to divorce is emphasized (e.g., divorce-related anxieties, how divorce affects parents' feelings and behaviors, concerns about the future, parental conflict). Further, a distinction is made between problems beyond children's control (e.g., parent reconciliation) and those within their control (e.g., appropriate ways of communicating feelings; Pedro-Carroll & Cowen, 1985). Unlike DAP, the focus of CODIP is on the child and does not include an intervention to change the social environment.

Evaluative data on CODIP have been quite encouraging. Compared with no-treatment controls, program participants were rated by parents as less shy and anxious and as learning better in school, and self-reports reflected less anxiety, more adaptive assertiveness, greater sociability with peers, greater skill at following rules, and greater frustration tolerance (Pedro-Carroll & Cowen, 1985). A second evaluation study compared CODIP participants with a demographically matched sample of peers from intact families. Children of divorce were less well-adjusted than their peers before the program but improved significantly after the intervention on teachers' reports of emotional/behavior problems and children's self-reports of anxiety, sociability, and self-confidence (Pedro-Carroll et al., 1986).

Pedro-Carroll and her colleagues have argued that CODIP is successful in part because it provides both emotional support *and* enhances the problem-solving skills of children of divorce. This is consistent with the notion that stress and coping preventive interventions need to enhance both problem- and emotion-focused coping skills. Affirmation of this idea awaits a component analysis of the effects of the different aspects of the program. Pedro-Carroll and Cowen (1985) also suggest that the program facilitates youngsters' abilities to match their coping to the perceived controllability of stressful situations (cf. Compas, Malcarne, & Fondacaro, 1988; Forsythe & Compas, 1987). Whether or not youngsters in CODIP learned to fit their coping with their appraisals of control and the possible beneficial effects of such matching need to be examined directly.

The positive effects of CODIP reflect an important distinction between stress and coping preventive interventions aimed at reducing problems and those designed to enhance personal competencies. Children of divorce are at risk for the development of emotional/behavior problems as a result of exposure to a stressor of extreme magnitude. This is reflected clearly in the pretreatment differences between the children of divorce and their peers from intact families noted by Pedro-Carroll et al. (1986). The parents of these children had been separated an average of 23 months in the Pedro-Carroll and Cowen (1986) study and an average of 48 months in the Pedro-Carroll et al. (1985) study. As such, the goal of the program centered around problem *reduction* rather than problem prevention per se. That such a reduction in emotional/behavior problems could be achieved by teaching coping skills indicates that ongoing stress associated with the divorce may contribute substantially to the maintenance of such problems. Whether preventive intervention programs implemented at the time of the divorce could prevent the development of such problems remains unclear.

The Transition Project

A very different approach to stress and coping preventive intervention is represented by the Transition Project described by Felner et al. (1982). The program was designed to address the increased risk for maladjustment associated with the normative life transition from junior high school to high school. Prior work by these researchers had established this transition as a time of increased vulnerability to various adjustment problems (Felner, Primavera, & Cauce, 1981). The Transition Project was unique in that it attempted to alter the social environment to facilitate students' adaptation during this transition.

The program featured two major components. First, the role of the homeroom teachers was restructured to provide a central link between students, parents and the rest of the school. This was designed to increase the amount of support experienced by students in their daily environment, increase students' feelings of accountability, decrease their sense of anonymity, and facilitate student access to information about school expectations, rules, and regularities. Second, the school environment was reorganized to reduce the amount of flux in the social setting and facilitate the restructuring and establishment of a stable peer-support system by assigning students to all of their primary academic subjects with the same set of classmates. Thus, rather than teaching youngsters skills to cope with psychosocial stress, the program was designed to reduced sources of stress in the social environment.

Project students and controls were compared on self-concept, perceptions of the social climate of the school, school attendance, and grade point averages. Whereas project students and controls did not differ in absenteeism or grade point average prior to the project, project students were absent less and achieved higher grade point averages than controls at the end of the transition year. Project students maintained relatively stable self-concepts during the year while controls showed declines in total self-esteem and in scholastic and social self-esteem as well. Finally, project students reported more positive perceptions of the school social climate than did controls.

The decline in grade point averages and self-concept scores as well as the increase in absenteeism observed in the control subjects can be interpreted as reflecting the stressful nature of the transition from junior high to high school. In contrast, by reducing the amount of change and flux in the social environment and providing more consistent peer and teacher social support, the project may have provided participants with an effective buffer against the stress associated with the transition and reduced the overall level of stress to which students were exposed. This interpretation of the effects of the program remains to be tested, as the number and intensity of stressful events were not measured directly.

Improving Social Awareness-Social Problem Solving

An alternative approach to helping students manage the stressors associated with a major school transition is the Improving Social Awareness-Social Problem Solving (ISA-SPS) Project (e.g., Elias et al., 1982). ISA-SPS is a 20-session school-based intervention program designed to help youngsters cope with stressors associated with the transition from elementary school to middle school (fifth to sixth grade). The program focuses on building several types of coping skills including sensitivity to one's feelings in problematic situations, means-ends thinking, planning and anticipation skills, and positive expectancies about personal competencies to solve problems and manage stress (Elias et al., 1986). The program is based on the assumption that the development of generalized coping strategies would be the most effective way to enhance adjustment to the many stressors encountered during the transition to middle school.

The program was analyzed by comparing project participants receiving the full intervention (instruction and application phases) with subjects receiving only the instruction phase and subjects in a no-treatment control condition on two factors: social problem solving skills and levels of perceived psychosocial stress. Youngsters receiving the full program reported fewer stressors, perceived those stressors that they did experience as less intense, and showed greater improvement in problem-solving skills than subjects receiving either partial or no treatment (Elias et al., 1986; Elias et al,. 1982). Further, social problem-solving skills were related to the perceived intensity of stress; greater problem-solving skills were associated with lower perceived difficulty with stress related to school and peers (Elias et al., 1986). Poor problem solvers reported high levels of intense stressors whereas good problem solvers reported more varied levels of intense stressors. The authors interpreted these findings as an indication that deficiencies in social problem-solving skills are associated with difficulties in coping with stress.

Directions for Future Research and Program Development

Although school-based stress and coping preventive interventions for children and adolescents are in the early stages of development, the results of the studies summarized here are quite promising and reflect a number of important facets of stress and coping theory and research. First, although most programs have an explicit focus on facilitating coping with major life events (e.g., parental divorce), they clearly address coping with the daily stressors and hassles associated with these major events. Given the significance of daily stress in the development and/or maintenance of emotional/behavioral problems, it would appear that these programs are addressing an important aspect of the stress process. Second, several programs have taken the developmental level of children into account in that they have targeted youngsters undergoing a normative life transition (e.g., junior high to high school) and have coordinated the intervention around this transition. Third, the levels of stress and symptoms in significant others in children's lives have been addressed in the DAP program in which single parents are assisted in the process of coping with the stress of divorce. Finally, both problem- and emotion-focused coping have been taught to children, and efforts have been initiated to facilitate youngsters' understanding of how these two types of coping may be useful in different stressful circumstances (Pedro-Carroll & Cowen, 1985).

Several aspects of the stress and coping process have received less attention in the development and implementation of preventive interventions. First, although transition-related interventions have had a developmental focus, the more general cognitive and social development of children typically has been overlooked. For example, the stresses associated with parental divorce and the types of coping skills children are able to employ may vary with social and cognitive maturity. Developmental changes such as these have not been taken into account in preventive interventions to facilitate coping, reflecting, as well, a more general absence of data on sources of stress and developmental changes in the nature of coping. Advances in interventions will depend further investigation of developmental factors in stress and coping. Second, interventions have not addressed possible gender differences in sources of stress and characteristics of coping. Differing needs of boys and girls may be an important factor to take into account in future intervention efforts. Third, the importance of facilitating change in the social environment, in addition to or in lieu of teaching coping skills to children, has received relatively little attention. Further studies are needed to analyze different components of child-focused and environment-focused interventions (cf. Stolberg & Garrison, 1985).

The programs described above have not included a comprehensive primary prevention effort designed to enhance the ability of a population of children and parents who are not at risk to cope with a wide range of stressful experiences of daily living. Our research group is presently conducting a controlled evaluation of an intervention designed to meet these goals—a comprehensive stress management program for children, parents, and teachers. This school-based program consists of eight class sessions for children dealing with a range of topics including the nature of stress, stress management as a matter of life style, decision-making, assertiveness, resisting peer pressure, and relaxation training (e.g., Ledoux, 1985). Parents and

teachers attend stress management workshops with a special emphasis on the school setting. The program is unique in that it focuses on
developing a generalized set of attitudes and coping skills in children
and others (i.e., parents and teachers) in their social environment.
The program has been delivered to over 3,000 children in grades 3
through 8 over the past five years and has been rated as extremely
valuable by the participants. Current evaluation efforts focus on the
development of problem- and emotion-focused coping skills, reducing levels of perceived stress, and reducing emotional/behavioral
problems in the participants.

Coping, Empowerment, and the Politics of Stress Management

If we assume that, in many instances, stressful events are a risk
factor for psychopathology and a threat to positive growth and adjustment, and further, that the ways individuals cope with stress can reduce the risk for maladjustment, then it is logical to enhance individuals' coping skills to reduce the threat to adjustment and well-being.
However, several significant problems arise when taking this approach. First, there has been an overemphasis on teaching "stress
management" skills to the exclusion of programs designed to reduced
sources of stress in the environment. This is particularly problematic
to the extent that emotion-focused coping skills are emphasized. In
such programs we are encouraging youngsters to adapt to their surroundings and reducing the demand on settings to decrease the levels
of stress they present to children. That is, we are committing the
fundamental error of person-focused interventions, that of blaming
the victim for his or her own problem (Ryan, 1971).

Second, interventions have failed to account for individual differences in their vulnerability to stress and the types of coping that might
prove effective in dealing with one's surroundings (cf. Lazarus &
Folkman, 1984, pp. 361–363). This problem has been noted above in
terms of failures to account for developmental and gender differences in sources of stress and characteristics of effective coping. However, this is also a problem in terms of our failure to account for
cultural and social class differences in these factors. All too often
studies of stress and coping have focused on white middle-class samples and overlooked the needs and preferred coping styles of ethnic
minorities and lower income groups.

Third, stress and coping preventive interventions have failed to
address the goal of empowering the populations they serve (e.g.,
Rappaport, 1981; 1987). Rappaport has argued persuasively that our

goals as community psychologists need to be broader than the prevention of mental and emotional disorder per se. We need to address the fundamental value of helping people, including children, to experience a greater sense of personal control and power in their daily lives. In order to accomplish this goal, stress and coping preventive interventions need to change not only the content of what is taught to children but also the process by which interventions are developed and conducted. Several authors have argued that the fundamental first step in any community intervention is to consult with members of the community to identify what they believe are their primary needs and problems and involve them in developing strategies to meet these needs and solve these problems. An alternative approach, and the one reflected in most interventions described here, is for professionals to develop a model of risk factors and an antidote to these risks, usually conceptualized in terms of the cognitions and behaviors that are useful in combating these risks. However, when developed from the perspective of the professional without extensive and meaningful contributions from members of the community, interventions may be out of touch with the real needs of those who are intended to be served. Further, such programs are likely to be couched in models that assume that individuals have no responsibility for either the causes of or solutions to their problems (medical models) or that individuals have responsibility for the causes of but not the solutions to their problems (enlightenment models; Brickman, Rabinowitz, Karuza, Coates, Cohen, & Kidder, 1982). These approaches are likely to carry a number of implicit messages that serve to undermine the ability of the program to increase feelings of personal control and power in individuals. The goals of empowerment and prevention are not contradictory (Rappaport, 1987). Rather, they can be seen as complementary objectives of a comprehensive stress and coping preventive intervention.

References

Botvin, G. J., & Dusenbury, L. (this volume). Substance abuse prevention and the promotion of competence.

Burke, R. J., & Weir, T. (1978). Sex differences in adolescent life stress, social support, and well being. *The Journal of Psychology, 98*, 277–288.

Brickman, P. Rabinowtiz, V. C., Karuza, J., Coates, D., Cohen, E., & Kidder, L. (1982). Models of helping and coping. *American Psychologist, 37*, 368–384.

Cohen, L. H., Burt, C. E., & Bjork, J. P. (1987). Life stress and adjustment: Effects of life events experienced by young adolescents and their parents. *Developmental Psychology, 23*, 583–592.

Compas, B. E. (1987a). Coping with stress during childhood and adolescence. *Psychological Bulletin, 101*, 393–401.

Compas, B. E. (1987b). Stress and life events during childhood and adolescence. *Clinical Psychology Review, 7*, 275–302.

Compas, B. E., & Banez, G. A. (1988). *Social-cognitive factors in vulnerability to stress in children and adolescents: The role of perceived competence and personal importance.* Manuscript submitted for publication.

Compas, B. E., Davis, G. E., & Forsythe, C. J. (1985). Characteristics of life events during adolescence. *American Journal of Community Psychology, 13*, 677–691.

Compas, B. E., Forsythe, C. J., & Wagner, B. M. (1988). Consistency and variability in causal attributions and coping with stress. *Cognitive Therapy and Research, 12*, 305–320.

Compas, B. E., Howell D. C., Phares, V., Williams, R., Giunta, C. (in press). Risk factors for emotional/behavioral problems in children and adolescents: A prospective analysis of children's and parents' stress and symptoms. *Journal of Consulting and Clinical Psychology.*

Compas, B. E., Howell, D. C., Phares, V., Williams, R., & Ledoux, N. (1989). Parent and child stress and psychological symptoms: An integrative analysis. *Developmental Psychology, 25*, 550-559.

Compas, B. E., Malcarne, V. L., & Banez, G. A. (in press). Coping with psychosocial stress: A developmental perspective. In B. Carpenter (Ed.), *Personal coping: Theory, research, and application.* New York: Praeger.

Compas, B. E., Malcarne, V. L., & Fondacaro, K. (1988). Coping with stressful events in older children and young adolescents. *Journal of Consulting and Clinical Psychology, 56*, 405–411.

Compas, B. E., Slavin, L. A., Wagner, B. M., & Vanatta, K. (1986). Relationship of life events and social support with psychological dysfunction among adolescents. *Journal of Youth and Adolescence, 15*, 205–211.

Cowen, E. L. (1980). The wooing of primary prevention. *American Journal of Community Psychology, 8*, 258–284.

Cowen, E. L. (1985). Person-centered approaches to primary prevention in mental health: Situation-focused and competence enhancement. *American Journal of Community Psychology, 13*, 87–98.

Elias, M. J., Clabby, J. F., Corr, D., Ubriaco, M., & Schuyler, T. (1982). *The improving social awareness-social problem solving project: A case study in school-based action research* (Action Research Workshop Report No. 4). New York: William T. Grant Foundation.

Elias, M. J., Gara, M., Ubriaco, M., Rothbaum, P. A., Clabby, J. F., & Schuyler, T. (1986). Impact of a preventive social problem solving intervention on children's coping with middle-school stressors. *American Journal of Community Psychology, 14*, 259–275.

Felner, R. D., Farber, S. S., & Primavera, J. (1983). Transitions and stressful life events: A model for primary prevention. In R. D. Felner, L. A. Jason, J. N. Moritsugu, & S. S. Farber (Eds.), *Preventive psychology: Theory, research, and practice* (pp. 119–215). New York: Pergamon.

Felner, R. D., & Felner, T. Y. (this volume). Primary prevention programs in the educational context: A transactional-ecological framework and analysis.

Felner, R. D., Ginter, M., & Primavera, J. (1982). Primary prevention during school transitions: Social support and environmental structure. *American Journal of Community Psychology, 10*, 277–290.

Felner, R. D., Primavera, J., & Cauce, A. M. (1981). The impact of school transitions: A focus for preventive efforts. *American Journal of Community Psychology, 9*, 449–459.

Forsythe, C. J., & Compas, B. E. (1987). Interaction of cognitive appraisals and coping with stress: Testing the goodness of fit hypothesis. *Cognitive Therapy and Research, 11,* 473–485.

Garrison, K. M., Stolberg, A. L., Mallonnee, D., Carpenter, J., & Antrim, Z. (1984). *The Single Parents' Support Group: A procedures manual.* Unpublished manual, Divorce Adjustment Project, Virginia Commonwealth University, Richmond, Virginia.

Glenwick, D. S., & Jason, L. A. (1984). Locus of intervention in child cognitive behavior therapy: Implications of a behavioral community psychology perspective. In A. W. Meyers & W. E. Craighead (Eds.), *Cognitive behavior therapy with children* (pp. 129–162). New York: Plenum.

Hammen, C., Marks, T., Mayol, A., & deMayo, A. (1985). Depressive self-schemas, life stress, and vulnerability to depression. *Journal of Abnormal Psychology, 94,* 308–319.

Holahan, C. J. & Moos, R. H. (1987). Risk, resistance, and psychological distress: A longitudinal analysis with adults and children. *Journal of Abnormal Psychology, 96,* 3–13.

Johnson, J. H. (1986). *Life events as stressors in childhood and adolescence.* Beverly Hills, CA: Sage.

Kessler, R. C., & McLeod, J. D. (1984). Sex differences in vulnerability to undesirable life events. *American Sociological Review, 49,* 620–631.

Kanner, A. D., Coyne, J. C., Schaefer, C., & Lazarus, R. S. (1981). Comparison of two models of stress measurement: Daily hassles and uplifts versus major life events. *Journal of Behavioral Medicine, 4,* 1–39.

Lazarus, R. S., & Folkman, S. (1984). *Stress, appraisal, and coping.* New York: Springer.

Ledoux, N. (November, 1985). *A comprehensive stress management program for elementary and secondary students and their families.* Paper presented at the Seventh National Conference on Child Abuse and Neglect, Chicago, IL.

Monroe, S. M. (1983). Major and minor life events as predictors of psychological distress: Further issues and findings. *Journal of Behavioral Medicine, 6,* 189–25.

Newcomb, M. D., Huba, G. J., & Bentler, P. M. (1981). A multidimensional assessment of stressful life events among adolescents: Derivation and correlates. *Journal of Health and Social Behavior, 22,* 400–415.

Pedro-Carroll, J. L., & Cowen, E. L. (1985). The Children of Divorce Intervention Program: An investigation of the efficacy of a school-based prevention program. *Journal of Consulting and Clinical Psychology, 53,* 603–611.

Pedro-Carroll, J. L., Cowen, E. L., Hightower, A. D., & Guare, J. C. (1986). Preventive intervention with latency-aged children of divorce: A replication study. *American Journal of Community Psychology, 14,* 277–290.

Rappaport, J. A. (1981). In praise of paradox: A social policy of empowerment over prevention. *American Journal of Community Psychology, 9,* 1–25.

Rappaport, J. A. (1987). Terms of empowerment/exemplars of prevention: Toward a theory of community psychology. *American Journal of Community Psychology, 15,* 121–148.

Rolf, J. E. (1985). Evolving adaptive theories and methods for prevention research with children. *Journal of Consulting and Clinical Psychology, 53,* 631–646.

Ryan, W. (1971). *Blaming the victim.* New York: Vintage Books.

Spivack, G., & Shure, M. B. (1982). The cognition of social adjustment: Interpersonal cognitive problem-solving thinking. In B. B. Lahey & A. E. Kazdin (Eds.), *Advances in clinical child psychology* (Vol. 5, pp. 323–372). New York: Plenum.

Spivack, G., & Shure, M. B. (1985). ICPS and beyond: Centripital and centrifugal forces. *American Journal of Community Psychology, 13,* 226–243.

Stolberg, A. L., Cullen, P. M., Garrison, K. M., & Brophy, C. J. (1981). *The Children's*

Support Groups: A procedures manual. Unpublished manual, Divorce Adjustment Project, Virginia Commonwealth University, Richmond, Virginia.

Stolberg, A. L., & Garrison, K. M. (1985). Evaluating a primary prevention program for children of divorce. *American Journal of Community Psychology, 13*, 111–124.

Thomson, B., & Vaux, A. (1986). The importation, transmission, and moderation of stress in the family system. *American Journal of Community psychology, 14*, 39–57.

Wagner, B. M., & Compas, B. E. (1988). *Gender, masculinity, and femininity: Moderators of adjustment to life stress during adolescence.* Manuscript submitted for publication.

Wagner, B. M., Compas, B. E., & Howell, D. C. (1988). Daily and major life events: A test of an integrative model of psychosocial stress. *American Journal of Community Psychology, 16*, 189–205.

Weissberg, R., Caplan, M. Z., & Sivo, P. J. (this volume). A new conceptual framework for establishing school-based social competence promotion programs.

Woolfolk, R. L., & Lehrer, P. M. (1984). *Principles and practice of stress management.* New York: Guilford.

PART IV

Obstacles and Avenues for School-Based Primary Prevention Programs

Have primary prevention efforts found a secure place within the schools? The preceding chapters attest to the fact that tremendous care and insight have been incorporated in the development of such school-based programs. Furthermore, the effectiveness of many of these preventive interventions is well-documented and recognized. But the security of these programs is less well-established, in large part due to the complexities of integrating both the varied models and the pragmatic contingencies that underlie classrooms, school systems, and intervention designs.

In this final section of the book, we consider various obstacles that have impeded a more comprehensive and effective incorporation of primary prevention efforts into our schools, and we examine alternative strategies for meeting the goals of prevention and promotion. Many of the concerns raised in earlier chapters are echoed once again, illustrating an emerging consensus regarding strategies needed for redirecting school-based efforts. The final message is optimistic—it is apparent that new models and strategies are coming into place that address current deterrents and increasingly take advantage of the rich resources that our schools provide to effect prevention and promotion.

In the first chapter, Jane Mercer, Professor of Sociology at the University of California, Riverside, considers barriers that have prevented our schools from focusing on primary prevention efforts. After spending many years analyzing the diagnostic and classification systems used in our educational system, she concludes that our schools will not shift their focus from pathology to prevention until we reject our indiscriminate use of a medical/diagnostic model and abandon the IQ paradigm.

Mercer takes us through her argument in a step-by-step fashion, exploring the roots of the medical/pathological model in special education, the symptoms-diagnosis-treatment triangle, a critique of the IQ

341

paradigm and an examination of the paradigm's consequences. Most importantly, in guiding us toward the future she presents us with two alternatives to present assessment practices, the edumetric paradigm and the learning process paradigm. These are models that she feels will move us away from cultural bias and distorted decision making toward a system in which the primary prevention of learning problems would be the norm.

In the next chapter we are called upon to take ecology seriously in the design, implementation, and evaluation of preventive interventions. Edison Trickett, Professor of Psychology, and Dina Birman, a doctoral candidate in clinical-community psychology, at the University of Maryland at College Park, elaborate upon the importance of working within the ecological context of schools and school systems to create preventive interventions that have both short- and long-term effectiveness.

Trickett and Birman analyze the components and influences of an ecological approach to intervention in the schools and in so doing, ask us to consider new goals and assumptions about community research, reminding us of issues raised by Felner and Felner in the first chapter of this book. To illustrate how an ecological perspective can guide preventive interventions, Trickett and Birman describe their collaboration with a high school in examining intercultural issues in adaptation to school. The authors demonstrate the ways in which an ecological perspective can generate data that, in turn, can be translated into preventive interventions, illustrating, as well, the application of these issues to individually based prevention efforts.

In the final chapter, Joel Meyers explores a host of opportunities and strategies for developing primary prevention efforts in the schools. Like Trickett and Birman, he emphasizes the critical need to develop and apply an understanding of the school culture. According to Meyers, Professor of Educational Psychology and Statistics and Director, Programs in School Psychology at the State University of New York at Albany, preventionists must form true collaborative partnerships with educators, with an eye toward integrating prevention efforts into the normal school curriculum and instructional process.

Meyers presents a school psychologist's perspective on current trends in education that have implications for primary prevention in schools before turning to general implications of the prevention literature for educational settings. He considers a variety of pragmatic approaches to implement prevention in schools, including a progression from secondary prevention to primary prevention, building upon mental health consultation, modifying special and remedial education services, implementing new assessment models, and altering the school routine to promote primary prevention. Most importantly, his recurring message is that "teachers represent a potentially powerful and untapped resource" for primary prevention efforts. Teachers themselves must be involved in developing school-based prevention efforts.

12

Why Haven't Schools Changed the Focus from Pathology to Prevention?: Conceptual and Legal Obstacles

Jane R. Mercer

Primary prevention refers to efforts to intervene before a pathological condition develops. Secondary prevention focuses on ameliorating the impact of a pathological condition once it has developed and, if possible, remediating it. Historically, special education programs in the public schools have focused on secondary prevention, the treatment of students who have been identified as disabled. Relatively little emphasis has been placed on primary prevention. Attempts to shift the focus of special educators from secondary to primary prevention have met with little success. Why has it been so difficult to shift the focus from pathology to prevention?

I argue in this paper that the major obstacles to primary prevention in public education are conceptual and intellectual. Education continues to cling to both a medical/diagnostic model when conceptualizing educational problems and a faulty assessment model, the IQ paradigm. Both, unfortunately, have been enshrined in state education codes and federal statutes. Unless we abandon our flawed paradigms and restructure our legal mandates, primary prevention for those students who do not have disabilities that are clearly biologically determined will remain beyond our grasp.

This chapter is not concerned with those disabilities that have a clearly identifiable biological basis; visual impairment, auditory impairment, cerebral palsy, epilepsy, and so forth. For such disabilities, the classic public health, medical model is appropriate. Rather, our focus is on that burgeoning category of children labeled *disabled* who have no identifiable physical anomalies—the so-called *learning dis-*

abled, communicatively handicapped and *mentally retarded*. In such cases, the medical-diagnostic model is NOT appropriate. Today, most of the children being served in special education programs have been labeled as learning disabled yet, as recently as 1970, the category did not even exist in the public schools. How can we explain this strange phenomenon? What exotic epidemic in the past decade has produced a generation in which 9% to 12% of the children are afflicted with a handicap that did not even exist in their parents' generation?

"Learning disabled" children are being identified within a medical/ diagnostic model solely on the basis of their academic performance in school relative to their presumed intelligence. Such "diagnoses" are being legitimized by a pattern of test scores on a small number of standardized instruments, that purport to discriminate between *intelligence* and *achievement*.

The position taken in this chapter is that *learning disability* is a socially constructed category. Two decades ago, similar children were perceived simply as *underachievers*. Now they have joined the company of the disabled. Although this category is viewed by practitioners as a medical-diagnostic entity and they use medical-diagnostic terminology when they discuss "learning disability," such thinking is inappropriate. The classification is not analogous to classifying students who have a hearing impairment or visual deficit, which are properly diagnosed from a medical model perspective. The "learning disabled" are identified using behavioral criteria, not biological symptomology. The tests used to identify these children are measures of what they have learned, not their biological status. The interpretation of those test scores is based on a faulty assessment paradigm, the "IQ paradigm." Until we sweep away the intellectual debris of that paradigm, progress toward primary prevention will be difficult.

Having summarized the thrust of this chapter, I will elaborate upon the components of my argument step by step.

Roots of the Medical/Pathological Model in Special Education

The earliest publicly financed special education programs were for children who had clearly identifiable biological anomalies, first the blind and the deaf and later the cerebral palsied and children with other physical handicaps. These children were readily identified using a medical/diagnostic model (Mercer, 1979). They could be sorted into relatively unambiguous categories according to their symptomotologies, and they required special educational interventions that were clearly related to their biological problems and were inappropriate for children who did not have those problems. It was relatively easy to persuade legislators and the public to provide extra funding to support special educational programs for children with physical impairments. Hence, the medical/pathological model became the primary, conceptual model for special education, and categorical funding programs associated with that model became the primary fiscal vehicle for supporting programs for handicapped children.

With the invention of "intelligence" testing, (Binet & Simon, 1905) and the importation of Binet's concepts to the United States by Lewis Terman and John Goddard shortly thereafter, psychologists believed they had a scientific instrument that could diagnose an individual's degree of intelligence. The new technology for the first time provided a mechanism for applying a medical/diagnostic model to the assessment of behavior. It provided a way to categorize what had formerly been uncategorizable—degrees of feeblemindedness. Indeed, a large, new category of disabled persons was socially constructed, labeled *morons,* and promptly became a focus of great national concern (Doll, 1972; Mercer & Richardson, 1975).

There was no legislative support for funding programs for morons, educational misfits, or backward children during the great depression of the 1930s and World War II. However, at the end of the war, educators and advocates successfully used the medical model to define learning problems as disabilities. Categorical labels proved an effective way to secure funding for programs for "mentally retarded minors," a handicapping condition diagnosed within a medical model using intelligence tests administered by a new category of professionals, the school psychologist. From that beginning, the medicalization of behavioral assessment gradually expanded to include other types of behavioral deviance unaccompanied by biological signs. Additional categories of disability were socially constructed: emotionally disturbed, communicatively handicapped, mildly retarded, learning disabled, and so forth, based on the IQ paradigm using the medical/diagnostic model. The medical/diagnostic model is an obstacle to primary prevention because of the symptoms–diagnosis–treatment triangle.

The Symptoms-Diagnosis-Treatment Triangle

The medical model, also called the *pathological* model, is symptom oriented. Borrowed from medicine, it is based on the assumption that *symptoms* are *caused* by some underlying biological malfunction. When symptoms occur, it is the task of the clinician to identify the causes of those symptoms and to work toward eliminating them or, at least, ameliorating their impact. Diagnosis is absolutely crucial to this endeavor. Certain patterns of symptoms indicate discrete pathologies that, typically, are given names so that clincians can communicate with one another about them, researchers can search for causes and cures, and, when treatments have been developed, practitioners can diagnose them and utilize the best available treatments with individual patients. The pathology is perceived as a characteristic of the organism, a condition that resides within the individual. A child *has* measles. A person *is* tubercular. Specific diagnoses lead to specific treatments.

No great difficulties arise when the symptoms–diagnosis–treatment triangle is applied to students who suffer from biological anomalies— the visually impaired, the hearing impaired, and the physically disabled. Difficulties arise when it is applied to socially constructed disabilities such as mild mental retardation, emotional disturbance, or learning disabilities.

In the medical/diagnostic model, correct diagnosis is crucial because it presumably leads to correct, differential treatment. However, treatments for students diagnosed as mildly retarded or learning disabled do not differ in form or substance from each other or from good teaching in any setting. There are no differential treatments for differential diagnoses (Heller, 1982). Nevertheless, when funding is based on the medical/diagnostic model, no funding is provided for interventions until a student has been "diagnosed," labeled categorically as having a particular handicap, and declared eligible for service. There can be no diagnosis until there are symptoms. By the time symptoms appear it is too late for primary prevention. The symptoms–diagnosis–treatment triangle creates a vicious circle when applied to socially constructed categories of disability. It precludes funding for students prior to diagnosis on the faulty assumption that diagnosis is necessary to treatment when, in fact, diagnosis is not relevant to treatment but is only relevant to funding!

The IQ Paradigm

Why is special education trapped in this vicious conceptual circle that requires labeling before treatment even though diagnosis is irrelevant to treatment? Why is it so hard to extricate special education from this conceptual morass and move toward primary prevention?

Special education is caught up in this costly, futile cycle because it has reified socially constructed disabilities, such as mild mental retardation and learning disabilities. Special educators and psychologists have come to believe that these socially constructed disabilities somehow exist in children awaiting diagnosis. Such reification occurs because the concepts of mild mental retardation and learning disability are secondary paradigms that are based on a faulty primary paradigm, the IQ paradigm.

A paradigm is a conceptual model that serves as a cognitive map to organize experience so that it has meaning and is comprehensible to the observer. Primary paradigms provide core assumptions about the nature of reality. They set the parameters within which intellectual discourse and innovation are likely to proceed in a given society. The assumptions of a basic paradigm are often implicit rather than explicit. Long-established paradigms are passed on to each succeeding generation as truth, as the taken-for-granted reality of everyday life. In many cases, assumptions are not consciously examined because they are accepted as self-evident, the way things *are*.

Secondary paradigms are those that build upon or flow from basic paradigms. They incorporate, implicitly, the basic paradigm because they are ancillary models that elaborate the basic structure. If the basic paradigm is faulty, then secondary paradigms built upon it will also be faulty and the entire interrelated structure will either require significant modification or abandonment. The IQ paradigm is a basic paradigm on which secondary paradigms, such as mental retardation and learning disability, have been constructed. The IQ paradigm has been the dominant model for explaining individual differences in performance in American society for approximately 75 years.

Major paradigms, such as the IQ paradigm, are not simply abstract systems of knowledge unrelated to social interaction. Individuals act on the basis of what they know to be true. Our society has created social structures, such as special education programs, to achieve purposes that make sense within the IQ paradigm. Persons in those structures are expected to deal with categories of disability, such as educable mentally retarded and learning disabled, that are conceptually and operationally dependent upon the IQ paradigm. They evolved as categories only after the IQ paradigm gained acceptance and they owe their existence to concepts and ways of thinking about human behavior made possible by the IQ paradigm and its ancillary models. It is no accident that the 1947 California statute that legally established educable mental retardation as a disability in public education also created the social role of the school psychologist to officially diagnose this disability, using intelligence tests and the role of the special education teacher to instruct persons so identified. Within three years, training programs were established at major universities to educate this new set of professionals. The complex special education structures of today were subsequently differentiated from these simple beginnings (Mercer & Richardson, 1975).

Jensen's (1980) exposition and defense of the IQ paradigm presents its fundamental elements and, in my opinion, clearly represents the implicit assumptions that undergird present testing practice and special education categories used in the public schools. For this reason, the following analysis relies heavily on his work. There are seven crucial premises in the IQ paradigm as described by Jensen. Following the presentation of each premise is a discussion of the flaws in that premise.

Premise 1. A fundamental premise of the IQ paradigm is that IQ tests measure intelligence. The primary evidence for this assumption comes from factor analysis. Regardless of the types of cognitive skills measured, a general factor *g* emerges. The *g* factor accounts for about 80% of the variance in *Stanford-Binet* items (Jensen, 1980, p. 219) and approximately half the variance in the *Wechsler Adult Intelligence Scale (WAIS)* (p. 216). Similarly large proportions of the variance in a wide variety of other standardized tests administered to a variety of different populations are accounted for by the first principal component, the general factor. Hence, a "working definition of intelligence is that it is the *g* factor" (p. 249), and its universal appearance in principal component analyses indicates that there must be some type of organic substrata of *g*.

Flaws in Premise 1: IQ tests do not *measure* intelligence. There is no known technology for *measuring* intelligence, mental abilities, aptitudes, mental potential or related constructs. The IQ test score measures what a person has *learned* (Cleary, Humphreys, Kendrick, & Wesman, 1975; Wesman, 1968). The *g* factor yielded by factor analyses of a wide variety of tests cannot be interpreted as evidence for the existence of intelligence as an entity separate from learning. The *g* factor can readily be explained by the fact that the materials in the tests are drawn from the same cultural pool, and an individual who has learned a lot about one aspect of a culture is likely to have learned a lot about other aspects of that culture. Biological explanations are unnecessary and untestable.

Premise 2. A second major premise of the IQ paradigm is that intelligence and achievement are separate dimensions, both conceptually and operationally. Although Jensen admits that there are "no clear-cut operational distinctions . . . between aptitude tests and achievement tests" (p. 239) he, nevertheless, believes that scores on the two types of tests reflect different dimensions. He argues that intelligence tests sample broader and more heterogeneous learning, measure cumulative knowledge from the individual's entire experience, contain an almost infinite variety of test items, and yield scores that are stable across time. Achievement tests, on the other hand, sample specific knowledge and skills that have been acquired recently through formal education, include a narrow band of items, and are more susceptible to instruction. Jensen believes the distinction between the two concepts is valid and that they can be distinguished operationally.

Flaws in Premise 2: Intelligence and achievement may be separable conceptually but they cannot be distinguished operationally. They are not separate dimensions. All tests are achievement tests in that they measure what a person has learned. Correlations between so-called intelligence tests and so-called achievement tests average between .8 and .9 (Jensen, 1980, p. 323), indicating that the measures have tremendous overlap, between 60% and 80% shared variance. In fact, Cleary et al. (1975) concluded that "There are no differences in kind . . . between intelligence and achievement, or between aptitude and achievement . . . it is possible for one man's intelligence test to be another man's achievement test. Thus Jensen categorized the National Merit Scholarship Examination as an intelligence test, but precisely the same items were used in the Iowa Tests of Educational Development for assessing achievement" (p. 21). The Stanford-Binet and the Wechsler scales are simply individually administered achievement tests, static measures of what persons have learned.

What a person learns is contingent upon many factors, not just intelligence. Following are some of the most important factors influencing learning. Learning depends upon the opportunity to learn through exposure to the cultural materials to be covered in the test. It depends upon the motivation to learn, once the opportunity has been presented. It depends upon using effective learning strategies so that the materials will be adequately comprehended and retained. It depends upon having the sensory equipment needed to learn, primarily adequate vision and hearing. It depends upon being in an emotional state that permits learning to take place. High anxiety, stress, depression, grief, and other debilitating emotions interfere with learning. With so many confounding factors, it is not possible to distinguish what persons have learned (their achievement) from their ability to learn (their intelligence).

Premise 3. Jensen argues that intelligence tests are valid because they have predictive validity. They correlate with a variety of criterion measures, such as school grades and academic achievement as measured by achievement tests. "By averaging various IQ and achievement test results over several years, the correlations between and among the tests approach . . . .80 and .90" (p. 323).

Flaws in Premise 3: Predictive validity is a form of pragmatic validity that is concerned with the usefulness of a test instrument in predicting the probability of success or failure at some future endeavor. To argue that intelligence tests have predictive validity because they are correlated with achievement tests is simply circular reasoning, a tautology, when we recognize that both types of tests draw their items from the same pool of items and both measure an individual's knowledge of the English language and core-culture. Intelligence tests are correlated with grades in school but achievement tests have just as high or higher correlations with school grades. Therefore, the correlation between intelligence tests and school grades cannot be treated as a unique relationship that proves that IQ tests measure intelligence. The many studies that have correlated IQ scores with achievement test scores and both types of tests with school grades provide evidence for the commonalities in the tests and in the school curriculum, nothing more.

Premise 4. Intelligence tests are not culturally biased because they have similar predictive validity for persons of different cultural backgrounds, that is, the regression lines predicting academic achievement test scores from intelligence test scores have similar slopes for different groups. The fact that the intercepts are lower for some groups because their mean performance is lower is not, according to Jensen, relevant to cultural bias. Differences in the average performance of different groups are not acceptable evidence of cultural bias in a test within the IQ paradigm.

Flaws in Premise 4: The fact that the regression lines predicting achievement test scores from intelligence tests are parallel for individuals from different sociocultural groups is further evidence that the two types of tests are simply measuring the same cultural materials, not evidence that IQ tests are measuring intelligence. It is the content of the tests and not the group to which the tests are administered that produces the parallel regression lines. The entire argument about predictive validity and parallel regression lines is highly circular and reveals nothing whatsoever about cultural bias in tests. What does reveal systematic bias in the tests is the fact, which no one disputes, that persons from minority groups tend to earn lower average scores on both so-called tests of intelligence and so-called tests of achievement. Minority groups had less exposure to the cultural materials in both types of tests, and score approximately two-thirds of a standard deviation below the majority group on both types of tests. Differences in average performance that parallel differences in exposure to the cultural materials in the test are evidence that the tests are culturally loaded. They are not equally valid for inferring the intelligence of socioculturally different populations.

Premise 5. Intelligence tests correlate highly with each other, an indication that they have concurrent validity. Correlations among IQ tests have an overall mean of about .67 (p. 315).

Flaws in Premise 5: Correlations among scores on intelligence tests prove only that various tests are measuring many of the same cultural materials and draw their items from a common item pool. It does not prove that any of those tests are measuring intelligence.

Premise 6. Intelligence tests are not culturally biased because they have comparable internal validity for different groups. They have similar reliability and stability for different groups and similar internal consistency. Factor analyses yield the same factors. Patterns of item difficulty are similar cross-culturally.

Flaws in Premise 6: The fact that intelligence test scores have similar reliabilities and stabilities in different groups, yield similar factors, and have similar patterns of item difficulty speaks only to the issue of internal not external validity. These findings assure us that, whatever the tests are measuring, they are measuring it in a comparable fashion for different groups. Such findings do not reveal what the tests are measuring. They say nothing about the external validity of IQ tests, that is, whether they are measuring intelligence in a culturally nonbiased manner.

Premise 7. There is no need to make allowances for cultural exposure. A single set of norms is appropriate for everyone. America is a relatively homogenous society based on the English language and cultural traditions. The amount of cultural loading in IQ tests is small and American society is sufficiently homogenous to interpret differences in test scores of different subpopulations as differences in intelligence.

Jensen (1980) is quite forthright in espousing the homogenous culture viewpoint. He argues that there is a continuum along which tests can be ranged from *culture specific* to *culture reduced.* Jensen ranks tests according to his perception of their cultural specificity and concludes that cultural loading has been overrated as a problem in intelligence testing. "Practically all our present standardized tests, culture-reduced or not, span as wide or wider a range of cultural distance as is found among any native-born, English-speaking racial and socioeconomic groups within the United States today . . . differences show up mark-edly only in foreign language groups and across quite remote cul-tures" (p. 642).

Flaws in Premise 7: American society is not culturally homogenous. It is highly pluralistic and is becoming more pluralistic each year. The IQ paradigm is based on the assumption that there is a single, homogenous cultural tradition in American society to which all per-sons have an equal exposure. This assumption simply does not square with the demographic facts of modern America.

Consequences of the IQ Paradigm

Two categories of disabilities in special education are creatures of the basic IQ paradigm. They can be regarded as secondary paradigms because their very existence depends upon the assumptions of the basic model.

Educable/Mild Mental Retardation is a category of disability that con-sists primarily of individuals who have no physical anomalies but are subnormal in intelligence as measured by a standard IQ test and are subnormal in adaptive behavior (Grossman, 1973). In actuality, adap-tive behavior is seldom systematically measured in diagnosing mental retardation (Heller, Holtzman, & Messick, 1982). Therefore, for all practical purposes, educable mental retardation is defined by a low score on an IQ test, for example, a score between approximately 55 and 69 on the Wechsler scales. "Trainable mental retardation" is ordi-narily accompanied by physical anomalies; although an IQ test is ad-ministered, it is not as crucial as in the identification of "educable mental retardation."

The social construction of the category of mild mental retardation (moron) based on the IQ paradigm has had the effect of defining large numbers of minority students as mentally retarded when they were, in fact, simply unfamiliar with the English language and the Anglo core culture. This mis-specification of the source of their academic difficul-ties resulted in many being labeled as disabled and being placed in programs that were not appropriate to their needs. Much has been written about the overrepresentation of minorities in classes for the mentally retarded (e.g., Heller et al., 1982; Mercer, 1973), and it is beyond the scope of this paper to review that literature.

Learning Disabilities are defined in a variety of ways in different jurisdictions. However, there is one element common to most definitions, that is, that there must be a significant discrepancy between *intelligence* and *achievement*. *Learning disabled* students are those who are performing academically at a level significantly below that expected on the basis of their measured intelligence. Obviously, this definition assumes that intelligence can be measured separately from achievement and that a discrepancy between the two scores reliably identifies a meaningful category of persons for whom there are educational interventions.

A critical feature of this definition is that it focuses on the discrepancy between the two scores rather than actual level of performance. Consequently, to be diagnosed as learning disabled, a student must have a relatively high IQ. Otherwise, the difference between the IQ and achievement scores might be too small to qualify as a reliable and significant discrepancy.

The IQ paradigm and its secondary paradigm, learning disability, becomes particularly mischievous when assessing students with limited English proficiency (LEP). In a study we have recently completed, of all the LEP students (N=1141) referred for special education assessment in seven educational jurisdictions in southern California, we found that 31% of the 551 LEP students who were labeled as *learning disabled* scored above 100 on the WISC-R Performance scale, and 69% scored below 100. On the other hand, only 16% of those declared ineligible for services scored above 100 while fully 84% scored below. It appears that those who score lowest and, presumably, have the greatest educational need have a lower probability of getting service than students who have higher scores and, presumably, have fewer educational problems. The least needy are getting the most services. Such illogical allocations of resources and inverted decisions are the direct result of applying the IQ paradigm in the assessment of LEP students.

Alternatives to Present Assessment Practices

If we abandon the medical-diagnostic model in the assessment of students whose difficulties are exclusively educational and stop utilizing the IQ paradigm and its secondary paradigms, major changes will be required in educational structures. Students would receive services based on educational need rather than based on some socially constructed disability identified by psychometric measures interpreted within a medical-diagnostic model. Assessment would focus on information needed to provide appropriate educational interventions. Funding would be based on educational need rather than pseudomedical categorization.

There are two promising paradigms that could replace the existing models: the edumetric paradigm and/or the learning process paradigm. Each will be described briefly.

The Edumetric Paradigm is based on the belief that IQ tests and other standardized tests administered by psychologists and other diagnosticians do not provide significant information for instructional planning or educational intervention. Educators can implement adequate educational programs for low-achieving children without standardized, norm-referenced tests.

Instead, educators should rely on edumetric tests, tests directly related to the curriculum. Such tests are criterion-referenced in terms of levels of performance established in the curriculum for students of various ages. They are, for the most part, teacher-generated. When used as an integral part of the teaching-learning-assessment process (as in precision-teaching and mastery-level learning), edumetric tests are very effective educational devices. Individual educational plans are based on direct knowledge of the student's performance level in the curriculum of that particular grade and school. There is no individual psychometric testing of any child for any purpose in this model and no diagnostic labeling by disability category. All educational decisions are based on edumetric test data and the teacher's professional judgment as an educator.

Each student is tested repeatedly, and there is continuous monitoring of academic progress. Once the basic student profile in academic skills has been established, the daily monitoring of student progress quickly identifies those students who are progressing at a satisfactory rate and those students who are moving more slowly. Additional assistance, such as time with the resource teacher, tutorial assistance from paraprofessionals or peer tutors, or assistance with learning English-as-a-second-language, is made available to those who are having difficulty. The type and amount of assistance is continuously adjusted, based on edumetric test data showing the student's progress through the curriculum. The need for special assistance is triggered by a teacher request. In this approach, language, per se, is not a major focus since English proficiency is constantly monitored in the language and reading curriculum and special assistance needed by those who have limited-English-proficiency is among the special services available in the school. The philosophy of such programs is based on direct instruction (Becker & Carnine, 1980).

The U.S. Office of Civil Rights conducted a nationwide study to identify schools that had developed the most effective educational programs for minority students. That study concluded that the most effective schools were making extensive use of edumetric testing in conjunction with some type of direct instruction, such as DISTAR, Exemplary Centers for Reading Instruction (ECRI), and Computer Assisted Instruction (CAI) (Cantalician Foundation, 1983).

The structural effects of the edumetric-only paradigm would be profound. It would eliminate the elaborate referral and assessment system that now consumes a great deal of time, energy, and resources. It would eliminate all special education categories based on the IQ paradigm and retain students formerly in those programs in the regular classroom. Special education personnel would be redeployed to provide interventions and support services needed by the regular classroom teacher in meeting the needs of all children who have educational problems that cannot be addressed in the regular classroom. Primary prevention would become the norm as students received immediate assistance based on their functional needs.

The Learning Process Paradigm is based on research and theory that comes primarily from cognitive psychology (Gelzheiser & Shepherd, 1986). It is based on the test-mediate-observe-retest approach. The rationale for this paradigm is as follows.

1. The learner plays an active role in learning and has the potential to exercise control of his or her own behavior. Most students who have difficulty learning are those who do not use effective learning strategies; they do not know how to learn. If teachers are to help students learn, they need to know what cognitive strategies a student is or is not using so that the teacher can remediate ineffective methods and teach students effective learning procedures.

2. Edumetric and psychometric testing provides information only on the end-products of learning. Alone, such testing yields almost no information on the learning process itself, such as the extent to which a student self-regulates learning, utilizes different learning strategies for different kinds of intellectual tasks, monitors his/her own learning, and corrects errors. Consequently, such tests do not provide the teacher with the primary information needed for effective intervention. Assessment should include an analysis of the learning processes being used by the student.

3. Cognitive processes that transpire between the input stimulus and the individual's response can best be studied as the student processes information in a learning situation. These processes become most observable when an intervention is attempted during assess-

ment. The assessor can then determine the student's ability to profit from instruction, can question the student about strategies used in solving different types of problems, and can ascertain the extent to which the student's lack of confidence in the efficacy of employing various strategies may be a factor in failure to learn.

4. Using findings from the analysis of a student's learning processes, prescriptions for intervention can be developed to teach the student specific strategies he/she can most effectively use for various learning tasks. An important part of the prescription for many students who have been failing academically is attributional retraining: convincing the student that lack of learning is the result of inefficient learning strategies and low effort rather than low ability. From the viewpoint of this paradigm, psychometric testing that convinces the student and/or the teacher that failure is the result of low ability is harmful.

Cognitive psychologists have identified a large number of cognitive processes that are important in efficient self-regulated learning. They may be grouped into three major categories: executive control skills, specific strategies, and attributional/motivational characteristics.

1. Executive control skills are also called *metacognitive processing skills*. They include understanding how to evaluate a novel problem, deciding what kind of plan is reasonable, comprehending what to do if the plan fails, and knowing how to check one's own performance. Metacognitions include awareness of one's own thinking processes and active involvement in identifying various options and modifying one's behavior accordingly.

2. Knowledge of specific strategies is essential to selecting those likely to be useful in learning various tasks. For example, the following are effective stratagies in reading comprehension: rereading a passage; skimming a passage in order to study it; paraphrasing a main idea to summarize important points; identifying the topic sentence; writing a topic sentence for paragraphs that have no topic sentence; hypothesizing about the next topic that will be discussed; asking oneself questions while reading; deleting trivia and redundancy; and identifying fundamental concepts. In math, checking one's arithmetic and determining if the answer is within logical limits are valuable strategies.

3. Attributional and motivational characteristics are very important factors in teaching students how to learn. Because of repeated failures, low achieving students tend to be inactive learners who do not persist in tasks. Therefore, it is important to ascertain a student's attributional characteristics and motivational status. To what does he/

she attribute success or failure? How important does he/she believe it is to use strategies in learning? What does the student believe is the probability of success if he/she expends effort on a task? Most students now labeled *mentally retarded* and *learning disabled* have negative antecedent beliefs about their own abilities and the probability of success if they try hard to achieve educationally. These negative attitudes impede their learning and must be understood and addressed in the intervention.

The basic technique for learning-process assessment is to present students with a problem or a reading task and ask them to think aloud as they solve the problem or read the passage. The teacher then uses direct instruction to teach specific learning strategies and to explain when a particular strategy is appropriate, why the strategy promotes learning, and why it merits extra effort. One technique uses public discussion of thinking skills and strategies to help students share their thoughts and feelings about the processes of learning. The goal of instruction is to guide students to plan learning, to select strategies, to monitor their own progress, to alter strategies that do not fit the task, to fill in missing information, and to know how much effort a strategy requires.

The traditional medical-diagnostic model and IQ paradigm do not provide any of the information necessary for teaching students how to learn. If the paradigm shift moves in the direction of learning process assessment, traditional referral and assessment procedures as well as traditional classification systems will no longer be needed. Primary prevention of learning problems would be the norm rather than the exception.

Conclusion

Paradigm shifts are major intellectual and policy events in which the prevailing paradigm is challenged by emerging paradigms. The prevailing assessment system is based on a medical-diagnostic view of assessment and an IQ paradigm that suffers from significant flaws. Based on the IQ paradigm, sets of socially constructed disabilities have been created that have very little relation to treatment or instruction and, furthermore, make many students in need of supplementary educational services ineligible for assistance, while providing special services to higher functioning students. Instead of enhancing educational decision making, the paradigm distorts the decision-making process. It is time to abandon the IQ paradigm, the disabilities created by that paradigm, and the categorical system created to serve those diagnosed as disabled within that paradigm and to move to primary prevention using other educational paradigms.

References

Becker, W., & Carnine D. (1980). Direct instruction: An effective approach to educational intervention with the disadvantaged and low performers. In B. B. Lahey & A. E. Kazdin (Eds.), *Advances in clinical child psychology: Vol 3* (pp. 429–473). New York: Plenum Press.

Binet, A., & Simon, T. (1905). Sur la necessite d'establir un diagnostic scientifique de etats inferiers de l'intelligence. *Annee Psychologique, 11*, 1–28.

Cantalician Foundation, Inc. (1983). *Technical assistance on alternative practices related to the problem of the overrepresentation of black and minority students in classes for the educable mentally retarded*. Report to the Department of Education, Office of Civil Rights, Contract No. 300–82–0191.

Cleary, T. A., Humphreys, L. G., Kendrick, S. A., & Wesman, A. G. (1975). Educational uses of tests with disadvantaged students. *American Psychologist, 30*, 15–41.

Doll, E. E. (1972). A historical survey of research and management of mental retardation in the United States. In E. P. Trapp & P. Himelstein (Eds.), *Readings on the Exceptional Child* (pp. 47–97). New York: Appleton-Century-Crofts.

Gelzheiser, L. M., & Shepherd, M. J. (Eds.). (1986). Competence and instruction: Contributions from cognitive psychology [Special issue]. *Exceptional Children, 53*(2).

Grossman, H. J. (Ed.). (1973). *Manual on terminology and classification in mental retardation* (Special publication series No. 2). Washington, DC: American Association of Mental Deficiency.

Heller, K. A. (1982). Effects of special education placement on educable mentally retarded children. In K. A. Kirby, W. H. Holtzman, & S. Messick (Eds.), *Placing children in special education: A strategy for equity* (pp. 262–299). Washington, DC: National Academy Press.

Heller, K. A., Holtzman, W. H., & Messick, S. (1982). *Placing children in special education: A strategy for equity*. Washington, DC: National Academy Press.

Jensen, A. R. (1980). *Bias in mental testing*. New York: The Free Press.

Mercer, J. R. (1973). *Labeling the mentally retarded*. Berkeley, CA: University of California Press.

Mercer, J. R. (1979). *SOMPA: Technical and conceptual manual*. New York: The Psychological Corporation.

Mercer, J. R., & Richardson, J. G. (1975). "Mental retardation" as a social problem. In N. Hobbs (Ed.), *Issues in the classification of children: Vol. 2. A sourcebook on categories, labels, and their consequences* (pp. 463–496). San Francisco: Jossey-Bass.

Wesman, A. G. (1968). Intelligent Testing. *American Psychologist, 23*, 267–274.

13

Taking Ecology Seriously: A Community Development Approach to Individually Based Preventive Interventions in Schools

Edison J. Trickett
Dina Birman

As evidenced by this book and recent bibliographies of preventive interventions (e.g., Buckner, Trickett, and Corse, 1985), schools are the sites for an extraordinary amount of work in the area of prevention. Most often, schools are the sites *for* rather than the objects *of* such interventions; that is, schools represent the place where the interventions occur but the interventions themselves are targeted directly at cohorts of children and adolescents who are deemed at risk for social or psychological maladaptation. Cowen (1985) has described such interventions as "person-centered"; they "enchance people's capacity to adapt effectively and to deal with stressful situations and events" (p. 31). Not only are they person-centered in terms of having individually based *goals* or outcome variables; they are individually based in terms of strategies of intervention. That is, intervention is aimed at groups of individuals directly, rather than at the role of the school in improving its ability to impact on at-risk groups of children and adolescents.

The primary purpose of this chapter is to place such individually based preventive interventions in context; specifically, to highlight the importance of the ecological context of schools and school systems hosting preventive interventions. The intent is to draw attention to the importance of designing, implementing, and evaluating preventive interventions with an appreciation of the ecological context in mind. We have very little data, for example, on how individually based preventive interventions affect the schools where they are implemented. Are the interventions irrelevant to the ongoing life of the school or do they leave a positive and/or negative residual that affects how children in the school are treated?

Taking ecology seriously requires the preventive interventionist to ask certain kinds of questions related to the ecology of schools hosting the interventions. What will happen to the school when the preventive intervention ends? What effect on the school will the preventive intervention have? How does the school itself affect the phenomenon of interest? And, how can the school become an ongoing part of the intervention? The punch line is that an ecological perspective can frame questions and suggest strategies that can facilitate the systemic impact of individually based preventive interventions.

First, a brief outline of an ecological approach will be presented. It will include both ecological concepts useful for assessing the school environment and a set of propositions about how an ecological perspective influences the implementation of preventive interventions. The final two sections concretize the implications of these concepts and propositions. One section presents a description of an ongoing school-based intervention using an ecological approach. In the last section illustrative topics are presented to show how an ecological perspective can be linked to individually based preventive interventions in the service of generating both knowledge and action relevant to the development of schools.

An Ecological Perspective on the School Context

In recent years, the term *ecology* has been increasingly used as a signal that individual and collective behavior are both shaped by and reflect the ecological context within which they occur. This suggests that preventive interventions are, in like manner, mediated by the social contexts hosting them. How long intervention effects last, whether or not programs are incorporated into the school curricula, and indeed, the very willingness of schools and school systems to allow outside intervention at all depends on the relationship of the preventive intervention to the ecological context.

In order to understand this context, a road map is needed to highlight what concepts to use and where to look for their manifestation. One cannot meaningfully design, implement, and assess preventive interventions intended to have systemic impact without a framework for understanding the system. Various perspectives on ecology have been developed in recent years, including Barker's behavior setting analysis and manning theory (Barker, 1968), Moos' social climate paradigm (Moos, 1974, 1979), and Bronfenbrenner's encompassing taxon-omy of the "ecology of human development" (Bronfenbrenner, 1979). Each provides somewhat different criteria for defining the important aspects of the ecological context. Each, however, affirms the power of the context to influence behavior.

The ecological metaphor of choice for the present chapter is that developed by James Kelly and elaborated on by his colleagues (Kelly, 1966, 1967, 1971, 1979a, 1979b, 1986; Kelly, 1979; Trickett, Kelly, & Todd, 1972; Trickett, 1984, 1986; Trickett, Kelly, & Vincent, 1985). It is useful because it was expressly developed to serve intervention as well as research goals. Further, it has been elaborated across a wide variety of topics germane to preventive interventions in schools, in-cluding how high school structure impacts on adolescent socialization (Kelly & Associates, 1979), mental health consultation to schools as a preventive intervention (Kelly, 1986; O'Neill & Trickett, 1982), ecologi-cal issues in social problem-solving research (Trickett et al., 1985), and the research relationship itself as a preventive intervention (Trickett et al., 1985). For these reasons it is an apt metaphor for discussing how preventive interventions *in schools* can become preventive interven-tions *for schools*.

The ecological metaphor rests on the elaboration of four ecological principles drawn from the study of biological communities and ap-plied to human communities such as schools. While these principles have been more extensively outlined elsewhere (see Kelly, 1966; Trickett, Kelly, & Todd, 1972), a brief review is useful in setting the stage for what follows. Table 13.1 outlines the four principles and their implications for the ecological assessment of the school.

Adaptation

The principle of adaptation focuses attention on the substance of the school environment; those structures, norms, attitudes, and poli-cies which, taken together, constitute the demand characteristics of the school. This principle alerts the preventive interventionist to as-sess what the school requires of students, teachers, and administrators as they cope with the school environment. What are the classroom norms for resolving interpersonal problems or for selecting popular and/or rejected children? How does a strict disciplinary code affect tolerance for divergent behavior in the classroom? These kinds of questions flow from a concern with what the school encourages and inhibits.

In addition to focusing attention on the substance of the school

TABLE 13.1 Principles of the Ecological Metaphor

Ecological Principle	Implications for Understanding the School Environment
(1) Adaptation	Attending to the adaptive requirements or demand characteristics of various settings in the school as experienced by various groups Particular attention to assessing structures, norms, attitudes, and policies
(2) Cycling of Resources	Conceptualizing aspects of the school in terms of the strengths and possible contributions to problem solving Viewing resources as including at least three elements: people, settings, and events
(3) Interdependence	Viewing the school as a social system of interconnected parts Assessing which aspects of the system are relevant to problem solving around a particular issue and how these parts are themselves connected
(4) Succession	Inquiring about how the history of the setting—its norms, traditions, and organizational structure—developed Attending to the setting's future aspirations and anticipatory problem-solving mechanisms

environment more broadly, the adaptation principle carries implications for the assessment of individual behavior. Specifically, individual behavior is viewed as transactional; that is, it is viewed as an effort by persons to cope with the demands of the school in terms of their own skills and interpretations of the school situation. Thus, an understanding of individual behavior requires simultaneous attention both to the individual and to the context in which the individual is behaving.

Cycling of Resources

The principle of cycling of resources, in field biology, refers to the ways in which biological communities develop, distribute, and use nutrients, or energy. In like fashion, a resource perspective on schools focuses on those manifest or latent resources that can aid the school in its problem solving and development. Resources may assume a variety of forms, including *persons* whose knowledge or skills are relevant to dealing with a particular issue, discrete *settings* in the school that are influential in creating policy or allowing groups to come together to solve problems, and *events* that help the school crystallize its identity and core values. Working from a resource perspective, we ask: What kinds of resources are necessary to deal with preventive issues? and Who in the school has talent relevant to their problem solution?

With respect to the assessment of individual behavior, a resource perspective focuses on the strengths and competencies of individuals that are relevant to the problem or issue at hand. Competencies may include energy to work on a cause, knowledge relevant to a problem, or being a link to external resources needed by the school. Uncovering such resources may be a complex task, for schools—like many other organizations—only activate a portion of the resources of the individuals in them.

Overall, however, a resource perspective on schools is critical to aiding their development. An assessment of resources is likewise important in deciding how to promote the adoption of a preventive intervention, for it is the resources in the school itself which will, of necessity, sustain it after the program ends or the grant concludes.

Interdependence

The principle of interdependence focuses on the interactive nature of the component parts of the school. In viewing the school as a social system, the interdependence principle stresses the value of looking for how policies differentially affect various groups in the school, and how change in one aspect of the school ripples throughout its other aspects. With respect to the introduction of preventive interventions into the school, this principle alerts the interventionists to assess how the preventive intervention may affect various components of the school in addition to those targeted by the intervention.

Like the previous principles, interdependence also carries implications for the assessments of individual behavior. Thus, the behavior of individuals in one setting such as a classroom is viewed within the context of the other settings the individual must function in, such as the home. One implication is that school behavior may reflect, in part, the congruence between school demands and home demands for adaptive behavior. This argues against assessing the impact of preventive interventions in a single setting such as the classroom and calls for research and interventions that systematically assess the multiple environments that individuals must negotiate.

Succession

The principle of succession focuses on the time dimension of schools, including both their institutional history and their hopes for future development. It reminds us that schools, like individuals, go

through cycles of definition and redefinition, of expansion and con-
traction, and that the current phase of the school affects how preventive interventions are received and implemented. Further, the principle of succession serves as a reminder that school traditions, policies,
and strategies for institutional survival have developed over time as
the school has faced varied environmental circumstances and pressures. How schools conceive of and process outside interventionists is
part of this historical development. Thus, the preventive interventionist uses the succession principle to inquire into how the school has
historically dealt with outsiders and how the preventive intervention
may serve the school's long range goals.

At the level of the individual, the succession principle alerts the interventionist to the economic, sociocultural, and familial contexts that
have influenced the world view of those who are the targets of the preventive intervention. It suggests that the technologies of intervention
may usefully be reviewed in terms of their implicit cultural values, for
the same intervention may be perceived and responded to quite differently by at-risk groups who themselves represent different world views.

Implications of an Ecological Perspective for Preventive Interventions in Schools

The ecological principles described above serve as a metaphor for
how to assess the environment of schools and/or school systems. They
provide an orienting framework and a set of questions useful in sizing
up the social context. They underscore the notion that the first order
of business for the ecologically oriented interventionist is an ongoing
commitment to understanding the environment where the intervention is implemented. The next series of issues involves how to conceptualize, implement, and evaluate preventive interventions in a way
that builds on and increases that understanding. Table 13.2 outlines a
series of goals and assumptions flowing from an ecological metaphor
that help to frame these tasks. Three related areas are specified: (1)
goals; (2) assumptions about community research and the research
relationship; and (3) some implications of an ecological perspective
for conceptualizing behavior and preventive interventions.

I. Goals

Table 13.2 lists three related goals underlying an ecological approach to preventive interventions. The superordinate goal is stated
first; namely, that development of the community or setting is the

TABLE 13.2 Implementing Ecology: Goals, Research Relationships and Conceptualization of Behavior/Intervention

I.	Goals	Implications for Implementation
(1)	The development of the community or setting as superordinate goal	Concern with evaluation and assessment of preventive interventions at the community level Commitment not only to the target population but the setting as well
(2)	Conservation, management, and enhancement of local resources as primary criteria for the success of the intervention	Analyze manifest and latent resources in the setting relevant to problem solving Design the preventive intervention in such a way that it becomes a resource to rather than a drain on the setting
(3)	Empowerment of citizens in the spirit of community development	Development of collaborative research relationship where there is reciprocal influence and power-sharing Promotion of collaborative structures for feedback, use of data, and future planning
II.	Research Relationships	Implications for Implementation
(4)	Community research is, by definition, an intervention	Approach the research relationship as an opportunity for promoting positive setting outcomes, rather than as an intrusion whose effects are to be minimized Attend to the structure of the relationship as a primary topic of discussion/negotiation
(5)	The research relationship mediates the range, validity, and local utility of the data	Give time and thought to the development of researcher credibility and mechanisms for testing the ecological validity of information gathered Maintain a sustained involvement over time to allow trust to develop and setting processes to unfold
(6)	Unintended consequences are bound to occur in community-based preventive interventions	Develop mechanisms to monitor the community or setting effects of the preventive intervention before, during, and after it occurs Include data gathering mechanisms sufficiently open-ended to detect potential unintended consequences

(continued)

TABLE 13.2—CONTINUED

III.	*Conceptualization of Behavior/ Intervention*	*Implications for Implementation*
(7)	Cultural pluralism is a positive and adaptive value	Explicit acknowledgement of the power of the ecological context to shape the world views of individuals raised in varied cultural contexts
		Value of assessing the implicit/ explicit values of the preventive intervention in terms of their cultural meaning for the recipients of the intervention
(8)	Preventive interventions are multiple, potentially additive, and at differing levels of analysis	Problem assessment investigates the differing levels of analysis of the setting and its context
		Interventions may require multidisciplinary collaboration and a mindset of using ongoing interventions as steps toward further efforts

primary task of ecologically oriented preventive interventions. Two broad aspects of this goal are salient; (a) that the recurrent concern for the preventive interventionist is how to craft the intervention for the setting's benefit, and (b) that the accountability of the interventionist be not only to the target population or to identifiable interest groups in the setting but to the setting itself. Thus, there is a consciousness of the context that surrounds the ways that interventions are conceptualized and carried out.

Supporting the overall goal of community development are two other interdependent goals: (a) that the conservation, management, and enhancement of local resources is a criterion for evaluating the success of preventive interventions, and (b) that the development of the setting can best be served by establishing collaborative relationships that empower members of the host community to participate in shaping the intervention. The first of these goals stresses the importance of understanding how the preventive intervention affects the resources of the setting. The guiding question is "can the intervention serve as a resource to, rather than a drain on, the setting hosting the intervention?" Were new skills imparted, were teachers energized to take on new issues, did the administration create new links to external agencies for outside funding, and did the school use data from the intervention for its own future planning? These kinds of questions spring from concern with local resource development as the goal of the intervention.

The third goal, stressing empowerment, is intimately connected to the issue of resource development, because the likelihood of successful resource development is enhanced to the degree that the intervention has been a result of a collaborative process between interventionist and setting. Collaboration, in this sense, extends beyond a sense of congeniality to encompass issues of shared decision making. Providing collaborative structures for shared decision making ensures that both the topics and the structure of the intervention reflect local concerns. It further increases the probability that the setting can continue interventions it perceives as useful without the presence of the outside interventionists.

Let us now turn to some assumptions that deal more directly with aspects of this intervention process.

II. Assumptions About Community Research and the Research Relationship

The assumptions about community research and the research relationship begin with the notion that research in community settings constitutes an intervention in the ongoing life of the setting. From an ecological perspective then, preventive interventions in schools, whether or not they are individually based, leave traces in the broader school environment. The preventive interventionist operating from this basic assumption asks certain kinds of questions that affect how the intervention proceeds. Is the proposed intervention congruent with the norms of the school? How should the relationship between the interventionist and the school be structured so that the impact of the intervention can be maximized? Most generally, how can the interventionist anticipate and remain aware of the systemic impact the intervention is having? The ecological principles outlined in the previous section provide a framework for approaching such questions.

Beyond these broad questions of the effect of the intervention on the school setting are issues of epistemology. The ecological perspective agrees with social scientists such as Argyris (1970) who assert that, in community research and intervention, the relationship between the data gatherer and the data provider affects both the reliability and the ecological validity of the data. Specifically, the relationship between interventionist and school affects the *range* of data made available to the interventionist, the *trustworthiness* of the data provided, and the degree to which the local setting can make *use* of the data. These three implications of the interventionist-school relationship are themselves related. Disclosure of information about various aspects of the school is likely to be greater under conditions of trust and commitment to the intervention, as is the degree to which the interventionist can trust what he/she is told. In like manner, schools find data useful to the degree that the data reflect on the perceived problems of the school. These problems are most likely to be conceptualized adequately when the relationship between interventionist and school is important and nurtured.

These larger issues of epistemology, however, also have tangible pragmatic consequences for the conduct and evaluation of preventive interventions. The nature of the relationship, for example, may affect whether or not the interventionist is informed about the negative side effects of the intervention, or whether school personnel think that the intervention has been a worthwhile idea. For example, the interventionist may not be made aware until too late that data-gathering protocol was not followed. The meaning the interventionist attributes to the data may be incomplete or misleading if not informed by how school staff intepret it. Most generally, then, this aspect of the ecological approach advocates paying careful attention to how the preventive interventionist structures the relationship with the school. It further promotes the value of maintaining a sustained involvement over time both to understand more fully how the school ecology affects the problems of interest and to allow trust to develop.

The third assumption of the research relationship is that any preventive intervention designed to influence individuals in a school will have unintended consequences. It may affect individuals in ways not predicted by the overt intervention goals; it may affect setting members not directly involved in the intervention; and it will certainly affect the school's interest in and use of the data, as well as the school's interest in future collaboration. Thus, an ecological perspective stresses the importance of: (a) thinking about the systemic ramifications of preventive interventions, and (b) developing structures or processes for feedback to detect such ramifications as they occur.

III. Implications for Conceptualizing Behavior and Preventive Interventions

While a variety of implications for understanding both individuals and interventions from an ecological perspective have been elaborated elsewhere (e.g., Bronfenbrenner, 1979; Kelly, 1966, 1986; Moos, 1979; Trickett & Mitchell, in press), the final two assumptions noted in Table 13.2 highlight the kind of thinking stimulated by the ecological metaphor. The first is the assertion that cultural pluralism is a positive and adaptive value. This assertion is not a context-free value position, but stems from an emphasis on behavior that acknowledges the power of the ecological context to shape the development of individuals. This context is viewed as multilevel (see Bronfenbrenner, 1979), and includes the levels of the broader culture, the family, the school, and the cultural backgrounds which individuals bring to the school setting.

While applicable across a variety of levels of analysis, special emphasis is placed here in the broad concept of culture as manifested in a pluralistic society. The ecological perspective stresses the power of an individual's culture to shape individual world views, including the ways in which preventive interventions are perceived and responded to. For example, in the area of interpersonal problem solving (IPS), Trickett et al. (1985) described the differential impact of the IPS curriculum in the predominantly White and wealthier suburbs and the predominantly Black and poorer inner city. Citing the experience of the Rochester group (e.g., Weissberg, et al., 1981), Trickett et al. (1985, p. 316) note that "the IPS curriculum created difficulties for inner-city children, which were not experienced in the suburbs. In the suburbs, for example, teachers felt that brainstorming alternatives (part of the IPS curriculum) helped children express ideas creatively, while urban teachers found that the same procedures produced mostly aggressive alternatives that negatively affected class discipline." Here, the same preventive intervention was responded to differently by individuals of differing racial and socioeconomic backgrounds.

On a system level, the emphasis on cultural pluralism alerts us to the degree to which schools and school systems value or devalue, use, misuse, or ignore the varied resources brought by individuals of varying cultural backgrounds. The ecological assertion is that schools that promote the expression of these cultural resources are themselves adaptive settings. They are adaptive not only in promoting the ability of cultural minorities to develop positive personal adaptations to the school, but in having available an increased range of resources that can be used to deal with school issues, problems or hopes for the future.

An emphasis on cultural pluralism serves as a reminder that the intervention itself is a cultural construction about what constitutes deviance, competence, and mental health. The interventionist needs to assess how the values of the intervention may be perceived through the cultural filters of its recipients.

Behavior reflects the influence of varying levels of the ecological environment, including interpersonal, organizational, and cultural. Because specific problems have multiple causes that reflect the contribution of variables at different levels of analysis, preventive interventions themselves may reflect multiple levels of intervention. Understanding the ecological complexity of settings, then, provides the data for attacking a problem in a variety of ways. For example, understanding that a problem may be manifested in teacher attitudes, lack of specific school resources, school policies that are insensitive to the problem, and county or state regulations expands the options for intervention efforts. It further allows one to investigate how interventions at one level of analysis may support or undermine what is happening at another level. Finally, it promotes the value that ecologically based preventive interventions are not technology driven; rather, they evolve from the specifics of the ecological context, blending technology with the demands of the school setting.

Overview

Tables 13.1 and 13.2 outline a mind-set for taking ecology seriously. The unrelenting focus is on: (a) the nature of the social context, most particularly, how we conceptualize the school environment, and (b) how the preventive intervention in that setting can positively enhance the setting's resources. The job of the ecologically oriented preventive interventionist is to develop an understanding of that context and embed the intervention in such a way that: (a) the intervention *findings* have ecological validity, and (b) the intervention *process* has constituent validity; that is, that it involves the data providers in such a way that they, too, trust the data.

Let us turn now to an emerging example of a preventive intervention building on this ecological perspective.

Intercultural Issues in Adaptation to High School: A Brief Ecological Example

An example of how this ecological perspective can guide preventive interventions is an ongoing collaboration between the University of Maryland and one of the local public high schools. We had been involved previously with the school on a research project and were interested in developing a longer term relationship for preventive intervention research and training. This particular project began a year and a half ago as part of a course called "Research as Intervention." The course is based on an ecological perspective and is designed to couple social science methodology and data-gathering skills with preventive intervention goals. Our approach has been to work with public schools on defining school-relevant problems. We then attempt to develop data on the problem in such a way that the substance of the data *and* the processes used to generate it contribute to the school's ability to deal with the problem.

Collaboration Around Problem Definition

As stated in Table 13.2, the superordinate goal of community development is enhanced by the development of a collaborative relationship where power to define issues and procedure does not rest primarily in the hands of the outside interventionist. The first issue, then, was to develop a process for defining the problem. Our initial approach was to meet with the principal, who steered us immediately to the guidance counselors to discuss possible areas of mutual interest. Doing so required that they outline their concerns and that we outline the kinds of interests and resources we could bring to the school.

After discussing several possible issues raised by school personnel, we agreed to collaborate on those arising as a result of an increase in international students entering the high school in recent years. This group of students constituted almost 20% of the high school's 2200 students, many of whom were at risk for academic failure, dropping out of school, and general school disengagement. Many spoke little or no English; some had come to the United States from war-torn countries and had experienced first hand the traumas of war; some were illegal and, having no local relatives, had to support themselves. And, of course, teachers and guidance counselors were frequently confronted with situations involving these students that were beyond their pedagogical skills and language abilities. Table 13.3 presents an overview of the international student population, and conveys a sense of the tasks facing the school. Over 60 different countries were represented, and over 40 different languages were spoken in the homes of these students.

On our side of the equation, the international student issue was relevant to the kinds of resources the university could offer, such as our program's experience in dealing with issues of cultural pluralism and the substantive professional interests of several graduate students who themselves were from various foreign countries and ethnic groups within this country. Further, the issue was not only one of increasing importance nationally as refugees and immigrants continue to move to the United States, it provided a problem well-suited

TABLE 13.3

Racial Composition of Babel High School

American Indian	5	.22%
Hispanic	172	7.73%
Asian	176	7.9%
White	916	41.2%
Black	955	42.9%
Total	2224	

Countries of origin of the foreign born students

Total number of countries of origin = 61

Countries of Origin:

Jamaica	72
El Salvador	55
India	43
Guiana	33
Korea	25
Siera Leone	18
Dominican Republic	18
Cambodia	17
Trinidad	14
Vietnam	12
Haiti	12
Guatemala	10
Other	131
Total	460

Languages spoken by the foreign born students

Total number of foreign languages spoken by the foreign students = 64

Languages:

English*	177
Spanish	122
Korean	25
Cambodian	17
Vietnamese	12
French	10

Enrollment in English for Students Speaking Other Languages Classes:

First semester 1986–87	127
Second semester 1986–87	138

---

*Although these students come from countries where English is spoken, such as Jamaica and India, they speak it with a different accent. For this reason, they experience many language difficulties in the classroom as well as with their American peers.

to an ecological framework, namely, the ways in which cultural differences mediated the adaptation of adolescents to high school. Thus, there was mutuality of interest around a school-defined problem. An equitable bargain was struck.

We discussed how to proceed, issues of confidentiality, and where the data gathering was headed. There was an immediate pull for some individually based intervention—developing a tutoring program, providing counseling for newly arrived students—and, among those teachers working most closely with international students, considerable frustration about how little school-wide interest there seemed to be in helping these students. Indeed, they viewed the principal himself as generally supportive but relatively unaware of the scope and complexity of the international student issue.

After a series of discussions with guidance and, now, the ESOL (English for Speakers of Other Languages) teachers, we agreed that, despite the potential immediate benefits of a tutoring or counseling program, the scope and complexity of the issue suggested a broader approach. This approach could, over time, involve a multilevel assessment of the problem and a general consciousness raising in the school about the effect of cultural differences on the educational process. While agreeable to this proposal to gather data across the system, school personnel were skeptical of its usefulness and convinced that they knew what we would find; i.e., that they knew the range of the data and, based on that knowledge, were not hopeful that it could be made useful. Still, we had developed a collaborative process that acknowledged the power of setting members to influence the agenda for a preventive intervention. Further, we were now accountable to them around our general ecological perspective on data gathering.

Ecological Influences on the Process and Content of Data Gathering

Having agreed upon a problem and a general way of proceeding, we used the principles outlined in Table 13.2 as a guide for our activities. While the overall goal still focused on the spirit of community development for the school more generally, three principles from Table 13.2 serve as examples of how the ecological perspective influenced both the process and content of our data gathering: (1) building an empowering relationship with various groups in the school environment; (2) developing a multilevel conception of the issues involving international students; and (3) assessing the school in terms of its manifest and latent resources. Let us consider each:

1. *The process of relationship building.* In the process of collecting

information about the international student issue we wanted to ensure that various groups in the school saw themselves as important both in defining the problems and having a potential role in solving them. To gain both credibility and a broad perspective on how school personnel were conceptualizing the issues, we interviewed school personnel across roles and ideological boundaries. We began with the ESOL teachers, with whom we had already developed a relationship, and we asked them to recommend other teachers whom they viewed as having differing perspectives on international students. We asked them to tell their colleagues that we were coming, thus using the internal network of the school to sanction our inroads into its culture.

Of particular interest to us were those teachers identified as being either uninterested in, or antagonistic to, international students so that, on a process level, we would not be perceived as interested only in what a select group thought and, on a content level, we could better understand the range of concerns present in the broader school culture. In similar fashion, we spoke with different groups of international students—Hispanics, Asians, and English-speaking students from the Carribean as well as White and Black U.S.-born students. It is useful to mention that having a research team that included Whites, Blacks, and bilingual graduate students was a great advantage in gaining access to data from a wide variety of students in the school.

Through this process an increasingly complex picture emerged of the issues, perceptions and misperceptions, and attitudes of various teachers and students about the school and each other. Most importantly, however, we had become known as an involved outside group, who now had personal contact with a large and representative number of teachers and students. We were seen in the school as having made a commitment to caring about the issue, not, at this point, as taking sides around how to deal with it. Further, we had told teachers that, at a later time, the data we gathered would be shared with them; that, in essence, both they and we were accountable to pursue the matter further.

2. *Developing a multilevel conceptualization.* The ecological perspective guided the content of our inquiry in addition to its process. Thus, an explicit intent of the interviews was to develop a multilevel approach to conceptualizing the transactions between international students and the school. For example, while it may be useful to know what the family situation of various international students might be, the important question for us involved the implications of family issues for the student's experience of school: that is, how family dynamics or norms affect classroom behavior, the use of school facilities, and peer interac-

tions. Further, we wished to know what concepts school personnel used to understand their experience with international students and how consistent these concepts were across teachers.

To structure our information gathering, we asked about four different aspects of the school environment stemming from the adaptation principle: (a) school *structures* (e.g., clubs, events, specialized roles) designed to support international student coping; (b) *norms* that affect students from different cultures in particular, such as teacher expectations about classroom behavior and student norms about interpersonal interactions and styles; (c) *attitudes* held by various groups in the school toward different groups of international students; and (d) *policies* of the school and school system as they affected both students and teachers.

Data gathered from this multilevel conceptualization validated its usefulness as a framework for investigating the transactions between international students and the broader school culture. These transactions emerged as complex and influenced by events occurring at differing levels of analysis. They further emphasize how important it is to view these students in context. For example, we found that many Hispanic students had to support themselves and their families by working long hours after school and on weekends. Indeed, it was not unusual for them to go from school to work, arriving home late at night to study. Because of this pattern many were too tired to be attentive at school and did not have time for homework. In class, they often turned to other Hispanic students to help them translate what the teacher was saying. Teachers, however, often brought a quite different perspective to their assessment of the behavior of these students. They were unaware of the out-of-school demands placed on many Hispanic students, and interpreted their classroom behavior as not caring about school—perhaps being on drugs—and preferring to socialize with other Hispanics rather than pay attention in class. In turn, Hispanic students expressed anger at being accused of being lazy or on drugs when they were in fact tired from their jobs.

The importance of understanding the influence of other levels of analysis can be found in how county and state policy affected the international student experience. For example, the county's policies on how to place international students—particularly those with meager educational histories who spoke no English—hinged on an interesting but difficult choice. Is it better to place students according to their prior educational level or according to age? The former would suggest placing a 16-year-old with 4 or 5 years of formal education in, perhaps, the fifth grade, while the latter might place the same student in high school but with a very serious deficiency in educational background. This county has chosen the latter policy, but it has complicated the pedagogical task of both student and teacher alike. Indeed, some of the frustrations voiced by teachers about international students stemmed from the difficulties they faced in teaching students who cannot possibly have the linguistic or educational prerequisites to pass their courses.

This pressure on teachers has been further heightened by the push for excellence and accountability in the state and the nation more broadly. Teachers are under increasing pressure to produce students who perform well on standardized tests. Since knowledge of English and a continuous educational background is a prerequisite to achieving this goal, and many international students are behind their U.S. counterparts in these areas, teachers view themselves as caught between the needs of these students and external criteria of accountability. This, too, has increased the tendency for teachers to express prejudiced or negative attitudes toward international students, not because of personal dislike so much as a reaction to policies that make these students an easy target for displaced anger.

Looking at these teacher-student interactions as policy related had important implications for intervention. First, it provided an alternative framework to the person-blame attributions about many teachers that we heard in our early meetings with the guidance and ESOL teachers. This framework increased the empathy of all teachers about the complexity of the situation facing them *and* the international students they teach. Second, defining the problem as at least partially policy-generated helped focus attention on intervention at the policy level rather than conjuring up the image of a T-group intervention. These, and many other findings, provided us not only with a rich picture of a complex phenomenon, but also with a variety of places and ways to intervene.

3. *Assessment of resources.* In addition to focusing on structures, norms, attitudes, and policies, we were simultaneously concerned about identifying resources in the school that could later be tapped for the purpose of preventive interventions. As elaborated elsewhere (Trickett, Kelly, & Vincent, 1985), resources include not only people, but settings and events that are part of the social context of the school. With respect to individuals as resources, for example, we looked for those adults in the school who expressed interest and concern about international students. We found many such individuals, including several whose interest was not widely known. Thus, there were latent as well as manifest human resources in the school, suggesting that one

intervention goal would be to develop mechanisms for these latent resources to act on their good intentions. In addition, we found that there was no clear relationship between who *ought* to be interested in international student issues and who *was* interested. Thus, the school librarian had developed specific programs for international students about how to use the library, while the teacher who taught psychology did not show interest in the particular psychological issues facing international students.

In addition to individuals, however, we sought out settings and events that could later serve as routes to preventive interventions. Among the settings, for example, were the international club and the student government. The international club, sponsored by one of the ESOL teachers, was designed to provide international students with a comfortable setting to meet as well as a forum for getting more involved in relevant school issues. Membership in this club, however, was dominated by the more acculturated and academically competent international students, thus posing a challenge in terms of its resource potential for more recently arrived international students. This fact did, however, aid in understanding some of the ways in which international students differentiated themselves in varying groups.

The student government was another resource whose potential exceeded its current helpfulness. Only Asian students were represented in this group, and there was no consensual interest in viewing the international students as posing special issues for the school. Rather, they were more likely to be viewed as one of many interest groups with no distinct claim on the agenda of the student government. Still, the student government represented a potentially useful setting if a broader consciousness about international student issues could be generated in the school.

On the teacher level, such settings as the in-service training time were explored as existing setting resources for discussion of international student issues. The general notion around existing settings, however, was to map out the various relevant settings in the school and assess what their distinctive contributions might be. A similar approach was used to seek out events, like the school's annual international dinner, which celebrated the cultural differences among international students and provided an opportunity for informal interaction among groups that seldom interacted during the school day.

The overall intent, then, was to develop a picture of the kinds of resources which were potentially available in the school. These resources proved to be both manifest and latent in terms of the degree to which they were broadly recognized in the school. Further, an assessment of settings and events suggested that while such potential resources existed, they were not mobilized to respond to international student issues. Implicit in the assessment of people, settings, and events was the notion that what was *not* found would be as important as what *was* found in directing intervention activities. Preventive interventions are creations designed to augment and energize existing resources.

Translating Data into Preventive Interventions and Teacher In-Service

While incomplete, the preceding is intended to provide a flavor for how an ecological perspective can generate data on which preventive interventions may be based. Three aspects of the ecological metaphor were highlighted: (a) attending to the development of a collaborative relationship with the school; (b) developing a multilevel approach to defining the problem; and (c) conducting a resource analysis. From the various kinds of information generated by these assessments come multiple possible interventions. How we have begun the process of translating these efforts into interventions is the next part of the story.

After having spent over a year developing relationships and gathering data, we are just starting to design interventions. Over the next few years, we intend to deal with issues of policy, bring outside resources into the school, and continue our efforts to understand how the international student issues shift and change as the international student population itself changes. The general intent will be to aid the school's ability to educate and learn from these students. We have, thus far, been involved in a teacher in-service training program and have aided the principal in documenting the rationale for increased resources from the school system. Each of these efforts springs from our work, but attacks issues at differing levels of analysis. A brief discussion of these activities follows in an effort to convey the spirit of the interventions.

The original idea to use a teacher in-service training session as a setting to discuss international student issues surfaced in a meeting between the principal and members of the "research as intervention" team. We on the team viewed it as a place to consolidate our findings, feed back information to teachers about what they, in individual interviews, had shared with us, and create a collaborative process around designing the experience. If successful, it would further serve as an event that could be built upon in the future.

The substantive goals of the in-service were framed by the issues raised by teachers and students in our interviews. Thus, as already mentioned, teachers were often unaware of the life circumstances of many international students and misinterpreted their classroom behavior. For example, lack of eye contact from Asian students was seen as a sign of respect by students but avoidance by teachers, as was the Jamaican students' silence rather than active classroom participation. Teachers were also generally unaware of the degree to which their frustrations were shared by other teachers. Based on these and other findings, the substantive goals of the in-service included: (a) helping teachers understand cultural pluralism, and how it is expressed in the classroom, and so ease their frustrations and the frustrations of international students; (b) recognizing the depth and complexity of issues facing international students, thereby fostering a stronger systemic commitment to caring about these students; and (c) providing a forum for teachers to share their concerns and renew their energy to attack the issues.

The process goals of the in-service were likewise driven by our data and the goal of collaboration and empowerment. Thus, we wanted to work with ESOL teachers, the principal, and external school system resources relevant to international student policy issues. We hoped that the in-service would heighten the visibility of the ESOL teachers as resources in the school, and we wanted the in-service to be a vehicle for setting future problem-solving processes in motion. Thus, the in-service would not be seen as an end in itself but as a step toward future work on international student issues. Consistent with these goals, the in-service was primarily planned with the ESOL teachers, using the findings of our work and their experiences as background.

1. *The in-service:* One of the first decisions of the group planning the in-service was to develop a small group format for the experience. A high school of 2200 students has a staff of over 130, and previous in-services conducted with all staff together had, with some exceptions, not been successful at engaging the interest and participation of teachers. Thus, a rotating format was developed where three successive groups, starting a half hour apart, would be involved in the same in-service, followed by a meeting of all the teachers for summarizing remarks, comments, and completion of an evaluation form.

In each of the three groups the format was the same. It began with one of the ESOL teachers addressing the group in Arabic—asking questions, motioning to the assembled teachers (now in groups of 30–40) to repeat phrases, and handing out an in-class homework assignment of math problems which, in Arabic, are read right to left rather than left to right. The purpose was phenomenological—to place the teachers immediately in the position of those students who neither spoke nor understood English well enough to grasp what was being said in classes. While the tone was light-hearted and often humorous, this exercise effectively conveyed the sense of bewilderment and uncertainty faced by many international students in class.

Following this, a second ESOL teacher showed a videotaped class discussion of international students in ESOL classes talking about their experiences at school. Several made comments about their difficulties in classes where the international students were far outnumbered by U.S. born students. Teachers listened hard to these candid comments, remarked when one of the videotaped students was known to them, and engaged in a brisk discussion with the ESOL teacher when the videotape concluded. They shared some of their classroom experiences and concerns and asked the ESOL teacher for her "insider" point of view.

Finally, graduate students from the University of Maryland who, themselves, represented differing ethnic groups, spoke about what they had learned from their interviews with international students and teachers. The experiences of Asian, Caribbean, and Hispanic students were contrasted in terms of the stereotypes surrounding them, their approach to teachers and education, their cultural backgrounds, and their relationship with and experience of black and white U.S. born students. The teacher interview data were then summarized for the teachers. These data reflected the broad educational concerns and frustrations reported by teachers, and provided a vehicle for sharing previously private information to them as a group. These presentations also stimulated discussions that could well have continued beyond the allotted time.

At the end of the three sequential small group meetings of teachers, the teachers convened in one large group. First, the county-wide director of guidance/placement of international students addressed the teachers on issues of placement. Placement of students had been frequently cited in the teacher interviews as being a source of concern and mystification. Thus, teachers needed both a context and a discussion of specific issues in order to understand why and how certain decisions were made. The county-wide director explained the constraints under which her office worked and invited the teachers to call her anytime if they had questions or concerns. Next, the head of the "Research as Intervention" project was introduced by the principal and discussed, more broadly, the hope that the current work and relationship with the school would continue into the future. Finally, the principal made some closing remarks, forcefully underscoring the importance of the issues involving international students and his commitment to helping the school cope with the situation. Evaluation forms suggested the overall success of the in-service, and a large number of teachers stated that they would be willing to devote more thought and energy to these issues in the future.

2. *Principal as resource finder:* Shortly after the in-service we submitted a final yearly report to the principal outlining our recommendations for next steps at the school. These included the need for such external resources as a bilingual guidance counselor and computers for ESOL classes, and also additional school attention to linkages with community settings serving various international groups, such as the University's Department of Education and International Student Office. Various school activities, such as an orientation program for incoming international students, ongoing guidance groups, and another in-service for the following year were recommended as well. Thus far, the principal has met with the ESOL teachers to discuss the recommendations in the final report, and has requested a variety of resources from the school board, using the report and his own experience as data. He is an active supporter of international student issues and is developing his own plans for dealing with these issues at the school. The intervention now includes system components as well, and we at the university are currently collaborating with him on plans for next year.

Ecology and Individually Based Preventive Interventions: Illustrative Topics

The example presented above can at best only provide the flavor of an ecological approach to the development of preventive interventions. Our intent was to position ourselves in such a way that we could learn about the school as a social context and design preventive interventions with that context in mind. In our work, we intentionally did not propose to begin with individually based preventive interventions as a way of affecting the school adaptation and psychological adjustment of international students. We chose to focus on the school and its many facets that affected the experience of these students. We further allowed ourselves the flexibility of collaboratively selecting the topic of concern and were free to adjust the process and content of our work to the needs of the school.

The ecological conditions confronting those involved with individually based preventive interventions are frequently different from those we created. More typically, these interventionists are interested in developing and testing a specific type of program in the school setting. Frequently, and particularly when such interventions are linked to the timetable of external funding, interventionists have neither the time, resources, or flexibility to develop either the relationship or knowledge of the school setting where the intervention occurs. Nor are they often able to alter the content of their proposed intervention in any significant way. There are many ways, however, that individually based preventive interventions can contribute to a better understanding of how local school ecology affects the particular preventive concerns of the interventionist, and many scientific as well as pragmatic reasons for taking ecology seriously.

In this concluding section we will argue that individually based preventive interventions can, in a variety of ways, illuminate ecological relationships and serve as a resource to the school in the service of community development. Though the intent is to implement a particular program with a specified group of targeted individuals, the research design, the process of data collection, and the building of a relationship with the school can be carried out in a way that takes ecology into account. Specifically, the ecological mind set alerts the investigator to certain kinds of questions. For example, how does the specific ecological context affect or define the problems which are the object of the intervention? Is the phenomenon expressed differently in schools that differ on identifiable ecological variables such as size, geographical location, average SES of the student body, racial composition, or organizational structure? What will happen to the intervention when the funding runs out? How can the school become part of the intervention? These kinds of questions focus on the setting itself and how the setting affects the problem and the intervention.

The following three topics from a potentially much longer list serve as examples of the kinds of issues raised by an ecological perspective. Taken together, they argue for the value of taking ecology seriously when designing and carrying out individually based preventive interventions in schools. They are summarized in Table 13.4.

1. The Value of Selecting Setting and Outcome Variables That Are Systemic as Well as Individual

(a) The selection of settings for individually based preventive interventions rarely surfaces as a conceptual topic in the literature. More frequently, ease of access accounts for the largest proportion of vari-

TABLE 13.4 Topics for Ecologically Oriented Preventive Interventions

Topic	Implications for Individually Based Preventive Interventions
1. Selecting setting variables and systemic outcome variables	Developing knowledge about representativeness of settings as well as subjects, and assessing the effect of the intervention on both the setting and the subjects
2. How the intervention is coupled with the host environment	Attention to the way the preventive intervention is structured or implemented in the host setting; environmental reconnaisance as prelude
3. Individually based preventive interventions and interventionists as resources for the school	Viewing the intervention as a means as well as an end and the preventive interventionist as a resource and linkage person to other resources useful for school problem solving

ance. However, in such interventions, attention to setting selection is important for at least two reasons: (1) to ascertain how contrasting ecologies affect the phenomenon of interest and (2) to counteract self-selection bias that influences the ecological validity and generalizability of the data.

The first issue highlights research questions that link individual behavior to its ecological context. For example, one important area of individually based preventive interventions involves the work of Coie and others on the implications of peer sociometric status for subsequent psychological adjustment. This work presents strong evidence for the predictive power of differing statuses assigned to children by their peers (see Coie, Rabiner, & Lochman, this book). An emphasis on setting selection within this body of work might lead to such questions as: Are the behaviors and attitudes that lead to peer acceptance or rejection similar in different types of schools serving children of varying races or social classes? Are the criteria for peer popularity mediated by the particular kind of classroom environment fostered by the teacher? Vincent (1986) has studied the latter issue and found some support for the notion that the behavioral determinants of peer popularity are related to the nature of the classroom environment; i.e., the same behavior is likely to be more valued by children in some kinds of classrooms than in others. Thus, attending to setting selection represents one way of linking individually based preventive interventions to their ecological contexts (see Moos & Trickett, 1979; Trickett et al., 1985; and Trickett & Mitchell, in press, for examples).

The second issue, that of self-selection bias, also highlights the relationship between intervention and context. It is aptly stated by Campbell and Stanley (1972, p. 19). "Consider the implications of an experiment on teaching in which the researcher has been turned down by nine school systems and is finally accepted by a tenth. This tenth almost certainly differs from the other nine, and from the universe of schools to which we would like to generalize, in many specific ways. It is, thus, nonrepresentative and the effects we find, while internally valid, may be specific to such schools." In sum, the generalizability of data gathered on individually based preventive interventions is potentially mediated by the larger ecology in which it occurs.

Both these issues support the value of attending to the ecology of schools per se in developing and implementing preventive interventions. Such a perspective embeds both the phenomenon and the intervention in a social context.

(b) The selection of systemic outcome variables is likewise an effort to understand the systemic ramifications of individually based preventive interventions. Such programs, particularly *because* they are powerful and persuasive, can be expected to affect the school more broadly. They may help redefine the norms around appropriate behavior and deviance, they may increase parental interest in the school, or they may cause teachers and principals to examine or re-examine policy. Wondering where such potential effects might occur alerts the interventionist to the ways in which other intervention *does* intrude into the system. It further increases the credibility of the interventionist because it shows that he/she knows what everyone in the school knows; namely that from the point of view of the school, the main effects of the interventions are not necessarily the findings, but how the intervention affects the ongoing life of the school.

2. Coupling the Intervention with the School Environment

A second topic involves paying attention to how the intervention is implemented in the school setting, how it is coupled with the ecology of the school. Our preceding discussion of the high school project has already given a flavor for how interventions can emerge from self-conscious attention to this process. The ecological perspective, as reflected in this example, advocates both a collaborative process and a lengthy "getting to know the school" as prelude to implementing an intervention. Thus, part of the issue of how the intervention is coupled with the school hinges on environmental reconnaissance and collaborative discussions.

The general importance of the issue for preventive interventions, however, is not only in the value of collaboration and its implications for trustworthy data. The meaning of the data itself is affected by how the intervention is linked to the ecological context. Consider the work by Ransen (1981) that reviews the short-term and long-term results of two conceptually similar intervention programs with the aged (Langer & Rodin, 1976; Schulz, 1976). Both programs were designed to test the "perceived control" hypothesis through enhancing residents' perceptions of personal control over aspects of their institutional lives. Both had similar positive short-term effects in stopping and, indeed, reversing aspects of physical and psychological decline.

However, follow-up showed marked differences between the two intervention programs. One study found that 18 months after termination of the program, residents in the experimental group remained happier, more socially active, and had a lower mortality rate than residents in the control group. In the other study, however, follow-up at 24, 30, and 42 months revealed a markedly different picture. Mean scores for the experimental group on indices of physical and psychological status were lower than those for the controls, and mortality was higher. "In sum," stated Ransen, "those residents who had benefited most from the intervention in the short run seemed to have suffered the greatest declines in the long run" (p. 18).

In an effort to understand these patterns, Ransen undertook a post hoc analysis of how the intervention programs were implemented in the two different settings. Several differences emerged, including whether those who delivered the intervention were insiders (e.g., the activities director) or outsiders (e.g., visiting college students), whether the intervention disrupted the ongoing social network of residents or kept it intact, and whether the project was designed to affect a broad or narrow range of expectations about control of one's institutional life.

On the basis of these analyses, Ransen drew the tentative conclusion that the differential long-term results reflected the different ways in which the programs were implemented. The same basic research program implemented differently in different settings is not, conceptually, the same program. How the research is coupled with the host environment thus becomes a salient topic for individually based preventive interventions. It carries implications not only for the short-term and long-term impact of the intervention, but for our attributions of why the intervention succeeded or failed. Attending to this issue thus contributes to theory development as well.

3. Becoming a Resource for the School: Interventions and Interventionists

Both preventive interventions and interventionists represent potentially important resources for the community development of the school. The interventions themselves, if linked to an understanding of local school ecology, can generate data and create processes that can illuminate school issues and enhance school problem-solving. Further, in the spirit of community development, interventionists can bring many kinds of resources to the school that can augment the intervention itself. Preventive psychologists have paradigms that can enrich teacher discussions about children and policies; interventionists are information links to external funding sources so needed by public schools today, and many have access to the myriad of human and technological resources that academic settings have to offer. Very importantly, they are currently involved in preventive work in schools and have the kind of solid, long-term relationship with schools and school systems that is a prerequisite for ecologically based work.

Taking ecology seriously involves the conceptual task of understanding the ecology of schools and school systems so that, as we design and execute preventive interventions, we can assess how they both shape and are shaped by the contexts in which they occur. Taking ecology seriously, however, also involves a reconceptualization of the role of the interventionist and the premises underlying his/her work. These premises include a longitudinal commitment to the systems where the work occurs, a concern with collaboration and empowerment, an appreciation of human diversity in conceptualizing behavior and interventions, and the intent to generate resources of help to the school as a social setting.

References

Argyris, C. (1970). *Interventions, theory, and method: A behavioral science view*. Reading, MA: Addison-Wesley.

Barker, R. G. (1968). *Ecological psychology*. Stanford: Stanford University Press.

Bronfenbrenner, U. (1979). *The ecology of human development: Experiments by nature and design*. Cambridge, MA: Harvard University Press.

Buckner, J., Trickett, E. J., & Corse, S. J. (1985). *Primary prevention and mental health: An annotated bibliography* (DHHS Publication No. ADM 85–1405). Washington, DC: Government Printing Office.

Campbell, D. T., & Stanley, J. C. (1972). *Experimental and quasi-experimental designs for research*. Chicago: Rand-McNally.

Cowen, E. L. (1985). Person-centered approaches to primary prevention in mental health: Situation-focused and competence-enhancement. *American Journal of Community Psychology, 13*, 31–48.

Kelly, J. G. (1966). Ecological constraints on mental health services. *American Psychologist, 21*, 535–39.

Kelly, J. G. (1967). Naturalistic observations and theory confirmation: An example. *Human Development, 10*, 212–22.

Kelly, J. G. (1971). Qualities for the community psychologist. *American Psychologist, 26*, 897–903.

Kelly, J. G. (Ed.). (1979a). *Adolescent boys in high school: A psychological study of coping and adaptation*. Hillside, NJ: Lawrence Erlbaum Associates.

Kelly, J. G. (1979b). 'T'ain't what you do, it's the way that you do it. *American Journal of Community Psychology, 7*, 239–61.

Kelly, J. G. (1986). An ecological paradigm: Defining mental health consultation as a preventive service. *Prevention in Human Services, 4*, 1–36.

Langer, E. J., & Rodin, J. (1976). The effects of choice and enhanced personal responsibility for the aged: A field experiment in an institutional setting. *Journal of Personality and Social Psychology, 34*, 191–98.

Moos, R. H. (1974). *Evaluating treatment environments: A social ecological approach*. New York: Wiley.

Moos, R. H. (1979). *Evaluating educational environments*. San Francisco: Jossey-Bass.

Moos, R. H., & Trickett, E. J. (1979). Determinants of classroom environments. In R. H. Moos (Ed.), *Evaluating educational environments* (pp. 159–182). San Francisco: Jossey-Bass.

O'Neill, P. T., & Trickett, E. J. (1982). *Community consultation*. San Francisco: Jossey-Bass.

Ransen, D. L. (1981). Long-term effects of two interventions with the aged: An ecological analysis. *Journal of Applied Developmental Psychology, 2*, 13–27.

Schulz, R. (1976). The effects of control and predictability on the psychological and physical well-being of the institutionalized aged. *Journal of Personality and Social Psychology, 34*, 191–98.

Trickett, E. J. (1984). Towards a distinctive community psychology: An ecological metaphor for training and the conduct of research. *American Journal of Community Psychology, 12*, 261–297.

Trickett, E. J. (1986). Consultation as a preventive intervention. In J. G. Kelly & R. Hess (Eds.), *The ecology of prevention: Illustrating mental consultation* (pp. 187–204). NY: Howard Press.

Trickett, E. J., Kelly, J. G., & Todd, D. M. (1972). The social environment of the high school: Guidelines for individual change and organizational development. In S. Golann & C. Eisendorfer (Eds.), *Handbook of community mental health* (pp. 331–406). New York: Appleton-Century Crofts.

Trickett, E. J., Kelly, J. G., & Vincent, T. A. (1985). The spirit of ecological inquiry in community research. In D. Klein & E. Susskind (Eds.), *Knowledge building in community psychology* (pp. 283–333). New York: Praeger.

Trickett, E. J., & Mitchell, R. E. (in press). An ecological metaphor for research and intervention in community psychology. In M. S. Gibbs, J. R. Lachenmeyer, & J. Sigal (Eds.), *Community Psychology: Theoretical and empirical approaches* (2nd ed.). New York: Wiley.

Vincent, T. A. (1986). *The relationship of classroom structure and classroom environment to peer interactions*. Unpublished doctoral dissertation, University of Maryland, College Park.

Weissberg, R. P., Gesten, E. L., Rapkin, B. D., Cowen, E. L., Davidson, E., Flores de Apodaca, R., & McKim, G. J. (1981). Evaluation of a social problem-solving training program for suburban and inner-city third grade children. *Journal of Consulting and Clinical Psychology, 49*, 251–61.

14

The Practice of Psychology in the Schools for the Primary Prevention of Learning and Adjustment Problems in Children: A Perspective from the Field of Education

Joel Meyers

The schools provide a logical focus for community resources interested in the primary prevention of psychopathology. Despite the intuitive appeal of this assumption, there is substantial resistance to implementing primary prevention in the context of public schools (e.g., Alpert, 1985; Meyers & Parsons, 1987). This chapter suggests that primary prevention would increase its chances for effective implementation in schools, if preventionists developed and used their understanding of the school culture, if they made a serious effort to work collaboratively with school professionals to develop preventive efforts, and if they took advantage of the ongoing ways in which prevention can be implemented within the normal school curriculum and instructional process, rather than emphasizing external primary prevention programs that are often costly and incompatible with school culture. This viewpoint does not imply that formal prevention programs brought into the schools are necessarily ineffective; however, a preoccupation with externally developed and imposed programs frequently misses the most important opportunities for primary prevention in the schools.

In an effort to clarify these points, this chapter is divided into three sections. The first section provides an overview of current trends in education that have implications for the ideas presented in the last two sections on primary prevention in schools. The second section considers ideas from the literature on primary prevention with implications for educational settings. The third section focuses on examples of pragmatic approaches to implement primary prevention in schools with particular consideration of ideas that have received little attention in the literature on primary prevention. A variety of school-oriented programs have been discussed frequently in the primary prevention literature, and a more detailed discussion of at least some of these can be obtained elsewhere (e.g., Alpert, 1985; Clarizio, 1979; Meyers & Parsons, 1987).

A School Psychologist's Perspective on Schools and Schooling

The implementation of externally imposed prevention programs that are separate from the rest of the educational system makes little sense when considering the purpose of schools, which is to teach skills so that children develop cognitively, academically, socially and emotionally. In effect, the goals of schools and primary prevention should be viewed similarly, since both are focused on teaching those skills necessary to promote learning and prevent the development of learning and adjustment problems. Yet, despite these similar goals, an unfortunate separation exists between primary prevention and other school programs. Perhaps the root of this problem is the traditional conflict between education and psychology. While educators have long resisted the input of psychologists, many psychologists have regarded the field of education with disdain. From the educator's perspective, psychologists have a relatively easy role in education. They develop ideas that may be interesting from their perspective, and they enter the school or the classroom briefly to test these ideas. When their ideas fail they have the luxury of walking away from the problem and they frequently blame the resistant system rather than examine their own failure seriously. When their ideas do work they typically leave to pick up another case or discontinue implementation to pursue publication before negative results begin to appear. In contrast, educators must face the day-to-day reality of dealing with difficult children, who refuse to conform to most theories. While they have the advantage of a long-term perspective that provides a realistic understanding about what works in schools, they are forced to confront their failures on a day-to-day basis that can be extremely frustrating. Further, rather than working individually or in small groups with difficult children, educators must face these children in large groups that are almost impossible to manage on a daily basis. Like the rest of society, most psychologists fail to appreciate the difficulty and the challenge of the job of teaching, and they fail to recognize that many of society's most effective "psychologists" are probably teachers.

Primary prevention's group focus may provide a vehicle to reduce the distance and conflict between education and psychology, but to accomplish this goal there may need to be some adjustments in our thinking about primary prevention. Writing about some inherent conflicts between classical thinking about primary prevention and education, Reynolds and Birch (1982) stated:

> Educational treatments . . . are concerned with teaching and learning, not recovery from defect or the simple prevention of problems. The educator prevents reading failure, for example, not by creating antibodies but by teaching reading or its prerequisites with greater resourcefulness and better effect to more children. Thus, to be educationally relevant and to engage the teacher, the treatment must involve learning and development. (p. 71)

Consistent with this orientation, Bardon (1983) has suggested a shift in " . . . priority from pathology (and its positive expression, mental health) to education, (with its positive emphasis on human effectiveness)" (p. 191). By focusing on educational attainment, rather than primary prevention, educators and psychologists might develop a common focus on human development, social competence, achievements and the environmental circumstances needed to facilitate these outcomes. These positive criteria may lead to more effective educational programs than the negative criteria traditionally associated with prevention. These positive criteria provide a common framework to facilitate problem solving by educators and may reduce conflicts and barriers to communication between education and psychology (Reynolds & Birch, 1982).

From this perspective it may be most effective to develop approaches to primary prevention that are closely linked to the ongoing structures and routines of school functioning. These approaches will be most succesful if they are viewed by teachers as consistent with the educational process, and if they can be implemented with minimal added expense and intrusiveness. Externally developed programs imported into the system would be minimized using this perspective.

The Need for Primary Prevention in Schools

Alpert (1985) pointed out that there were 3.2 million children under age 18 who have major emotional problems, with only 10–15% of these children receiving even minimal mental health services. She also reported that of 7 million children with major learning problems less than 50% receive the needed educational services. Based on these estimates, 6.2 million children with learning and adjustment problems receive absolutely no services at all. Serious questions can be raised regarding the actual psychological and/or educational services received by the remaining 4.0 million children (see Meyers, Parsons, & Martin, 1979; Reynolds, 1982; and Ysseldyke, et al., 1984, for criticisms of these psychological and educational services). The need for alternative prevention oriented models of service delivery becomes even more apparent from a consideration of current approaches to remedial and special education.

Problems with Remedial and Special Education

Several years ago I had the opportunity to negotiate with several urban school districts regarding their approaches to the delivery of special education services. One school district reported a waiting list for testing children with suspected learning and adjustment problems that included 16,000 children. I was informed (facetiously, I hope) that this resulted in a request that psychologists evaluate three children each day using a test battery that was limited to three subtests from the WISC-R, an unscored Bender, and the "House" from the House-Tree-Person. Perhaps equally astonishing was that in a district where there was a substantial concern for nondiscriminatory assessment, the three recommended subtests from the WISC-R included the Vocabulary and Information subtests from the Verbal Scale. Needless to say, it is not possible to provide meaningful psychological or special education services in a school district where there is such a restricted view of psychology and education. While this may be an exaggerated example, it does reflect an image of the truth which exists in many school districts across the country. Many school systems require psychologists to perform one or more psychological evaluations each day (Goldwasser, Meyers, Christenson, & Graden, 1983). When professional services are defined by counting numbers of cases, an emphasis is placed on quantity rather than quality of services, and this may be a problem throughout the full range of educational services.

Special education and prevention. Madeline Will (1986) suggested that schools fail to meet the needs of children with learning problems. She noted an increase of one million children classified as learning disabled during the 10 year period from 1975 to 1985, and she concluded that unless alternative models of special education are developed, the number of children labeled learning disabled and the widespread experience of school failure will continue to increase. Consistent with a preventive framework, she argued that alternative models must provide vehicles for regular class teachers to receive support from special educators, and must promote techniques to meet individual needs in the regular classroom as the barriers between special and regular education are removed.

PL 94–142 mandated the right of all handicapped children to a public education in the least restricted environment. This means that all children must receive an education in the setting that is as similar as possible to the regular classroom environment and still provides a maximally effective education. Mainstreaming is most frequently implemented by combining regular classroom instruction with special education service in a resource room setting. This model of pulling children out of the regular classroom is used for a variety of other special services as well, such as remedial math and remedial reading. Unfortunately, these pull-out programs have a variety of negative consequences. They reduce the relationship between special, remedial, and regular education, as teachers from one program are not necessarily aware of what occurs in the other program. The result is an artificial separation between these programs, as well as special programs that may differ from and even conflict with the education presented in the regular classroom. Given this unnecessary separation, regular education is not likely to take advantage of the knowledge and expertise of special educators or school psychologists, even though these professionals could help to reduce the incidence of school failure (e.g., Allington, Stuetzel, Shake, & Lamarache, 1986; Haynes & Jenkins, 1986; Johnston, Allington, & Afflerbach, 1985; Meyers, et al., 1979).

Pull-out programs can also reduce the time allocated to instruction as too much time must be spent moving from class to class. An investigation of the reading instruction provided in resource room programs (Haynes & Jenkins, 1986) reported that: (a) there was minimal time devoted to direct reading activities in the resource room (average = 9.95 minutes/day); (b) there was tremendous variability in the amount of direct reading provided in resource rooms (range = .41 minutes to 29.4 minutes/day); (c) there was less time spent on direct reading activities in the resource room than in the regular classroom; and (d) the total amount of direct reading time for handicapped students (resource and regular class combined) equaled the time spent in direct reading by nonhandicapped children who did not have to leave the regular class. It is, therefore, not surprising that Allington et al. (1986) found no additional instructional time for students in remedial reading, or that remedial reading teachers spend most of their time distributing and correcting work rather than instructing. Allington has also found that pull-out programs may actually reduce the amount of time students with learning problems spend actively engaged on task. Children removed from the regular class for remedial reading spent about 10 less minutes per day engaged in reading, and those in resources room programs spent about 40 fewer minutes per day engaged in reading (R. Allington, personal communication, March 12, 1987).

Despite their current dominance in special and remedial education, pull-out programs are inconsistent with a preventive orientation since they do not maximize the opportunity for the special education teacher to provide instruction to or influence the instruction of ineligible students who are educated in the regular classroom, many of whom may be at risk of developing learning and adjustment problems. These ineligible children do not have access to the special attention that might prevent the development of these problems. Structural changes that reduce the tendency to categorize and remove children from the mainstream must be developed to achieve goals associated with the prevention of learning and adjustment problems (Will, 1986), and a variety of such potential changes will be considered later in this chapter.

Research on Schools and Schooling

During the past 10 to 20 years there has been an explosion in educational research with significant implications for educators, psychologists, and the lay public, including those interested in primary prevention. A consistent conclusion from this research is that a variety of factors in the learning environment can have a substantial impact on students' achievement. This research is summarized below in relation to three topics: academic engaged time, direct instruction, and the environmental context for learning.

Academic Engaged Time. Academic engaged time refers to the amount of time a student spends actively involved in academic learning tasks. Recent research on this topic has been stimulated by the notion that students in school may spend too much time in nonacademic activities thus losing significant opportunities for learning. Despite the intuitive appeal of this concept and consistent evidence that academic engaged time of students relates positively to learning (Graden, Thurlow, & Ysseldyke, 1982; Rosenshine & Berliner, 1978), many students spend surprisingly little school time actively engaged in academic tasks (e.g., Graden, Thurlow, & Ysseldyke, 1982, 1983).

For example, Graden et al. (1983) found that of the 6 hour and 30 minute elementary school day, students spent about 3 hours and 30 minutes in class, with about 30 minutes of class time allocated to nonacademic activities. The remaining 3 hours (182 minutes) were allocated to academic activities (Reading = 63 minutes, Math = 43 minutes, Language = 28 minutes, Social Studies = 18 minutes, Science = 11 minutes, Spelling = 10 minutes, Handwriting = 9 minutes). Although 182 minutes were allocated to this academic instruction, children actually spent considerably less time *actively* engaged in academic learning tasks—an average of only 47 minutes per day (Writing = 26 minutes, Reading = 11 minutes, Talk/Academic = 4 minutes, Read Aloud = 2 minutes, Academic Game = 2 minutes, Answer/Academic = 1 minute, Ask/Academic = 1 minute). The remaining 135 minutes per day were spent in activities such as searching for materials, waiting for instructions and a variety of inappropriate behaviors. Given these data, it is difficult to imagine how children learn to read in school, particularly given that the average child may spend only 13 minutes per day reading aloud or silently. The implications for primary prevention are obvious. If schools increased the amount of time students spend engaged in academic tasks they would have the potential to promote more effective learning and to prevent the development of learning problems.

While the concept of academic engaged time is important, an over-reliance on this variable can result in an oversimplified view of the teacher as a time-manager (e.g., Allington et al., 1986). An effective teacher must be much more, and therefore, in addition to considering academic engaged time, it is equally important to consider the academic task (Doyle, 1983). The data reported by Graden et al. (1983) provide some insight into the typical tasks provided in public schools: 57% of the time allocated to classroom activities was focused on Readers, Worksheets and Workbooks, while only 6% was allocated to Discussion. This suggests an approach to education based on a passive view of the learner, whose task is to get the correct answer without working actively to develop alternative ways of thinking about the subject.

The difficulty level of curriculum materials is also important since they must be at the appropriate level for each child. Further, the materials selected must be congruent with the teacher's learning goals (Rosenfield, 1988).

Direct Instruction. Direct instruction focuses on procedures designed to provide clear academic goals, to monitor student performance, to use questions that are easy enough to ensure a high percent of correct responses, to provide immediate feedback to students concerning their academic performance, to provide structure imposed by the teacher, and to provide management strategies designed to facilitate academic engaged time (e.g., Becker & Carnine, 1981; Rosenshine & Berliner, 1978). Research on this model is related generally to the growing body of teacher effectiveness literature which has found that the above procedures produce positive educational outcomes (e.g., Anderson, Evertson, & Brophy, 1979; Becker & Carnine, 1981; Good & Beckerman, 1978).

Environmental Context for Learning. The environmental context for learning is particularly important in determining educational effectiveness. Barr and Dreeben (1983) and Slavin (1987) have documented that the levels of school organization as well as social organization of classroom instruction can have powerful effects that modify the relationships between various educational variables and learning outcome. Their work suggests, for example, that factors such as scheduling and grouping procedures, the use of cooperative learning groups, relationships between regular and special education teachers, and the principal's attitudes toward children with learning and/or adjustment problems may have important effects on various educational interventions. Although Barr and Dreeben (1983) and Slavin (1987) may be focused more on the specific details of schools, these findings are similar to work in the prevention literature that has demonstrated that environmental factors have an important effect on organizational efficacy (e.g., Barker & Gump, 1964; Moos, 1979) and that effective preventive interventions can be developed to modify organizational climate (e.g., Felner & Felner, this book).

Goals and Values in Education

Many people would support a broad role for schools and would assert that they are designed to prepare children and youth for living within and contributing to the well-being of the community. Yet, the reality of most schools is much more restrictive as the primary goal is to facilitate the educational and intellectual development of children.

For example, when Ed Zigler was Director of the Office of Child Development, he "learned that it was inadequate to state that children should be fed because they are hungry. He learned to say instead that children should be fed in order to facilitate learning" (reported in Alpert, p. 1115).

Another primary characteristic of schools is that their boundaries are relatively closed to external input and that they are resistant to change (e.g., Sarason, 1971). This is a particular problem in the context of prevention since schools are likely to resist efforts to develop innovative preventive education programs (Meyers & Parsons, 1987). Further, as Sarason (1971) has documented so cogently, the politics of schools can lead to miscommunication between innovators and educators when each interprets the innovation as meeting their own needs without thinking clearly about the other's perspective. Too often there is a rush towards acceptance of a proposed innovation without the careful planning necessary for success, and teachers often are not consulted during program development, even though they are frequently the personnel crucial to implementation. When innovative programs are imposed on teachers, this exacerbates the natural resistance to change within the educational system. Therefore, even when teachers correctly implement mandated procedures during research or program implementation, they rarely continue implementation after the project's conclusion (Meyers & Parsons, 1987).

Implications of the Prevention Literature for Educational Settings

A variety of ideas from the prevention literature have potential implications for education. Two of the most frequently discussed approaches to primary prevention are particularly important in this context and these include approaches to build competence and those designed to modify the environment. Not only have these approaches been discussed extensively in the general prevention literature (e.g., Albee, 1982; Cowen, 1983, 1985), but they have been discussed explicitly in terms of their applications to school settings (i.e., Alpert, 1985; Clarizio, 1979; Meyers & Parsons, 1987; and throughout this volume). A third major approach described by Alpert (1985) involves community based prevention efforts. She described ways in which the school can serve as a center for the family, school, and community as they work together to promote primary prevention. She suggested, for example, that the school could serve as an Information and Referral Registry for the community (Zigler, Kagan, & Muenchow, 1982), and as a resource to provide a variety of innovative programs for parents and pre-parents (e.g., Alpert, 1985; Alpert, Richardson, & Fodaski, 1983). One idea with equally important implications for schools, empowerment (i.e., Rappaport, 1981), has been discussed less extensively in relation to schools, and its implications are considered in more detail in this section.

Empowerment and Prevention in Schools

Rappaport (1981) argued that an empowerment model may be more comprehensive and powerful than other models of primary prevention. He suggested that primary prevention derives from a needs-based model in which people are viewed as dependent, and society is responsibile for meeting the needs of these people. While prevention is viewed as potentially efficient, since it can prevent these needs from occurring, it does not encompass advocacy which is a rights-based, rather than a needs-based, model of social services. As Rappaport (1981) indicated, advocacy derives from a legalistic and due process view of people as citizens. A model that views people as citizens with rights has very different implications than traditional preventive models that view people as depending on society to meet their needs. Rappaport (1981) stated that both models are incomplete, and he argued that a social change theory based on empowerment is more comprehensive because it is based simultaneously on a model that considers both the needs and rights of people.

> Empowerment implies that many competencies are already present or at least possible. . . . Prevention implies experts fixing the independent variables to make the dependent variables come out right. Empowerment implies that what you see as poor functioning is a result of social structure and lack of resources that make it impossible for the existing competencies to operate. It implies that in those cases where new competencies need to be learned, they are best learned in a context of living life rather than in artificial programs where everyone, including the person learning, knows that it is really the expert who is in charge. . . . (Rappaport, 1981, p. 16).

Empowerment suggests that people be given the opportunity to control their own lives, and this is substantially different from preventive philosophy which suggests that the professional solve the problem before it occurs. This implies a dramatic restructuring of the relationship between professionals and those they serve so that the values of the community (and the clients), rather than those of professionals, dictate professional intervention (Alpert, 1985). As Rappaport (1981) has documented, a variety of social science research suggests that control over one's own life can be a potent variable, and this includes research on: locus of control, learned helplessness, ascribed versus achieved status, attributions, the impact of perceived labels, beliefs about powerful others, group cohesiveness, self-help groups and other community organizations. Moreover, empowerment is a theoretical perspective that is dramatically different from the theories about learning and education that are dominant in most schools. A serious consideration of this framework by schools would result in dramatically different approaches to education with significant preventive implications.

The theoretical perspective dominant today views education as a top-down process. Much like the needs-based theory underlying primary prevention, schools view students (and their parents) as children with needs that are determined by the school. The school also determines the best approaches to meet these needs. The direct instruction model reviewed earlier, is an example of an instructional approach that has received considerable recent attention and that provides structured procedures imposed by the teacher, rather than using student input. The result is an educational technology in which the student is treated as a passive recipient, rather than an active participant who exercises control in learning. In contrast, one educational example that illustrates the potential preventive implications of empowerment theory for educational technology is the Instructional Leadership Project (P. Sunshine, personal communication, May 15, 1986).

Instructional Leadership Project. The Maryland State Department of Education has developed and implemented an innovative approach for schools in their efforts to deal with disruptive youth. I became familiar with this program when serving as a consultant to it in 1982 and 1983. The premise of the project was that rather than responding to disruptive behavior primarily with a variety of behavior management strategies, a more effective procedure would be for the schools to develop approaches to curriculum and instruction that would be more effective at involving students and holding their interest. This meant that it was important to gather information from students to help determine the direction for developing the educational program. This was done by obtaining student perceptions of school climate. In addition, it was assumed that the most effective way to accomplish the needed changes was by ensuring the active involvement of the teaching staff.

The active participation of the teaching staff required a shift from the top-down hierarchical leadership patterns found in most secondary schools, towards more collaborative approaches. Training in collaborative leadership techniques was provided to the administrators associated with the target schools. Secondary schools were selected since the problems with disruptive student behavior were most extreme in these settings, and the administrators involved in this training included principals, assistant principals and all chairs of academic departments (e.g., English, math, science, etc.). As a follow-up to this training, the State Department provided each participating school with a consulting professional to help the administrators implement this new collaborative approach to leadership. This added support was particularly important for department chairs who were asked to change their role dramatically. The majority of departmental chairs involved in this project had previously viewed their roles as primarily clerical. Now they were asked to exercise educational leadership. The collaborative approach to leadership was implemented initially by asking the teaching staff at each school to help determine staff development activities, rather than having in-service programs imposed on them. This led to active involvement in many other aspects of school functioning and decision-making throughout the school year including decisions about the agenda for staff meetings, curriculum development, disciplinary policy, community relations, etc.

This project resulted in positive changes in the school climate of the participating schools, as well as in a substantial reduction in discipline problems. Moreover, there were improvements in curriculum and instruction in an effort to facilitate academic and cognitive gains as well. It was concluded that the success of this project was due to the participating schools' ability to change their approach to school leadership so that both teaching staff and students became more actively involved in a variety of instructional decisions. Because top-down school management procedures were replaced with collaborative approaches, students and teachers gained a sense of empowerment that facilitated students' decisions to attend school more regularly, to behave less disruptively in school, and to attend to the instructional process more seriously and consistently. The results of this project are consistent with much of the work in the prevention literature that suggests that ecological change can be a powerful way to prevent the development of psychopathology (e.g., Meyers & Parsons, 1987; Moos, 1979), and one reason for this outcome may be the sense of empowerment that was facilitated for both students and staff.

Pragmatic Approaches to Implement Prevention in Schools

The literature is filled with a range of innovative and promising primary prevention programs and as noted earlier in this chapter most of these programs can be conceptualized as either an approach to competence enhancement or environmental modification. For example, competence enhancement programs include approaches to train interpersonal cognitive problem-solving skills (e.g., Elias et al., 1986; Shure & Spivack, 1982; Weissberg et al., 1981), to help children cope with divorce (e.g., Stolberg & Garrison, 1985), and to provide cognitive stimulation through early education programs (e.g., Johnson & Breckenridge, 1982; Lazar, Darlington & Associates, 1982). Environmental modification programs include approaches designed to increase social support for students entering elementary school, junior high (Bower, 1964), and high school (Felner, Ginter, & Primavera, 1982), to facilitate cooperative social interaction (Johnson & Johnson, 1980; Wright & Cowen, 1985), and to modify school and class climate (Moos, 1979). (See the earlier example in this chapter concerning the Instructional Leadership project.) Research on these programs is important as it helps to document the potential effect of various approaches to primary prevention. However, a primary reliance on such programs may ignore some important realities of the schools and may contribute to the resistance to primary prevention in schools.

The future of primary prevention in schools is dependent upon the development of pragmatic approaches that may overcome resistance and that have a realistic chance of being implemented and institutionalized as a routine component of school practice. While some of these approaches have been widely disseminated, many have not been considered sufficiently in the literature on primary prevention. These include: (a) moving from secondary prevention to primary prevention; (b) mental health consultation as a model for service delivery in schools; (c) special and remedial education services as primary prevention; (d) new models of assessment; and (e) modifying the school routine to promote primary prevention. more effective procedure would be for the schools to develop approaches to curriculum and instruction that would be more effective at involving students and holding their interest. This meant that it was important to gather information from students to help determine the direction for developing the educational program. This was done by obtaining student perceptions of school climate. In addition, it was assumed that the most effective way to accomplish the needed changes was by ensuring the active involvement of the teaching staff.

From Secondary to Primary Prevention

Jason and Ferone (1981) indicated that one potentially effective strategy to implement primary prevention is to establish effective secondary prevention programs first, and follow these with primary prevention efforts. This can be effective since secondary prevention may be accepted more readily by schools. This viewpoint has received support elsewhere (Meyers & Parsons, 1987), and a variety of commonly used approaches to secondary prevention are mentioned briefly below.

Emory Cowen's (1980) primary mental health project developed in the Rochester schools is an excellent example of a secondary prevention program. It uses screening to identify children showing early signs of emotional difficulty who are at risk of developing more serious problems, and it trains paraprofessionals to provide preventive treatment to children identified as at risk. A long term evaluation in a variety of school settings across the country has begun to establish the generalized efficacy of its specific procedures (Cowen, 1980; Cowen, Gesten, & Wilson, 1979; Cowen et al., 1983), and this project has and continues to have important effects on the delivery of psychological services in the schools. Other approaches to secondary prevention include comprehensive approaches to screening, assessment, and intervention concerning a variety of school learning and adjustment problems (Barclay, 1983), and learning problems (Hagin, 1980). Mental health consultation is also a commonly used procedure that is viewed by some as being consistent with secondary prevention (Jason & Ferone, 1981).

Initiating prevention efforts with secondary prevention is a useful guideline, but it would be a mistake to adhere to it too rigidly, since the key is to be sure to meet the perceived needs of the system. There are certainly many situations where a system perceives a need for secondary rather than primary prevention. There may be others, however, where the need for primary prevention is expressed from the outset. In the investigation by Jason and Ferone (1981), a survey was administered to the school staff asking their perceptions of the value of various mental health services without focusing on particular school problems. Although these educators reported a preference for secondary prevention services, a different pattern of responses might have been obtained if different questions had been asked. For example, if educators were asked their opinions about approaches to serious school problems (e.g., disruptive youth, drug abuse, school drop outs, etc.), the responses might have been more favorable to primary prevention. This has often been true of needs assessments conducted by practicing school psychologists and other professionals in schools (e.g., Lennox, Flanagan, & Meyers, 1979; Parsons & Meyers, 1984).

Mental Health Consultation

It has always surprised me that mental health consultation is not seen more often as a major approach to primary prevention. Perhaps one reason for this is that those techniques associated with what Caplan (1970) described as client-centered consultation are focused on secondary prevention. There are, however, a variety of approaches to mental health consultation focused on the teacher, the classroom, and the school system that have clear implications for primary prevention. Furthermore, mental health consultation is an approach to service delivery that is relatively well-accepted in schools (e.g., Curtis & Meyers, 1985), providing a unique opportunity to promote primary prevention through an ongoing component of the school routine in many settings.

The goal of consultation is to help the educator solve a current work problem and to respond more effectively to similar problems in the future. It is a problem-solving process that occurs between a help-giver (the consultant) and a help-seeker or consultee who has responsibility for another person (i.e., a student). Mental health consultation in the schools typically involves an educator as the consultee, and many school personnel have assumed the role of consultant, for example, school psychologists (e.g., Curtis & Meyers, 1985), special education teachers (Idol, Paolucci-Whitcomb, & Nevin, 1986) speech and language pathologists (e.g., Frasinelli, Superior, & Meyers, 1983), counselors (e.g., Dinkmeyer & Carlson, 1973), and others (e.g., Meyers et al., 1979). School consultation procedures have been described in some detail (e.g., Alpert & Meyers, 1983; Bergan, 1977; Brown, Pryzwansky, & Schulte, 1987; Conoley, 1981; Curtis & Meyers, 1985; Gutkin & Curtis, 1982; Meyers et al., 1979; Parsons & Meyers, 1984), and considerable recent research evaluating the process and outcome of consultation supports the relative efficacy of this approach (e.g., Alpert & Yammer, 1983; Curtis & Meyers, 1985, Mannino & Shore, 1975; 1983; Medway, 1979; 1982; Meyers et al., 1979).

Consistent with empowerment theory, collaborative methods of interaction are most likely to result in successful consultation (Curtis & Meyers, 1985), and certain preventive outcomes of consultation have been reported. Consultation can result in improved professional skills for teachers (Gutkin, 1980; Zins, 1981); more accurate teacher attitudes regarding the severity of children's problems (Gutkin, Singer, & Brown, 1980); improved teacher information and understanding of children's problems (Curtis & Watson, 1980); improved teacher ability to provide concrete behavioral descriptions (Curtis & Watson, 1980); benefits to non-target children in the same classroom (Jason & Ferone, 1978; Meyers, 1975); and reduction in special education referrals and placements (Graden, Casey, & Bonstrom, 1985; Ritter, 1978).

Consultation services can be focused at three distinct levels: (a) the child (i.e., Level I), (b) the teacher or classroom (i.e., Level II), and (c) the school as a system (i.e., Level III) (e.g., see Curtis & Meyers, 1985; Meyers et al., 1979). Traditional models have emphasized secondary prevention by focusing the attention of professionals on the first level (i.e., the child), while providing less attention to the potential for primary prevention afforded by the classroom and the school. Mental health consultation is a model that is especially pragmatic in its potential to facilitate primary prevention, because it can emphasize both the classroom and the school (i.e., Levels II & III). This is appealing since consultation has been proposed as an important basis for service delivery by various school professionals, including school psychologists, as noted above.

Case Example of the Consultation Model. The following example (see Meyers & Pitt, 1976) illustrates the consultation model and shows how this model can be used to facilitate primary prevention even when specific clients have been referred. In this example, a school psychologist was consulting to a parochial school containing kindergarten through eighth grade. This school was located in a small-town parish located near a large city. It included 14 classroom teachers, 3 supplementary teachers, and 422 students in addition to the psychologist who worked there one day per week. Many students had one or more siblings at the school and the parish had a stable population of families who had attended the same church for years. The members of this parish knew each other well.

The initial consultation contract had been negotiated informally with the school principal. Level I consultation (child-centered consultation) was the only approach to consultation sanctioned by the prinicpal, and it was understood that the consultant's primary activity would be to assist teachers with problems in classroom management in an effort to support the goal of secondary prevention.

During one school vacation a sixth grade boy died a tragic accidental death. The school sent condolences to the family, but made no official response within the school. As a result teachers were uncertain how to handle the situation, and discussion with students was frequently avoided. Within a month, a seventh grade boy was injured fatally in a car accident.

In the period immediately following the deaths several new problem behaviors were observed. (1) There was an increase in the number of children sent to the principal or referred to the consultant as discipline problems, and it was reported that acting out, lying, and other disruptive behavior had increased. Further, several efforts to consult with teachers about reducing their discipline problems (i.e., Level I consultation) were unsuccessful, and these problems just mounted. (2) There was a series of bomb scares at the school with at least some connection to the deaths. The boy responsible for one bomb scare was caught, he had been a friend of one of the deceased children and had perpetrated the bomb scare as a result of his confused feelings about his friend. The consultant recommended counseling for the boy and a sensitive supportive approach by the teacher (Level I consultation), but these recommendations were rejected initially. The principal indicated that the child should be expelled from school, and the teacher reported that he could not be supportive and reinforce such negative behavior. (3) There were superstitious rumors and fantasies among the students. The kindergarten teacher reported to the consultant that her students had "seen" parts of the boys' bodies in the dark church basement, and a variety of people in the community believed that since evil occurs in threes a third child would die. According to this rumor, the third child was expected to be an eighth grader named Mary (following the sixth grader named Chris and the seventh grader named Joseph). There were two eighth grade girls named Mary. At this point, the consultant arranged a meeting with the principal.

In this meeting the consultant pointed out the effects the deaths were having on the children's behavior in school. The consultant pointed out, further, that as a result of this systemic problem, his most recent efforts (i.e., Level I consultation) had been unsuccessful. In other words, it was suggested that the crisis over the deaths interfered with his ability to help the teachers with classroom management. In effect, the consultant "renegotiated" the consultation contract so that Level III consultation (system-centered consultation) could be used to help the school deal more effectively with the bereavement process, an approach to primary prevention.

It was agreed that a teacher workshop on this topic would be an effective way to help the school cope with this crisis (Level III consultation). Two goals were set for the workshop: (a) to help the teachers understand that the increase in disturbing behaviors might be part of the bereavement process; and (b) to help the teachers encourage students to express their feelings about death and related issues. Following this Level III consultation, the system was more effective in dealing with the process of bereavement. Several teachers indicated their positive experiences discussing feelings about death with their classes, and there was a decrease in discipline problems.

As noted earlier, this organizational problem (the crisis regarding bereavement) had interfered with effective consultation using Level I (i.e., the bomb scare student, and the classroom management problems). Subsequent to the workshop those teachers who referred disruptive children were able to concentrate on the recommendations and consultation returned to its previous level of effectiveness. Similarly, the Level I consultation regarding the youngster who had made the bomb scares now reached a successful conclusion. Soon after the bereavement workshop the principal volunteered her revised opinion that the youngster should be maintained in the school, and the teacher agreed that perhaps he could provide the needed supportive relationship for this youngster.

Another significant change began to occur after the organizational consultation. Teachers began to bring their own professional problems to the consultant (i.e., Level II consultation) rather than being limited to discussions of specific student cases. As a result, the consultant met with the principal and indicated this general trend without revealing teacher names. At this point the principal was able to envision the potential value of the consultant responding to these teachers' needs, and she willingly sanctioned Level II consultation (i.e., teacher-centered consultation). This example illustrates how consultation can be used to initiate services at the level of secondary (and tertiary) prevention prior to gaining acceptance for primary prevention provided through teacher-centered and system-centered consultation.

Mainstreaming, Teacher Consultation and Primary Prevention

While some authors suggest that mainstreaming may have negative effects due to resultant rejection and social isolation of handicapped children in the regular class, there is a considerable body of contrary evidence demonstrating that mildly handicapped children can be taught effectively in mainstream classes (e.g., see Bogdan, 1983; Johnson & Johnson, 1980, 1981; Knowles, Auferheide, & McKenzie, 1982; Leinhardt & Pallay, 1982; Madden & Slavin, 1983; Slavin, 1984; Wang, 1981; Wang, Peverly, & Randolph, 1984). These approaches can have implications for the primary prevention of learning and adjustment problems.

Most prior mainstreaming research has investigated approaches in which children labeled as handicapped spend part of their day in a segregated special education setting and the remainder of the day in a regular education setting. Although generally supportive of mainstreaming, this research has certain limitations in terms of prevention because placement in the regular class is limited, and because there is no systematic effort to provide consultative support to the regular class teacher who must work with the difficult child. Approaches to full time mainstreaming are more appealing in terms of their long term implications for prevention.

One line of research on full time mainstreaming has been initiated by Slavin (1984), whose most recent work combines the use of cooperative learning models with individualized instruction in the regular classroom using an approach he describes as Team Assisted Instruction. This approach has the potential for primary prevention of both learning and adjustment problems because it provides social support through cooperative learning, and it seeks to meet the academic needs of all children in the regular class through individualized instruction. The goals of primary prevention are met by offering these services to all children in the regular class, rather than restricting them to handicapped children in a restrictive setting. Despite some research design problems, Slavin found the Team Assisted Instruction model had significant positive effects on both the achievement and attitudes of the mildly handicapped children as well as the other children in these classrooms.

Margaret Wang's work (e.g., Wang & Birch, 1984; Wang et al., 1984) has provided another useful model. Wang et al. (1984) investigated the effects of the Adaptive Learning Environments Model (ALEM) which is used to provide individualized instruction to mildly handicapped children who are mainstreamed full-time. This investigation included all of the teachers with mainstreamed children from five schools (a total of 26 teachers). A careful evaluation revealed that teachers, in fact, implemented the program to a significant degree and that degree of implementation related to measures of classroom process, student achievement and student attitudes for both handicapped and nonhandicapped. Similar to the results of Slavin's research, these positive effects for nonhandicapped children are promising in terms of their preventive potential. While the ALEM model was described as including consultation between the special and regular class teacher, no details were reported regarding the process of implementing consultation or its relative efficacy; similarly, Slavin (1984) did not document the consultative components of his program. There is, however, a substantial body of research that documents consultation procedures in special education which have implications for primary prevention.

With the advent of Public Law 94–142, many children with special educational needs have been assigned to mainstream classrooms. In this context, consultation is of potentially greater value as a method of service delivery, particularly as an approach to be used by resource room or remedial teachers (e.g., Evans, 1980). Several consulting teacher models have been proposed including the resource room teacher as consultant (e.g., Evans, 1980), the school consultation committee (e.g., McGlothlin, 1981), the teacher-assistance team model (Chalfant, Pysh, & Moultrie, 1979), the prereferral intervention system (Graden, Casey, & Bonstrom, 1985) and the consulting teacher model (e.g., Knight, Meyers, Paolucci-Whitcomb, Hasazi, & Nevin, 1981). The Vermont consulting teacher program is an excellent example because it has been implemented over an extended period of time with encouraging results (see Egner & Lates, 1975; Knight et al., 1981; McKenzie, 1972).

Moreover, when integrated with models of full-time mainstreaming, ongoing consultation to the regular class teacher provides opportunities to prevent the development of learning and adjustment problems in non-handicapped children in the classroom.

New Models of Assessment

A substantial impediment to primary prevention is that psychologists tend to maintain a view of behavior that focuses on the individual and ignores relevant systemic factors. For example, most psychological reports rely primarily on constructs attributed to the child (i.e., ability, personality, behavior, etc.), while ignoring systemic factors such as the curriculum and the instructional process. Since psychoeducational assessment is a primary component of the role of psychologists in schools, one potentially powerful way to facilitate primary prevention is to shift to a model of assessment that emphasizes the contributions of the environment rather than the child's characteristics. The use of such models will redirect the way psychologists and educators think about children, particularly in schools where tests seem to determine the curriculum, the approach to instruction, and even our views of the causes of behavior (Meyers, 1988b).

Consider, for example, traditional norm-referenced assessment instruments such as standardized intelligence tests. It has been noted that the purposes of these tests is to compare people, to predict educational performance, and to assist in placement decisions. These tests do not lead to instructional or behavioral prescriptions, and in fact, the only prescriptive outcome of such assessment is to sort students into various educational groups based on uniform conceptions of ability, academic learning and instruction. This is consistent with a medical model view of disability, and in contrast to social construction models, this approach does not lead to instructional and/or curricular procedures to modify the child's behavior. Rather than leading to the prevention of learning and adjustment problems, this traditional norm-referenced approach may even promote disability (Gelzheiser, 1987).

It is not the norms per se that present the primary problems associated with norm referenced measures, but rather, it is the assumption that the test measures qualities that are not influenced by the environment, or the assumption that the environment has been equivalent for all students. If there were different assumptions about the environment, then assessment would be designed to answer questions about the match between the child's learning styles and relevant instructional environments. This orientation could lead to preventive interventions with the potential to prevent the development of learning and adjustment problems. Moreover, the use of assessment models and instruments to answer questions related to intervention will encourage individuals involved in education to develop a conception of behavior that suggests that learning and adjustment problems are, indeed, preventable. This attitudinal shift could have a major influence in facilitating the acceptance and implementation of preventive programs in educational settings.

One such model has been proposed, and it focuses on the characteristics of the child, the task, the setting and the interactions between these three factors (Meyers, Pfeffer, & Erlbaum, 1985). This model is referred to as process assessment and is based on a conceptual framework and assessment techniques that emphasize the link between assessment and the environment, the link between assessment and intervention, and the process of learning. By emphasizing the interactions between these factors, process assessment views behavior as dependent on the environment and as modifiable, depending on the match between the individual's characteristics and those of the setting. It is also a model that views education as a process in which the learner must be an active participant rather than a passive recipient, and it supports the contention that a variety of environmental interventions can help to prevent the development of learning and adjustment problems (Meyers, 1988a).

Process assessment uses assessment techniques that raise questions about the child's learning process (i.e., Meyers, 1988a), and since these types of assessment procedures have implications for curriculum and the instructional process, they have implications for the prevention of learning and adjustment problems as well. Methods for the direct assessment of family process have been suggested also as an appropriate component of process assessment (e.g., Meyers, et al., 1985) since the family is an important environmental factor. Methods that answer questions about communication, decision making, power structure, and interaction within the family have immediate preventive implications suggesting that these factors may be an important part of the learning and adjustment of all children. Similarly, a variety of assessment instruments have been proposed to measure the social-cognitive skills discussed within the Interpersonal Cognitive Problem Solving Model (Shure & Spivack, 1978), and these methods have been proposed as appropriate tools for the process assessment model (Meyers & Lytle, 1986). The Preschool Interpersonal Problem Solving Test assesses children's ability to generate alternative solutions to social problems (Shure & Spivack, 1978), the What Happens Next Game assesses the child's ability to conceptualize the consequences of different interpersonal behaviors (Shure & Spivack, 1978), and the Means Ends Problem Solving Procedure measures the individual's ability to orient him- or herself to a goal and to conceptualize the means for moving towards that goal (Spivack, Shure, & Platt, 1981). By using assessment instruments that examine these social skills, preventive educational implications arise regarding the importance of these skills for all children. By using process assessment models and instruments, psychoeducational diagnosticians will stimulate the use of preventive, educational interventions by a variety of educators.

Modifying the School Routine to Promote Primary Prevention

There are a variety of pragmatic approaches designed to modify the school routine that are particularly relevant because they can be implemented readily by the regular classroom teacher, rather than requiring mental health specialists to implement prevention in schools. These include modifications of curriculum and instruction, and the use of the classroom to build resistance to stress. As teachers take an active role in primary prevention it will have a greater potential for long lasting effects.

Modifying the curriculum to promote primary prevention. Sylvia Ashton-Warner's (1963) book *Teacher* is an excellent example of an approach to promote primary prevention (as well as good education) through modifications in the school curriculum. She described her experiences as a teacher of 5-year old Maori and white children in a provincial New Zealand school. Her initial educational efforts with this population were frustrated due to the inappropriateness of the traditional curriculum materials that focused on a vocabulary that was not relevant to the children's life experience. These students saw school as irrelevant and maintained a passive stance that minimized their opportunities for growth and development, as well as academic learning. Ashton-Warner's educational success with this population began when she abandoned the traditional curriculum and worked with the children to develop a set of relevant vocabulary that became the basis for her new curriculum. Children were reported to bring in words that traditionally would have been excluded from the curriculum as they touched on some of the taboo subjects of their daily lives such as violence and sex. The children became more actively involved in the educational process resulting in more effective learning, and it can be argued that this prevented future learning problems. In addition, by developing a curriculum with substantial emotional meaning to these children, there was an opportunity to work preventively on social and emotional issues, and this may have helped to prevent some adjustment problems.

Today's schools, as well, might benefit from substantial changes in curriculum. Unfortunately, the curriculum is controlled, too often, by text book companies rather than by educators at the local level. Education might work more efficiently and promote preventive goals if there were more variability in curricula across schools so that the curriculum was designed to meet the needs of the specific children with whom it is used. In addition to Ashton-Warner's (1963) principle of developing curriculum materials from the child's own experience, a variety of additional principles might be considered in modifying the curriculum, and examples are provided below.

Reading, writing, language development and even social and emotional development as well as a variety of other educational factors might receive more effective attention by using literature as the basis for the curriculum, rather than being limited to texts from reading series. This would provide more challenging reading material, which is likely to be inherently more interesting, and which may focus on a variety of cognitive, social and emotional themes for children, resulting in more active involvement in learning. In addition this could avoid some of the inherent problems with reading series that have some of the same negative effects as standardized tests. Since reading series present material on a continuum from pre-primer levels to more advanced grade levels, the placement of a student in one book from the series provides the child with a label as either a good reader or a poor reader. Anyone who has worked in an elementary school classroom knows that children are keenly aware of the labeling effects associated with particular books in the series.

Curriculum materials can be developed to facilitate the youngster's active involvement in learning by stressing metacognitive theory and the cognitive strategies children use in a variety of academic, cognitive and even social problem solving situations. Curriculum materials as well as instructional activities can be built around this assumption (e.g., Meyers, 1988a). This concept can be applied to instruction in math where children's problem solving strategies and the use of logic are particularly important to successful performance, to science where the scientific method represents a problem solving sequence that is similar to the strategic behavior invoked in a variety of problem solving situations and to reading where strategic behaviors can facilitate comprehension (Meyers, 1988a; Meyers & Lytle, 1986). Consistent with this orientation, social problem solving can be conceptualized from a cognitive perspective viewing social problem solving skills as cognitive skills that can be taught (e.g., Shure & Spivack, 1982). This orientation has led to the development of a variety of curricular materials, commonly cited in the prevention literature, that can be used in school settings to teach interpersonal cognitive problem solving skills (e.g., Shure & Spivack, 1982).

Modifying instruction to promote primary prevention. The discussion about curriculum modification has clear implications for instruction as well, as was illustrated in the discussion of Ashton-Warner's (1963) work. The ideas underlying the development of alternative curriculum materials have implications for alternative instructional procedures which in both instances are based on the goal of increasing the learner's active involvement. Another excellent example is Shure and Spivack's (1982) Interpersonal Cognitive Problem Solving Skills.

Despite a variety of positive findings (e.g., Elias et al., 1986; Shure & Spivack, 1982; Weissberg et al., 1981), Durlak's (1983) review raised substantial questions about the efficacy of various approaches to social skills traning. It has been suggested that the positive effects of social skills training programs may require environmental support for the learning that occurs during formal instruction (Gesten & Jason, 1987). This is consistent with Trickett's (1984) view that the field of social skills training (along with the more general field of primary prevention) has not taken into account the potential significance of ecological factors (see Trickett & Birman, in this volume). Shure and Spivack (1978; 1982) have developed an approach referred to as dialoguing that is responsive to at least some of these ecological questions. In addition to providing instruction based on the curriculum materials that have been developed, dialoguing considers the learning environment by providing an approach to child management for the teacher and/or parent to supplement formal cognitive training. The teacher (or parent) uses instances of problem behavior, where interpersonal-cognitive skills are not used effectively, as opportunities to reinforce those concepts discussed in the curriculum and as an opportunities to try out relevant skills from curriculum. Thus, for example, dialoguing helps the child to identify the problem that occurred, to conceptualize a variety of alternative responses that could have been attempted, to conceptualize the potential consequences of these alternatives and to try out at least one of the alternatives, rather than focusing attention on blame and punishment. This provides greater opportunity for learning that extends beyond the classroom situation to real life, and for the primary prevention of adjustment problems in the long run.

Using the school routine to build strens.[1] William Hollister coined the term *strens* to suggest that competence in reacting to stress can be built by providing successful exposure to minor stressful experiences (Phillips, Martin, & Meyers, 1972). The term *strens* was used to signify the individual's strength in dealing with stress, and it is related to Janis' (1958) conception of psychological innoculation. Approaches to the development of strens in school children that can be implemented effectively by teachers have been discussed elsewhere (Meyers & Parsons, 1987).

For example, Meyers and Parsons (1987) have described four developmental crises as having particular significance in school settings: school entrance, school achievement pressure, transition from elementary to secondary school, and the transition toward independence. In addition, the transition to high school has been described as a particularly important transition (Felner, Primavera, & Cauce, 1981).

School entrance incorporates a variety of opportunities for preventive education. This is one of the first opportunities for the child to learn to cope with separation, change in routine, and competition for success. The pressure for school achievement is heightened in the middle years of elementary school, often in fourth grade, as the demands for independent work and the sheer amount of homework and class work are increased dramatically. This is a point where achievement anxiety may be exacerbated or may appear for the first time, and the teacher has an opportunity to teach coping skills that may be particularly effective using a cognitive and/or cognitive-behavioral framework (e.g., Cavallaro & Meyers, 1986). Transition from elementary school to secondary school is particularly difficult. Not only are important physiological changes beginning to occur at this time, but social relations begin to change dramatically. Similar problems can be involved in the transition to high school (Felner, et al., 1981). Programs reported by Bower (1964) and Felner, et al. (1982) are promising approaches to facilitate the transition to junior and senior high school so that these transitions provide a maximum opportunity for growth and primary prevention. Finally, the transition toward independence must occur during the high school years since high school graduates must learn to function as independent adults in our society. This stage provides opportunities to teach coping skills for problems associated with drugs, sex, alcohol and social relations that have the potential for powerful preventive effects (Meyers & Parsons, 1987).

Conclusions

While many factors may be important in shaping effective prevention programs in schools, this chapter has stressed that preventionists must develop a thorough understanding of school culture and use this understanding as they implement prevention in schools. In particular, it may be important to recognize the teacher's difficult job and to work collaboratively with educators to formulate effective primary prevention for the schools. This requires that conferences considering the primary prevention of learning and adjustment problems in schools (e.g., the conferences supported by the Vermont Conferences on the Primary Prevention of Psychopathology) make a conscious effort to include a variety of educators as partners in planning and implementation. As a result, educators will learn more about the good ideas that preventionists have to offer to the field of education, and preventionists will learn more about the effective primary prevention activities that are ongoing in the schools but not necessarily referred to as *primary prevention*. If this sort of dialogue is not initiated, then we may unwittingly "prevent" the primary prevention of psychopathology in schools.

Serious efforts to work collaboratively with educators should be based, in part, on an awareness that teachers represent a potentially powerful and untapped resource for the primary prevention of learning and adjustment problems in schools. A collaborative framework suggests a deemphasis on externally developed programs implemented by outsiders, along with an emphasis on preventive techniques that are, or can be, embedded in the school routine. Prevention should be viewed as a part of education, rather than a separate appendage, and this may require serious attention to the preventive implications of various school resources that have not typically been thought of in terms of primary prevention (e.g., the discussions of consultation, assessment, secondary prevention, and special education presented in this chapter). Further, empowerment provides a pragmatic conceptual basis for preventive techniques that is perfectly compatible with this collaborative framework.

A final caution may be in order for those in the mental health fields interested in providing primary prevention in the schools. We should maintain a sense of humility and awareness of our lack of knowledge about how to make systems change. Rather than criticize schools, which are sometimes seen as "resistant to change," it may be more fruitful to devote professional energy to the development of theory and technology to facilitate systemic change. Furthermore, as Alpert (1985) has suggested, it may be most challenging and most productive to pursue this theory development by experimenting with our ideas about change in our own institutional settings.

Note

1. This section is derived from an earlier report (Meyers & Parsons, 1987).

References

Albee, G. W. (1982). Preventing psychopathology and promoting human potential. *American Psychologist, 37*, 1043–1050.

Allington, R., Stuetzel, H., Shake, M., & Lamarache, S. (1986). What is remedial reading? A descriptive study. *Reading Research and Instruction, 26*, 15–30.

Alpert, J. L. (1985). Change within a profession: Change, future, prevention, and school psychology. *American Psychologist, 40*, 1112–1121.

Alpert, J. L., & Meyers, J. (Eds.). (1983). *Training in consultation.* Springfield, IL: C. C. Thomas.

Alpert, J. L., Richardson, M. S., & Fodaski, L. (1983). Onset of parenting and stressful events. *Journal of Prevention, 3*, 149–159.

Alpert, J. L., & Yammer, M. D. (1983). Research in school consultation: A content analysis of selected journals. *Professional Psychology, 14*, 604–612.

Anderson, L., Evertson, C., & Brophy, J. (1979). An experimental study of effective teaching in first-grade reading groups. *Elementary School Journal, 79*, 193–223.

Ashton-Warner, S. (1963). *Teacher*. New York: Simon & Schuster.

Barclay, J. R. (1983). Moving toward a technology of prevention: A model and some tentative findings. *School Psychology Review, 12*, 228–239.

Bardon, J. I. (1983). Psychology applied to education: A specialty in search of an identity. *American Psychologist, 38*, 185–196.

Barker, R. G., & Gump, P. (1964). *Big school, small school*. Stanford, CA: Stanford University Press.

Barr, R., & Dreeben, R. (1983). *How schools work*. Chicago: University of Chicago Press.

Becker, W. C., & Carnine, D. W. (1981). Direct instruction: A behavior theory model for comprehensive educational intervention with the disadvantaged. In S. W. Bijou & R. Ruiz (Eds). *Behavior modification: Contributions to education* (pp. 145–210). Hillsdale, NJ: Lawrence Erlbaum Associates.

Bergan, J. R. (1977). *Behavioral consultation*. Columbus, OH: Merrill.

Bogdan, R. (1983). A closer look at mainstreaming. *The Educational Forum, 47*, 425–434.

Bower, E. M. (1964). The modification, mediation and utilization of stress during the school years. *American Journal of Orthopsychiatry, 34*, 667–674.

Brown, D., Pryzwansky, W. B., & Schulte, A. C. (1987). *Psychological consultation: Introduction to theory and practice*. Boston: Allyn & Bacon.

Caplan, G. (1970). *The theory and practice of mental health consultation*. New York: Basic.

Cavallaro, D. M., & Meyers, J. (1986). Effects of study habits on cognitive restructuring and study skills training in the treatment of test anxiety with adolescent females. *Techniques: Journal for Remedial Education and Counseling, 2*, 145–155.

Chalfant, J. C., Pysh, M. V., & Moultrie, R. (1979). Teacher assistance teams: A model for within-building problem solving. *Learning Disabilities Quarterly, 2*, 85–96.

Clarizio, H. F. (1979). Primary prevention of behavioral disorders in schools. *School Psychology Digest, 8*, 434–445. (Service No. ED 134–591).

Conoley, J. (Ed.). (1981). *Consultation in schools*. New York: Academic Press.

Cowen, E. L. (1980). The primary mental health project: Yesterday, today and tomorrow. *The Journal of Special Education, 14*, 133–154.

Cowen, E. L. (1983). Primary prevention in mental health: Past, present, and future. In R. D. Felner, L. A. Jason, J. N. Moritsugu, & S. S. Farber (Eds.) *Preventive psychology: Theory, research and practice* (pp. 11–30). New York: Pergamon.

Cowen, E. L. (1985). Person-centered approaches to primary prevention in mental health: Situation-focused and competence enhancement. *American Journal of Community Psychology, 13*, 31–48.

Cowen, E. L., Gesten, E. L., & Wilson, A. B. (1979). The primary mental health project (PMHP): Evaluation of current program effectiveness. *American Journal of Community Psychology, 7*, 293–303.

Cowen, E. L., Weissberg, R. P., Lotyczewski, B. S., Bromley, M. L., Gilliland-Mallo, G., DeMeis, J. L., Farago, J. P., Grassi, R. E., Haffey, W. G., Weiner, M. J., & Woods, A. (1983). Validity generalization of a school-based preventive mental health program. *Professional Psychology: Research and Practice, 14*, 613–623.

Curtis, M. J., & Meyers, J. (1985). Best practices in school-based consultation. In A. Thomas & J. Grimes (Eds.), *Best practices in school psychology* (pp. 74–94). Kent, OH: National Association of School Psychologists.

Curtis, M. J., & Watson, K. (1980). Changes in consultee problem clarification skills following consultation. *Journal of School Psychology, 18*, 210–221.

Dinkmeyer, D., & Carlson, J. (1973). *Consultation*. New York: Wiley.

Doyle, W. (1983). Academic work. *Review of Educational Research, 53*, 159–199.

Durlak, J. A. (1983). Social problem-solving as a primary prevention strategy. In R.

Felner, L. Jason, J. Moritsugu, & S. Farber (Eds.), *Preventive psychology: Theory, research and practice* (pp. 31–48). New York: Pergamon.

Egner, A. N., & Lates, B. J. (1975). The Vermont consulting teacher program: A case presentation. In C. Parker (Ed.), *Psychological consultation: Helping teachers meet special needs* (pp. 31–53). Reston, VA: Council for Exceptional Children.

Elias, M. J., Gara, M., Ubriaco, M., Rothbaum, P. A., Clabby, J. F., & Schuyler, T. (1986). Impact of a preventive social problem solving intervention on children's coping with middle-school stressors. *American Journal of Community Psychology, 14*, 259–276.

Evans, S. (1980). The consultant role of the resource teacher. *Exceptional Children, 46*, 402–404.

Felner, R. D., Ginter, M. A., & Primavera, J. (1982). Primary prevention during school transitions: Social support and environmental structure. *American Journal of Community Psychology, 10*, 277–290.

Felner, R. D., Primavera, J., & Cauce, A. M. (1981). The impact of school transitions: A focus for preventive effort. *American Journal of Community Psychology, 9*, 449–459.

Frasinelli, L., Superior, K., & Meyers, J. (1983). A consultation model for speech and language intervention. *ASHA, 25*, (11), 25–30.

Gelzheiser, L. M. (1987). Reducing the number of students identified as learning disabled: A question of practice, philosophy, or policy? *Exceptional Children, 54*, 145–150.

Gesten, E. L., & Jason, L. A. (1987). Social and community interventions. *Annual Review of Psychology, 38*, 427–460.

Goldwasser, E., Meyers, J., Christenson, S., & Graden, J. (1983). The impact of PL 94–142 on the practice of school psychology: A national survey. *Psychology in the Schools, 20*, 153–165.

Good, T. L., & Beckerman, T. M. (1978). Time on task: A naturalistic study in sixth grade classrooms. *Elementary School Journal, 78*, 192–201.

Graden, J., Casey, A., & Bonstrom, O. (1985). Implementing a prereferral intervention system: II. The data. *Exceptional Children, 51*, 487–496.

Graden, J., Thurlow, M., & Ysseldyke, J. (1982). *Academic engaged time and its relationship to learning: A review of the literature* (Monograph No. 17). Minneapolis: University of Minnesota, Institute for Research on Learning Disabilities.

Graden, J., Thurlow, M., & Ysseldyke, J. (1983). Instructional ecology and academic responding time for students at three levels of teacher perceived behavioral competence. *Journal of Experimental Child Psychology, 36*, 241–256.

Gutkin, T. B. (1980). Teacher perceptions of consultation services provided by school psychologists. *Professional Psychology, 11*, 637–642.

Gutkin, T. B., & Curtis, M. J. (1982). School-based consultation: Theory and techniques. In C. R. Reynolds & T. B. Gutkin (Eds.), *The handbook of school psychology*, (pp. 796–828). New York: John Wiley.

Gutkin, T. B., Singer, J. H., & Brown, R. (1980). Teacher reactions to school based consultation services: A multivariate analysis. *Journal of School Psychology, 18*, 126–134.

Hagin, R. A. (1980, September). *Prediction, prevention, presumption*. Division 16 distinguished service award address presented at the annual meetings of the American Psychological Association, Montreal.

Haynes, M. C., & Jenkins, J. R. (1986). Reading instruction in special education resource rooms. *American Educational Research Journal, 23*, 161–190.

Idol, L., Paolucci-Whitcomb, P., & Nevin, A. (1986). *Collaborative consultation*. Rockville, MD: Aspen Systems.

Janis, I. L. (1958). *Psychological stress*. New York: Wiley.

Jason, L. A., & Ferone, L. (1978). Behavioral versus process consultation interventions in school settings. *American Journal of Community Psychology, 6*, 531–543.

Jason, L. A., & Ferone, L. (1981). From early secondary to primary preventive interventions in schools. *Journal of Prevention, 1*, 156–173.

Johnson, D. L., & Breckenridge, J. N. (1982). The Houston Parent-Child Development Center and the primary prevention of behavioral problems in young children. *American Journal of Community Psychology, 10*, 305–316.

Johnson, D. W., & Johnson, R. (1980). Promoting constructive student-student relationships through cooperative learning. In M. R. Reynolds & R. Bentz (Eds.), *Extending the challenge: Working toward a common body of practice for teachers* (pp. 1–54). Minneapolis: University of Minnesota National Support Systems Project, University of Minnesota.

Johnson, R., & Johnson, D. W. (1981). Building friendships between handicapped and nonhandicapped students: Effects of cooperative and individualistic instruction. *American Educational Research Journal, 18*, 415–424.

Johnston, P., Allington, R., & Afflerbach, P. (1985). The congruence of classroom and remedial instruction. *Elementary School Journal, 85*, 465–477.

Knight, M. F., Meyers, H. W., Paolucci-Whitcomb, P., Hasazi, S. E. & Nevin. A. (1981). A four-year evaluation of consulting teacher service. *Behavioral Disorders, 6*, 92–100.

Knowles, C., Auferheide, S., & McKenzie, T. (1982). Relationship of individualized teaching strategies to academic learning time for mainstreamed handicapped and non-handicapped students. *The Journal of Special Education, 16*, 449–456.

Lazar, I., Darlington, R. B., & Associates. (1982). Lasting effects of early education: A report from the Consortium for Longitudinal Studies. *Monograph of the Society for Research in Child Development, 47* (2–3, Serial No. 195).

Leinhardt, G., & Pallay, A. (1982). Restrictive educational settings: Exile or haven? *Review of Educational Research, 52*, 557–578.

Lennox, N., Flanagan, D., & Meyers, J. (1979). Organizational consultation to facilitate communication within a school staff. *Psychology in the Schools, 16*, 520–526.

Madden, N. A., & Slavin, R. E. (1983). Mainstreaming students with mild academic handicaps: Academic and social outcomes. *Review of Educational Research, 53*, 519–569.

Mannino, F. V., & Shore, M. (1975). The effects of consultation: A review of empirical studies. *American Journal of Community Psychology, 3*, 1–21.

Mannino, F. V., & Shore, M. F. (1983). Trainee research in consultation: A study of doctoral dissertations. In J. L. Alpert & J. Meyers (Eds.), *Training in consultation* (pp. 185–199). Springfield, Ill: C. C. Thomas.

McGlothlin, J. E. (1981). The school consultation committee: An approach to implementing a teacher consultation model. *Behavioral Disorders, 6*, 101–107.

McKenzie, H. S. (1972). Special education and consulting teachers. In F. Clark, D. Evans, & L. Hammerlynk (Eds.), *Implementing behavioral programs for schools and clinics* (pp. 103–125). Champaign, IL: Research Press.

Medway, F. J. (1979). How effective is school consultation: A review of recent research. *Journal of School Psychology, 17*, 275–282.

Medway, F. J. (1982). School consultation research: Past trends and future directions. *Professional Psychology, 13*, 422–430.

Meyers. J. (1975). Consultee-centered consultation with a teacher as a technique in behavior management. *American Journal of Community Psychology, 3*, 111–121.

Meyers, J. (1988a). Diagnosis diagnosed: Twenty years after. *Professional School Psychology, 3*, 123–134.

Meyers, J. (1988b). Reactions diagnosed. *Professional School Psychology, 3*, 153–156.

Meyers, J., & Lytle, S. (1986). Assessment of the learning process. *Exceptional Children, 53*, 138–144.

Meyers. J., & Parsons, R. D. (1987). Prevention planning in the school system. In J. Hermalin & J. Morell (Eds.), *Prevention planning in mental health* (pp.11–150). Beverly Hills, CA: Sage Publications.

Meyers, J., Parsons, R. D., & Martin, R. (1979). *Mental health consultation in the schools.* San Francisco: Jossey-Bass.

Meyers, J., Pfeffer, J. & Erlbaum, V. (1985). Process assessment: A model for broadening assessment. *Journal of Special Education, 19*, 73–89.

Meyers. J., & Pitt, N. (1976). A consultation approach to help a school cope with the bereavement process. *Professional Psychology, 7*, 559–564.

Moos, R. H. (1979). *Evaluating educational environments.* San Francisco: Jossey-Bass.

Parsons, R. D., & Meyers, J. (1984). *Developing consultation skills.* San Francisco: Jossey-Bass.

Phillips, B. N., Martin, R. P., & Meyers, J. (1972). Interventions in relation to anxiety in school. In C. D. Spielberger (Ed.), *Anxiety: Current trends in theory and research* (pp. 409–464). New York: Academic Press.

Rappaport, J. (1981). In praise of paradox: A social policy of empowerment over prevention. *American Journal of Community Psychology, 9*, 1–25.

Reynolds, M. C. (1982). The rights of children: A challenge to school psychologists. In T. R. Kratochwill (Ed.), *Advances in school psychology: Vol. 2* (pp. 97–118). Hillsdale, NJ: Lawrence Erlbaum.

Reynolds, M. C., & Birch, J. W. (1982). *Teaching exceptional children in all America's schools* (2nd ed.). Reston, VA: The Council for Exceptional Children.

Ritter, D. (1978). Effects of a school consultation program upon referral patterns of teachers. *Psychology in the Schools, 15*, 239–243.

Rosenfield, S. (1988). *Instructional consultation.* New York: Pergamon Press.

Rosenshine, B. V., & Berliner, D. C. (1978). Academic engaged time. *British Journal of Teacher Education, 4*, 3–16.

Sarason, S. B. (1971). *The culture of the school and the problem of change.* Boston: Allyn & Bacon.

Shure, M. B., & Spivack, G. (1978). *Problem solving techniques in childrearing.* San Francisco: Jossey-Bass.

Shure, M. B., & Spivack, G. (1982). Interpersonal problem-solving in young children. A cognitive approach to prevention. *American Journal of Community Psychology, 10*, 341–356.

Slavin. R. E. (1984). Team assisted individualization: Cooperative learning and individualized instruction in the mainstream classroom. *Remedial and Special Education, 5*, 33–42.

Slavin, R. E. (Ed.). (1987). School and classroom organization (Special Issue) *Educational Psychologist, 22*, (2).

Spivack, G., Shure, M. B., & Platt, J. J. (1981). *Means-ends problem solving: Stimuli and scoring procedures supplement.* Philadelphia: Department of Mental Health Sciences, Hahnemann Medical College & Hospital.

Stolberg, A. L., & Garrison, K. M. (1985). Evaluating a primary prevention program for children of divorce: The divorce adjustment project. *American Journal of Community Psychology, 13*, 111–124.

Trickett, E. J. (1984). Toward a distinctive community psychology: An ecological metaphor for the conduct of community research and the nature of training. *American Journal of Community Psychology, 12,* 261–280.

Wang, M. C. (1981). Mainstreaming exceptional children: Some instructional design and implementation considerations. *The Elementary School Journal, 81,* 194–221.

Wang, M. C., & Birch, J. W. (1984). Comparison of a full-time mainstreaming program and a resource room approach. *Exceptional Children, 51,* 33–40.

Wang, M. C., Peverly, S., & Randolph, R. (1984). An investigation of the implementation and effects of a full-time mainstreaming program. *Remedial and Special Education, 5,* 21–32.

Weissberg, R. P., Gesten, E. L., Carnrike, C. L., Toro, P. A., Rapkin, B. D., Davidson, E., & Cowen, E. L., (1981). Social problem-solving skills training: A competence building intervention with second to fourth grade children. *American Journal of Community Psychology, 9,* 411–423.

Will, M. C. (1986). Educating children with learning problems: A shared responsibility, *Exceptional Children, 52,* 411–415.

Wright, S., & Cowen, E. L. (1985). The effects of peer teaching on student perceptions of class environment, adjustment and academic performance. *American Journal of Community Psychology, 13,* 417–413.

Ysseldyke, J. E., Reynolds, M. L., Weinberg, R. A., Bardon, J. I., Heaston, P., Hines, L., Ramage, J., Rosenfield, S., Schakel, J., & Taylor, J. (1984). *School psychology: A blueprint for training and practice.* Minneapolis: National School Psychology Inservice Training Network.

Zigler, E., Kagan, S. L., & Muenchow, S. (1982). Preventive intervention in the schools. In C. R. Reynolds & T. B. Gutkin (Eds.), *The Handbook of School Psychology,* (pp. 774–795). New York: Wiley.

Zins, J. (1981). Using data-based evaluation in developing school consultation services. In M. J. Curtis & J. E. Zins (Eds.), *The theory and practice of school consultation* (pp. 261–268). Springfield, IL: C. C. Thomas.

Contributors

Howard S. Adelman, Ph.D., is Professor of Psychology at the University of California, Los Angeles, where he also served as Director of the Fernald Laboratory and Clinic, a research and demonstration center for children with learning and behavior problems, from 1973 to 1986. He has authored numerous articles and two books in the field of learning disabilities and was co-director of a project concerned with the early identification and prediction of psychoeducational problems in children.

Dina Birman, M.A., is a doctoral student in clinical/community psychology at the University of Maryland, College Park. Her professional interests center on issues of acculturation and adaptation with particular emphasis on the intersection of sociocultural processes and feminist psychology. She has conducted research on the acculturation process of Soviet emigres to the United States and helped to plan a national conference on human diversity as reflected in psychological theory and research.

Lynne A. Bond, Ph.D., is Professor of Psychology and Dean of the Graduate College at the University of Vermont. Her research has focused on early child development, family interaction, and strategies for optimizing early childhood development. She is coprincipal investigator of Listening Partners, a preventive/promotive intervention to foster the cognitive and socioemotional development of isolated, rural mothers and their children. Bond has chaired a number of the Vermont Conferences on the Primary Prevention of Psychopathology and is principal investigator of a clinical training grant designed to train trainers of primary prevention.

Gilbert J. Botvin, Ph.D., is Associate Professor in the Department of Psychiatry, Cornell University Medical College where he is Director of

423

the Laboratory of Health Behavior Research. His current research focuses on preventive interventions to reduce smoking in youth and adolescents, and he is currently principal investigator on four research projects in this area. His work has led to the development of the Life Skills Training Program, a preventive intervention program for smoking and substance-abuse prevention.

Marlene Zelek Caplan, Ph,D., is Associate Research Scientist in the Department of Psychology at Yale University. She has coauthored two preventive mental health training programs for young adolescents. Her major research interests include social development in childhood, the development of conflict resolution skills, and the correlates and predictors of problem behaviors in early adolescence.

Ana Marie Cauce, Ph.D., is Assistant Professor of Clinical Community Psychology, University of Washington. Her research has involved social support networks in young children and adolescents, as well as evaluations of social support programs in community settings. She has been examining, also, the development of social competence in poor and ethnic minority youth, and the ecological correlates of development in this population. Cauce is currently principal investigator of a project supported by the National Institute for Child Health and Human Development/NIH that explores an ecological model of well-being in minority adolescents.

John D. Coie, Ph.D., is Professor of Psychology at Duke University, where he was Director of Clinical Training from 1976 to 1982. His research interests include the prediction of adolescent and adult disorders from childhood problems, children's peer relationships, and the development of preventive intervention paradigms with socially rejected children. He has authored numerous articles and served as principal investigator on several research projects related to these interests.

Bruce E. Compas, Ph.D., is Associate Professor of Psychology at the University of Vermont. His research has focused on stress, coping, and maladjustment in children, adolescents, and families. He was principal investigator on a project funded by the William T. Grant Foundation that investigated stress and coping in young adolescents and their parents and evaluated a primary prevention program that taught coping skills to children and parents. His current work, funded by NIMH, investigates sources of risk for emotional/behavioral problems in children of cancer patients and processes of coping and adjustments in cancer patients and their families.

Linda Dusenbury, Ph.D., is Assistant Professor of Psychology in the Department of Public Health, Cornell University Medical College. Since the beginning of her career, her research has focused on primary prevention. Her current work involves substance abuse prevention and competence promotion with urban minority adolescents, both in school settings and in shelters for the homeless.

Robert D. Felner, Ph.D., is Professor of Psychology and Director of Clinical Training at the University of Illinois, Urbana-Champaign. He is senior investigator on a series of primary prevention efforts focused on both the development of essential competencies in children and adolescents and the modification of social systems to enhance coping and adaptation. He has authored many articles, books, and chapters concerning broad-based antecedent conditions that predispose children to a variety of problematic outcomes. One of his ecologically focused school-based programs was selected as an exemplary model of primary prevention by the Task Force on Community Psychology of the American Psychological Association in 1986.

Tweety Yates Felner, M.A., is a doctoral student in Early Childhood/Special Education at the University of Illinois, Urbana-Champaign. She was formerly on the faculty in the School of Education at Auburn University. Her primary research interests are in early intervention and prevention programs for at-risk children and parent-child interaction patterns.

Normand Ledoux, Ph. D., is Children's Services Coordinator and Coordinator of Stress Management Programs for the Northeast Kingdom Mental Health Services. He is currently involved in the delivery of direct services to children and families and school consultation. In 1983 he developed the Comprehensive Stress Management Program for Children and Families, a school-based primary prevention program.

Jean Ann Linney, Ph.D., is Associate Professor of Psychology at the University of South Carolina, and is currently coprincipal investigator on a research project investigating the prevention of substance abuse in high risk adolescents. She recently received an award for Outstanding Contribution to School Psychology from the South Carolina Association of School Psychology and is a Program Consultant to the South

Carolina Department of Youth Services. Dr. Linney was elected President of the Division of Community Psychology of the American Psychological Association in 1988.

John E. Lochman, Ph.D., is Assistant Professor of Medical Psychology at the Duke University Medical Center. His current research is focused on the development, implementation, and evaluation of intervention programs with aggressive children.

Rolf Loeber, Ph.D., is Associate Professor of Psychiatry at the University of Pittsburgh School of Medicine, Western Psychiatric Institute and Clinic, where he is Codirector of the Child Conduct Problems Program. He has published extensively on the prediction and prevention of delinquent, antisocial, and aggressive behavior. He is presently coprincipal investigator on several research projects concerning these topics.

Jane R. Mercer, Ph.D., is Professor of Sociology at the University of California, Riverside. She has directed numerous research projects and published extensively in the areas of multiethnic education, the development of the System of Multicultural Pluralistic Assessment (SOMPA), and factors contributing to adjustment and achievement in racially desegregated public schools. Mercer served as an expert witness on the Larry P. case concerning the use of IQ tests to segregate minority students in public education.

Joel Meyers, Ph.D., is Professor of Educational Psychology and Statistics and is Director, Programs in School Psychology, at the State University of New York at Albany. A past president of Division of School Psychology of the American Psychological Association, he has authored numerous books and articles that address mental health consultation in schools, models of assessment, and the relationship between anxiety and learning. Meyers is currently codirecting a project funded by the U. S. Office of Special Education that examines alternative approaches to mainstreaming, and in particular, strategies that encourage teachers to collaborate with one another in solving educational problems.

Vicky Phares, M.S., is a doctoral student in Clinical Psychology at the University of Vermont. Her primary research interests include stress, coping, and development in children, adolescents, and families; different perspectives in the assessment of children's emotional/behavioral problems; subjective distress felt by young adolescents about their self-reported emotional/behavioral problems; and fathers' effects on child psychopathology.

David L. Rabiner, Ph.D., is Assistant Professor of Psychology at the University of North Carolina at Greensboro. He is currently examining interventions that are designed to affect positively children's social expectations and peer group adjustments.

Mary Jane Rotheram-Borus, Ph.D., is Associate Clinical Professor of Medical Psychology in the Division of Child Psychiatry, Columbia University. She has been principal investigator on a number of major research projects, including investigations of the development of ethnic identity during adolescence, the prevention of suicide attempts among runaways, the prevention of AIDS among youth with high risk behaviors, and assertiveness training with elementary school children. This latter project was selected as an exemplary model of primary prevention by the Task Force on Community Psychology of the American Psychological Association in 1986.

Lawrence J. Schweinhart, Ph.D., has worked at the High/Scope Educational Research Foundation since 1975 where he designed and for three years coordinated the graduate program for early childhood specialists. He is director of High/Scope's Voices for Children Project, an effort funded by the Carnegie Corporation to disseminate to policy makers and the general public research-based information on early childhood programs. He is codirector of the longitudinal Perry Preschool Study and Preschool Curriculum Comparison Study. These studies and others like them have generated considerable public interest in early childhood education for economically disadvantaged children.

Patricia J. Sivo, M.A., is a Clinical/Community Psychology doctoral student at Yale University. Her research concerns the relationships among stress, coping, and substance use in adolescence. She has been involved also in the evaluation of substance-abuse prevention programs for young adolescents.

Debra S. Srebnik is a Clinical Psychology doctoral student at the University of Vermont. Her principle area of research is in social support conceptualization and intervention applications. She is also involved in research concerning stress and coping in adolescents. Currently, she is working on a program focused on the prevention of eating disorders and body image dissatisfaction in college women.

Magda Stouthamer-Loeber, Ph.D., is Assistant Professor of Psychiatry and Psychology at the University of Pittsburgh. Her research focuses on the development of antisocial behavior in children and adolescents, especially the concealing of antisocial behaviors such as stealing and lying.

Edison J. Trickett, Ph.D., is Professor of Clinical/Community Psychology, University of Maryland, College Park. With an extensive background in consultation and evaluation activities, he is well-known for his innovations in models of community intervention. His research has focused on the elaboration of ecology as a paradigm for community psychology. His current work involves the ecology of cultural pluralism and human diversity as it affects research processes, methods, and questions.

Sam J. Tsemberis, Ph.D., is Assistant Clinical Professor, Department of Psychiatry, New York University School of Medicine. He teaches and practices therapy with an emphasis on ethnic and immigration issues. The former chairperson of the Greek-American Behavioral Sciences Institute, he is currently editing a book on social and clinical issues in the Greek American Community.

David P. Weikart, Ph.D., is president and founder of the High/Scope Educational Research Foundation and coordinator of the international IEA Preprimary Project. He has supervised early childhood education and research projects for over 20 years, including High/Scope's Perry Preschool Study and the Preschool Curriculum Comparison Study, High/Scope's participation in Project Follow Through, the evaluation of Head Start's Developmental Continuity Project, and a series of early childhood special education training projects.

Roger P. Weissberg, Ph.D., is Associate Professor of Psychology and the Child Study Center at Yale University. He has written extensively in the areas of primary prevention and school-based social competence promotion. Currently, he is funded by the William T. Grant

Foundation Faculty Scholars Program in Children's Mental Health to design and evaluate preventive mental health programs for young adolescents. As cochair for the William T. Grant Consortium on the School-Based Promotion of Social Competence, he is developing an agenda for effective ways to develop and evaluate preschool through high-school social competence promotion programs.

Name Index

Subject Index

NOTES

NOTES

NOTES

NOTES